RE-ORGANIZATION OF NORTH-EAST INDIA
FACTS AND DOCUMENTS

By the Same Author

- Illegal Migration from Bangladesh
- India and Central Asia: A Shared Past
- India and Central Asia: Classical to Contemporary Periods
- India: Caste, Culture and Traditions
- Naga Identity
- Problems of Ethnicity in the North-East India
- Rashtriya Samasyaen: Chinta Avem Chintan (Hindi)
- Small State Syndrome in India

About the Author

The author is an educationist, activist and scholar specializing in North-East India, Tribes and Castes, Tribal languages, Central Asia and Islam.

RE-ORGANIZATION OF NORTH-EAST INDIA
Facts and Documents
(Revised and Enlarged Edition)

B.B. Kumar

CONCEPT PUBLISHING COMPANY PVT. LTD.
NEW DELHI-110059

ISBN-13: 978-93-5125-301-3

First Published 2017
Revised and Enlarged Edition

Published and Printed by

Concept
Since 1974

Concept Publishing Company Pvt. Ltd.
Regd. Office:
A/15-16, Commercial Block, Mohan Garden,
New Delhi-110059 (INDIA)
Phones : 25351460, 25351794, *Fax* : 091-11-25357109
E-mail : publishing@conceptpub.com
Website: www.conceptpub.com

Cataloging in Publication Data—DK Courtesy: D.K. Agencies (P) Ltd. <docinfo@dkagencies.com>

Kumāra, Braja Bihārī, 1941- author.
Re-organization of North-east India : facts and documents / B.B. Kumar. -- Revised and enlarged edition.
pages cm
Includes bibliographical references and index.
ISBN 9789351253013

1. India, Northeastern--Politics and government. I. Title.

DS483.8.K86 2017 DDC 954.1 23

DEDICATED TO
THE MEMORY OF

Professor V. Venkata Rao

PREFACE TO THE FIRST EDITION

The emergence of Seven North-Eastern States — Assam, Nagaland, Meghalaya, Manipur, Tripura, Mizoram and Arunachal Pradesh — was the result of the Re-organization of North-East India and the dismemberment of Assam due to diverse historical, social, cultural, ethnic, linguistic, administrative and constitutional factors. The existing frame-work of linguistic and bigger states was challenged for the first time in North-East resulting into the formation of Nagaland. The processes further continued and Meghalaya, Manipur, Tripura, Mizoram and Arunachal Pradesh were born. The initial attempt to satisfy various ethnic groups by giving District Level Autonomy could not satisfy them.

The need of an additional instrument for Regional Planning was actually felt after the Re-organization of the region into smaller states. This necessitated the establishment of North-East Council.

The book deals with the Re-organization of North-Eastern India in light of various facts and the documents. The historical, administrative and constitutional documents are given in the Annexures for reference and further use.

The author shall heartily welcome any comment and criticism on this book from any corner.

B.B. Kumar

PRE

Nort
pra
day
states
Mizoram, N
was made for
of the Const
Distric coun
became state
the distu
were al

S

Schedu
such col
the Sixth
includes
related

L

Compa
book.

PREFACE TO THE REVISED EDITION

North-East India, before independence, had the State of Assam, the princely states of Manipur and Tripura, and Khaṣi syiemships of present day Meghalaya. The region was gradually reorganized to have seven states, namely, Assam, Arunachal Pradesh, Manipur, Meghalaya, Mizoram, Nagaland and Tripura. Originally, the provision for autonomy was made for the four tribal districts of Assam under the Sixth Schedule of the Constitution of India. This provision continued; the number of District Councils under Sixth Schedule increased even after the districts became states. The book dealt with the reorganization of the region and the district councils under the Sixth Schedule. The related documents were also given in the annexures.

Some more areas were brought under the provisions of the Sixth Schedule after the reorganization of the region. At the same time some such councils were also created which did not fall under the purview of the Sixth Schedule. The present revised and enlarged edition of the book includes information about the creation of such tribal councils and the related documents also.

Lastly, I thank Shri Ashok Kumar Mittal of the Concept Publishing Company (P) Ltd., for timely publication of this enlarged edition of the book.

B.B. Kumar

CONTENTS

1

INTRODUCTION

North-East India consists of the States of Assam, Nagaland, Meghalaya, Manipur, Tripura, Arunachal Pradesh and Mizoram. This area is strategically placed. It has international boundaries with China, Burma, Bangladesh and Bhutan. Except for Brahmaputra, Surma and Imphal Valleys, most of the area is hilly.

The valleys are predominantly inhabited by Hindus and Muslims. Christianity has taken deep roots in Nagaland, Meghalaya, Mizoram and the hills of Manipur. Most of the people of Arunachal follow Buddhism and Animism. Nocte Nagas follow Vishnuite faith. Tripuris are mostly Hindus.

Assamese and Bengali spoken in Brahmaputra and Surma Valleys, are Indo-Aryan languages. Nagamese is a pidgin based on Assamese, which is slowly becoming a creole. Languages on Tibetan border in Arunachal Pradesh such as Mompa and Memba are dialects of Tibetan. A large number of dialects of Central Arunachal Pradesh such as Nishi (previously known as Dafla), Apatani, Hill-Miri and numerous Adi (previously known as Abor) dialects like Padam, Miniyong, Galong, Bokar, Ashing, Bori, Marke, Lodung, Milang, Pailibo, Panggi, Pasi, Ramo, Shimong, Tagin and Tangam differ very little from each other and are mutually intelligible. Mishing (Miri) of Assam also comes under this category.

Three Mishmi dialects of Lohit District of Arunachal namely Taraon (Digrau), Idu (Chulikata) and Mizu (Kāman) differ very much from each other. Akas and Sherdukpens speak distinct languages. The same is true with Khamtis and Singphos.

An area of great linguistic variety is located on Indo-Burma border from Tirap district of Arunachal through Nagaland to North, East and West Hill districts of Manipur, where about three dozen Naga dialects are spoken. Except for Konyak of Nagaland and Wancho of Arunachal and Angami and Chokri of Nagaland, almost all the Naga dialects differ considerably from each other. These languages not only differ phonetically, lexically and syntactically from each other, but practically each of them also show dialectical variations. As for example, Tangsa Naga language has about one dozen dialects such as Moklum, Longcang, Havi, Mosang, Moran, Tikhak, Panthei (Hoshang), Jogli (Yogli), Kimsing, Bongran, Longri and Longphi. Nocte Naga is a distinct language.

The language of northern and central Nagaland like Ao, Sangtam, Chang, Phom, Yimchunger, Khiamngan and Lotha and that of southern Nagaland like Angami, Sema, Rengma, and Chakhesang (Kheja, Chokri and Pochury) show considerable point of contact and similarities, Zemi, Liangmei and Rongmei Naga languages and Karbi (also known as Mikir) of Assam show link with the Bodo and Kuki-Chin languages. Tangkhul, Mao, Maram, Maring, etc. of Manipur link Naga and Kuki-Chin languages.

Numerous Kuki-chin dialects spoken in southern Manipur, Mizoram and parts of Tripura and Assam are divided into Old and New Kuki groups. Most of the Kuki-chin clans claim their languages to be distinct due to non-linguistic reasons as there is practically very little difference between the languages spoken by them. However, Kom, Anal, Gangte, Vaiphei, Purum, Hiroi (Lamgang), Koireng, etc. come under old Kuki and Simte, Thadou (known as Kuki in Nagaland), Haokip, etc. are known as New Kuki dialects. Meithei (or Manipuri) and Mizo (previously known as Lushai) are also Kuki-chin languages. Manipuri is a literary language. Mizo is developing very fast. Aimol, Allam, Banjogi, Baite, Paite, Chimbok, Chibon, Cha, Chinmei, Chiru, Kolrhen, Kom, Khami, Khyangsho, Langrong, Lakher, Lai Paite, Pankhu, Ralte, Rangkhol, Jiroi-Lamgang, Siyin, Sokte, etc. are other Kuki-chin groups. Numerous Boro languages — such as Boro, Dimasa Kachari, Laluing, Rabha, Hojai, Koch, etc. of Assam, Garo of Meghalaya, Kok-Borok (Tripuri) and Reang of Tripura differ very little from each other.

All these languages spoken in North-East India are Tibeto-Burman languages.

Khasi language of Meghalaya belongs to Austric family Ahom (now dead) and Khamti which were considered to belong to Siami-Chinese family in reality belongs to Austro-Thai. This is a major departure from earlier stand.

Mundas, Santhals and Hos (Tea-garden labourers) speak Munda dialects of Austric family. Kurukh (or Oraon) and Sadari (Nagpuri) spoken in the tea gardens are Dravidian and Aryan languages respectively.

It is true that there is great linguistic variety in this part of the country, but it is also equally true that our emphasis in all these years was to search for the differences rather than to search for the thread of unity running through them.

The people of this region followed different kinds of polity, which may be summed-up as follows:

(i) In Assam, Manipur, Tripura, Cachar and Jayantia hills there existed monarchies. While the areas under Ahom, Cachar and Jayantia kings were merged in the British State of Assam. Manipur and Tripura continued to have their kings under British paramountcy.

(ii) The Khasis, Mizos, Sema and Konyak Nagas, etc. had their tribal chiefs. While there was moderation and dilution of Khasi Syiems' powers by the super imposed democratic system, the Mizo Chiefs had perfect autocratic power.

(iii) Most of the tribes had their village tribal councils with different degrees of political, administrative and judicial powers.

(iv) Some tribals, like Angami Nagas followed ultra-democratic norms in running their village and community affairs.

The tribes of North-East India are rich in colour and variety in their dresses and customs, social structures, norms, beliefs, values, material culture, etc.

Some of the tribes such as Angami and Chakhesang Nagas, Apatanis and Mompas followed advanced terraced cultivation with indigenously developed methods of irrigation. Most of the others followed primitive methods of Jhuming.

The Nagas prefer to have their villages on hill tops, whereas many other tribes prefer to settle near river-banks. Availability of abundant fertile land, water sources and security conditions were supreme factors in the selection of the village sites.

The houses built by different tribes differ in their sizes, materials used and in other details. In the extreme north, many tribes such as Mompas, Khambas and Membas build stone houses. Their neighbours in the south use bamboo and wood for house construction. The houses of the Adis and a large number of tribes are of platform type. They have anthropozoological latrines. Aos, Kukis, Mikirs, etc. also have machang type houses. The Angamis build their houses on ground. Lotha houses are of Machang type, but they often cover it with earth. The Changs build their houses partly on ground with part of the house extending on raised platforms. The same is the case with many Kuki tribes.

Many tribal-chiefs such as Adi, Angami and Sema chiefs have larger houses, while some have smaller ones. Use of nails or metals is taboo in house-building in the case of a large number of tribes. Some tribes like Angamis keep domestic animals inside the house, while some others like Semas do not do so. Many tribes such as Rengmas build their granaries outside the village. Many tribes such as Akas prefer to build it near their houses.

Khasis build their houses on raised plinths on the ground.

Some tribes build houses on two sides of the streets. Some have scattered houses without following a proper village design.

The design and the colour of the clothes used and the dresses of various tribes greatly vary. Most of the tribes have settled habits and they have old and very big villages. Some others like Kuki-chin tribes, Karbis, Semas, etc. had migratory habits with usually smaller villages.

Most of the tribes are patriarchal and patrilocal, and nuolocal after the birth of first child. Khasis and Garos are matriarchal. They usually have the nuclear family.

The degree of modernization and literacy varies from tribe to tribe. The literacy is highest in Mizoram and lowest in Arunachal Pradesh.

The Ahoms followed paik-system and revenue was collected in terms of labour. The same was true with Manipur. Thus, cash was in a very limited circulation. British introduced cash economy, but huge money circulation started only after independence.

The phenomenal growth of schools, colleges, universities and professional institutions is a post-Independence phenomena. There were limited number of schools and colleges and no university in the region before independence. Gauhati University was started only after Independence. The Nagaland, Mizoram and Arunachal Pradesh had no college before 1947.

The rail link was cut off due to partition and was restored only after Independence. New roads were constructed in every part of the region. The construction of new roads got impetus after Chinese aggression.

The region was pioneer in the field of tea and petroleum production. However, industrialization continued to be slow, rather very slow and many industrial schemes were not successful.

North-East Region During Independence

The North-East India at the time of Independence consisted of:

1. The province of Assam, which has the following districts:

(a) Brahmaputra Valley Districts:

(i) Goalpara,
(ii) Kamrup,
(iii) Nowgong,
(iv) Darrang,
(v) Sibsagar, and
(vi) Lakhimpur.

(b) Surma Valley Districts:

(i) Cachar, and
(ii) Sylhet.

(c) Hill Districts:

(i) Garo hills,
(ii) United Khasi and Jaintiya hills,
(iii) Naga hills, and
(iv) Lushai hills.

2. The North-East Frontier Tracts consisting of:

(a) Balipara frontier tract later on divided into:
(i) Kameng Frontier Division, and
(ii) Subansiri Frontier Division,
(b) Abor Hills district later on named as Siang Frontier Division,
(c) Mishni Frontier district later on named as Lohit Frontier Division,.
(d) Tirap Frontier, and
(e) The Naga or Tuensang Frontier Tract.

3. The Princely States were:

(a) Manipur,
(b) Tripura, and
(c) Khasi states.

The predominantly Muslim areas of Sylhet district were transferred to East Pakistan (now Bangladesh) at the time of independence — after a referendum. The eight thanas of that district, which form Karimganj district now, were merged with Cachar district. A portion of Duar area, which was taken from Bhutan after Bhutanese war by the British was transferred to that country after independence as per the decisions of the Assam Legislative Assembly and Parliament.

Adjustments and Re-organization After Independence

After independence, an attempt was made to provide limited autonomy to the hill districts of Assam under the provisions of the Sixth Schedule of the Constitution. The Naga Hills district did not accept the same and the District Council was never formed there. The Nagas followed the path of violence and insurgency and a section of them wanted to secede. This led to gradual emergence of Nagaland State. The Mizo Hill district gradually became Mizoram State, following almost the path of Nagaland. The State of Meghalaya was formed by a peaceful democratic process. Thus, there was gradual dismemberment of Assam leading to the formation of Nagaland, Meghalaya and Mizoram. The Assam ultimately was confined to Brahmaputra and Surma Valleys and the two hill districts, namely, Karbi Anglong and North Cachar Hills districts.

The North-East Frontier Agency, i.e. NEFA was already a distinct Administrative unit at the time of independence. It gradually emerged as the State of Arunachal Pradesh by a most painless Constitutional process.

The Manipur and Tripura were princely states when the independence dawned. They became Group-C states and had their Territorial councils. Gradually, they acquired Union Territory status and finally became states after re-organization of North-East region.

Thus North-East India ultimately has now the following seven States:

1. Assam,
2. Nagaland,
3. Meghalaya,
4. Manipur,
5. Tripura,
6. Arunachal Pradesh, and
7. Mizoram.

Most of the states are very small and the need of the supplementary regional planning was acutely felt due to various reasons. Thus, North-Eastern Council was formed to help the States in formulating and executing plans of inter-state nature in certain areas, such as power generation and communication. The North-Eastern Council is an advisory body.

The various aspects of the re-organization of the region and the emergence of States is discussed in detail in the various chapter. There are separate chapters on the Sixth Schedule and the North-Eastern Council.

All the important regulations, Acts and Orders are given in the Annexure for reference and study.

The principle of linguistic states was successfully challenged in North-East India. The autonomy movements leading to re-organization of the region were violent and of secessionist nature in certain areas. In other areas the people adopted peaceful democratic means of achieving the Statehood.

2

FRONTIER DURING THE BRITISH DAYS

The British passed Inner Line Regulation, 1873 (Annexure I) to prohibit entry of all British subjects, or any class of British subjects in the area within the inner line without proper pass — issued by competent authority. The Government was authorized to apply Inner Line Regulation by notification in Calcutta Gazette in any or more of the districts of Kamarup, Darrang, Nowgong, Sibsagar, Lakhimpur, Garo Hills, Khasi and Jaintiya Hills, Naga Hill, Cachar and Chittagong Hills — or in specified areas of the same. The inhabitants of the areas beyond Inner Line were denied property rights or business interest without Government Orders.

The aim of the British Government was to isolate the people of the Hills and to prevent interaction between hills and plains, and they were successful in their game. The freedom movement did not get strong roots in the areas within Inner-line due to their policy of segregation.

Inner-line Regulation was applied to the districts of Darrang and Lakhimpur in 1875-76 and accordingly the inner-line was specified. The people of the plains inhabiting the areas beyond the specified boundaries of the said Inner-line were not allowed to enter inside without passes issued by competent authority. Trespassers were liable to legal action.

The British thought that these unsophisticated and rude tribes should not and can not be administered by applying Regulations and Acts prevailing in the plains. Thus, they thought it necessary to administer the areas within Inner-line in an unsophisticated rude and rough manner by issuing Regulations. The Scheduled Districts Act of 1874 (Annexure II) authorized the Government to act accordingly. The Assam Frontier Tract Regulation was passed in 1880 under the authority of the Scheduled Districts Act of 1874 (Annexure II). The Chief Commissioner of Assam was authorized as per the said Regulation to prohibit or permit, with the prior consent of the Governor General, the operation of any law or part thereof passed by the Government of India and to propose rules for the administration of the Frontier Tracts, which, when approved by the Governor-General-in-Council would have the force of law. The Chief Commissioner of Assam passed Rules for the administration of justice in the Lakhimpur Frontier Tract in 1886 under the authority of the Scheduled Districts Act, 1874 (Annexure II). It may be pointed out that Chief Commissionership of Assam was created only in 1874. The North-East Region formed part of Bengal prior to that. In 1905, Assam was tagged with Eastern Bengal, but with annulment of partition of Bengal, its status was restored in 1912. It became a Governor's province in 1921. These changes in the status of Assam did not effect the status of North-East Frontier Tracts adversely.

The North-Eastern Frontier Tract remained un-administered and practically unknown prior to 1912. The British followed the non-interventionist policy in-spite of the demand of forward policy by the local officers. The policy of annexation was opposed on financial ground. It was not only taken as economically wasteful, but also politically immature. They also felt that such step might also cause political disturbances on the frontier and thereby seriously affect the supply of labour to the tea estates causing great loss to the industry.

Prior to 1912, the tribes of North-Eastern Frontier Tract, (now Arunachal Pradesh) were divided into two administrative sections. The Central and Eastern Section known as Balipara Frontier Tract was placed under the Deputy Commissioner of Darrang. These tracts were kept out of general administration and were governed through regulations. The Chief Commissioner of Assam was authorized by the Assam Frontier Regulation, 1880 to administer hill tracts of Assam directly. He passed rules for the administration of Justice in Lakhimpur Frontier Tract. The Chief Commissioner administered these areas with the help of Political Officers, their assistants and the native village authorities appointed by them. For detail, the "Rules for the Administration of Justice in the Dibrugarh Frontier Tract, 1886" (Annexure IV) may be seen.

The British appointed an Assistant Political Officer at Sadiya in 1882 so that to consolidate their authority. They opened a number of fairs to attract the hill people in as early as 1860. The fairs at Sadiya and Udalguri attracted thousands of people from hills and helped the British in promoting friendly relations with them. In spite of all these, the administration did not penetrate deep into Arunachal due to following facts:

(a) The British thought it un-profitable and un-economic to spend on administration of Arunachal, which was sparsely populated and devoid of communication facilities.
(b) They did not have adequate knowledge about the land and the people of Arunachal.

It was only in 1911-12 that the hills of Arunachal were surveyed and mapped during Abor expedition. The area, which was unknown became gradually known. This helped in change of British policy towards Arunachal Pradesh. The other factor was, continuous violence by the tribals climaxing into murder of Williamson and his followers in 1911. The new administrative arrangements after 1912 resulted into re-organization of Arunachal Pradesh into following administrative units:

(i) The Central and Eastern Unit under a Political Officer with headquarters at Sadiya.
(ii) The Lakhimpur Frontier Tract under the Deputy Commissioner of the Lakhimpur district.
(iii) The Western unit under a Political Officer with the headquarters at Charduar.

The administrative control of these three areas was vested in the Government of Assam. The Rules of administration of justice which was initially passed for Lakhimpur Frontier Tract only was promulgated in all the three sections of the Assam Frontier Tracts in 1914. The Deputy Commissioners (replaced by Political Officers in the Frontier Tracts except in Lakhimpur) became both magistrates and judges in these Frontier Tracts. The Chief Commissioner of Assam rather than the Calcutta High Court was the highest court of justice for them. This personalized form of administration of justice for these unsophisticated people was practically the same as was done by traditional institutions.

In 1919, the Western section was renamed as Balipara Frontier Tract and Central and Eastern Section as Sadiya Frontier Tract. The name of Lakhimpur Frontier Tract was not changed.

The Government of India Act, 1915 was amended in 1919 (Annexure VII). After the promulgation of the same in 1920, the administration of the North-East Frontier was vested in the Governor of Assam as the Deputy of the Governor-General of India, rather than in the Government of Assam. These areas were declared "Backward Tracts" as per the provisions of the said Act. This position continued till 1935, when Government of India Act, 1935 was passed (Annexure VIII). The

Government of India (Excluded and Partially Excluded Areas) Order, 1936 (Annexure IX) was promulgated as per the provisions of the Act of 1935 and these areas were declared excluded areas. Like 1920 order, these areas continued to be under the direct charge of the Governor of Assam, who administered them in his discretion, through the Political Officers of Sadiya and Balipara and the Deputy Commissioner of Lakhimpur. These areas were kept out of the purview of the Acts passed by Central or State legislatures unless the Governor directed in favour of its application or part of the same subject to exceptions or modifications as he though fit.

Tirap Frontier Tract was constituted by taking away parts of Lakhimpur and Sadiya Frontier Tracts in 1943. The new Tract was placed under the charge of a Political Officer with headquarters at Margherita. The Balipara Frontier Tract was divided into Sela Sub-agency and Subansiri area in 1943 and Sadiya Frontier Tract into Abor Hills district and Mishmi Hill district in 1948 after independence.

Thus, we find that the North-East Frontier Tracts (now Arunachal Pradesh) already acquired its distinct personality when the independence dawned in 1947.

As already stated above, the administration of these areas was carried on by the Governor of Assam acting in his discretion. He functioned in this matter independently of his Council of Ministers and was assisted by the Secretary to the Governor in doing so. The Secretary to the Governor was the head of the Governor's Secretariat which was established in Shillong in 1937.

It was decided to bring these areas under normal administration in 1943 and accordingly an Advisor to the Governor for these areas was appointed in 1943. He was concerned with the administration of the excluded areas and helped the Governor in this matter, who functioned as the agent to the Governor-General of India.

The application of Inner Line Regulation, 1874 to the North-East Frontier Area gave the boundary between Arunachal and Assam. This Inner-line was only a boundary inside the country. The outer-line was the boundary between India and Tibet. This line was demarcated and authenticated by Shimla Convention of 1914. The documents were signed by Indian and Tibetan Authorities. The British plenipotentiary, Sir Arther Henry McMahon signed the treaty from Indian side and, therefore, the boundary is known as McMahon line. It is the traditional and natural boundary running through Indo-Tibetan watershed. Sir Arther Henry McMahon initialled the document, which is valid as per General convention on the Law of Treaties, Article 12(2). The Tibetan delegate Lonchen Shatra put his full signature and also mentioned his lineage. It may be pointed out that initialling is not only difficult, but is also supposed to be discourteous and insulting act according to Tibetan customs and usages.

Two books were published by pro-Chinese British Scholars on McMahon Line. The books were "McMahon Line (1966)" by Alstair Lamb and "India's China War (1970)" by Neville Maxwell. Lamb protested against initialling of the document and in protest not only used the word "initial" in the American edition of his book, but also in the English edition. This un-English spelling in the English edition of the book was carried to lodge the protest.

The Maxwell's book describes Shimla agreement variously as "After-thought", "mysterious", "conspiratorial", "fraudulent", "fake" and "spurious". He forgot the fact that China never denied the existence of Shimla Agreement (Indian White Paper, page CR 26; Chinese Red-paper, page 30). Maxwell in 1930. This fact is well known and there is nothing secret about the same. In this connection it may be noted that:

(i) The Shimla Agreement was signed in a tripartite convention of India, Tibet and China in which Chinese delegate Ivan Chen did not put his initials. The Tibet was represented in the convention as a Sovereign State and it had the right to sign or refuge to sign and agree on its own jurisdiction. Tibet and India signed the agreement and the same was fully enforceable between the signatory parties as it only decided about their liabilities and rights and not about that of the China. Thus, legality of the document can not be doubted.
(ii) As already staled, the Chinese leaders have repeatedly accepted the fact that the agreement was signed by British-Indian and Tibetan delegates.
(iii) Unabated trade between India and Tibet during pre-Independence and post-Independence period was possible due to agreement signed by both parties. The trade was not illegal one and the legality of the trade depended on the validity of the agreement signed between the two parties.
(iv) When Shimla agreement was not included in 1930 edition of *Aitchison's Treaties and Engagements* (the print of which was soon withdrawn) then British officials in India — specially Olaf Caroe and Hugh Richardson — strongly advised for its inclusion in the same. Alastair Lamb and Neville Maxwell

> declare them to be imperialists for such advice. This act of Lamb and Maxwell convinces their fellow travellers in the Indian Universities that Lamb and Maxwell were guided by British sense of justice. Unfortunately, they do not realize that the aim of such innocent looking British scholars was to create further discord between India and China. Lamb and Maxwell fully knew that empire is not going to gain or lose by their innocent looking protests, but India is going to pay the price. The problem with Indian Scholarship is that they are the product of translation culture; they lack originality, are basically the consumers and not the producers of ideas, have multiple obsessions; enjoy camps at the cost of the nation. Most of the fellow travellers of Lamb and Maxwell in India know very little about Arunachal's history and culture. They feel that their so called objectivity shall be suspect if they talk about Chinese imperialist design in Tibet. They lack basic understanding to understand that Eastern Himalaya does not only have watershed, but also a line of cultural divide. Even Tibet is far far nearer to India in its culture, religion, literature, language, script, polity, mythology, way of life, etc. than with China.

It is unfortunate that this country and its poor people pay heavily for upkeep of their intellectuals and elites, who always fail them. India enjoyed special privileges and right in Tibet due to Shimla agreement. The Government failed to even refer to that document when they quietly surrendered everything to China in 1954, while signing the agreement with China on Tibet. This was certainly a great diplomatic blunder.

The Government of India Act, 1919 and declaration of backward areas were the results of the Montague Chelmsford Report (1917). Similarly, the Act of 1935 and subsequent declaration of excluded and semi excluded areas was the after-math of the Simon Commission Report. The British officers played active roles behind the screen in all these developments.

The British officers wanted to isolate entire hill areas of North-East from the plains from the very beginning, but their efforts gained ground after the freedom movement under the leadership of Mahatma Gandhi gained momentum. The attempt of Robert Reid, the Governor of Assam to get a crown colony carved out of the hill areas including North-East Frontier Tracts, Naga Hills, Mizo Hills, Chittagong Hill Tract, etc. was a part of well —thought out secret strategy. Some British officials tried again in 1941 to carve out North-Eastern Frontier Province comprising hill areas of India and Burma. The efforts of these British officers to separate these hills did not bear fruit due to the fact that British were deeply involved in Second World War and independence came too soon after the war.

When British left India in 1947, entire Arunachal Pradesh and Tuensang and Mon districts of Nagaland were excluded areas. Areas like Naga Hills district and Mizo Hills district were included in the list of partially excluded areas at that time.

3

THE SIXTH SCHEDULE AND THE DISTRICT LEVEL AUTONOMY

Introduction

The Cabinet Mission under the Chairmanship of Sir Stafford Cripps suggested the formation of Advisory Committee on the Rights of Citizens, Minorities and Tribal areas. Thus, when Constituent Assembly was set-up as per the proposals of the Cabinet Mission, then it also formed an Advisory Committee on Tribal Areas under the Chairmanship of Sardar Vallabhbhai Patel to consider the problems of Assam and the tribal areas. The Advisory Committee formed a sub-committee under the Chairmanship of Gopi Nath Bardoloi, the then Chief Minister of Assam (then known as Prime Minister of Assam). Two Members were co-opted by Bardoloi Sub-Committee from each hill district of Assam except from Frontier tracts.

Bardoloi Committee

When Simon Commission toured India, almost all hill districts submitted their various demands. Bardoloi Sub-Committee Functioned in that background. Most of the memoranda to the Simon Commission asked for more local autonomy. These demands were echoed in the memoranda and petitions submitted to Bardoloi Committee also. The Committee toured extensively in the hills and collected views and opinions of different shades from large number of people.

The demands of autonomy for hill districts was made at the time of independence from most of the districts.

Khasis demanded the formation of a federation of Khasi Syiemships and Jaintiya Doloiships under the province of Assam. They wanted four members in Assam Assembly and a 29 member Federated State Council including four women to be elected by adult franchise. They wanted an

Executive Council consisting of three members with veto power. As per their demand Assam Legislative Assembly was to be denied power to legislate on any subjects for Khasi-Jaintiya Hills.

Garo National Union came out with similar proposals, such as the formation of Garo Hills Union with 25 members (including two women) National Council, elected by adult franchise with powers to legislate and collect taxes. The five members Executive Council should have powers to prepare budget, fix salaries, appoint officers and police-force, shall have certain emergency powers, etc. They demanded four members in the Assam Assembly and one cabinet member. No legislation of Assam Assembly shall apply to Garo Hills without the consent of the Executive Council.

Bardoloi Committee toured extensively throughout the tribal areas and collected the opinions of the people and considered their demands. They submitted their recommendations, which were almost entirely accepted by Constituent Assembly. The recommendations of the Committee find place in the Sixth Schedule of the Constitution.

The Sixth Schedule

There was a lot of debate on the tribal situation in North-East India and the report of the Bardoloi Sub-committee in the Constituent Assembly. Ultimately, the Constituent Assembly accepted the report and the recommendations were incorporated in the form of fifth and Sixth Schedule in Article 244 of the Constitution. The Fifth Schedule incorporates provisions for the administration and control of the Scheduled Tribes and areas of other states, the Sixth Schedule has similar provision for the Scheduled Tribes and areas of Assam.

Part A of the Sixth Schedule has Constitutional provisions for district level autonomy for the Garo Hills, the United Khasi and Jaintiya Hills, the Lushai Hills, the Naga Hills, the North Cachar Hills and the Mikirs Hills. It provided for the constitution of District Councils for them. There was provision for the Constitution of Regional Councils for the Balipara Frontier Tract, Sadiya Frontier Tract, Tirap Frontier Tract, Abor Area and the Naga Tribal Area of the North-East Frontier Tracts in Part B of the Sixth Schedule. These Constitutional provisions gave greater autonomy to the Tribal Districts and Tracts.

The District and Regional Councils

The Sixth Schedule of the Constitution provides detailed frame about the working of the District Councils and Regional Councils — including their constitution, their powers to make law, administration of justice in autonomous districts and regions, etc. The Sixth Schedule was considerably modified by the Act 55 of 1969 and Act 81 of 1971. The modified Schedule is attached in Annexure XIX. It is not applicable in Jammu & Kashmir as per Constitution Jammu & Kashmir Order, 1954.

The District Councils and the Regional Councils were given certain legislative, executive and judicial powers under the provisions of the Sixth Schedule. They were empowered to make laws with respect to —

(i) the allotment, occupation or use, or the setting apart of land — other than reserved forest land;
(ii) the management of forests other than reserved forests;
(iii) the use of land or water course for agricultural purpose;
(iv) the regulation of the practice of Jhum or other forms of shifting cultivation;
(v) the matters related to village or town administration, including village or town police and public health and sanitation;
(vi) the establishment of village or Town Committees or Councils and their powers;
(vii) the appointment or succession of chiefs;
(viii) the inheritance of property;
(ix) social customs; and
(x) marriage.

They are empowered to make regulations for the control of money lending and trading by non-officials.

They are also empowered to do the following:

(i) to constitute courts for the trial of suits and cases between the parties, belonging to the scheduled tribes;
(ii) establishment and management of primary schools;
(iii) to determine the language and the manner in which the primary education shall be imparted in the primary schools in the district;
(iv) establishment and management of dispensaries, markets, cattle-ponds; and
(v) maintenance of roads and water-ways, etc.

The Governor was empowered to make rules for the first constitution of District Councils and Regional Councils in consultation with the existing Tribal Councils or other representative tribal organizations within the autonomous districts or regions. Such rules shall provide for —

(i) their composition and allotment of seats;
(ii) delimitation of territorial constituencies for election purpose;
(iii) qualification for voting, preparation of electoral rolls;
(iv) the qualification of members;
(v) the terms of office of members of Regional Councils;
(vi) matters related to elections/nominations of members;
(vii) the procedure and conduct of business; and
(viii) the appointment of officers and staff etc.

The Special Powers of the Governor

The Governor of Assam was given special powers about the District and Regional Councils. He was endowed with the powers of the suspension of the resolutions of the Councils and supersession, dissolution or suspension of the Councils. It was necessary to receive assent of the Governor on the rules, regulations and laws passed by the Councils. He was also empowered to appoint commission of inquiry into the administration of the councils. These provisions were made as a safeguard.

Unique Status

The Sixth Schedule gave unique Status to the tribal areas of North-East India. As per the provision of the Sixth Schedule:

> "No Act of the State Legislature in respect of tribal affairs shall apply to any autonomous districts unless the District Councils so direct. On the other hand these areas were given full share in the State Legislature and State Cabinet."

Drawbacks in the Functioning

One of the drawbacks in the functioning of the councils specially the District Councils was the lack of Constitutional provision for the coordination of their activities with that of the State Government and thereby making them to work independently of the State Government.

There meetings were not held regularly.

There was instability and constant in-fighting within the District Councils in most of the cases.

The councils and specially the District Councils did not make full use of their legislative, executive and judicial powers.

The District Councils did not properly use their taxation powers. In this connection it may be said that District Councils did not try to mobilize resources properly and relied more and more on government grants. All the avenues of taxation were not tapped properly and their taxation powers were sparingly used. The levied taxes were collected half-heartedly and there was leakage of revenue leading to resource crunch.

It is observed that the control of the District Councils were often perpetuated in selected hands. In Mikir Hills, most of the Chief Executive Members and Executive Members came from handful of families related by blood.

The Naga Hills district of Assam did not have the District Council from the very beginning. Tuensang had a Regional Council, which continued to function for more than a decade after formation of Naga Hills Tuensang Area (NHTA) and the state of Nagaland. Later on the Regional Council of Tuensang was abolished.

The District Councils of Garo Hills, Khasi Hills and Jaintiya Hills continued to function even after the formation of the state of Meghalaya comprising Garo Hills District and United Khasi and Jaintiya Hill District.

The Lushai Hills district of Assam (later on renamed as Mizo Hills) gradually became the state of Mizoram. The Mizo Hills District Council not only continued to function even after the Statehood, but the provisions of Sixth Schedule were further extended and District Councils were also given to Lakher and Chakma people of the state.

As per the provisions of the Manipur (Hill Areas) District Councils Act, 1971, (included in the Annexure XXXII), new District Councils were established in the hill districts of Manipur in early seventies. The same was done for the hill areas of Tripura during eighties. Thus, we find that not only the District Councils continued to exist even after the formation of new hill states, but even their number multiplied in all the hill states except Nagaland and Arunachal Pradesh. The District Councils also continued to function in Karbi Anglong district (earlier known as Mikir Hills district) and North Cachar Hills district of Assam as usual.

The Sixth Schedule was made to provide reasonable autonomy to the hill districts of Assam. The creation of hill states maximized the autonomy and thus there was no need to continue the existing system where districts became states. The district councils were very costly instruments, where most of the funds continued to be consumed under salary, T.A., etc. and very little fund was left for development works. Much remains to be done in the field of administration of justice according to customary laws even after the establishment of district courts in many states as early as in 1952. Needless to say the district councils have failed to a great degree to perform the task, for which they were created.

The creation of Nagaland increased the appetite of tribals of the districts of Assam for more and more political power. The need of the hour was statesmanship, pragmatism and elastic approach. Amendments in Sixth Schedule might have saved Assam from dismemberment at that hour. However, it did not happen. The district council lost their utility after creation of hill states and yet they continued to exist everywhere.

4

EMERGENCE OF NAGALAND STATE

The Nagaland was inaugurated as the sixteenth state of the Indian Union on 1st December, 1963 by the President Dr. S. Radhakrishnan. The Nagaland's statehood was a departure from the existing norms of state formation in India and gave birth to new trends in Indian politics, specially in the politics of North-East India. The following points in this connection are worth nothing:

(i) The states were formed on linguistic lines on the recommendations of the State Re-organization Commission of 1956 and also after that. The Nagaland was the first state, which was not formed on linguistic lines.

(ii) The State Re-organization Commission and Indian leaders believed in bigger states prior to the formation of Nagaland. Nagaland was the first state with smaller area and smaller population.

(iii) It was for the first time that the economic viability was not the main consideration in the formation of a state and the state was to run mainly on the grants received from the consolidated fund of India.

(iv) The Nagaland was the first state in India which had the insurgency and underground movements in the background of its formation. The insurgency of Nagaland was the fore-runner of insurgency in other parts of the country.

(v) The formation of Nagaland gave birth to the never ending demands for smaller states on ethnic lines in North-East India and elsewhere. The insurgency by Mizo National Front under the leadership of Laldenga, and the formation of Mizoram was much on the same line as we witnessed in Nagaland. The formation of Nagaland encouraged All Party Hill Leaders Conference to demand a hill state. The Manipur and Tripura leaders, who demanded statehood were also encouraged by the formation of Nagaland. Thus, the formation of Nagaland was fore-runner of the re-organization of North-East India and the formation of smaller states elsewhere.

(vi) The Sixth Schedule based on Bardoloi Committee recommendations was framed to give district level autonomy. The formation of Nagaland made it ineffective.

The Autonomy Movement in Nagaland

The Naga Club was established in 1918 with Naga Government employees. This was the first organization of its kind in Nagaland. The Naga Hills District Tribal Council was formed in 1945 on the nucleus of Naga Club. The aim of the said organization was to work for rehabilitation and reconstruction of war devastated areas of Naga Hills. The Naga Hills District Tribal Council very soon got itself transformed into Naga National Council. The 29 member Council had representatives from almost every Naga tribe. The Council very soon became the political platform of the Naga people. It may be pointed out that the initiative of Mr. C.R. Pawsey, the then Deputy Commissioner of Naga Hills district in the formation of Naga Hills District Tribal Council is well-known. The Naga National Council in its meeting on 19th June, 1945 drafted a memorandum about the future of Nagas to be submitted to His Majesty's Government. Some resolutions of the said memorandum, which was approved by the general body meeting of the Naga National Council are given below:

> "The Naga National Council stands for the solidarity of the Naga tribes including those of the un-administered areas."
>
> "The Council strongly protests against the grouping of Assam with Bengal".
>
> "The Naga Hills should be constitutionally included in an autonomous Assam in a free India with local autonomy and duly safeguarded for interests of the Nagas".
>
> "The Naga tribes should have a separate electorate".

The above cited resolutions clearly indicate that Nagas wanted to remain as part of Assam in free India. The idea of self-determination was an after-thought and its protagonists gradually got the full control of the Naga National Council. The Naga National Council drafted another resolution on 10th February, 1947 to be submitted to His Majesty's

Government and the Government of India. The memorandum approved by its general body demanded self-determination for the Nagas. They asked for setting-up an interim government for ten years, at the end of which Nagas would be free to decide the form of government of their liking.

The argument of the N.N.C. for self-determination was based on the following:

(a) Ethnic distinctiveness.
(b) Distinct social life, way of living, laws and customs, etc.
(c) Different religion-Animism and Christianity.

The leadership of N.N.C. passed in the hands of A.Z. Phizo just before Independence and the demand of the right of self-determination was voiced under his leadership. The moderates' voice of "Nagas under Autonomous Assam in free India" was never heard again from the platforms of N.N.C.

It is necessary to discuss the background under which such developments were taking place and the forces in operation in Naga Hills just before Independence.

(i) Kohima was on the fore front of Second World War. This exposed Nagas to the latest technology of the world. The circulation of money considerably increased. The elites among them had already Western education and were converted to Christianity. All this brought modernization in Naga Society, although the number of modernized Nagas continued to be small for 10-15 years.
(ii) The process of greater identity formation — the Naga identity as distinct from individual tribal identity — had already begun. At least the elites were thinking in terms of Naganess. The force of parochialization was becoming weaker.
(iii) The British officers were successful in isolating hills and plains of North-East India. This is why, the freedom movement could not have any considerable impact and following in the hills.
(iv) Some British Officers were secretly trying to separate hills of India and Burma and form a separate political unit. Robert Neil Reid, then Governor of Assam, J.H. Hutton, Deputy Commissioner of Naga Hills district and J.P. Mills, Advisor to the Governor subscribed to the idea of separation. They strongly favoured creation of North-East Frontier Province under British

protection, Andrew Çlow, the Governor of Assam and Sir Reginald Coupland, a British constitutional expert favoured the formation of Crown colony comprising hills of North-East India and Burma. According to Coupland, "the inhabitants of both areas are alike in race and culture, and in no sense belonged to the Indian or Burman Nation". There were certainly many takers of such ideas among the tribals of North-East. The freedom came too early for the British officers to get their dreams of separation realized.

(v) The partition of India generated hope in the minds of a section of hill people that a similar partition was possible.

(vi) The National leaders were too busy in solving post-Independence problems and in constitution making, and had no time to work for removing the fear of dominance from the minds of a section of hill people. The fear in the minds of a section of Nagas, that their identity, religion and culture would be endangered; and that their lands shall be forcibly occupied, and they may be out numbered by the people of the plains in their own land, was to be removed.

(vii) It was natural for a section of the elite to be over ambitious, and to dream to have new opportunities in nations of their choice and to work for secession.

As already mentioned, February 1947 memorandum by N.N.C. to His Majesty's Government asked for a ten year's interim government for the Nagas followed by self-determination. The memorandum further said that a constitution drawn-up by people not knowing the Nagas would be "unsuitable and unacceptable" to them. The N.N.C. leaders insisted that Bardoloi Committee should accept the points raised in their memorandum and incorporate them in their report. Needless to say that the Committee could not agree to their demands. Ultimately, District Councils, were not constituted in Naga Hills district.

Hydari Agreement

Sir Akbar Hydari, the Governor of Assam visited Kohima on 26th June, 1947 and had wide ranging discussion with Naga leaders and C.R. Pawsey, Deputy Commissioner, Naga Hills. A nine point agreement was worked out to solve the Naga problem.

The agreement provided for the basic safeguards for Naga culture and way of life.

The Nagas also were assured about the preservation of Naga customary laws and rights over their lands and resources.

Hydari agreement conceded that the N.N.C. would be responsible for collection of land revenue and house-tax and that they would control for what they would pay. "Bringing all the Nagas under one administration" was also a demand, which was included in the agreement.

The 9th clause of the agreement talked of ten year's period of special responsibility of the Governor of Assam as the agent of the government of India to ensure the due observance of the nine point agreement and that at the end of the ten years period the Nagas would be asked whether they required the above agreement to be extended for a further period or a new agreement for the future of the Naga people to be arrived at. The N.N.C. interpreted the last point to mean that they may have right to opt out of India after 10 years. The official interpretation was to mean more acceptable arrangements for the smooth functioning of autonomy. It resulted into disagreement and ultimately Hydari agreement broke-down.

Civil Disobedience and Violent Phase

A.Z. Phizo led a series of delegations to Delhi to press for his demand of sovereign Nagaland. Naga delegations met Mahatma Gandhi once and Nehru several times at several places. Nehru and U Nu Prime Ministers of India and Burma visited Kohima in 1953. The Naga leaders wanted to submit a memorandum to the P.M., which was not allowed. This led to famous walk-out by the Nagas from the meeting organized to welcome the two Prime Ministers. Nehru was mortified. President Rajendra Prasad and Congress president Dhebar Bhai refused to meet them after Kohima incident.

Earlier in 1952, the following happenings boosted the morale and image of the secessionists and highly demoralized the administration:

(a) Non-participation of the Nagas in District Council formation under provisions of the Sixth Schedule of the Constitution.
(b) Successful boycott of the 1952 general elections by the Nagas of the Naga Hills district.
(c) Plebiscite conducted by Phizo in May to August 1951, in which 99 per cent Nagas are said to have voted for Naga independence.

The hard-liners started civil disobedience movement soon after, in which some of the activities launched were the following:

(a) Non-payment of house-tax.
(b) Non-cooperation with the government in its development schemes.
(c) Refusal to supply labour and food items to touring officers.
(d) Boycotting national and official celebrations.
(e) Return of red blankets — the badges of their authority by Gaon-Burras to the Deputy Commissioner.
(f) Forced resignation of school teachers.
(g) Forced withdrawal of students from schools, etc.

In the beginning, the movement remained mostly non-violent, as proclaimed by Phizo. However, it could not remain so and, very soon violent clashes started taking place. The climax reached in around 1956.

The fear of India and the Indians loomed large in the minds of the unsophisticated Nagas. The sustained publicity campaign launched by highly intelligent person like. T. Sakhrie strengthened and sustained it. The movement was going on under the leadership of A.Z. Phizo, who had unmatched determination and tenacity. There were many other factors also, which contributed towards the success of the civil disobedience. Lack of imaginativeness, rigidity in handling the Naga affairs, undue harshness, etc. helped N.N.C. in getting more and more support of the Nagas. It was unfortunate that a person like Gopi Nath Bardoloi could not live longer to solve the problems of Assam. With his pragmatic and elastic approach and far-sightedness, perhaps, it was possible for him to save Assam from disintegration.

The N.N.C. was the only political forum of all shades of Naga's opinion, before it went into the total control of Phizo. Young educated people continued and still continue to be a force in the politics of the hill areas of North-East India and Naga Hills and Tuensang were no exception. Most of such people were moderates, but they used to leave the platform for government jobs and failed to register their prolonged presence and to guide the opinion. This is how the N.N.C. went easily in the control of Phizoites Moderates and their opinion could not be heard from the platform of N.N.C. after February 1947. Although, N.N.C. was under the full control of Phizo and his followers, the voice of the moderates continued to be heard in Naga inhabited area. The Reforming Committee of the Naga National Council and three Naga People's Conventions and Naga Nationalist Organization (the party which won 1964 Nagaland Legislative Assembly elections), etc. represented moderate view-points.

As already stated violent activities started in early fifties in Naga Hills. The underground slowly spread their activities in Tuensang also.

In fact, Tuensang saw the simultaneous growth of administration and underground activities in early fifties.

The attempts to recruit young men in the armed underground ranks resulted into the mobilization of an army of 5,000 men by the end of 1955. Their number further increased soon after. The government recruited armed village guards. Murder, arson, loot and intimidation of moderates and government servants continued unabated. The village guards and Assam police failed to control the situation. Army was called in the hills in 1956. The Naga Hills Disturbed Area Ordinance and Assam Maintenance of Public Order were promulgated in Naga Hills. After replacement of Assam police Battalions by Indian Armed Forces, Special Powers Act was also enforced. A period of intense violent opposition started. The rebels operated in the cover of dense forests. It was a new experience for the armymen to fight a guerilla battle in an area devoid of communications. Most of the army battalions were new to the scene while the rebels knew every inch of it.

The Chief of the Army Staff issued official instructions in 1955, according to which military operations were not to be conducted on war footing. The instruction issued was the following:

> "You must remember that all the people of the area in which you are operating are fellow-Indians. They may have a different religion, they may pursue a different way of life, but they are Indians, and the very fact that they are different and yet part of India is a reflection of India's greatness. Some of these people are misguided and have taken to arms against their own people, and are disrupting the peace of this area. You are to protect the mass of the people from these disruptive elements. You are not there to fight the people in the area, but to protect them. You are fighting only those who threaten the people and who are a danger to the lives and properties of the people. You must therefore, do everything possible to win their confidence and respect and to help them feel that they belong to India".

The insurgents formed the Federal Government of Nagaland in March 1956. They also framed their Constitution which runs as follows:

> "Nagaland is a people's sovereign republic. This has been so from time immemorial. There will be a parliament with 100 *tatars* (M.Ps.), the president will be elected by the people and his cabinet will consist of 15 *Kilonsers* (Ministers)".

"Nagaland will maintain permanent military neutrality. There will be no standing army for the maintenance of law and order. There will be a department of Home Guards headed by a Chief to function in a dual capacity of police and patriot soldier."

They further declared:

"Land belongs to the people and it will remain so. There will be no land tax, and other forms of taxation will be formulated by different administrative units".
"All forms of trade, business, industry, transport and other public utility will be free and will be in the hands of the people".
"Religion will be free".
"Each Naga village is a republic in its own right. Each Naga family or tribe occupies its own distinct region, and shall continue as before to exercise full authority over its own affairs, including land, community organization, social and religious practices and customs".
"Men and women above 22 years of age, will have equal rights of voting".
"There will be equal wages for equal work irrespective of sex".

There was provision for the appointment of *Angs* (i.e. Governors), Advisors, Deputy Commissioners, Magistrates, Ambassadors, Judges, etc. in underground set-up. They had a Commander-in-Chief of the military organization of Home Guards, and men of all other ranks. The arms and ammunitions consisted of those left behind in Second World War and arms and ammunitions captured in raids and seized from individuals.

They also established an underground Federal High Court:

The innocent villagers were the worst sufferers in the conflict. Dissentions started surfacing soon in the ranks and files of the underground. T. Sakhrie and some others resigned from the N.N.C. Sakhrie was cruelly murdered. The efforts started afresh to end the state of belligerence. People disliked violence and conflict and they took courage and started mobilizing public opinion in favour of peaceful settlement of the problem.

In the meantime, 1957 general elections were held and three Nagas — Khelhose Seina, Chubatemsu Ao and Subedar Satsuo Angami — filed nominations and got elected as MLAs of Assam Assembly unopposed, Mr. Khelhose was appointed Deputy Minister. All of them resigned on

1st December, 1957, when a separate unit — Naga Hills-Tuensang Area was formed.

First Naga People's Convention

An All Tribes Naga People's Convention was convened from 22nd to 26th August, 1957, under the chairmanship of Dr. Imkongliba Ao, J.B. Jasokie was its secretary. It was attended by 1760 delegates and over 2,000 visitors from every Naga tribe. The convention denounced violence and advocated settlement of Naga problem through negotiation. The underground Nagas did not join the convention. The demand for Independence was formally given up and the following main demand were made:

(a) Creation of single administrative unit comprising of Naga Hills district of Assam and Tuensang Frontier Division of NEFA.
(b) Restoration of the reserved forests carved out of the Naga Hills district in 1921.
(c) Declaration of general amnesty.
(d) Certain administrative changes as interim measure.

A nine member delegation of the Naga People's Convention under the leadership of Dr. Imkongliba Ao met the Governor at Shillong and the Prime Minister in New Delhi to present their resolutions soon after the convention.

Formation of Naga Hills Tuensang Area

Nehru was sympathetic to their demands and conceded their main demands. The Naga Hills-Tuensang Area (NHTA) came into being on 1st August, 1957. The Assam Government granted general amnesty. It is worth-nothing that the Nagas of Manipur in a largely attended meeting under the chairmanship of Mr. Anal, a prominent Congress leader passed a resolution to merge Naga areas of Manipur also in the new political set-up.

Naga Hills-Tuensang Area was formed basing on the Naga Hills-Tuensang Area (Administrative) Regulations, 1957 promulgated by the President of India in exercise of the powers conferred by Article 240 of the Constitution read with sub-paragraph (2) of paragraph 18 of the Sixth Schedule to the Constitution.

Some important articles of the regulation are re-produced below:

> "The Naga Hills-Tuensang Area shall be divided into three districts to be called Kohima District, Mokokchung District and Tuensang District, each comprising the areas respectively set out against it in the Schedule".
>
> "The administration of Naga Hills Tuensang Area shall be carried on by the Governor of Assam as the agent of the President''.
>
> "The Central Government may appoint a Commissioner for the Naga Hills-Tuensang Area to assist the Governor of Assam; and the Governor may appoint a Deputy Commissioner for each of the districts therein and the Deputy Commissioners shall perform their functions under the supervision and control of the Commissioner".

The existing provisions of law and taxation were to continue in the NHTA till modifications were made by competent authority.

The Second and Third Naga People's Conventions

The Second Naga People's Convention was held in Ungma village in Mokokchung district in May 1958. There were protests and threats from the underground. A Laison Committee was appointed to contact the underground people, but there was no response from their side. Ultimately, the convention appointed a Drafting Committee to formulate their demands. The Drafting Committee prepared a 16 point memorandum for the constitution of a separate state within Indian Union. The Third Naga People's Convention was held in Mokokchung from 22nd to 26th October, 1959. It approved the draft of the sixteen point memorandum.

The Naga People's Convention delegates met the Governor of Assam at Shillong in April 1960 for preliminary discussion. This was followed by a meeting of 15 members and four consultants representing all the Naga tribes, with the Prime Minister in July 1960. The Prime Minister accepted their demands in principle. Their main demand was the establishment of Nagaland state.

Some important points of the memorandum are the following:

1. The name of the state shall be Nagaland.
2. The Ministry-in-Charge shall be External Affairs Ministry.
3. The provision for separate Governor and Secretary with headquarters within Nagaland; special responsibility of the Governor with regard to Law, Order and Police only during transitional period.

4. Council of Ministers responsible to the Naga Legislative Assembly.
5. Naga Legislative Assembly.
6. Two representatives in Lok Sabha and one in Rajya Sabha.
7. *Acts of Parliament*
   "No Acts or Law passed by the Union Parliament affecting the following provisions shall have legal force in Nagaland unless specially applied to it by the majority vote of the Naga Legislative Assembly".
   (i) The Religious or Social practices of the Nagas.
   (ii) Naga Customary Laws and Procedure.
   (iii) Civil and Criminal justice so far as these concern decision according to Naga Customary laws.
   (iv) The ownership and transfer of land and its resources.
8. Local Self-Government for each tribe with provisions for:
   (i) The Village Council
   (ii) The Range Council
   (iii) The Tribal Council
9. Administration of justice in each tribe through the following Courts of Justice:
   (a) (i) The Village Court
   (ii) The Range Court
   (iii) The Tribal Courts
   (b) Appellate Courts:
   (i) The District-*cum*-Sessions Court and the Supreme Court of India.
   (ii) The Naga Tribunal.
10. Separate administrative and legal provision for Tuensang district for ten years; Representation in Assembly through nomination by the Regional Council.
11. Financial assistance from Government of India as lump-sum grant from consolidated fund of India for development and administration.
12. Re-transfer for Reserved Forests.
13. Consolidation of Contiguous Naga Areas.
14. Separate Naga Regiment.

15. The Constitution of Interim Body for three years subject to re-election as a transitional measure to run the administration till Nagaland State is formed.
16. Continuance of the provisions of Inner Line Regulation.

Most of the points of the memorandum were accepted by Government of India with slight modification. Practically, they got everything. They got one member each for Lok Sabha and Rajya Sabha. Article 371A of the Constitution provided special safeguards regarding their religious and customary usages and procedures.

Formation of Interim Body

The Interim Body was formed for three years with 45 members representing all the tribes of Nagaland as per provisions of the Nagaland (Transitional Provision) Regulation, 1961 (No. 2 of 1961). It started functioning w.e.f. 18th February, 1961. It elected five-member Executive Council consisting of P. Shilu Ao, as Chief Executive Councillor and Hokishe Sema, J.B. Jasokie, R.C. Chitan Jamir and Akum Imlong as Executive Councillors. Dr. Imkongliba Ao, who took most prominent part in the Naga People's Convention activities was elected as the first chairman of the Interim Body.

The underground did not approve the activities of Naga People's Convention and the formation of Interim Body and the Executive Council. The members of these bodies were threatened and worst possible words like "Traitors" and "Stooges" were used for them by the underground people. Dr. Imkongliba Ao, who was the architect of negotiations and peaceful settlement was assassinated just after few months of the formation of Interim Body in his home-town, Mokokchung. The Interim Body elected T.N. Angami as Chairman and M. Kithan as its Deputy Chairman after his death.

The Interim Body had the strange combination of old and young, experienced and un-experienced, the government servants, and ex-underground. Shilu Ao, Hokishe Sema, and M. Kithan were government servants. People like Jasokie and Zulekhemba Ao were ex-underground. Levi, retired head clerk of Deputy Commissioner's office was also an ex-government servant.

Formation of Nagaland State

The Parliament passed the Constitution (Thirteenth) Amendment Act, 1962 to provide for the formation of Nagaland in September 1962 as the

Sixteenth Slate of the Republic of India. The State of Nagaland Act, 1962 provided constitutional and legal frame work for the new state (attached in Annexure XXIII).

As already stated, the state was inaugurated on 1st December, 1964 by the President Dr. S. Radhakrishnan. The Interim Body and the Executive Council started functioning as the Nagaland Legislative Assembly and Nagaland Cabinet and the Chairman of the Interim Body as the Speaker after the state inauguration, till the Assembly elections were held in early 1964.

There was provision for 60 members in the Nagaland Assembly as per the Act. However, fewer members were to be nominated by Tuensang Regional Council for 10 years. There were 46 members in the first Nagaland Legislative Assembly, 40 elected from Kohima and Mokokchung districts and six nominated by Tuensang District Regional Council. The Minister-in-charge of Tuensang Affairs was chosen from among the MLAs of Tuensang district.

5

EMERGENCE OF MEGHALAYA

Introduction

The state of Meghalaya was carved out of Assam with the United Khasi and Jaintiya and the Garo Hills districts. It consisted of the following areas at the time of Independence:

1. The Garo Hills district;
2. The British portion of the United Khasi and Jaintiya Hills district; and
3. The Khasi Syiemships.

Rev. Nichols Roy was the first person to ask for the integrated Khasi States comprising of the Khasi Syiemships and British portion of the United Khasi and Jaintiya Hills district. He suggested the formation of Legislative Council, and executive Council and a federal court. At the same time he wanted their representation in Assam Legislative Assembly and Assam Cabinet. He further suggested that "no legislation of Central or provincial legislature shall be extended to their area without the consent of the executive council of the federated States." He wanted continued linkage of the Khasi and Jaintiya Hill with the stale of Assam and opposed the idea of the Crown colony. These proposals submitted to the Cabinet Mission in 1946, were slightly modified and submitted to the Bardoloi Sub-committee. Stanley D.D. Nichols Roy later on changed his stand favoured the Hill State proposal in his communication to the State Re-organization Commission.

The Bardoloi Committee recommendations were accepted by the Constituent assembly and District Councils were formed in the Garo Hills and the United Khasi and Jaintiya Hills districts. However, this did not satisfy the tribals who continued to ask for more autonomy.

Hill State Demand

Capt. Williamson Sangma called a conference of the people of autonomous hill districts of Assam on 6 October, 1954 at Tura to consider the demand of a hill state. The conference decided to submit a memorandum to the State Re-organization Commission for the creation of Eastern Hill State. Accordingly a lengthy memorandum was submitted to the State Re-organization Commission to press for their demand for separate hill state. The memorandum emphasized their differences from the plains people and blamed Assamese for trying to impose their culture and language on the hill-tribes and for attempts to dominate in legislature and services. They also pointed out that the autonomy granted under Sixth Schedule was not real and substantial. The Assam Government refuted the charges.

Earlier, in a conference of the members of the Executive Committees of the autonomous District Councils held at Shillong on 16 June, 1954 under the Chairmanship of B.M. Roy, Chief Executive Member of the United Khasi and Jaintiya Hills district Council, the demand of the Eastern Hill State was voiced by Capt. Sangma. The meeting was attended by all except the members of the Mikir Hills District Council. It was called to discuss the matters of mutual interest, but the discussions were confined to the following topics:

(i) Formation of the Eastern Hill State consisting of all the hill areas and the contiguous areas inhabited by people of the same stock.

(ii) More autonomy to the District Councils by amending the Sixth Schedule.

They suggested English to be the state language to be replaced by Hindi in due course.

The proposal of Capt. Sangma was opposed by the members of the North Cachar Hills and Lushai Hills District Councils, who wanted greater autonomy for the districts, rather than the hill state. However, his opinion was accepted later on in the meeting.

The State Re-organization Commission and Its Recommendations

The hill leaders demanded the formation of hill state in their memorandum to the State Re-organization Commission. The Assam Government not only wanted to retain all its areas, but also demanded the inclusion of Manipur, Tripura and the districts of Cooch Bihar, Jalpaiguri and

Darjeeling in the same. The S.R.C. did not concede to the demand of hill state. It did not recommend the inclusion of sub-Himalayan North Bengal in Assam either. However, the merger of Manipur and Tripura with Assam was recommended by the S.R.C. The Government of India did not concede on that point and *status quo* was maintained.

The 1957 general elections were fought on the issue of separate hill state. The Garo National Council, the East India Tribal Union and U.M.F.O. captured ten seats and Indian National Congress only one in the hills in the Assembly election. The success in election encouraged the hill leaders and the agitation continued.

The Prime Minister Pt. Nehru sent Home Minister Mr. G.B. Pant for reconciliation, who suggested a formula to settle the issue. In the mean time, B.P. Chaliha became the Chief Minister and E.I.T.U. agreed to join his government on the advise of Pt. Nehru. Sangma joined the Ministry. Mr. Sangma established cordial relation between hills and plains, and settled the border issue. He established Tribal Affairs Advisory Committee, which recommended amendment of the Sixth Schedule. The idea of separate state was almost given up by Capt. Sangma.

The official Language bill declaring Assamese as state language gave the hill people opportunity to start the hill state struggle afresh. The creation of Nagaland also encouraged them to do so.

The Birth of All Party Hill Leaders Conference

The announcement of B.P. Chaliha, Chief Minister of Assam that the official language bill would be introduced in the next session of the Assembly generated mixed response. The Assamese welcomed the announcement, but the Bengalis did not like it. It resulted into language riots in Assam, in which both the communities suffered badly. Capt. Sangma was still in the cabinet and Chaliha advised him to call the meeting of the hill leaders to ascertain their views on the issue. The conference passed unanimous resolution to oppose the official language bill and formed All Party Hill Leaders Conference. They also formed a Council of action. Chaliha was unprepared and surprised. APHLC opposed Assamese on the plea that it was spoken only by 50 per cent people of the state and tribal shall be forced to learn four languages and as many scripts after the passage of the bill. The APHLC declared on 22 August, 1960, that they would separate from Assam if Assamese was made the official language. The situation was violent, tense, complex and volatile. There was no meeting point between irreconcilable demands of three communities. The Assamese wanted Assamese as the sole official language, Bengalis wanted Bengali as the second state language and the tribals wanted the continuance of English until replaced by Hindi. The bilingual formula suggested by Home Minister was rejected by the Assamese. He wanted the use of Assamese and Hindi both as the state language. He suggested the continuance of English until replaced by Hindi. Needless to say that the efforts of the Home Minister was not fruitful.

In spite of tremendous opposition from hill districts (except Mikir Hills and North Cachar Hills districts) the official language bill was introduced in the Assembly on 18th October, 1960. The APHLC decided on 2nd November, 1960 to fight for hill state by peaceful and Constitutional methods. It demanded North-East Frontier State consisting of the tribal areas of Assam, Manipur and Tripura. Their main demand included the following for the hill State:

(i) A separate Governor;
(ii) A Council of Ministers;
(iii) 60-member unicameral assembly elected by adult franchise from single member constituency;
(iv) Three Rajya Sabha members;
(v) One Lok Sabha member from each district and two from NEFA;
(vi) Separate High Court;
(vii) A separate University;
(viii) A Public Service Commission;
(ix) Retention and strengthening of District and Regional Councils; and
(x) English as the state language.

When APHLC delegates met Pt. Nehru, then he assured the continuance of English in the Secretariat and the use of medium of instruction of their choice. He thought that smaller states are not economically viable and their developments would be adversely affected. The Home Minister raised certain issue such as the non-contiguity of the geographical areas of the hill districts and the complimentary nature of the economy of the hills and plains of Assam. Prime Minister wanted to provide maximum internal autonomy, sufficient budget for development and their representation in the National Development Council meetings. He put forward Scottish Plan for them.

Scottish Plan

The main features of the Scottish Plan are given below:

1. Regional committee consisting of all the MLAs from the hill districts with certain power.
2. Statutory state council for looking after planning and development funds.
3. The Committee of MLAs from hills to scrutinize the applicability and extension of legislations to the hill areas; the Committee to function under the Cabinet Minister in-charge of the hill affairs.
4. A Cabinet Minister and one or more Deputy Ministers from among the MLAs from the hills to be in charge of the subject concerning the hill areas.
5. Separate budget for the hill areas.
6. More powers to the District Councils.
7. The Governor's verdict to be final in case of the disagreement between the Assam Assembly and the Regional Committees.
8. The appointment of the Commission of inquiry.

The Scottish Plan failed to satisfy the tribals. It did not tackle the language problem and fell far short of the expectations of the hill leaders. The experience with the Advisory Council was not happy and the proposed statutory state council was the new edition of the same. The Scottish Plan did not provide for separation of administration and had enough scope of conflict and friction.

The Prime Minister did not accept the demand of separate state. The Scottish Plan, as already stated, was rejected by 'APHLC'. However, District Congress Committees of the Garo and U.K. & J. Hills accepted the plan. A phase of petioning and non-violent agitation by the APHLC followed. The APHLC fought 1962 elections on Scottish Plan issue and most of its candidates won. As the Hill state demand was not conceded after the election, APHLC asked its MLAs to resign. Many of the MLAs did not follow the party directive in this case and they did not resign.

In the by-election of July 23, 1963 the APHLC did not do as well as in 1962 elections. Moreover, there were defections in the party. The APHLC candidate lost to MNF candidate in 1963 by-election. Mizo Union left APHLC soon after. There was no APHLC in North Cachar Hills soon after its formation as its leaders deserted it. Mikir Hills did not join it from the very beginning.

The APHLC whose area of operation gradually shrunk to only two districts of Assam was offered autonomy by the Prime Minister under what is known as the Nehru Plan. Most of the provisions of the plan were same as those offered under Scottish Plan.

Nehru Plan

Some important provisions under the Nehru Plan are given below:

1. Amendment of Sixth Schedule to give more powers to the District and Regional Councils.
2. A Regional Council for all the hill districts, the laws affecting hill areas to be referred to the council for approval.
3. Each hill district to have one M.P. (Lok Sabha) and one MLA for every 40,000 population.
4. A Cabinet Minister in charge of hill areas and a Minister of State and 1 or 2 Deputy Ministers.
5. Control of Hill Ministry over education, agriculture, horticulture, forests, health and administration of justice.
6. Separate wing of Secretariat for hill affairs.
7. The Hill Minister shall (i) have control over making of plan; (ii) have access to Planning Commission; (iii) control expenditure on the subjects under him; (iv) be responsible for the preparation of the budget with the help of a financial advisor; (v) central grants given under Article 275 and revenue collected in hills; (vi) regulate appointments, postings and transfers under his charge; and (vii) determine the official language.
8. Continuance of Constitutional provisions safeguarding the interests of the hill people.
9. Provision for separate university.
10. Measures to be taken to quicken development.
11. Appointment of a commission to work out details if hill people accept the plan.

The plan provided for the infringement of the rights of Assam Legislative Assembly and the Chief Minister. As per Nehru Plan, the people of the plains practically would have no say in the affairs of the hill men, whereas hill-men shall continue to have say in their affairs as the MLAs of Assam. The number of cabinet birth provided to hill people continued to be too less under the given plan.

After a lot of bickerings, the Nehru Plan was accepted by the hill leaders on 17th April, 1964. The Pataskar Commission was appointed to work out the details of the Nehru Plan.

Pataskar Commission

The Pataskar Commission recommendations were more or less the same as proposed by B.P. Chaliha from time-to-time and fell far short of the promises given by the Prime Minister. He emphasized more on the strengthening of District Councils; did not recommend for a separate wing of secretariat; did not recommend full authority in the matters of planning, budgeting and control of expenditure in the hands of the hill people and considered the issue from administrative rather than political view-point. The abolition of Regional Council, the discretionary powers of the Governor in settling issues in case of dispute between the Regional Committees and the Assembly were out-dated propositions. The readings of Pataskar Commission recommendations remind us of the Bardoloi Committee. The whole exercised seemed to be out-dated.

As was expected, Pataskar Commission recommendations were accepted by the Assam Government but rejected by the hill leaders. The latter re-iterated their demand for the creation of North-Eastern Frontier State.

Failure of Pataskar Commission report to yield anything resulted in a series of attempts to solve the complex tribal problem till ultimately the State of Meghalaya was born, first as an autonomous State under Assam and then as a full-fledged State of the Indian Union. A brief discussion about the various plans and schemes suggested from time to time is given below:

The Nanda Committee Recommendations: A Cabinet Committee under the Chairmanship of G.L. Nanda, the then Home Minister, recommended the formation of sub-state with separate Legislative Assembly and the Council of Ministers under Assam. It was not accepted by the hill leaders.

Federal Plan: The Federal Plan, which was the brain-child of Vishnu Sahay, the Governor, suggested the formation of Federated States of Assam including Hill States, Manipur, Tripura and if possible NEFA. The plan envisaged equal status for all the federating units. The plan failed to evoke positive response. It was for the first time that a re-organization based on equal status for hills and plains was announced.

The Mehta Plan was the next to be proposed and rejected. It also suggested maximum district level autonomy. It was rejected by the APHLC. The North Cachar Hills and the Mikir Hills districts welcomed it.

The APHLC threatened direct action on 20th December, 1967 if hill state was not granted The threat was repeated again. The Government of India announced the plan of re-organization. It is summed up below:

1. The autonomous State of Meghalaya shall consist of the Garo Hills and the U.K. & J. Hills districts. The North Cachar and

the Mikir Hills were free to join the hill state if 2/3 members of their District Councils vote for the same.

2. The Hill State was to have a legislative assembly and council of ministers.
3. It would have power to levy and collect taxes on mineral, passengers, goods, land revenue, excise duty, agricultural income tax and entertainment tax.
4. Fifty nine subjects of the state list was to be transferred to hill state and remaining seven including state highways, major irrigational and flood control projects, etc. hydro electric projects and navigation to Assam. Some subjects of the concurrent list such as conservation of forest, agricultural scheme of common benefit, acquisition and requisition of property was given to the hill state.
5. The executive power and the subjects assigned to the hill state shall be co-extensive.
6. The bills passed by the legislatures would need the Governor's assent.
7. There would be a joint cadre of all India services. Police and public order list would remain with Assam to enable the state to maintain unified administration.
8. The hill state would continue to have representation in Assam Legislative Assembly and Cabinet. The Assembly and the standing committees of the same shall have its jurisdiction over subjects of common interest in the plains.
9. There shall be common High Court, Public Service Commission and the Electricity Board for Assam and the hill state.
10. The District Councils would be given more powers.
11. The Shillong would continue to be the capital of both the states.
12. The autonomous state would continue to be the part of Assam.

The plan was not accepted by the Assam Government on the ground that it would endanger unity, integrity and security of the country. The APHLC accepted it on 28th January, 1969.

As announced by Government of India, the Constitution (Twenty Second Amendment) Act, 1969 was introduced in Lok Sabha. It received the assent of the President of India on 25th September, 1969. A New Article (Article 244A) was inserted in the Constitution as per Article 2 of the Act, Article 275 of the Constitution was amended, which empowered the new state to use the grants in aid received from the consolidated funds of India. Article 37IB was inserted in the Constitution of India as per the new Act (The copy of the Act is given vide Annexure XXIV).

The Mikir Hills and North Cachar Hills districts did not join the autonomous state of Meghalaya. The Mizos delinked them from APHLC quite early and wanted to have their own separate state. Thus, only two districts of Assam remained with the new state.

The futility of the experiment was proved very soon and the Government of India realized it. The autonomous state of Meghalaya was inaugurated on 2nd April, 1970 and the North-Eastern Areas (Re-organization) Act, 1971 (Annexure XXVII) conferred full-statehood to Meghalaya, alongwith Manipur and Tripura within two years from that date. Meghalaya got statehood without sheding blood, through peaceful and non-violent means.

6

ARUNACHAL PRADESH AS A STATE

Early Administrative Arrangements

The Arunachal Pradesh, which became a distinct administrative unit in 1874 as per Regulation 3 of 1873 gradually became a Union Territory and then a State of the Indian Union. The administration of the area was vested in the Governor of Assam according to the Government of India (Excluded and Partially Excluded Areas) Order, 1936 (see Annexure IX). This arrangement continued upto 1947. A change was brought in that year, when India (Provisional Constitution) Order, 1947 vested administration of the area in the Government of Assam (attached vide Annexure XIII) in place of Governor of Assam.

Sadiya Frontier Tract was divided into two administrative units in 1948, namely the Abor Hills district and the Mishmi Hills district. The plains portions of the Balipara Frontier Tract, Tirap Frontier Tract, Abor Hills district and Mishmi Hills district were transferred to Assam in 1951.

The administration of the area was vested in the President of India as per the Constitution of India and the said power of the President was delegated to the Governor of Assam (Annexure XII). The administrative officers of the tracts were the political officers and their assistants.

The Representation of the People Act, 1950 made provision for their representation in the Parliament (Annexure XV). In 1954, the North-East Frontier Areas (Administration) Regulation, 1954 was passed (Annexure XIX) which renamed the North-East Frontier Tracts as North-East Frontier Agency (i.e., NEFA). The boundaries of the different tracts were defined and their names were changed as given below:

Old Name	*New Name*
1. Balipara Frontier Tract	1. Kameng Frontier Division
2. Subansiri District	2. Subansiri Frontier Division

3. Abor Hill District	3. Siang Frontier Division
4. Mishrai Hill District	4. Lohit Frontier Division
5. Tirap Frontier Tract	5. Tirap Frontier Division
6. Naga Tribal Area	6. Tuensang Frontier Division

In 1957, Tuensang Frontier Division was taken out from NEFA and merged with Naga Hill district to form Naga Hills-Tuensang Area, i.e. NHTA.

After fixing the boundaries and renaming the Frontier Tracts as Divisions, Government of India took a significant step of shifting their headquarters from the plains to the interior hills. Bomdila at an altitude of 9,000 ft. was made the headquarters of the Kameng Frontier Division. Similarly, the headquarters of Subansiri, Siang, Lohit and Tirap Frontier Divisions were shifted to Ziro, Tezu, Along and Khela, respectively. The headquarters of the Tuensang Frontier Division was established in early fifties in Chang Naga village of Tuensang. The administrative set-up continued to be very small till early sixties. The development work was yet to start in proper perspective.

The Chinese Aggression and After

The massive Chinese attack on India in October 1962 exposed our defence weaknesses. The Chinese forces virtually walked over our territory without any resistance and our forces withdrew everywhere. The China, however, declared unilateral cease-fire soon after and withdrew, but not completely. It retained certain pockets of our territory south of McMahon Line.

The Chinese aggression had the following impacts:

(a) The North-East Frontier Agency, i.e. NEFA became well-known throughout the country.
(b) It made the Government of India realize its defence weaknesses.
(c) The strategic importance of the area was realized.
(d) The importance of rapid economic development; construction of roads, bridges; opening of new administrative centres, administrative and military out-posts, schools, hospitals, posts-offices, banks, etc. was deeply felt by the government.

The Government of India sincerely worked for the development of the area after 1962 and there was rapid development in almost every field.

The North-East Frontier Agency (Administration) Regulation, 1965 *(Annexure XX)*

The North-East Frontier Agency (Administration) Regulation was passed by the Parliament in 1965. The regulation brought following changes in the existing frame:

(a) There was change in the names of Divisions, which were termed as districts, as given below:

	Old Name	*New Name*
1.	Kameng Frontier Division	Kameng District
2.	Subansiri Frontier Division	Subansiri District
3.	Siang Frontier Division	Siang District
4.	Lohit Frontier Division	Lohit District
5.	Tirap Frontier Division	Tirap District

(b) The designation of the administrative officers were changed.

Old Designation	*New Designation*
Political Officer	Deputy Commissioner
Additional Political Officer	Additional Deputy Commissioner
Assistant Political Officer	Assistant Deputy Commissioner

This was a positive step towards updating the administration of the area. This process continued swiftly and the administration of NEFA was shifted from the charge of Ministry of External Affairs to that of the Home Ministry. It may be pointed out that NEFA and Nagaland continued to be under External Affairs Ministry only for the convenience of the Prime Minister, Pt. Nehru and his special interest in these areas. He was External Affairs Minister and wanted to handle the affairs of these areas himself.

The administrative set-up of the state witnessed rapid growth after that. The Agency had 25 subdivisions and 81 circles by the end of the sixties. The headquarters of NEFA was transferred from Shillong to Itanagar in Subansiri district. Today, there are 21 districts in Arunachal Pradesh.

The Erring Committee and the Introduction of Democratic Process

As stated earlier, the Governor of Assam has discretionary powers in regard to the Frontier Tracts upto independence in 1947. He was divested of his discretionary powers and the same was vested in the Government of Assam just after independence. The power of the Governor was again restored on 26th January, 1950.

The North-East Frontier Agency continued to be without democratic institutions, except for the village level traditional bodies upto the middle of the sixth decade of the last century. NEFA had no Legislative Assembly and Parliament made laws for the Agency, The lone member in Lok Sabha was nominated by the President. The laws made by Assam Legislative Assembly were not applicable in the agency area. The law made by Parliament were applicable only if specific orders for their application were brought out.

The Government of India appointed Erring Committee to suggest ways and measures to introduce and develop democratic institutions in NEFA. The Erring Committee recommendations are summed up below:

1. There should be village council at the village level which should be entrusted with judicial, developmental and general functions. The existing Village Councils should be recognized. The Village Council members should be elected according to customary laws.
2. The Anchal Samitis should be established in each block under the chairmanship of the Sub-Divisional Officer to look after executive and developmental functions assigned to them.
3. A Zilla Parishad consisting of 24-30 members should be formed in each district under the chairmanship of the Deputy Commissioner in place of the District Development Committee.
4. An Agency Council with 20 members — four members from each district — should be formed in NEFA. The Erring Committee recommendations were accepted by Government of India and accordingly the North-East Frontier Agency Panchayati Raj Regulation was passed in 1967 (Annexure XXI).

The Panchayati Raj Regulation provided three tier system of local self-Government starting from village through block to district level. The system was unique for Arunachal Pradesh in many respects. Some of the important aspects of the same are given below:

(a) It was for the first time that the people of Arunachal got opportunity to participate in democratic process.
(b) It gave opportunity of upward mobility of village leadership upto Agency level through Anchal and district levels.
(c) It provided opportunity to train the local elite in modern state-craft and made them capable of running the affairs of not only

the Arunachal Pradesh State Government but also the Central ministries. Today, Arunachal Pradesh is one of the best run states in the country.

(d) Initially, the experiment was one of the guided democracy types. The head of the Anchal Samiti, Zilla Parishad and Agency Councils were the Sub-Divisional Officer, the Deputy Commissioner and the Governor, respectively.

Chapter II of the North-East Frontier Panchayati Raj Regulation, 1967 had articles on declaration of blocks, constitution of Anchal Samitis and their incorporation, alteration in area of block, composition of Anchal Samiti, disqualification for membership, President and Vice-president, term of office, vacancies among members of Anchal Samiti, resignation of office and filling up of casual vacancies, oath of office, officers and employees of Anchal Samiti, motion of no confidence, power of Governor to remove Vice-president or member of Anchal Samiti, meetings of Anchal Samiti, no confidence motion, committees, proceedings not to be invalid, general meetings, and travellings and daily allowances of the members of the Anchal Samitis.

The functions and powers of Anchal Samitis are also given in detail. It has articles on functions of Anchal Samitis, control of Anchal Samiti on certain properties, transfer of any work or management of any institution to or from Anchal Samiti, public charitable dispensaries and hospitals, establishment and maintenance of dispensaries and hospitals, improvement in sanitation, power to do certain acts in the event of an epidemic, disinfection of buildings and articles, removal of persons suffering from infection of contagious diseases to hospitals.

The regulation gives powers to the Anchal Samiti to close markets, the licensing of market, to take steps to ensure water supply, power to compulsory vaccination, power to make contribution to Gram Panchayats, power to protect crops. It provided the power of entry of Anchal Samiti officers in the Anchal Samiti offices or in any house or land as per provisions of the Regulations, establishment and maintenance of bungalows and *sarais* — and offering awards.

The Anchal Samitis were given powers: (i) to raise funds by appropriate ways; (ii) of raising of loans and formation of a sinking fund; and (iii) of application of Anchal Samiti Fund as per the provisions of the regulation.

The Regulation provided for the power of taxation, recovery of taxes and other duties, power of collection of tax or revenue due to Government of the Anchal Samiti.

There are provisions of appeal against levy of taxes, etc. to the Deputy Commissioner. The Governor may, by notification, suspend the levy or imposition of any tax, fee or surcharge and may at any time in like manner rescind such suspension. The Governor has also the power to increase taxation. The Governor may, if he deems fit place certain properties under the direct management and control of Anchal Samitis.

There are detailed provisions for the maintenance of accounts and auditing, preparation of budget estimates of the Samiti and submission of annual administrative report of the Anchal Samiti to the Deputy Commissioner.

There are articles on constitution and composition of Zilla Parishads, term of office of members of Zilla Parishad, President and Vice-president of Zilla Parishad, resignation of vice-president or member, and the functions and meetings of the Parishad in Chapter III.

Chapter IV deals with constitution, function, and the meetings of the Agency Council. The articles on control of Gram Panchayats and Anchal Samitis, and miscellaneous subjects are included in Chapters V and VI respectively. The regulation has also two schedules.

There was happy combination of elected, nominated and ex-officio members of the Panchayati Raj institutions of Arunachal Pradesh. This system under the dynamic guidance of K.A.A. Raja, Chief Commissioner, was instrumental in emergence of young, energetic, vibrant and responsible political leadership.

The Union Territory Status

The North-East Frontier Agency was made a Union Territory with a Chief Commissioner as per the provisions of the North-Eastern Areas (Reorganization) Act, 1971 (*vide* Annexure XXVII) on 21st January, 1972. K.A.A. Raja the Advisor to the Governor was made the Chief Commissioner.

The Pradesh Council was constituted in NEFA after it became a Union territory in January 1972. It consisted of twenty representatives from five districts (four members from each of the districts) the members of the Parliament and three nominated members representing minor unrepresented tribes. It had a chairman, a secretary and 26 members. The administrator was the ex-officio chairman. The Pradesh Council was an advisory and deliberative body, but its advices were mostly carried out as there was very cordial relation between emerging political elite and the bureaucracy. K.A.A. Raja was a man of high integrity and foresight and his innovativeness helped in painless growth of political institutions in Arunachal Pradesh.

There was provision of the appointment of five councillors from among the twenty Pradesh Council members and the same was to be done by nomination by the Chief Commissioner. The Chief Commissioner rather than nominating the councillors got one councillor elected informally by the four members of each district and then the total five members by the Pradesh Council. He then nominated them formally as councillors. Needless to say that this created mutual confidence and harmony between the Pradesh Council members and the Chief Commissioner.

The Arunachal Pradesh was provided one Lok Sabha and one Rajya Sabha seat as provided by the North-Eastern Areas (Re-organization) Act, 1971 and the same were to be filled up by the nomination by the Governor/President. Mr. Raja, rather than nominating the members directly, got them elected by the electoral colleges. The Rajya Sabha member was elected by Agency Council members. The Lok Sabha member was elected by all the members of the Zilla Parishads. Thus, electoral college for Rajya Sabha and Lok Sabha members consisted of 20 and 118 members only when Arunachal Pradesh sent members to the Upper and Lower Houses of Parliament for the first time.

As per Regulation 4 of 1971, the Administrator was to consult one or all the councillors from time to time. In theory, the views expressed by the councillors were supposed to be recommendatory in nature. The Chief Commissioner started the convention of arriving at decisions by having consensus between him and the councillor(s). There was no provision for transfer of portfolios to the councillors in the regulation, but Chief Commissioner did it and did it successfully. He made the councillors *de-facto* Ministers. He consulted each of them and allotted development department only after consulting.

Multiple Screening of Leaders

The only political organizations that existed in Arunachal Pradesh prior to 1967 were village level organizations. The statutory organizations from village to Agency level were only established after Regulation 3 of 1967 was passed on the basis of Erring Committee Report. In the given system, the members were elected by the villagers in traditional way to their respective village Panchayats. The Village Panchayat members were electing members for the Anchal Samiti from among them. Similarly, Anchal Samiti members were electing Zilla Parishad members and the latter were sending four members from among them to the Agency Council. A Councillor was elected from among the Agency Councillors. Thus, one had to get him elected five times for reaching to the top. This process of multi-stage filtration was unique in any state of India. This gave the new and young leaders of Arunachal the desired experience and maturity.

The Agency Council as the apex body continued to function from 1968 to 1972. Its place was taken by Pradesh Council in 1972, when Arunachal Pradesh became a union territory as per the provisions of North-Eastern Area (Re-organization) Act, 1971. The Pradesh Council consisted of the following members:

(i) All the M.Ps.
(ii) All the Vice-Presidents of the Zilla Parishads.
(iii) Three members elected from each of the Zilla Parishads.
(iv) Three persons nominated by the administrator to represent un-represented tribes.

Adult franchise was introduced in 1972 in Arunachal Pradesh.

The Advisor to the Governor was the chairman of the Agency Council. The Chief Commissioner was the Chairman of the Pradesh Council. They developed the convention of electing panel of five Vice-Chairmen — one from each district — to chair the sessions of the Pradesh Council one after another in the absence of the chairman.

The capital of Arunachal Pradesh was shifted to Itanagar in Subansiri district from Shillong after it acquired the union territory status. It was not a painless process; as the employees developed vested interests in their stay at Shillong and wanted to resist any attempt to shift the capital. One important feature of the emerging leadership of Arunachal Pradesh was the relatively young age of the councillors. Their average age was only 32. Prem Khandu Thungon, who later on became the Chief Minister of Arunachal Pradesh was only 29 years old in 1974, when he was a councillor. Arunachal administration sent the councillors in different parts of the country for gaining experience and wider outlook. Thus, emerging leaders of Arunachal gradually and rapidly became ready to manage the state.

Extension of the Area of the High Court

The area of Guwahati High Court was extended to Arunachal as provided in Section 32 of the North-Eastern Areas (Re-organization) Act, 1971.

The Elections, Adult Franchise and the Political Parties

The Universal Adult Franchise was introduced in Arunachal Pradesh in 1972 for Village Panchayat elections. However, the people of Arunachal Pradesh participated in Universal Adult Franchise only in January 1980 General Election for the election of their MLAs. The people went to polls again for the Assembly election during 1985 and after that at regular intervals for both the Assembly and Parliament elections.

There were no political parties in Arunachal Pradesh prior to the introduction of elections based on adult franchise and the introduction of Legislative Assembly and the cabinet. The All India National Congress and the. People's Party of Arunachal Pradesh were the first parties to have their foot-holds. Later on, Janata Party were also introduced in Arunachal Pradesh.

Salaries and perks were given to the councillors in Arunachal Pradesh before the establishment of the Legislative Assembly. Their perks included accommodation, cars and travelling costs. Salaries were paid to council members also.

Arunachal Pradesh as a State

The Pradesh Council was converted into provisional legislative council till the election of 30 members Legislative Assembly in 1975. The Councillors became Ministers, P.K. Thungon became the first Chief Minister of Arunachal Pradesh. It is already mentioned that councillors of Pradesh Council in Arunachal Pradesh were already functioning as Ministers. Their formal appointment as ministers was the recognition of their successful and satisfactory performances. The first Council of Ministers in Arunachal was a cohesive team. Arunachal continued to have such teams.

When Mizoram was granted statehood in 1986 after the agreement between Government of India and Laldenga, then people of Arunachal Pradesh also wanted to have the same. The Government of India readily agreed to grant statehood to Arunachal. In fact Arunachal Pradesh had every thing which a state was supposed to have; its 40 members assembly, its Council of Ministers, a common High Court, its own capital, representation in Parliament and unique history of Administrative and Constitutional growth. The leadership already proved beyond doubt that they have the capacity to run the state. They were capable and deserved statehood. Creation of Mizoram only hastened the process.

The Government of India decided to create the state of Arunachal Pradesh. Accordingly, state of Arunachal Pradesh Bill, 1986 and the Constitution (Fifty fifth) Amendment Bill were introduced in the Lok Sabha in December 1986. The first bill provided for the creation of the state with forty members Assembly and the Council of Ministers. There was provision for safeguarding the religious, social and customary practices of the people of Arunachal Pradesh in that bill. The Governor of Arunachal Pradesh was given special responsibility of maintaining law and order situation. This provision, however, was made because of sensitive location of the state and was to be used very sparingly.

The second Bill was introduced to make Constitutional adjustments to facilitate the creation of Arunachal Pradesh state.

After passing the bill, Lok Sabha sent it to Rajya Sabha and the President. Arunachal Pradesh was inaugurated as 24th State of the Indian Union by Rajiv Gandhi in 1987. The creation of full-fledged state hastened the process of development in Arunachal Pradesh.

7

MIZORAM: FROM DISTRICT TO A STATE

Introduction

The Lushai Hills was conquered by the British in stages. The trend of British annexation in Lushai Hills was the same as that in Naga Hills. The Lushai tribals (now known as Mizos) continued to raid British territories. Punitive actions followed every raid and in course of time the entire Lushai Hills was conquered by the British. The Chief Commissioner of Assam proposed to the Government of India on 17th July, 1897 to transfer South Lushai Hills from Bengal to Assam. He also proposed to merge Demagiri with South Lushai Hills. He suggested the merger of North and South Lushai Hills into a single district of Assam with headquarters at Aizawl and Major Shakespeare as its first Superintendent and Political Officer with effect from 1st October, 1897.

The two districts were accordingly united and placed under Assam with effect from 1st April, 1898. The administration of the district was vested in the Chief Commissioner, the Superintendent and his assistants and in the Chiefs and Headmen of the villages.

The district was declared as an excluded area as per the provisions of Government of India Act, 1935. It was a district of Assam, when India became free in 1947.

Formation of District Council

Lushai Hills took full advantage of the provisions of the Sixth Schedule of the Constitution and the Lushai Hills District Council was formed along with other District Councils of hill districts of Assam.

Early Political Activities

Mizo Union was the first political party of Mizoram, which was established on 9th April, 1946. The party was started by R. Vanlawma the founder general secretary for solving, many local problems of the district; which are listed below:

(i) Unlike any other districts of the country this district has a Superintendent as the head of the Civil and Police administration. Thus, the functions of the District Magistrate (or Deputy Commissioner) and Superintendent of Police were merged in one and were handled by the same officer. This made some of the Superintendents autocratic and oppressive specially when state administration blindly supported them.

(ii) The Mizos had chieftainship. Their chiefs had autocratic powers and they were often supported by the Superintendent in outrageous acts.

(iii) The Lushai Hills district was denied representation in legislature, because it was an excluded area.

The Mizo union pledged to work for the (i) abolition of Chieftainship; (ii) representation of the Mizos in the State and Central legislature; and (iii) improvement of the social and economic conditions of the Mizos.

The party had large followers. Later on, there was split in the party and a section merged with Indian National Congress. The other group became secessionist.

The U.M.F.O. was established by Lalmavia. He was an ex-armyman, who, later on, joined Burmese Civil Service. He wanted that Lushai Hills should join Burma. He could not succeed in enlisting the active support of U Nu in his scheme. After that he started U.M.F.O. and worked for the secession from India. The popularity of Mizo Union, which wanted to stay in India, demoralized Lalmavia. Ultimately, he became the supporter of the North-Eastern Hill State within Indian Union and merged his party with East India Tribal Union.

There were many other parties in Mizoram, but Mizo National Front or M.N.F., which was a late comer in Mizo political scene played crucial role in the formation of Mizoram State.

Mizo Participation in Hill State Movement

A section of Mizos became protagonists of North-Eastern Hill State at a later stage, but most of them wanted more autonomy under Sixth Schedule. When members of the executive councils of the autonomous District Councils of Assam met at Shillong on 16th June, 1954 under the chairmanship of B.M. Roy, the Chief Executive Member of United Khasi and Jaintiya Hills District Council to consider the formation of

Hill State, the views on separate hill state were not acceptable to the Chief Executive Members of the Lushai Hills and North Cachar Hills District Councils. They wanted to have more autonomy for the District Councils rather than a hill state. They never thought in this direction for considerably long period.

When All Party Hill Leaders Conference was formed in 1960, then the political leaders of Mizoram also joined it. They fought 1962 General Election from APHLC ticket and got elected. However, most of them did not follow APHLC directive and therefore, did not resign their assembly seats after the election. One of the candidates who resigned on the party directive lost his seat to MNF candidate in the 1963 bye-election. When APHLC delegation met Central Home Minister in November 1960 to discuss their demand for the creation of hill-state, then one of the objections raised by the latter was that the Hill areas were not geographically contiguous to one another. Saprawnga was representing Mizo Hills district as a delegate. He spontaneously reacted that Mizo Hills may back out from Hill State demand in that case and it should get a state of its own. Perhaps, this sparkled the imagination of Mizos to have a state of their own and the day came very soon when Mizos were no more with the APHLC and it became the party of the Meghalayans only.

The Rise of Mizo National Front

Whenever bamboos flower and bear fruits, the number of rats multiply enormously and crops are eaten by them, creating famine situation resulting into starvation deaths. It happens almost after every fifty years in Mizoram and Mizos call it *Mautam Tampui* (*mau* = bamboo, *tampui* = havoc of famine). In 1959 also *mautam tampui* occurred in Mizoram. The Assam Government was given advance warning about the famine, but they failed to take timely and adequate measures to combat the worsening situation. There were starvation deaths and this angered Mizos. The Mizo Cultural Society founded by John F. Maniliana tried to help the starving people, but could not do much in this direction. Mizo National Famine Front was formed in 1959 to organize relief work. R. Dengthuama and Laldenga were president and secretary respectively, of the new organization. Mizo National Famine Front was convened into Mizo National Front, a political party on 22nd October, 1961 with Laldenga and R. Valawma as its first elected president and secretary respectively.

Laldenga was inspired by the Phizo and the N.N.C. The formation of Nagaland state encouraged him to launch armed rebellion in Mizoram. He modelled MNF on the lines of NNC. Later on, a break away group of MNF, turned itself as MNC, i.e. Mizo National Council like Naga National Council.

Laldenga was a primary school teacher before Second World War and a Haviklar clerk during the war. He joined District Council office as an accountant in 1952. He resigned his job of accountant so that to escape the charge of misappropriation of District Council funds. He was defeated in District Council elections in early sixties.

Laldenga was a fine orator and he had a mesmerizing gaze. He took full advantage of the following factors to make MNF popular:

(i) MNF under the leadership of Laldenga took full advantage of people's anger against Assam Government for not taking adequate famine relief measures in spite of prior warning.

(ii) It took full credit for fighting the famine and helping the suffering people.

(iii) The District Council and the Mizo Union leaders who were controlling the District Council had initially very good relation with the Congress. However, they were very angry with B.P. Chaliha, Assam Government and I.N.C. party after their prior advice about famine relief work were ignored by the latter. Laldenga fully utilized the rift between the Mizo Union and the Congress and the angry statements of the District Council and Mizo Union leaders against Assam government for the halting and inadequate relief measures.

(iv) The Mizo Union and the Congress parties were responsible for the abolition of Chieftainship. It is alleged that the compensations were not given to the chiefs observing equity. Educated chiefs got more in comparison to uneducated ones. Although government paid handsome compensation, many chiefs spent the money in no time and became paupers. The pauperization of chiefs made them angry with the government and the Mizo Union. MNF under the leadership of Laldenga easily enlisted the support of the disgruntled chiefs.

(v) MNF enlisted the support of discharged men of the 2nd battalion of the Assam regiment, who were dissatisfied because regiment was disbanded without making any provision for their re-habilitation. They formed the part of underground army of M.N.F. later on.

(vi) Lack of proper economic planning left a large section of people unemployed and dissatisfied. They became supporters of MNF in due course.

(vii) Lack of dynamism and proverbial vacillation on the part of the Chief Minister and his playing politics in Mizo Hills affairs helped the MNF. The Chief Minister pampered MNF in order to make Mizo Union weak, inspite of being informed about the treasonable activities of the MNF.

(viii) MNF continued to talk of non-violent methods to be adopted by them. On the other hand, their efforts for armed rebellion continued unabated. The government was caught unaware when MNF staged armed rebellion. They could realize very late that they were hood-winked and the talk of constitutional and non-violent Gandhian methods by Laldenga had no meaning for him.

(ix) The Mizos also did not like Assamese as the official language and Mizo Union joined APHLC earlier on this issue.

(x) Pakistan continued to help Mizo rebels by giving them military training and by supplying them arms and ammunitions.

Under above circumstances, Laldenga's open preaching for independence found receptive ears and hearts and he was never stopped from doing so by the Assam government. The almost open and very long international border with Burma and East Pakistan helped MNF in organizing insurgency.

A point which is important and pertinent and needs to be mentioned here is, that our governments have always followed wrong *modus operandi* in tackling such problems, which used to send wrong signals that violence may pay and one may reach the corridors of seat of power through violence. The MNF and Laldenga really came to the seat of power through violence and rebellion.

The MNF fought District Council and Assembly elections during 1962 and after that also, but mostly lost the battle to Mizo Union. Even Laldenga lost District Council elections. They, however, could win a bye-election in 1963. The Mizo Union always wanted to stay in India and Mizos voted for it. It was due to mishandling of Mizo affairs that MNF could win a section of Mizos for secessionist cause.

The MNF openly preached secession and no action was taken against it. In a memorandum submitted to the Prime Minister on 30th October, 1965, it said:

"Mizos from time immemorial lived in complete independence without foreign interference. Chiefs of the different clans ruled over separate hills and valleys with supreme authority and their administration was very much like that of Greek city stales of the past . . . they are a distinct nation, created and moulded and nurtured by God and Nature. The Mizos had never been under Indian Government. . . ."

"Solely (due) to their political immaturity, ignorance and lack of consciousness of their fate, the representatives of the Mizo Union choose integration with free India".

"During fifteen years of contact and association with India, the Mizo people had not been able to feel at home with Indians, or in India, nor have they been able to feel that their joys and sorrows have really ever been shared by India. They do not feel, therefore, Indians. Being created a separate nation, they cannot go against the nature to cross barriers of nationality. They refused to occupy a place within India as they consider it to be unworthy of their national dignity and harmful to the interests of their posterity".

"The only aspiration and political cry is the creation of Mizoram, a free and sovereign State to govern herself to work out her own destiny and to formulate her own foreign policy".

"Though Mizos are head-hunters and belong to a martial race, they will adopt non-violent methods if independence is not granted".

Armed Rebellion

The MNF was not only preaching independence, but was also preparing to achieve it through armed revolt. They recruited and trained thousands of persons, many of them ex-army men for violent struggle and just in four months time after submission of above mentioned memorandum, they captured Aizawl and issued the Declaration of Independence, which sounded somewhat like Declaration of American War of Independence. It reads as given below:

"In the course of history, it becomes invariably necessary for mankind to assume their social, economic and political status to which the laws of Nature's God entitle them. We hold this truth to be self-evident that all men are created equal and that they are endowed with inalienable fundamental human rights and dignity of human persons and to secure these rights, governments are instituted among men deriving their just powers from the consent of the governed, and whenever any form of government becomes destructive of them, it is the right of the people to alter, change, modify and abolish it and institute a new government laying its foundation on such forms as to them shall seem most likely to effect their rights and dignity. The Mizos created and moulded into a nation and nurtured as such by Nature's God, have been intolerably dominated by the people of India in contravention to the laws of nature".

A bomb exploded at the electric veng, Aizawl on 28th February, 1966. After a few hours, on 1st March, 1966, an hour after midnight, the Aizawl sub-treasury was attacked and ₹ 64,000 and some arms and ammunitions were looted. Actually three plateless jeeps and a truck were parked in front of the sub-treasury and armed men overpowered the treasury guards and looted it. They put out the Aizawl Telephone Exchange and declared independence.

The revolt was properly planned and it broke out simultaneously in all the important towns of Mizo Hills. Kolasib, Champai, Saireng, etc. were captured on March, 3 and Lunglei on March 5, 1966. The sub-treasury was also looted at Lunglei. The S.D.O. (Civil) was captured. The Assam Rifles at Lunglei was also over-powered.

The Mizo Hills district was completely captured by the rebels. Assam Rifles and Assam Police failed to meet the situation. Army had to be called in.

The rebels also formed their underground government Mizoram Sawrkar, as they called it — with a president, a parliament, a speaker, and the council of ministers. They declared the establishment of National Judiciary (National Refinement Court) and National Army, (Mizo National Army).

The formation of four Divisions, each under a Chief Commissioner, and four Sub-Divisions in each Division, each under a Deputy Commissioner was announced. All received the uniform salary of ₹ 15 per month.

We find a parallel in the *modus operandi* of underground movement in Nagaland and Mizoram. Laldenga and MNF copied everything, with slight modification here and there, from Phizo and NNC.

There were many factors, which helped Laldenga and MNF in getting an upper hand in Mizo Hills affairs. We have already discussed those points. What helped MNF most was the apathy of Assam government. Thousands of people participated in the uprising and things were planned meticulously. It is most surprising that Assam Government remained highly ignorant and inactive and was caught napping when even the final scene of the drama was being enacted.

Counter-Measures and Pacification

The Army was called in aid of the civil power. The Government of Assam declared Mizo Hills district as a disturbed area under the Assam Disturbed Areas Act, 1955. The Armed Forces (Assam and Manipur) Special Power Act, 1958 was also applied. The MNF was declared as an unlawful organization on 6th March, 1966, by Government of India and was banned under Defence of India Rules.

The army started its operation as soon as it was requisitioned. It captured Aizawl on 5th March, 1966 and moved towards Lunglei under air cover. The Lunglei was spared from being bombed on the intervention of Church leaders and it was captured without resistance. All the towns were re-captured by army within a month. The MNF vice-president requested D.C. to arrange talk between the Government and the rebels- on 7th March, 1966. The D.C. asked them to surrender.

The hard-core of MNF retired to deep valleys and inaccessible hills and forests after army captured all the towns. The army also proposed to the Government of India to hand over the district to the Defence Ministry. The Government of India did not agree. Then army worked out Operation Security by regrouping of villages. The aim of the grouping of the villages was:

(a) to facilitate effective military operation against the rebels;
(b) to segregate them from the masses;
(c) to provide protection to the villagers;
(d) to facilitate economic development;
(e) to provide social services to all; and
(f) to provide communication facilities.

The army claimed that the grouping of villages helped the villagers. It certainly helped them and also helped army in combating insurgency.

However, villagers suffered a lot of hardship during the regrouping. It is alleged that compensations were given to few persons only. The shifting was compulsory rather than voluntary and the villagers had to suffer physically and psychologically while leaving their old villages and parental homes inspite of their migratory habits. Mizoram had a large number of very small villages scattered throughout the hills and not connected by roads and it was not possible for the army to protect them unless they were re-settled near the roads. This was the logic behind the regrouping of villages.

Although back-bone of the underground movement was broken by army operation, insurgency continued. The army had to continue counter-insurgency measures for prolonged period. The government stepped up development efforts and social welfare activities. This had the desired effect and a large number of underground came overground. There was split in MNF and most of the intellectuals deserted it. There was confusion and demoralization in the rank and file of MNF. The people wanted peace. The emergence of Bangladesh deprived the underground of their support base.

Union Territory Status

The desirability of awarding union territory status was felt by many people after the start of underground activities. Mizoram was awarded Union Territory Status on 21st January, 1972 as per the provisions of the North-Eastern Areas (Re-organization) Act, 1971. Mizoram also got its Legislative Assembly and Council of Ministers as per the Act of 1971.

The first two Ministries led by the Congress and the People's Conference tried to bring MNF to conference table. There efforts bore fruit and an accord was signed between the Union Home Secretary and MNF Chief Laldenga on 1st July, 1976. The agreement could not be implemented due to some reasons, leading to another phase of insurgency, counter-insurgency and pacification.

The talks were called off in 1978 and MNF stepped up its hostile activities against security forces, civil officials and non-Mizos. This resulted into ban on MNF and its allied organizations and arrest of Laldenga on 8th July, 1979.

Fresh effort by Mizoram Pradesh Congress (1) resulted in resumption of talks and dropping of charges against Laldenga after 1980, but the talks broke down due to Laldenga's demands of greater Mizoram and constitutional safeguards for Mizoram of Jammu & Kashmir type.

The Congress (I) Ministry headed by Lalthanhawla came to power in Mizoram in 1984, Lalthanhawla was committed to the cause of peace, harmony and development. MNF also wanted the resumption of peace talks. Laldenga was called back from London to Delhi on 29th October, 1984. After a lot of deliberations and series of discussions and consultations, a memorandum of settlement was signed on 30 June,

1986 by R.D. Pradhan, Central Home Secretary; Laldenga, MNF Chief and Lalkhama, Chief Secretary, Government of Mizoram.

After the peace accord MNF deleted the clause of "Independence and secession from India" and other objectionable clauses from its constitution. The underground MNF and MNA personnel surrendered with arms and ammunitions. The Government of India took steps to confer statehood on Mizoram and to rehabilitate the surrendering personnel of the MNF and MNA. The ban on MNF was lifted. MNA was disbanded.

The Statehood

The State of Mizoram Act, 1986 and Constitution (53rd Amendment) Act conferred Statehood on Mizoram. An interim Congress-MNF coalition government was formed on 21st August, 1986 with Laldenga as Chief Minister and Lalthanhawla as Deputy Chief Minister as per the understanding between the Government and MNF. The Chief Minister, Lalthanhawla resigned earlier after the State Act was passed to facilitate the formation of the new coalition government.

The journey of Mizoram from a district to a state took 39 years. It is one of the smallest states of the Indian Union both in terms of area and population but, has a bright future and a lot of promise for Mizos and India as a whole.

8

THE CONSTITUTIONAL GROWTH OF MANIPUR AND TRIPURA

Introduction

The Manipur and Tripura were Princely States during pre-independence period. Although, the two states had their kings, but the real power in, the states were vested in the British Political Agents and Darbar. Ironically, the Chairmen of the Darbars were not the kings, but the British Officers. In Manipur, Raja had practically no say in the administration of tribal areas, and limited power in many other matters such as in financial matters. The Political Agent was empowered to refer any matter or any decision of the Maharaja of Manipur to the Government of Assam in consultation with the latter. Similar power was vested in Political Agent in Tripura also.

Developments after Independence

A series of administrative, political and constitutional developments took place in Manipur and Tripura after the dawn of Independence in India.

The State Constitution Acts

The Maharajas and their followers in both Manipur and Tripura tried to take full advantage of the exit of the British from Indian political scene. Attempts were made in both the States to pass State Constitution Acts and to restore their Sovereignties.

The State Constitution Acts tried to give democratic frame to the respective monarchies. However, everything was done in a hurry leading to a lot of confusion.

The Manipur State Constitution Act, 1947, provided for the establishment of a State Assembly with 3/5 members from the valley and 2/5 from the Hills. No party could muster majority in the 53 members Assembly and a coalition Government was formed after 1948 elections. K.C. Chakravorty, Legal Remembrancer was appointed Chairman of the Assembly, who had to resign after some time due to discontentment about his appointment as he was not a member of the Assembly. The Constitution was silent on the appointment of ministers. The matter had to be referred to the Legislatures to decide whether they were to elect Ministers from among them?

The Legislature and the Coalition Government Ministry in Manipur was abolished soon after the merger Agreement was signed by the Maharaja and the State joined Indian Dominion. The same thing happened in Tripura also.

The paramountcy lapsed in 1947 and the Raja entered into a Standstill Agreement with the Government of India in August, 1947. On 21st September, 1947, the Maharaja acceded to the Indian dominion and the State of Manipur was merged with the same. He ceased to be the head of the state. The Government of India appointed a Chief Commissioner as the Head of the State on 15th October, 1949. On 22nd January, 1950 Manipur was declared as a Chief Commissioner's Province. The Head of the State was designated in 1969 as Lt. Governor and in 1972 as the Governor. As per Part-C States Act 1950, the Territorial Council Act, 1956 and the Government of Union Territories Act, 1963, the Head of the Slate was Administrator. He could be a Chief Commissioner or Lt. Governor as determined by the President at the time of appointment.

The status of Manipur and Tripura rapidly changed with effect from 1950 to 1972. The two States became Part-C States as per Part-C States Act, 1950, on 22nd January, 1950. The States Re-organization Commission, 1956 suggested their merger with Assam, but Government of India did not do so. They were given their Territorial Councils in 1956 as per Territorial Council Act, 1956 and Union Territory Status in 1963 as per the provisions of Union Territories Act, 1963.

The Statehood was conferred to Manipur and Tripura as per North-Eastern (Re-organization) Act, 1971.

A brief discussion about these developments follows:

Advisory Councils

After the merger of Manipur and Tripura with the dominion of India, their Legislative Councils were abolished. The Government of India provided Advisory Councils in 1950 for these states, which consisted of the Chief Commissioner and Members nominated by the Central

Government on the advice of the Chief Commissioner. 15 Member Advisory Council for Manipur was inaugurated on 9th October, 1950. This was done as per the provisions of Part-C States Act, 1950.

The Part-C States Act laid down that the President may for Manipur . . . constitute a Council of Advisers consisting of such number or members as he may think fit for the purpose of assisting the Chief Commissioner in the discharge of his functions under Article 239 as may be specified by the President and the notification constituting such a Council shall define the powers to be exercised and the procedures to be followed by the Council. Similar provision was also made for Tripura.

Besides the Advisory Council there was also an Electoral College, consisting of 30 members for the election of a member to Rajya Sabha. The elections to the electoral college were held in 1952, and the electoral college was abolished after the election to the Rajya Sabha was over.

Any resident of a Part-C State above the age of 21 was eligible for nomination as a member. Each Adviser was paid a salary of ₹ 500 per month and sumptuary allowance of ₹ 150 per month. The Chief Commissioner consulted the Advisers on any matter concerning the administration of the state and on matters of policy, but the advisers had no right to interfere with the day to day administration and the function of the council was limited to general policies and development programme.

The members of the council were free to interpellate on subjects with certain limitations. The Chief Commissioner could refuse to give any information in public interests. He could also disallow discussion on any subject. The council met once in three months and the Chief Commissioner presided over the meetings of the council.

As per Part-C States Act, 1950, the Parliament delegated the legislative, power in respect of the Part C States to the Central Government and the Central Government could extend laws in force in any Part-A State to Manipur with such restrictions and modifications as it thought fit.

After the re-organization of states in 1956, Part C States ceased to exist and in their place, Territorial Councils were established under the Territorial Council Act, 1956.

In 1956, the State Re-organization Commission recommended the merger of Manipur and Tripura with Assam. But the proposal was opposed by all the political of two states and the same was not done.

Territorial Council Act, 1956

The political and constitutional position of the union territories was not equal to that of the states. The former shall be administered by the President through the Administrator designated as Chief Commissioner or Lt. Governor. The President could make legislation in the form of Regulation for the peace, order and good government of the union territories. He appointed the Governor of a neighbouring state as the Administrator of the territory and required him to act in relation to the territory independently of his responsibility for the state of which he happened to be the Governor and without aid and advice of the Council of Ministers.

The union territory did not have the legislative and executive powers of the Constitution like the states. It had no right to express its views on the formation or alteration of the name and boundaries of the existing state (Art. 3) and there was no provision for the membership of the Presidential Electoral College for the members of the Territorial Council (Art. 35); Constitutional Amendments were not referred to them for ratification, and the distribution of powers under the federal rule was not applicable to any union territory.

The Territorial Council Act, 1956 laid down that for each union territory there shall be a Territorial council. The strengths of the Manipur and Tripura Territorial Councils were fixed at 30. The Central Government could nominate not more than two non-official persons. The first members of the Council should be elected on the basis of adult franchise holding office for a term of five years. The Territorial Council was a body corporate and had perpetual succession and a seal. It should elect a chairman and a vice-chairman from among its members. The members of the Territorial Council should register electors. The Territorial Council came into existence on 16th August, 1957 in Manipur. In Tripura also it was established in the same month.

The council had the power to remove its Chairman by a 2/3 vote of the total membership of the council.

Although the term of the council was fixed at five years, but it could be dissolved at any time before the expiry of its normal term.

The members of the Territorial Council were entitled to receive such salaries and allowances as determined by the Union Government.

The quorum for meetings was one fifth of the total strength of the Council. It should meet at least once in two months.

Powers and Functions of the Territorial Council

The council must maintain movable and immovable property, construct, repair, and maintain roads, bridges and buildings, undertake planting and preservation of trees, control of traffic, construct ropeways and tramways, establish hospitals, dispensaries and markets, supply water for domestic purposes, undertake establishment and management of primary and secondary schools, the training of teachers, the award of scholarships, and public health.

The council was not concerned with the maintenance of law and order, administration of justice, police, collection of taxes and forests, as such functions were not transferred to Territorial Council.

The council could levy taxes on professions, trade, calling and employment and tolls on bridges with the previous sanction of the Central Government. It received grants of various kinds, matching grant, general grants, etc.

It must submit its financial statement to the Central Government through the Administrator.

It should send the budget to the Administrator after it was passed by it. The Administrator might return the budget to it for modification, if it failed to make adequate provision for certain services. When the budget is returned the council should consider the proposals made by the Administrator and return the same to him for his assent.

The chairman of the council should furnish the Administrator with a copy of the proceedings of the meeting of the council and such other informations required by him. The latter had the power to suspend the execution of any resolution or orders of the council, prevent the doing of any act which was about to be done or was being done in pursuance of or under the cover of any provision of the law. He may suggest the suspension or the dissolution of the council to the President. The Central Government could supersede the council if it was convinced that it was not competent to discharge its duties under law, or if it persistently defaulted in the discharge of its duties or acted unconstitutionally.

The Administrator appointed the Chief Executive Officer. In reality the council selected the officer with the approval of the Administrator.

Union Territoryhood

Manipur and Tripura were converted into Union Territories under the Union Territory Act, 1963 and their existing Territorial Councils were converted into Territorial Assemblies. The Chairman of the Territorial Council was appointed as the Chief Minister of the Union Territory. Certain political parties such as C.P.I. and Socialist Party in Manipur started agitation for the establishment of Legislative Assemblies. The Legislative Assemblies were accordingly established by converting existing Territorial Councils into Legislative Assemblies as per the provisions of Government of Union Territories Act, 1963. Manipur and Tripura Legislative Assemblies with 30 elected and two nominated members started functioning in July 1963.

The tenure of the Assembly was five years. The quorum for meeting was one third of the total strength of the Assembly. It had its own Speaker and Deputy Speaker. The Chief Minister was appointed by the President and other Ministers were appointed by the President on the advice of the Chief Minister. They held office during the pleasure of the President. The Assembly had power to make laws for the whole or any part of the Union Territory with respect to any of the matter enumerated in the State list or the Concurrent list in the Seventh Schedule of the Constitution. This did not derogate from the powers conferred on Parliament by the Constitution to make laws with respect to any matter for a union territory or any part thereof. In case, if any provision of a law made by the Legislative Assembly of the union territory was repugnant to any provision of a law made by Parliament, than the law made by the Parliament prevailed.

The money bills could be moved in the Assembly only on the recommendation of the Administrator. After a bill had been passed by the Legislative Assembly, it was presented to the Administrator who reserved it for the consideration of the President, who could direct the Administrator to return the bill together with a message for reconsideration.

The Administrator in each financial year, with the previous approval of the President, presented a financial statement of the estimated receipts and expenditures, showing separately,

(a) the sums required to meet expenditure charged upon the Consolidated Fund of the union territory; and
(b) the sums required to meet other expenditures proposed to be made from the Consolidated Fund of the union territory.

Most of the expenditures such as the emoluments and allowances of the Administrator and expenditures relating to his office were charged from the Consolidated Fund of India.

The Legislative Assembly formed during U.T. stage continued after statehood. A candidate for membership of the Legislative Assembly must be a citizen of India, of not less than 25 years of age and take the prescribed oath before the date fixed for the scrutiny of the nomination papers.

The Legislative Assembly should meet once in six months and as often as is necessary. The Governor shall from time to time summon, prorogue or dissolve the Legislative Assembly. It may be noted here that a convention has come into being namely that the Governor should act on the advice of the Chief Minister. However, if the Chief Minister refuses to advise him under certain circumstances, the Governor may summon the legislature to test whether the Chief Minister has the necessary majority in the Assembly.

Powers and Functions of the Assembly

The Assembly of the union territory has the power to elect and remove the Speaker and the Deputy Speaker of the Assembly, by a vote of no confidence. The Assembly has also power to approve or disapprove the annual payment of loans advanced to the union territory from the Consolidated Fund of India including interest, sinking fund charges, redemption charges and other expenditures concerned therewith, the salaries and allowances of the Speaker and Deputy Speaker of the Legislative Assembly, the salaries and allowances of the Judicial Commissioner, any sum required to satisfy any judgement, decree or award of any court or Arbitration Tribunal, expenditures incurred in the discharge of his special responsibilities and finally any other expenditure declared by the Constitution or by law made by Parliament to be charged.

Expenditures charges on the Consolidated Fund were not submitted to the vote of the Legislative Assembly, but they could be discussed in it. The estimates of other expenditures were submitted in the form of demands for grant to the Legislative Assembly. All demands for grants could be made on the recommendation of the Administrator.

The Administrator could submit a supplementary budget if the amounts already provided are not sufficient to meet expenditures already sanctioned.

Thus, the Legislative Assemblies of Manipur and Tripura under the Act of 1963 had no exclusive power to make laws with respect to any matter included in the State List II or the concurrent list of the Seventh Schedule. Parliament had the paramount power to legislate with regard to any matter included in the State List in relation to Manipur and Tripura.

The Statehood

There was agitation for Statehood in Meghalaya, Manipur and Tripura. The North-Eastern Areas (Re-organization) Act, passed by the Parliament during the December Session of 1971, conferred statehood on all three of them. Thus, Manipur and Tripura attained full statehood alongwith Meghalaya in January 1972.

The journey from Part-C State level to full-fledged statehood was passed by Manipur and Tripura together. The statehood was achieved by Mizoram and Arunachal Pradesh after these two states, which ultimately culminated into Re-organization of North-East India into seven states.

9

NORTH-EASTERN COUNCIL AND THE REGIONAL PLANNING

North-Eastern Council was established as an additional instrument of regional planning on 1st August, 1972 by the Central Government as per the North-Eastern Council Act, 1971 passed by the Parliament (attached *vide* Annexure XXVIII). There were five states and two union territories (now seven states) in the region at that time and most of them were very small.

There were many reasons for establishing North-Eastern Council as a device for regional planning. Some of them are noted below:

(1) Although the region has seven political units, the area is geographically compact and strategically located with international borders with China (Tibet), Burma, Bangladesh and Bhutan with narrow land strip linking it with the rest of the country. The region as a whole needs integrated development.

(2) Most of the North-Eastern states are too small and economically unviable depending on Central Government's fund for development. They lack the capacity to invest sum for huge development projects. The North-Eastern Council was to provide common-infrastructure for the region.

(3) There was need for the states to cooperate and work in unison in many fields such as transport, power generation and flood control. It is often difficult in this region to travel from one part of a state to another part of the same without passing through a second state. Therefore, inter-state road transport need to be developed rapidly. It was not possible to do so with the meagre state resources nor is it possible today. Conversion of metre gauge into broad gauge railway line was equally essential for rapid economic growth of the region.

(4) The region continued to be poor in power generation and

consumption inspite of huge power generation potential. Power generation and distribution need huge sums and it is not possible to, meet the same by poorer and smaller states. Moreover, the power generation and consumption potentials were not located in the same states and, therefore, needed regional planning.

(5) North-East India need inter-state planning in many other fields, such as irrigation and agricultural development, manpower development, man-power planning and training, etc. Establishment of North-Eastern Regional Institute of Science and Technology (NERIST), Itanagar, Law Research Institute at Guwahati, etc. are the steps taken by the NEC in positive direction.

(6) A common forum to co-ordinate so that to avoid overlapping and duplication of development activities and wastage of resources by providing expert guidance was needed in the region. The NEC may safely perform the role. It may act as think tank and clearing house in fields of academic and social planning.

As envisaged, the NEC formulates regional plans to meet the above mentioned needs. The regional plan prepared and implemented by North-Eastern Council are in addition to the state plans and the former supplement the latter.

The credit goes to North-Eastern Council for successful formulation and implementation of a large number of useful projects in the region such as Kapili and Loktak power projects, construction of inter-state roads, survey and construction of new railway lines linking various states, railway gauge conversion, technical advices, etc.

Initially, there were apprehensions about the intentions of the Central Government and North-Eastern Council was taken as a device to curtail the powers of the states and to be used for interfering into their internal affairs by Central Government. Gradually, Government of India could convince them that the NEC would be primarily an Advisory Body and the states and union territories were free to join or not to join it. The idea to form the council was conceived as early as in 1968, but the same could be established four years later due to the reason given above. The draft act of 1970 was thoroughly revised in the NEC Act of 1971 and even then Nagaland did not join it in the beginning.

As it stands today, apart from all the seven states of the region Sikkim also have joined the NEC and their Governors and Chief Ministers are included as the members of the council. Initially, Governor of

Assam was the chairman, but now one of the Governors does the job. The NEC has its own Secretariat at Shillong. It has a Secretary, a Planning Advisor, a Financial Advisor, a Security Advisor, etc. The Chief Secretaries of the States meet once in six months to review the progress made during the period and to formulate new plans.

As stated earlier, NEC is an Advisory body as per the NEC Act of 1971. It advises and helps the states in making state plans. It prepares and implements plans in the matters of common interests such as generation of powers, inter-state transport, the economic and social planning and flood control. It is authorized to formulate proposals leading to balanced development of the region and forward them to the Central Government.

The proposal of regional plans are prepared in addition to the state plans. The schemes/proposals included in the unified and co-ordinated regional plans must benefit two or more states of the region. The functions of the council have been clearly defined in the Act (*see* the Annexure XXVIII). The NEC has played effective role in many fields which has certainly helped the growth of the region. The positive role played by the NEC in some of the fields is given below:

(i) The survey and extension of new railway lines to Arunachal Pradesh, Manipur, Mizoram, Tripura, Meghalaya and Nagaland. The first four states have already rail link now. Assam and Nagaland already had it.
(ii) Railway gauge conversion.
(iii) Detailed investigation and survey of potentials of power schemes.
(iv) Construction and commissioning of power projects such as Kapili Power Project.
(v) Survey and construction of inter-state roads.
(vi) Funds for the development of agriculture, industry and manpower development.
(vii) Reservation of seats for students in various Technical Institutions of the country.
(viii) Soil conservation and Jhum control schemes.
(ix) Foundation of seed potato farms at Tawang (Arunachal Pradesh), Sialkosh (Mizoram) and Laitkara (Meghalaya).
(x) Fruit nurseries at Dirang (Anunachal Pradesh), Maran (Manipur).
(xi) Ginger station at Thingdaw (Mizoram).

(xii) Swine Husbandry and Pork procession unit, Assam Agricultural University, Jorhat.
(xiii) Fish seed farms.
(xiv) Fish breeding farms.
(xv) Fisheries Training Institute, Joy-Sagar, expansion programme, etc.
(xvi) Technical expertise for coffee, rubber and cardamon plantation, etc.
(xvii) The North-Eastern Handicraft and Handloom Development Corporation.
(xviii) Sericulture Training Institute-expansion work.
(xix) Silk reeling unit in Tripura.
(xx) Regional Mulbery seed station in Meghalaya and Manipur.
(xxi) Regional Munga seed station, Kharama, N.C. Hills, etc.
(xxii) Graduate Nursing College, Guwahati.
(xxiii) Regional Medical College, Imphal, expansion programme.
(xxiv) Design and Technical Development Institute, Guwahati.
(xxv) Regional Police Training Institute, Barapani.
(xxvi) The College of Physical Education, Tripura (documentation centre at NEC secretariat).
(xxvii) Regional Students Hostel, Shillong and Engineering College Hostel, Agartala.
(xxviii) Law Research Institute, Guwahati High Court.
(xxix) Surveys by Satellite remote sensing survey.
(xxx) Various training programmes.
(xxxi) Various programmes for the development of agriculture, industry, minerals, power, etc.
(xxxii) Providing experts/technical expertise, etc.

The list is in no way exhaustive and can be multiplied. Thus, NEC is doing immense service to the region and is a very useful regional forum.

10

AUTONOMY MOVEMENTS AND FURTHER RE-ORGANIZATION OF NORTH-EAST INDIA

North-East India, as discussed elsewhere in the book, had the State of Assam, the Princely States of Manipur and Tripura and Khasi Syiemships when India attained freedom. The princely States merged in the country as it happened in other parts of India. The Constitution of India provided for the tribal autonomy under the Sixth Schedule of the Constitution. Accordingly, following Autonomous District Councils with legislative, judicial and budgetary powers were constituted:

1. United Khasi and Jaintia Hills District Council (UKJHD) with headquarters at Shillong;
2. Garo Hills District Autonomous Council (GHDAC) with headquarters at Tura;
3. United Mikir and North Cachar Hills District Council (UMNCHDC) with headquarters at Diphu; and
4. Mizo Hills District Council (MHDC) with headquarter at Aizawl.

The district council was not formed in the Naga Hills district of the then Assam as Nagas declined to have it. Moreover, a section of the Nagas started insurgency under the leadership of the Naga National Council under its leader Z.A. Phizo. The over-ground Naga leadership worked out a settlement with Government of India, which resulted into the formation of "Naga Hills-Tuensang Area (NHTA)", a Centrally Administered Territory in 1957 by merging Naga Hills district of Assam and Tuensang division of North-East Frontier Agency (NEFA; now Arunachal Pradesh), which emerged as full-fledged State of Indian Union in December 1963. It became the 16th State of the Indian Union.

The introduction of the bill declaring Assamese as the State language of Assam led to the agitation of separate Hill State comprising of the hill districts of Assam. The agitation led to the formation of Meghalaya as a sub-State and then as a full-fledged State. It consisted of the two hill districts of the Meghalayan plateau — United Khasi and Jaintia Hill district and Garo Hills district. The remaining two districts of Assam did not join the new State.

Two separate Autonomous District Councils were formed when the United Mikir and North Cachar Hill district was bifurcated into two separate districts. The demand for the statehood, however, continued to be raised in the two regions from time to time. The nomenclature of the two has changed according to the names used by the two tribes themselves. As the Mikirs call themselves Karbi, the name of their district now is "Karbi Anglong, and that of the autonomous council is Karbi Anglong Autonomous Council (KAAC)". Similarly, North Cachar Autonomous District Council was named Dima Hasao Autonomous District Council (DHADC) as it was named after Dima (Dimasa, Dimasa Cachari) tribe.

The movement by the Bodos of the Brahmaputra valley for the creation of Bodoland State led to the creation of Bodoland Territorial Council (BTC). The agitation for the full-fledged Sate still continues. Some other autonomous tribal councils for half a dozen different communities have also been created in the Brahmaputra valley, but those tribal councils are not functioning under the provisions of the Sixth Schedule of the Constitution of India.

The Mizo Hills district of Assam witnessed the secessionist movement under Mizo National Front led by Lal Denga. The district became a Centrally Administered Territory, and then a full-fledged State as a result of Mizoram accord with rebel leader. The States of Manipur, Tripura and Arunachal Pradesh became full-fledged States as a result of the State Re-organization in 1971. Manipur and Tripura, like many other princely states became Group C states before States Re-organization of 1956. Then they became Centrally Administered Territories before attaining Statehood. Arunachal became a Centrally Administered Territory, and then a State. Sikkim was not considered to be the part of North-East India. It has, however, been made a member of the North-Eastern Council located in Shillong. Thus, we have following eight States in North-East India:

1. Assam,
2. Arunachal Pradesh,

3. Manipur,
4. Meghalaya,
5. Mizoram,
6. Nagaland,
7. Sikkim, and
8. Tripura.

The Sixth Schedule of the Constitution was envisaged to provide tribal autonomy within the State of Assam. But the autonomous district councils continued to operate even after the formation of the State of Meghalaya. Not only that, in Meghalaya, where there were two Autonomous District Councils earlier, the number of the same increased to three after the split of United Khasi and Jaintia Hills district. In Assam, the split of United Mikir and North Cachar Hills leading to the formation of two separate Autonomous Councils, and establishment of Bodoland Territorial Council, ultimately resulted into three such councils.

Thus in Assam, we have following three Autonomous Councils constituted in terms of the Sixth Schedule:

(i) Karbi Anglong Autonomous Council (KAAC).
(ii) Dima Hasao District Autonomous Council (DHDAC).
(iii) Bodoland Territorial Council (BTC).

The Karbi Anglong Autonomous Council (KAAC) covering the Karbi Anglong district of Assam with headquarters at Diphu has 30 members including 26 elected and four nominated members. The executive council consists of a Chief Executive Member and 10 Executive Members.

Dima Hasao District Autonomous Council (DHDAC) covering Dima Hasao district with headquarters at Maibong has the provision of 23 elected and four nominated members (total twenty-seven members). The executive council consists of a Chief Executive Member and 9 Executive Members.

Bodoland Territorial Council (BTC) covering the districts of Baksa, Kokrajhar, Chirang and Udalguri districts of Assam has total number of 46 members, which include 30 Scheduled Tribe, five from non-tribal communities, five open for all other communities, and six nominated members. The Executive Committee consists of a Chief Executive Member and 15 Executive Members. It has total Population of 36,37,562, including 34,23,612 rural and 2,13,950 urban population.

The two Autonomous Councils of Assam, KAAC and DHDAC, have legislative powers in addition to Subjects entrusted in Para 3 of the

Schedule VI of the Constitution. KAAC has also the powers to legislate on additional 20 subjects which were agreed in the MoU signed in 1995. Apart from the above thirty more subjects have been entrusted to KAAC for their administration.

The BTC, in addition to Subjects entrusted in Para 3 of the Schedule VI has powers to legislate on additional 40 subjects which were agreed in the Memorandum of Settlement on Bodoland Territorial Council (BTC) signed in 2003 among Government of India, Government of Assam and Bodo Liberation Tigers.

KAAC and DHDAC have also the judicial Powers as enumerated in paras 4 & 5 of the Schedule VI of the Constitution.

Meghalaya

1. In Meghalaya, there are following three Autonomous Councils in terms of the Sixth Schedule of the Constitution covering the entire State except the Shillong Municipal area:

   (i) Khasi Hills Autonomous District Council (KHADC),
   (ii) Garo Hills Autonomous District Council (GHADC), and
   (iii) Jantia Hills Autonomous District Council (JHADC).

The Khasi Hill Autonomous District Council (except Shillong Municipal Area, with headquarters at Shillong has (i) East Khasi Hills District, (ii) West Khasi Hills District, and (iii) Ri Bhoi District under its jurisdiction.

The Jantia Hill Autonomous District Council covers only Jantia Hills District.

The Garo Hill Autonomous District Council has the (i) East Garo Hills District, (ii) West Garo Hills District, and (iii) South Garo Hills District under its jurisdiction.

These Autonomous Councils have the legislative, judicial and executive powers. These have powers to legislate on the Subjects described in para 3 of the Sixth Schedule. They have the judicial powers enumerated in paras 4 and 5 of the Schedule VI of the Constitution. The population of the three district council areas is 23.1 lakh out of which 19.91 lakh is tribal.

Mizoram

The Mizo Hills District Council (MHDC) ceased to function after the creation of Mizoram State. But three other tribes, namely, Chakmas, Lai and Mara, demanded and got their autonomous councils. The three Autonomous District Councils, constituted in terms of the Sixth Schedule in Mizoram, are the following:

(i) Chakma Autonomous District Council (CADC),
(ii) Mara Autonomous District Council (MADC), and
(iii) Lai Autonomous District Council (LADC).

These District Councils cover two administrative districts on the southern part of the State, namely, Lawngthlai to the west of the Kolodyne river, and Saiha falling to the east of the river. As per the memorandum signed between Government of India and Mizo National Front (MNF), certain amendments, as given bellow, were made in the Sixth Schedule vide the 67th Amendment of 1988:

(i) Sub-clause 3 was inserted in Paragraph 9, stating that the Governor may direct that the share of royalties to be made over to District Council shall be so made over within one year from the date of any agreement under sub-paragraph (1).
(ii) Paragraph 10 was amended to prescribe that no person resident in the district shall carry on any trade, whether wholesale or retail, except under a license issued by the District Council.
(iii) The Lakher Regional Council and the Pawi Regional Council were re-named as the Mara Autonomous District Council and Lai Autonomous District Council respectively w.e.f. 1st May, 1989 through notifications issued by the Government of Mizoram.

Chakma Autonomous District Council (CADC) has a Chief Executive Member and five Executive Members. Mara Autonomous District Council (MADC) has a Chief Executive Member and seven Executive Members. Lai Autonomous District Council (LADC) has a Chief Executive Member and seven Executive Members.

All the three Autonomous Councils have legislative powers on subjects entrusted in Para 3 of the Schedule VI. In addition 20 more subjects have been entrusted to Autonomous Councils for their administration. The judicial powers enumerated in paras 4 and 5 of the Schedule VI are also applicable to these Autonomous Councils.

Tripura

The only one Autonomous Council in Tripura, namely, Tripura Tribal Areas Autonomous District Council (TTAADC) was set up on January

18, 1982. Following the 49th Amendment of the Constitution of India, the TTAADC was brought under the provisions of the Sixth Schedule of the Constitution w.e.f. 1.4.1985. Thus, Tripura tribals also got an autonomous council for them. It covers and have jurisdiction over the total area of all the four revenue districts of the State. The State has thirty-five Rural Development (RD) Blocks, out of which nineteen R.D. Blocks are within the Sixth Schedule area and the remaining eighteen R.D. Blocks are within jurisdiction of both Sixth Schedule and Panchayati Raj Institutions (PRI) areas.

The principal objective of setting up the TTAADC is to empower the tribal people to govern themselves to bring all round development to them and protect and preserve their culture, customs and traditions.

The Autonomous Council has thirty members, out of which there are twenty-eight elected and two nominated members. Twenty-six elected members come from the Scheduled tribe communities of the State. The Executive Council consists of a Chief Executive Member and eight Executive Members.

The Autonomous Council has legislative powers on the subjects described in para 3 of the Sixth Schedule. Besides, 19 subjects have been entrusted by the State Government to the TTAADC for their administration. It has the judicial powers enumerated in para 4 and 5 of the Schedule.

Arunachal Pradesh does not have any autonomous council. **Autonomous Councils not functioning under the provisions of the 6th Schedule Autonomous.**

Hill District Councils in Manipur

In accordance with the powers vested on the Governor of Manipur as per the Manipur (Hill Areas) District Council Act, 1971, passed by the Parliament paving the way for establishment of six Autonomous District Councils in Manipur, following six Autonomous Districts Councils were constituted in Manipur on 14th February, 1972:

(i) Chandel Autonomous District Council,
(ii) Churachandpur Autonomous District Council,
(iii) Sadar Hills Autonomous District Council, Kangpokpi,
(iv) Manipur North Autonomous District Council, Senapati,
(v) Tamenglong Autonomous District Council, and
(vi) Ukhrul Autonomous District Council.

The first election to the autonomous district councils was held in 1973. The last elections were held in 2010. The act mentioned above has been so far amended thrice. The first amendment to the Act, made in 1975, envisaged removal of the Chairman of the District Council by the Government for reasons to be recorded in writing upon passing of a resolution by the District Council by a simple majority of the total membership of the Council. The second amendment, made in 2006, envisaged the following features:

(i) Notifying areas as urban areas for the purpose of development plan and to execute the works; and
(ii) Allotment/transfer/lease of land by a resolution passed by the District Council.

The third amendment to the Act was made in 2008, which envisaged the following changes:

(iii) Increase in membership from18 to 24;
(iv) Election Commission of the State to be entrusted election to HDC;
(v) Constitution of Executive Committee; and
(vi) Addition of 9 entries to the list of powers of the autonomous Hill Districts Council.

Functions of the District Councils

Section 2 of the Act vests the following powers with the Autonomous Hill District Council (the words in italics have been added by the third amendment to the Manipur (Hill Areas) District Council Act, 1971):

(i) the maintenance and management of such property, movable and immovable, and institutions as may be transferred to that Council by the Governor;
(ii) the construction, repair and maintenance of such of the roads, bridges, channels and buildings as may be transferred to that Council by the Governor;
(iii) the establishment, maintenance and management of schools up to Class VIII;
(iv) the establishment, maintenance and management of dispensaries and Primary Health Sub-Centres;
(v) the establishment and maintenance of cattle pounds including such functions under the Cattle-trespass Act, 1871 as may be transferred to that Council by the Governor;

(vi) the establishment; maintenance and management of markets and fairs and the construction, repair, and maintenance of all buildings connected therewith;

(vii) water supply and sanitation schemes;

(viii) the construction, repair and maintenance of embankments and the supply, storage and control of water for agricultural purposes including irrigation schemes;

(ix) the preservation, reclamation and conservation of soil;

(x) animal husbandry and veterinary dispensaries;

(xi) the management of such ferries as may be entrusted to the charge of that Council by the Governor;

(xii) the initiation, inspection and control of relief works;

(xiii) the allotment, occupation or use, or the setting apart of land, other than land acquired for any public purpose or land which is a reserved forest, for the purpose of agriculture or grazing or for residential or other non-agricultural purposes or for any other purposes likely to promote the interests of, the inhabitants of any village or town situated within the autonomous district for which that council is constituted;

(xiv) the management of any forest not being a reserved forest, minor forest produce including fuel and fodder;

(xv) the regulation of the practice of Jhum or other form of shifting cultivation;

(xvi) Fisheries;

(xvii) co-operatives;

(xviii) sports and youth affairs;

(xix) adult and non-formal education;

(xx) horticulture and floriculture;

(xxi) rural housing and schemes under rural development including tribal development;

(xxii) *khadi* and village industries and cottage industries;

(xxiii) small scale industries;

(xxiv) non-conventional energy sources;

(xxv) library and cultural activities;

(xxvi) any other matter which the Administrator may, in consultation with the Hill Areas Committee, entrust to the District Council in the field of agriculture, animal husbandry, community development, social and tribal welfare, village planning or any other matter.

Assam Autonomous Tribal Councils

Assam, apart from three Autonomous Councils established under the provisions of the Sixth Schedule, have following sis Tribal Autonomous Councils established under the State laws:

(i) Rabha Hasong Autonomous Council (RHAC), Dudhnai;
(ii) Mishing Autonomous Cauncil (MAC), Dhemaji;
(iii) Tiwa Autonomous Council (TAC), Marigaon;
(iv) Deori Autonomous Cauncil (SAC), Lakhimpur;
(v) Thengal Kachari Autonomous Council (TCAC), Titabor; and
(vi) Sonowal Kachari Autonomous Council (SKAC), Dibrugarh.

While the formation of different autonomous councils were followed by agitation and aggressive demands, one of them was granted even when no demand was made for the same. In the same way, the Chief Minister, Tarun Gogoi has announced his decision to create Garo Autonomous Council; he has also announced that the formation of the Autonomous Councils for the Kumar, Madahi, Sut, Hajong and Scheduled Castes is already under the active consideration of his Government.

We may have an idea about the structural frame work and other details about the councils by going through the annexure detailing Missing Autonomous Council.

ANNEXURES

THE ADMINISTRATIVE AND CONSTITUTIONAL DOCUMENTS

ANNEXURE I

Inner Line Regulation, 1873

Preamble *WHEREAS* the Secretary of the State for India in Council has by resolution in Council declared the Provisions of Act XXXIII of Victoria, Chapter 3, Section 1, to be applicable to the districts of Kamrup, Darrang, Nowgong, Sibsagar, Lakhimpur, Garo Hills, Khasi & Jaintia Hills, Naga Hills, Cachar and Cheettagong Hills.

AND WHEREAS the Lt. Governor of Bengal has proposed to the Governor-General-in-Council a draft of the following Regulation, together with the reason for proposing the same, for the peace, and good government of the said districts.

AND WHEREAS the Governor-General-in-Council has taken such draft and reasons into consideration and has approved of such draft and the same has received the Governor General's assent.

The following Regulation is now published in the Gazetteer of India and will be published in the Calcutta Gazette and thereupon will have the force of law under their by third of Victoria, Chapter III.

Commencement 1. This Regulation shall extend to the districts named in the preamble, and shall come into force on the 1st November, 1983.

Local Extent 2. It shall be lawful for the Local Government of Bengal with the previous sanction of the Governor-General-in-Council to prescribe, and from time-to-time after by notification in the Calcutta Gazette, a line to be called 'The Inner Line' in each or any of the above named districts. The Local Government by notification in the Calcutta Gazette, prohibit all British subjects, or any class of British subjects, or any persons, sending in or passing through, such districts, from going beyond such line without a pass under the hand and seal of the executive officer to such district, of such officer as he may authorize from time-to-time cancel or very such prohibition.

3. Any British subject or other person so prohibited who goes beyond 'the Inner Line' fixed in accordance with section 2 of the Regulation after its notification in the Calcutta Gazette, without a pass shall be liable, on conviction before a Magistrate to a find not exceeding ₹ 100 for the first offence, and to a fine of not exceeding ₹ 500 or to simple or rigorous imprisonment for a term of not exceeding three months, or to both for each subsequent offence.

4. The Local Government may from time-to-time, prescribe, by notification in the Calcutta Gazette, a form of pass for each district, and may in such form of pass fix such restrictions or conditions a Local Government may deem fit, and may require the payment of such dues and fees for such passes as to the Local Government may seem proper. Any holder of such pass shall on breach of any such restriction or condition be liable on conviction to a fine not exceeding ₹ 100 for a first offence and to a fine not exceeding ₹ 500, or to simple or rigorous imprisonment which may extend to seven months, or to both, for each subsequent offence.

5. Any rubber, wax, ivory, or other jungle product found in possession of any person convicted of an offence under this Regulation may be confiscated to the Government by an order to be passed at the time of conviction by the Magistrate.

6. The Chief Executive Officer of any district comprised in any notification as aforesaid may subject to the approval of the Local Government authorize, by a written instrument under his hand, any public servant to arrest and bring before him with the least practicable delay.

Firstly — Any person prohibited from crossing the Inner Line prescribed for such district if such person, shall be found beyond the line and when asked to produce his pass shall refuse or be unable to do so.

Secondly — Any person to whom a pass may have been granted, and who has committed any infraction of its conditions.

7. It shall not be lawful for any British subject, or other persons not being native of the district comprised in the preamble of this Regulation to acquire any interest in the land or the product of land beyond the said Inner Line without the sanction of the Local Government as such officer as the Local Government shall appoint in this behalf. Any interest so acquired may be dealt with as the Local Government or if said officer shall direct. The Local Government may also by notification, in the Local Gazette, extend the prohibition contained in this section to any class of persons natives of the said districts, and may from time-to-time in like manner cancel or vary such extension.

Offence and Punishment

8. Whenever, without the written permission of the officer authorized by the Local Government to grant such permission will or captures or attempts to kill or capture, or abets the killing or capturing of, a wild elephant in any of the districts to which this Regulation extends, shall be liable to a fine not exceeding ₹ 200 for each elephant so killed or captured, and any elephant so killed or captured shall be confiscated to Government provided that no person who kills or abets the killing of an elephant in protection of himself, his houses or his crops shall be liable to punishment; and provided also that every person who in an elephant shall not be liable to fine, but shall be bound to surrender such captured elephant to the Government, or to pay such royalty thereon as the Local Government, may from time-to-time direct.

9. It shall be competent for the Local Government to make rules for the issue of licences to kill or capture elephant, and for all purposes connected with the capture of elephants.

10. The prosecution for every offence punishable under section 8 of the Regulation shall be

commenced within 6 months after the offence is committed.

Power to Punish 11. Offences against this Regulation may be tried by Magistrates of the First or Second class and shall be bailable.

ANNEXURE II

Act No. XIV of 1874

The Scheduled Districts Act, 1874

An Act to ascertain the enactments in force in various parts of British India, and for other purposes.

Preamble *WHEREAS* various parts of British India have never been brought within, or have from time-to-time been removed from, the operation of the General Acts and Regulations and the jurisdiction of the ordinary Courts of Judicature;

AND WHEREAS doubts have arisen in some cases as to which Acts or Regulations are in force in such parts and in other cases as to what are the boundaries of such parts;

AND WHEREAS among such parts are the territories specified in the first schedule hereto annexed, and it is expedient to provide readier means than now exist for ascertaining the enactments in force in such territories and the boundaries thereof, and for administering the law therein;

(It is hereby enacted as follows:)

Short title 1. This Act may be called the Scheduled District Act, 1874.

Local extent This Act extends in the first instance to the whole of British India other than the territories mentioned in the first schedule hereto annexed, and it shall come into force in each of Scheduled Districts on the issue of a notification under section 3 relating to such district.

Interpretation clause In this Act the term 'Scheduled District' means the territories mentioned in the first schedule hereto annexed; and from the date fixed in the resolution next hereinafter mentioned, it shall also include any other territory to which the Secretary of State for

India, by resolution in Council may declare the provisions of the XXXIII of Victoria, Chapter 3, Section 1, to be applicable.

Repeal of enactments

2. The enactments mentioned in the second schedule hereto annexed shall be repealed.

Notification of enactments in force in Scheduled Districts

3. The Local Government * * * * may from time to time, by notification * * in the local Gazette * * —

[a] declare what enactments are actually in force in any of the Scheduled Districts, or in any part of the any such district;

[b] declare of any enactment that it is not actually in force in any of the districts or in any part of any such district; and

[c] correct any mistake of fact in any notification issued under this section:

Provided that a declaration once made under clause [a] or clause [b] of this section shall not be altered by any subsequent declaration other than a declaration under clause [c] of this section.

Effect of notification under Section 3

4. On the issue, under section 3, of a notification declaring what enactments are in force, or not in force in any Scheduled District, the enactments so notified shall be deemed to be in force or not in force, according to the tenor of the notification, in such district, and every such notification shall be binding on all courts of law.

Power to extend enactment to Scheduled District

5. The Local Government * * * may, from time to time, by notification * * * in the local Gazette * * * extend to any of the Scheduled District or to any part of any such district, any enactment which is in force in any part of British India at the date of such extension.

Modification of enactment in their application to Scheduled District

5A. In declaring an enactment in force in a Scheduled District or part thereof under section 3 of this Act, or in extending an enactment to a Scheduled District or part thereof under section 5 of this Act, the Local Government * * * * may declare the operation of the enactment to be subject to such restrictions and modifications as that Government thinks fit.

Appointment of officers and Regulation of their procedure

6. The Local Government may from time to time —

[a] appoint officers to administer civil and criminal justice and to superintend the settlement and collection of the public revenue, and all matters relating to rent and otherwise to conduct the administration, within the Scheduled District;

[b] regulate the procedure of the officers so appointed; but not so as to restrict the operation of any enactment for the time being in force in any of the said districts; and

[c] direct by what authority any jurisdiction, powers or duties incident to the operation of any enactment for the time being in force in such district shall be exercised or performed.

Continuance of existing rules and officers

7. All rules heretofore prescribed by the Governor-General-in-Council or the Local Government for the guidance of officers appointed within any of the Scheduled Districts for all or any of the purposes mentioned in section 6, and in force at the time of the passing of this Act, shall continue to be in force unless and until the Governor-General-in-Council or the Local Government, as the case may be otherwise directs.

All existing officers so appointed previous to the date on which this Act comes into force in such districts shall be deemed to have been appointed hereunder.

Settlement of question as to boundary

8. Whenever any question arises as to the line of boundary between any of the Scheduled Districts and other territory, such officer as the Local Government or (where the said district and the other territory are not subject to the same Local Government) as the Governor-General-in-Council from time-to-time appoints, may consider and determine such line of boundary; and the order made thereon by such officer, if confirmed by the Government which appointed him, shall be conclusive in all Courts of Justice.

Place of imprisonment or transportation

9. Any person liable to be imprisoned or to be transported beyond sea under any order or sentence passed by any officer appointed under section 6 may (subject to such rules as the Local Government may from time to time prescribe in this behalf) be imprisoned in such jail or transported to such place as the Local Government directs.

Extension to Satna strip of Acts relating to public gambling and salt

10. Act No. III of 1867, * * * and No. XXV of 1869 are hereby declared to be in force in the tract of land ceded to the British Government in the year 1863 and lying between the Railway Station at Satna and the eastern boundary of Jabalpur District.

Saving of criminal jurisdiction over European British subjects, and savings of other laws

11. Nothing contained in this Act or in any notification issued under the power hereby conferred shall be deemed —

[a] to affect the criminal jurisdiction of any Court over European British subjects, or

[b] to affect any law other than laws contained in Acts or Regulations or in Rules made in exercise of powers conferred by such Acts or Regulations.

The First Schedule

[See Section 1]

Part 1

Scheduled Districts, 5 Madras

1 — In Ganjam

Part X

The Chief Commissionership of Assam

The Second Schedule

[See Section 2]

Number and Years	*Title*
3 * * * *	
4 XXXVII of 1855	An Act to remove from the operation of the General Laws and Regulations certain districts inhabited by Santhals others, and to place the same under the superintendence of an officer to be specially appointed for that purpose.

Scheduled District [1874 : Act XIV]

Presidency or Province	*Scheduled District*	*No. and Date of Notification*	*Gazette in which the Notification is published*
Assam	The Chief Commissionship of Assam	1651, dated 3rd, November, 1877. Dated 7th Nov., 1877	India 1877 Pt. 1, p. 662 Assam, 1877 Pt. 1, p. 383
	The Lushai Hills [formerly known as the North and South Lushai Hills] and Rutton Puiya's villages, including Demagiri, in the Chittagong Hills Tracts	921 p., dated 1st April, 1898	India, 1898 Pt. 11, p. 345 Assam, 1898, Pt. 1, p. 379

1874 : Act XIV Scheduled Districts

APPENDIX B

Territories which have become Scheduled District by virtue of the concluding portion of the third paragraph of section 1 of the Scheduled District Act, 1874, namely, those to which the Secretary of State for India has, by resolution in Council, declared the provisions of the Government of India Act, 1870 [XXXIII Vict., ch. 3] section 1, to be applicable.

1	*2*	*3*	*4*
Presidency of Province	***Territories***	***Date from which Resolution took effect***	***Gazette of India in which the Resolution is published***
Assam	The North Lushai Hills The South Lushai Hills	6th September, 1895	1895, Pt. 1, p. 935

Regulation 2 of 1880

The Assam Frontier Tracts Regulations, 1880[1]

Preamble *WHEREAS* it is expedient to provide for the removal of certain frontier tracts in Assam inhabited or frequented by barbarous or semi-civilized tribes from the operation of enactments in force therein. It is hereby enacted as follows:

Short title 1. This regulation may be called the Assam Frontier Tracts Regulation, 1880.

Local extent It extends to such frontier tracts within the territories [for the time being][2] administered by the Chief Commissioner of Assam (as he)[3] may, by notification in the [local Gazette][4] from time-to-time direct;

Commencement And it shall come into force in each of such tracts on such day as (he) in like manners directs in this behalf.[5]

Power to direct that enactments shall cease to be in force 2. When this Regulation has been extended in manner hereinbefore prescribed to any tract, the Chief Commissioner may from time to time[6] * * * * by notification in the Local Gazette, direct that any enactment in force in such tract shall cease to be in force therein,[7] but not so as to affect the criminal jurisdiction of any Court over European British subjects.

Settlement of question as to boundary 3. Whenever any question arises as to the line of boundary between any tract to which the provisions of this Regulation have been extended as aforesaid and the adjoining territory in British India, such officer as the Chief Commissioner of Assam from time-to-time appoints may consider and determine such line of boundary; and the order made thereon by such officer, if confirmed by the said Chief Commissioner, shall be conclusive.

NOTES

1. **Local Extent :** This regulation extends to such frontier tract in Assam as the Governor-General-in-Council may, by notification, direct [see s.1] and may similarly be extended by him to the Garo Hills District, the Khasi & Jaintia Hills District and any portion of the Nowgong District [see Reg. 3 of 1884 s.1 post].

   The Regulation has been extended by such notifications to the districts of the Garo Hills, the Khasi & Jaintia Hills and the Lushai Hills [including the areas transferred from the Cachar District in 1904], the Mikir Hills Tract [in the Nowgong District], the North Cachar Hills, the Sadiya, Balipara and Lakhimpur Frontier Tracts, the area added to the Lakhimpur Frontier Trade by Notification No. 2847 A.P. dated 12th August, 1929, the Naga Hills District, the Melomi Primi area added to the Naga Hills District, the tract added to the Naga Hills District by Notification No. 6492 Arunachal Pradesh, dated 23rd November, 1927, the area transferred to the Balipara Frontier Tract by Notification No. 1470 Arunachal Pradesh, dated 26th February, 1931, see Vol. III, Appendix II, Table C.

   The Regulation has [with the exception of the second and third paragraphs of section 1, the words "in manner hereinbefore prescribed" in section 2, and the words "as aforesaid" in section 3], been extended to the Mokokchang Sub-division [including the area added to it by Notification No. 68P, dated 1st February, 1910] of the Naga Hills District by Notification under the Scheduled District Act, 1874 [XIV of 1874].
2. The words in square brackets were inserted by Assam Frontier Tracts Regulation [1880] Amendment Regulation, 1898 [2 of 1898].
3. Substituted for the words "the Governor-General-in-Council by section 2 of the Devolution Act XXXVIII of 1920.
4. Substituted for the words "Gazette of India" by Act XXXVIII of 1920.
5. The concluding paragraph of s. 1 which was repealed by the Assam Frontier Tracts Regulation [1880] Amendment Regulation, 1898 [2 of 1898] s. 2[2] is omitted. It ran thus:

   "Every notification extending this Regulation to any tract shall specify the boundaries by which such tract is separated from the adjoining territory in British India."
6. The words "with the previous sanction of the Governor-General-in-Council" was omitted by Act XXXVIII of 1920.
7. For a list of enactments which have been barred in areas to which this Regulation extends, see Manual of Local Rules and Orders in force in Assam see Vol. III, Appendix II, Table C.

   For reference to rules under the Scheduled District Act, 1874 [XIV of 1874], for the administration of the said areas and of the Eastern Duars in the Goalpara district, Manual of Local Rules and Orders in force in Assam see Vol. III, Appendix I, Table 1.

ANNEXURE IV

Rules for the Administration of Justice in the Dibrugarh Frontier Tract, 1886

(Amended up to 1913)

I. GENERAL

1. The administration of the Dibrugarh Frontier Tract is vested in the Chief Commissioner of Assam, the Political Officer, Central and Eastern Sections, North-East Frontier, his Assistants, and the native village authorities, or such other officer or officers as the Chief Commissioner may see fit from time-to-time to appoint in that behalf, subject to the restrictions and rules hereinafter recorded.

2. The Political Officer shall nominate and appoint the village authorities, if any, subject to the confirmation of the Chief Commissioner, and shall assign to them their respective functions under these rules, and define, so far as may be necessary the local limits within which such duties shall be exercised by each, respectively, and may cancel or modify any such order. When no village authorities have been so nominated and appointed, the powers and duties assigned to them by these rules shall be exercised and performed by the Political Officer or by such other officers as he may depute for this purpose.

II. POLICE

3. The ordinary duties of Police in respect of crime will be discharged by the village authorities. They shall arrest all criminals and maintain peace and order within their respective local limits.

4. It shall be the duty of the village authorities to report to the Political Officer or such other Officer as may be authorized by him in that behalf, at the earliest practicable moment, all crimes, violent deaths, and serious accidents occurring within their respective local limits, and all occurrences, whether within or beyond such limits, which may come to their knowledge and which are likely to affect the public peace; and to deliver up offenders as soon as may be to the officer authorized to try them.

5. The village authorities shall watch and report, or apprehend and deliver up, all vagrants or bad and suspicious characters found within their respective local limits.

6. On the occurrence of any heinous crime[1] or of offences under the Arms Act or Excise Act within their local limits, the inhabitants of the village shall at once, if possible, apprehend the offender, and in any case shall at once inform the chief village authority, who, if the offender has not been apprehended, shall proceed without delay to the place where the crime occurred, and enquire into the matter. He shall further, as soon as possible, report any such offence as may be duly authorized by him in that behalf, whether the offender has been apprehended or not.

7. The village authorities may pursue an offender fleeing beyond their jurisdiction and arrest him, but shall not ordinarily attempt to arrest an offender beyond their own jurisdiction without the cognizance and cooperation of the village authorities within whose limits the offender has fled. When an offender is traced from one jurisdiction to another, it will be sufficient to point him out to the village authorities within whose limits he may be found, aiding them, if required, to effect his capture.

8. When the village authorities are unable to arrest an offender, they shall apply to the Political Officer or such other officer as may be duly authorized by him in this behalf for the aid of the regular police.

9. All inhabitants of the tract are bound to aid the village authorities when required to do so for the maintenance of order or apprehending offenders, and are liable to fine for failing to give such assistance; the fine to be adjudged by the chief village authority to the extent of his powers in criminal cases, or by the Political Officer or his assistants. And if it appears that the community is to blame, and that particular offenders cannot be discovered, a fine may be imposed upon the community, but by the Political Officer only.

10. Misconduct on the part of the village authorities in police matters shall be punishable by fine which may extend to ₹ 500, or by simply imprisonment to the extent which would be awardable under the Penal Code or other law for a like offence, or by both. Imprisonment may be awarded *in lieu* of fine in accordance with the provisions of the Penal Code or any other law in force.

11. An appeal shall lie from all orders of the chief village authority in police matters to an Assistant Political Officer authorized by the Political Officer in that behalf, and from him to the Political Officer, whose orders are final; but the Chief Commissioner may at any time call for the proceedings, and modify or reverse any order of the Political Officer.

III. CRIMINAL PROCEDURE

12. Criminal justice shall be ordinarily administered by the Political Officer and his assistants and by the Chief village authority duly authorized in this behalf.

13. The Political Officer shall be competent to pass sentence of death, transportation, or imprisonment up to the maximum amount provided for the offence, of whipping and to fine up to any amount : Provided that all sentences of death or transportation or imprisonment for a term of seven years and upwards shall be subject to the confirmation of the Chief Commissioner.

The Chief Commissioner or Political Officer may call for the proceedings of any officer subordinate to him and reduce, enhance or cancel any sentence passed or remand the case for retrial; but no offence shall be punished by a sentence exceeding that awardable under the Indian Penal Code. The Assistant Political Officers shall exercise such powers not exceeding those of a Magistrate of the first class as defined in the Criminal Procedure Code, as they may be invested with by the Chief Commissioner.

14. The Chief village authorities may themselves dispose of the cases of persons residing within their jurisdiction charged with the following offences:

Theft.
Injury to property to whatever kind.
Injury to person not endangering life or limb.
House-trespass.
Affronts of whatever kind.

15. The Chief village authorities may impose a fine for any offence which they are competent to try up to a limit of ₹ 50 and may award restitution or compensation to the extent of the injury sustained. Fines may be enforced by distraint of the property of the offender.

16. The Chief village authorities may not decide in cases:

(a) where their father, mother, son, daughter, their wife, or the children, husbands, or wives of any of these are concerned; or
(b) where the defendant does not reside within their jurisdiction;
(c) where the offence is one against the State or of causing death or danger to life or limb, or of robbery of any sort with violence or

of arson or of making or passing counterfeit coins or of making fraudulent documents, or offences under the Arms Act or Excise Act, and generally any offences of a heinous nature.

17. The Chief village authorities shall decide all cases in open Darbar in the presence of at least three witnesses and of the complainant and accused whose attendance they are empowered to compel.

18. The Chief village authority may carry out his decision as soon as pronounced, unless the accused person appeals. If the sentence is fine, and the accused person does not pay, he shall be sent to the Political Officer or any assistant authorized by him in that behalf to be dealt with while the fine is being realized.

19. Either party may appeal from the decision of the chief village authority at the time the decision is pronounced. The case shall then be tried *de novo*.

20. An appeal shall lie from the decision of an Assistant Political Officer to the Political Officer if preferred within thirty days.

21. No appeal shall lie as a matter of right from any sentence passed by the Political Officer involving less than three years' imprisonment. An appeal shall lie to the Chief Commissioner against sentences of three years' imprisonment and upwards, and from all sentences of death or transportation. Appeals must be presented within thirty days of the date of the order appealed against excluding the time required for procuring copy of the order : Provided that an appeal from a sentence of death shall be preferred within seven days from the date of the sentence.

22. The Political Officer and the Assistant Political Officer shall be guided in regard to procedure by the principles of the Criminal Procedure Code so far as they are applicable to the circumstances of the district and consistent with these rules. The chief exceptions are —

(a) Verbal orders of notice only shall be requisite in any case except when the regular Police are employed, or when the person concerned is not a resident of or in the tract at the time; but orders or summonses shall in every case before a fixed day, and the order shall be made known to the person concerned or to some adult member of his family, and failing this shall be openly proclaimed at the place where he is, or was last known to be, in sufficient time to allow him, if he sees fit, to appear.

(b) The proceedings of the Chief village authorities need not be recorded in writing nor shall it be necessary that examinations before the Political Officer and the Assistant Political Officer be signed by the parties examined; but the Political Officer may require the chief village authorities to report their proceedings in any way which appears to him suitable.

(c) There shall be no preliminary enquiries by regular or village police unless the Political Officer or Assistant Political Officer see fit to direct one.

(d) Recognizance to appear shall not be taken unless it appears necessary to the Political Officer or Assistant Political Officer.

(e) Examinations and proceedings generally shall be recorded in English only.

(f) Oaths shall be administered to parties and witnesses in cases where the accused is charged with murder, but not in other cases unless the Court or either party so require. It is, however, at all times optional with the Court to put witnesses on oath; but witnesses, whether on oath or not, shall be punishable for giving false evidence. In all cases where oaths are administered, all persons shall be sworn in the mode most binding on their conscience.

IV. CIVIL PROCEDURE

23. The administration of civil justice in the Dibrugarh Frontier Tract shall be conducted by the Political Officer, the Assistant Political Officer and the Chief village authorities.

24. The Chief village authorities may try cases in which plaintiff and defendant are living in their jurisdiction without limit as to amount, but with the following reservations.

25. The Chief village authorities may not try suits in which their fathers, mothers, sons or daughters, uncles or aunts, sisters or brothers, the children of any of the foregoing, their wives, or persons in the above relationship to a wife, or any near relative, are concerned.

26. All suits shall be decided in open Darbar in the presence of the parties, and at least three respectable witnesses.

27. The Chief village authorities shall have power to compel attendance of parties to any suit and witnesses, and to fine up to a limit of ₹ 50, persons failing to attend when ordered to do so. They have power to award all costs, also compensation to defendants for unfounded or vexatious suits bought against them.

28. All proceedings shall be *viva voice*, but the Political Officer may require the Chief village authorities to report their proceedings in any way which may appear to him suitable. After hearing both parties and their witnesses, if any, they shall, with or without the opinion of assessors, as they may see fit, forthwith pronounce a decision.

29. The Chief village authorities may carry out their decisions at once, if necessary, by distraint of any property belonging to the person found liable, to pay (unless appeal is made, or security given to the Chief village authority's satisfaction); but if an appeal is made at the time of decision, the Chief village authority shall send-up the parties and their witnesses to the Political Officer or any other officer authorized by him in that behalf forthwith, as soon as may be. He shall either accompany them himself or send at least one respectable person who has been present at the trial with them.

30. The Political Officer and the Assistant Political Officers shall not ordinarily hear any suits triable by the Chief village authorities; but suits which under these rules the chief village authority cannot try shall be tried by the Political Officer or an Assistant Political Officer.

31. The Political Officer and the Assistant Political Officers shall in all cases coming before them, in which the parties are indigenous inhabitants of the frontier tract, endeavour to induce them to submit their cases to a *panchayat*. In that event, each party shall name an equal number of arbitrators, and the Court shall either choose, or leave the arbitrators to choose, an umpire. The name and residence of the arbitrators and umpire and the matter in dispute shall be recorded before their proceedings commence, and the Court shall direct the chief village authority, or some other person, to assemble the *panchayat* and witnesses within such reasonable period as the Court may fix. When the case has been decided, the umpire shall appear with the parties before the Court, which shall proceed to record the decision and enforce it as its own. From such decision there shall be no appeal.

32. On appeals to the Political Officer from a decision of the Chief village authority, a record shall be made of the matter in dispute, and of the decision of the Chief village authority, if necessary, the Court shall examine the parties, and, if the decision appears to be just, it shall be affirmed and enforced by the Court as its own. If, on the other hand, the Court sees grounds to doubt the justice of the decision, it shall try the case *de novo*, or refer it to a *panchayat*, as provided above.

33. Decrees against persons resident beyond the jurisdiction of the Court in the Dibrugarh Frontier Tract, if satisfaction cannot be obtained within the Dibrugarh Frontier Tract, shall be transferred for execution to the Court having jurisdiction.

34. Houses, needful clothing, or cooking utensils, or implements whereby the owner or his family subsists, shall not be attached, sold, or transferred in execution of decree, unless the house or other things above exempted is the actual subject matter of the suit. Land may be sold or temporarily transferred where custom admits of individual right in it being recognized.

35. There shall be no imprisonment for debt, excepting when the Political Officer is satisfied that fraudulent disposition or concealment of property has taken place. In such case the debtor may be detained for a period not exceeding six months.

36. The Chief Commissioner or Political Officer may, on application or otherwise, call for the proceedings of any case decided by any officer subordinate to him and pass such orders as he may deem fit.

An appeal shall lie to the Political Officer against any decision of an Assistant Political Officer, and to the Chief Commissioner against an original decision of the Political Officer, if the value of the suit be rupees five hundred or over, or if the suit involves a question of tribal rights or customs, or of right, or possession of, immovable property : Provided that the petition of appeal accompanied by a copy of the order appealed against by a clear statement of the grounds of appeal be filed within thirty days from the date of decision, excluding the time required for obtaining a copy of the decision. An appeal which lies to the Chief Commissioner may be pretended to the Political Officer, who shall, if it be in order and presented in due time, endorse upon it the date of receipt and transmit it with the records of the case to the Chief Commissioner.

The decree of the Appellate Court shall be transferred to the Court passing the original order for execution as a decree of its own.

37. The Courts of the Chief Commissioner, Political Officer and Assistant Political Officers, shall be guided by the spirit, but not be bound by the letter, of the Code of Civil Procedure.

38. No professional pleader or *mukhtar* shall be allowed to appear in any case except with the sanction of the Court. Near relatives may appear for persons incapacitated by age, sex, or sickness.

39. Oaths shall not be administered to parties or witnesses in suits unless the Court or either party to a suit so requires. In all cases where oaths are administered, all persons shall be sworn in the manner most binding on their consciences. It is at all times optional with the Court to put witnesses on oath; but witnesses, whether on oath or not, shall be punishable for giving false evidence.

40. The Political Officer is empowered to try suit up to any amount. The Assistant Political Officers shall hear and decide original civil suits up to a value of ₹ 1,000, and shall hear and decide appeals from the decision of the chief village authorities up to a value or ₹ 500.

NOTE

1. **Heinous crimes are :** Arson, Cattle stealing, Counterfeiting coin or passing it, Dacoity, Forgery, House breaking, Murder, Rape, Rebellion, Robbery, Riot, Wounding to the danger of life or limb.

ANNEXURE V

Regulation 3 of 1914

The Assam Frontier Tracts Regulation, 1884[1]

A regulation to empower the extension of the Assam Frontier Tracts Regulation, 1880, to certain tracts in Assam, and *to declare that Act 10 of 1 872* [*the Code of Criminal Procedure shall be deemed never to have come into force in the Garo Hills District, the Naga Hills District and the Khasi & Jaintia Hills District*[2]].

WHEREAS it is expedient to take power to extend the Assam Frontier Tracts Regulation 1880, to certain tracts within the territories administered by the Chief Commissioner of Assam which though not frontier tracts within the meaning of that Regulation, are inhabited or frequented by barbarous or semi-civilized tribes:

1. *AND WHEREAS it is also expedient to remove doubts which have raised as to whether when the Garo Hills Act, 1874*[3], *to the territories to which the Garo Hills Act 1869 had previously applied or been extended, namely the Garo Hills District, the Naga Hills District and the Khasi and Jaintia Hills District :*

It is hereby enacted as follows:

Power to extend Regulation II of 1889 to certain districts

1. Notwithstanding anything contained in the Assam Frontier Tracts Regulation, 1889, the Chief Commissioner may extend that Regulation,[4] in the manner prescribed in Section 1 thereof, to the Garo Hills District, the Khasi & Jaintia Hills District and such portion of the Nowgong District as the Chief Commissioner[5] may direct as if the same were frontier tracts.

Act 10 of 1872 declared never to have been in force in certain district

2. *Act 10 of 1872 [the Code of Criminal Procedure] shall be deemed never to have come into force in the Garo Hills District the Naga Hills District or the Khasi & Jaintia Hills District.*

NOTES

1. **Short Title** — This short title was given by the Amending Act, 1897 [V of 1897] Sec. III.
   Local Extent — This Regulation extends to the Garo Hills, Khasi & Jaintia Hills and Nowgong Districts.
2. The matter printed in italics is now obsolete. Act X of 1872 was repeled and re-enacted by Act X of 1882 which again has been repealed and re-enacted by Act V 1898 [the Code of Criminal Procedure, 1898]. The operation of the latter Act excluding Section 144 has been barred [except as to jurisdiction over European British subjects], by Notification under the Assam Frontier Tracts Regulation, 1880 [II of 1880], in all areas in which that Regulation is in force including the Garo Hills, the Mikir Hills Tract in the Nowgong District, the Naga Hills including the areas added to it by notifications nos. 68P., dated 1st February, 1910 and 6492 A.P., dated the 23rd November, 1927 and the "Melomi Primi area," the Khasi & Jaintia Hills excluding the area for the time being comprised within the Municipality or Cantonment of Shillong, the Lushai Hills District, the North Cachar Hills [the North Cachar Sub-division of the Cachar District] except the town of Shillong and the Sadiya, the Balipara and the Lakhimpur Frontier Tracts including the areas added to these tracts by Notification Nos. 7280 A.P., dated 8th December, 1921, 7281 A.P., dated 8th December, 1921 and No. 1470 A.P., dated 26th February, 1931 and 2897 A.P., dated 26th April, 1928, see Vol. III, Appendix II, Table C.
3. General Act Vol. II [Fifth edition].
4. For places to which the Assam Frontier Tracts Regulation, 1880 [II of 1880] has been extended see footnote 1 thereto, *ante*.
5. Substituted for the words "Governor-General-in-Council" by section of the Devolution Act XXXVIII of 1920.

ANNEXURE VI

Notification by the Government of India

Foreign and Political Department

No. 631 P. dated the 8th March, 1876

Under the provision of Section 2 of Regulation V of 1873 (Regulation for the peace and government of certain districts on the eastern frontier of Bengal) the Governor-General-in-Council hereby notifies that the line described below shall be the Inner Line under the Regulation in the district of Darrang: From the eastern boundary of the district of Kamrup, that is, from the pillar No. 98 in the Bar Nadi, the line shall follow in a easterly direction, the southern boundaries of Bhutan [including the countries of the Kariapara and Charduar Bhutia] and of the Aka and Duffla Hills as defined by the Revenue Survey in the years 1872-74-75 and demarcated by pillars Nos. 98 to 160 inclusive. From pillar No. 160 the line shall run in a southern-easterly direction to the point where the Balum River cuts the northern boundary of the Singlijan waste land grant No. 18. Thence the line shall follow the eastern boundary of the Singlijan grant No. 18 where the boundary cuts the Duffla Gar. Thence the line shall follow the Duffla Gar to a point on the Mora Sessa River, being the north-westerly extremity of the 'Inner Line' of the Lakhimpur district as notified in the Gazette of India page 452 of the 4th September, 1875.

No. 2427 P. dated the 30th Sept., 1875

Under the provision of Section 2 of Regulation V of Bengal Eastern Regulation 1 of 1873 (Regulation for the peace and government of certain districts on the eastern frontier of Bengal) the Governor-General-in-Council hereby notifies that the line described below shall be the Inner Line under the Regulation in the district of Lakhimpur. From the eastern boundary of the district of Darrang, that is, from a point on the Mora Sessa River the line shall follow the course of the Rajgarh Ali to the Subansiri river. It shall deviate from the Rajgarh Ali so as to follow the western, northern and eastern boundaries of the Harmati No. 95 and Joyhing No. 65 waste land grants. From the Subansiri to a point on the Sessi river marked by a masonry pillar it shall follow a line to be hereafter marked out along the foot of the Abor Miri Hills. From the masonry pillar on the Sessa river it shall follow the patrol path of Dimu outpost; thence along the patrol path to Pubha outpost. From the Pubha outpost it shall follow the patrol path to the confluence of the Lalli and the Brahmaputra rivers; thence it shall follow the right bank of the Brahmaputra and Dibang rivers to the junction of latter river with the Sessiri opposite to the Sessiri outpost. From the Sessiri outpost to the Dikrang outpost the line shall follow the patrol path; thence to the masonry pillar on the right bank of Brahmaputra river to the confluence of the Noa Dihing with that river; then it shall follow the left bank of the Noa Dihing river to its confluence with the Kherampani river; thence along the right bank of the Kherampani and Dihing river to the confluence of the latter river with Namsang river; thence along the left-bank of the Namsang river to a masonry pillar near the Kukanjuri with the Taurack tea garden to a masonry pillar on the right bank of the Dessang river near the latter garden. Thence along the right bank of the Dessang as far as the Lucdorgorh Ali.

No. 977 EB. dated the 25th Sept., 1914 In modification of Foreign Department Notification No. 990, dated the 22nd April, 1884, and in exercise of the powers conferred by Section 1 of the Assam Frontier Tracts Regulation, 1880, the Governor-General-in-Council is pleased to direct that the Regulation shall extend to the tract comprising the hills inhabited or frequented by Abors, Miris, Mishmis, Singphos, Nagas and

Khamtis and separated from the Lakhimpur district by the line specified below:

From Siplumukh on the Subansiri east along the ridge of the outer range to peak Dipa [2,820]; thence due east to the Sinyang river; thence east along the range to the longest source of the Dijmur river; thence down the Dijmur river to its confluence with the Buri Suti; thence east along the left bank of the Buri Suti to the Sengajan road; thence south-east along the Sengajan road to the Brahmaputra; thence east along the right bank of the Brahmaputra to a point opposite the mouth of the Likajan; thence across the Brahmaputra and along the Likajan; the Dholla Nadi, and the Hakhati Nadi (both of which are local names of the Likajan), to its source at a bhil or lake ....; thence across the bhil still eastwards to the Dirak river; thence south-east up the left bank of the Dirak river to a point due of Bisa, ...; thence due south along a demarcated line to the Dihing river so as to include Bisa's village; thence along the Dihing river to its confluence with the Magantaun river; thence along the Magantaun river; to its confluence with Khasanpani; thence along the Khasanpani to its confluence with the Buri Dihing (or Namphuk) river; thence up the Buri Dihing (or Manphuk) river to its confluence with the Namgoi; thence up the Namgoi river to the demarcated point where it turns southwards; thence along a demarcated line to the high peak H of Honkap Bum range; thence south-east along a demarcated line to the Namchik river; thence along the Namchik river to its confluence with the Khatangjan stream; thence up the Khatangjan stream for about 1,000 yards to a Naga path which breaks off westwards at the junction of the Likrajan and Khatangjan streams; thence along the Naga path passing through the villages of Loungto and Wangnon to the point where the path runs into the right bank of the Tirap river; thence up the Tirap river to a demarcated point; thence in a north-east by easterly direction along the watershed between Burma and Assam to a peak market "Balum" [6,795]; thence along the same range to the Nongyong lake.

The tract described above shall be styled the "Central and Eastern Sections, North-East Frontier Tract".

No. 987 EB. dated the 25th Sept., 1914 In modification of Foreign Department Notification No. 990, dated the 22nd April, 1884, and in supersession of Notification No. 11768J, dated the 1st November, 1906, the Governor-General-in-Council, in exercise of the powers confered on him by section 1 of the Assam Frontier Tracts Regulation, 1880, (II of 1880) is pleased to direct that the said Regulation shall extend to the tract inhabited or frequented by Singphos, Nagas and Khamtis and separated from the Lakhimpur district by the line specified below:

From the point on the Dirak river where the boundary between the Saikhowa and the Buri Dihing mauzas begins in a south-westerly direction along the western boundary of the Buri Dihing mauza to the Dibru river; thence west along the Dibru river to its confluence with the Moranjan; thence up the Moranjan to a point one and a half miles to the east of the Dibru-Sadiya Railway; thence along a demarcated line to a point on the Dihing river one and a half miles to the east of the Dibru-Sadiya Railway; thence up the Dihing river to its confluence with the Tirap river; thence up the Tirap river to its confluence with the Likra Kha stream; thence up the Likra Kha to the point where it turns south; hence along a demarcated line to the upper waters of the Namdang river; thence down the Namdang river to a pillar to the south of the Namdang coal mines; thence along a demarcated line westward across the Makum stream to the Dirak river; thence up the Dirak river to a pillar; thence along a demarcated line to a pillar on the Tirap river; thence down the Tirap river to the point where the Naga path passing through the villages Loungto and Wangnon meets the river; thence along this path passing through the angnon and Loungto village sites, in that order, to the confluence of the Likrajan and Khatangjan streams; thence down the Khatangjan for about a thousand yards to its confluence with the Namchik river; thence east along the Namchik river to a demarcated point at the bend of that river before it turns harply to the south; thence north-east along a demarcated line to peak H on the Honkap Bum range; hence east along a demarcated line to the point on the Namgoi river where it turns south; thence from his demarcated point down the Namgoi river to its confluence with the Namphuk [Buri Dihing] river; thence down the Buri [or Namphuk] river to its junction with the Khasanpani; thence along the Khasanpani to its confluence with Magantaun river; thence along the Magantaun river to its confluence with the Buri Dihing river upto and excluding Bisa's village; thence due north along a demarcated line to pillar on the left bank of the Dirak river; thence along the left bank of the Dirak river to the point where he boundary between the Saikhowa and Buri Dihing Mauzas begins.

The tract described above shall be styled the "Lakhimpur Frontier Tract".

No. 979 EB. of 25-9-1914, as amended by No. 279 A.P. dated the 2nd Nov., 1935

In exercise of the powers conferred by section 1 of the Assam Frontier Tracts Regulation, 1880, (II of 1880) the Governor-General-in-Council is pleased to direct that the Regulation shall extend to the tract comprising the hills inhabited or frequented by Bhutias, Akas, Daflas, Miris and Abors and separated from the Darrang and Lakhimpur districts by the line specified below:

From the Subansiri river westwards along the Inner Line to the Dikrang river; thence down the Dikrang to a demarcated line past the Borpathar stockade to demarcated point on the Dubia Nadi; thence along the Kauri Ali embankment to the Gogra road; thence along the Gogra road to the north-east corner of the Singlijan grant; thence along the Inner Line and the west boundary of the grant to the south-west corner of the grant; thence along a straight line to junction of the Bihmari and Baroi rivers; thence along a straight line to the north-east corner of the Rangagarh tea garden; thence along the northern boundary of the garden to its north-west corner; thence along a straight line to the junction of the Dikai and Borgang rivers; thence along a straight line to the north-east corner of grant No. 536; thence along the northern boundary of the grant to its north-west corner; thence along a straight line to the Chiladhari river; thence along the southern boundary of the Nauduar forest reserve to the Borelli river; thence along the southern boundary of the Charduar forest reserve and a demarcated line running through a portion of the cadastral village of Buragaon to the Forest Guard's quarters at Likra; thence along the southern boundary of the reserve to its south-west corner; thence along a straight line to the north-east corner of Kunderbil Garden; thence along a straight line to pillar No. 108 on the Inner Line; thence along the Inner Line to its junction with the eastern boundary of the Khalingduar reserve forests; thence along the eastern boundary of the Reserve to its south-east corner on the Bhola river; thence along the southern boundary of the Reserve and a line running parallel with the Inner Line between pillars 101 and 99 to a point on the boundary between the Darrang and Kamrup districts one and a half miles south of boundary pillar No. 98.

The tract described above shall be styled the "Western Section, North-East Frontier Tract".

No. 8052 P. dated the 13th Oct., 1917 In exercise of the powers conferred by section 2 of the Bengal Eastern Frontier Tracts Regulation, 1873 (V of 1873), and in supersession of all previous on the subject, the Governcr-General-in-Council with the previous sanction of the Governor-General-in-Council, is pleased to prescribe the line described below as the *Inner Line in the Balipara Frontier Tract:*

From the eastern boundary of the district of Kamrup, that is, from pillar No. 98 on the Bor Nadi, the line shall follow in an easterly direction the southern boundaries of Bhutan (including the countries of the Kariapara and Charduar Bhutias) and of the Aka and Duffla Hills as defined by the Revenue Survey in the years 1872-73-74-75, and demarcated by pillars Nos. 98 to 160 inclusive. From pillar No. 160 the line shall run in a south-easterly direction to the point where the Balum River cuts the northern boundary of the Singlijan waste land grant No. 18. Thence the line shall follow the eastern boundary of the Singlijan grant No. 18 to the point where boundary cuts the Duffla Gar. Thence the line shall follow the Duffla Gar to a point on the Mora Sesa Nadi. From this point along the Rajgarh Ali to the Dropang (Durpang) Nadi thence by the shortest line north to the hills and skirting the foot of the hills to point idstream of the Dikrang river .... thence along the Lakhimpur district boundary to the west bank of the Subansiri river as ....

....

....

For subsequent modifications of the boundaries Frontier Tracts, see ....

No. 7281 AP of December 8, 1921
No. 2632 AP of May 21, 1925
No. 5691 AP of November 9, 1926
No. 2874 AP of April 26, 1928
No. 3146 AP of May 7, 1928
No. 5763 AP of August 12, 1929
No. 1975 AP of March 1, 1932
No. 6778 AP of November 2, 1934
No. 6779 AP of November 2, 1934
No. 278 AP of January 20, 1934

For excluding areas from operation of enactment, see Numbers 6780 AP, 6782 AP and 6783 AP, all the four of November 2, 1934.

Notification No. 4956P, dated the 18th August, 1916

The Sadiya Frontier Tract

In exercise of the powers conferred by Section 5 of Scheduled Districts Act, 1874 [XIV of 1874], and with the previous sanction of the Governor-General-in-Council, the Chief Commissioner is pleased to extend the undermentioned enactments to the Central and Eastern Section of the North-east Frontier Tract, namely:

1. The Indian Penal Code, 1860 [XLV of 1960].

[See Assam Gazette of 30th August, 1916, Part II, Page 1335]

Notification No. 4958P, dated the 18th August, 1916

Lakhimpur Frontier Tract

In exercise of the powers conferred by Section 5 of Scheduled Districts Act, 1847 [XIV of 1974], and with the previous sanction of the Governor-General-in-Council, the Chief Commissioner is pleased to extend the undermentioned enactments to the Lakhimpur Frontier Tract, namely:

1. The Indian Penal Code, 1860 [XLV of 1860].

Notification No. 4960P, dated the 18th August, 1916

Western Section North-east Frontier Tract

In exercise of the powers conferred by Section 5 of Scheduled Districts Act, 1974 [XIV 1874], and with the previous sanction of the Governor-General-in-Council, the Chief Commissioner is pleased to extend the undermentioned enactments to the Western Section of the North-East Frontier Tract, namely: 1. The Indian Penal Code, 1860 [XLV of 1860].

Government of India Act, 1915, as Amended by Government of India Act, 1919

13 [52A. [1] The Governor-General-in-Council may, after obtaining an expression of opinion from the local Government and the Local Legislature affected, by notification, with the sanction of His Majesty previously signified by the Secretary of State in Council, constitute a new Governor's province, or place part of a Governor's province under the administration of a Deputy-Governor to be appointed by the Governor-General, and may in such case apply, with such modifications as appear necessary or desirable, all or any of the provisions of this Act relating to Governor's provinces, or provinces under a Lieutenant-Governor or Chief Commissioner, to any such new province or part of a province.

[2] The Governor-General-in-Council may declare any territory in British India to be a "Backward Tract" and may, by notification, with such sanction as aforesaid, direct that this Act shall apply to that territory subject to such exceptions and modification as may be prescribed in the notification.

Where the Governor-General-in-Council has, by notification, directed as aforesaid, he may, by the same of subsequent notification, direct that any Act of the Indian Legislature shall not apply to the territory in question or any part thereof, or shall apply to the territory or any part thereof subject to such exceptions or modifications as the Governor-General thinks fit, or may authorize the Governor-General-in-Council to give similar directions as respects any Act of the local Legislature.

Government of India Act, 1935

Section 91

[1] In this Act the expressions "Excluded Area" and "Partially Excluded Area" mean respectively such areas as His Majesty may by order in Council declare to be excluded areas or partially excluded areas.

The Secretary of State shall lay the draft of the order which it is proposed to recommend His Majesty to make under the sub-section before Parliament within six months from the passing of this Act.

[2] His majesty may at any time by Order in Council —

[a] direct that the whole or any specified part of an excluded area shall become, or become part of, a partially excluded area;

[b] direct that the whole or any specified part of a Partially Excluded area shall cease to be a Partially Excluded area or a part of such an area;

[c] alter, but only by way of rectification of boundaries, any Excluded or Partially Excluded Area;

[d] on any alteration of the boundaries of a province, or the creation of a new province, declare any territory not previously included in any province to be, or to form part of, an Excluded Area or a partially Excluded Area, and any such order may contain such incidental and consequential provisions as appear to His Majesty to be necessary and proper, but save as aforesaid the Order in Council made under sub-section [1] of the section shall not be varied by any subsequent order.

Section 92

[1] The executive authority of a province extends to Excluded and Partially Excluded areas therein but, notwithstanding anything in this Act, no Act of the Federal Legislature or of the Provincial Legislature, shall apply to an Excluded Area or Partially Excluded area unless the Governor in giving such a direction with respect to any Act may direct that the Act shall in its application to the area, or to any specified part thereof, have effect subject to such exception or modifications as he thinks fit.

[2] The Governor may make regulations for the peace and good government of any area in a province which is for the time being an excluded area, or a partially excluded area, and any regulations so made may repeal or amend any Act of the Federal Legislature or of the Provincial Legislature, or any existing Indian law, which is for the time being applicable to the area in question.

Regulation made under this sub-section shall be submitted forthwith to the Governor-General and until assented to by him in his discretion shall have no effect and the provisions of this part of this Act with respect to the power of His Majesty to disallow Act shall apply in relation to any such regulations assented to by the Governor-General as they apply in relation to Acts to a Provincial Legislature assented to by him.

[3] The Governor shall, as respects any area in a province which is for the time being an excluded area, exercise his functions in his discretion.

ANNEXURE IX

The Government of India (Excluded and Partially Excluded Areas) Order, 1936

At the Court at Buckingham Palace The 3rd day of March, 1936

Present

The Kings Most Excellent Majesty in Council

WHEREAS by sub-section [1] of section 91 of the Government of India Act, 1935 (hereafter in this order referred to as "the Act"), His Majesty in Council is empowered to declare what areas are to be Excluded Areas and Partially Excluded Areas within the meaning of the Act:

AND WHEREAS draft of this Order has been laid before Parliament in accordance with the provisions of sub-section [1] of section 309 of the Act and an Address has been presented to His Majesty by both Houses of Parliament praying that an Order may be made in the terms of this order:

NOW, THEREFORE, His Majesty, in the exercise of the powers conferred on him as aforesaid and of all other powers enabling him in that behalf, is pleased by and with the advice of the Privy Council to order, and it is hereby ordered as follows:

1. This order may be cited as "The Government of India (Excluded and Partially Excluded Areas) Order, 1936".

2. The areas specified in Part I of the Schedule to this Order shall be the Excluded Areas, and the Areas specified in Part II of that Schedule the Partially Excluded Areas, within the meaning of the Act.

3. Any reference in the said Schedule to any district, administration area or estate shall be constructed as a reference to that district, area or estate as existing on the first day of January, nineteen hundred and thirty six.

M.P.A. HANKEY

ASSAM

The North-East Frontier (Sadiya, Balipara and Lakhimpur) Tracts.
The Naga Hills District.
The Lushai Hills District.
The North-Cachar Hills Sub-division of the Cachar District.

Regulation 1 of 1943

The North-East Frontier Tract (Internal Administration) Regulation, 1943

Preamble *WHEREAS* it is expedient for the good Government of the North-East Frontier (Sadiya, Balipara and Lakhimpur) Tracts to establish therein a further unit of Administration.

Now, therefore, in exercise of the powers conferred by sub-section (2) of section 92 of the Government of India Act, 1935, the Government of Assam is pleased to make the following Regulation:

Short Title and commencement 1. This regulation may be called the North-East Frontier Tracts (Internal Administration) Regulation, 1943.

(2) It shall come into force on such date as the Governor may by notification in the official Gazette appoint.

Administrative boundaries 2. So much of the Sadiya Frontier Tract as is contained within the boundaries set out in the First Schedule and so much of the Lakhimpur Frontier Tract as is contained within the boundaries set out in the Second Schedule shall cease to be under the administrative control respectively of the Political Officer, Sadiya Frontier Tract, and the Deputy Commissioner, Lakhimpur, and shall henceforth under the designation of the Tirap Frontier Tract be jointly under the administrative control of an authority to be designated the Political Officer, Tirap Frontier Tract.

Application of law 3. All laws for the time being in force in the Sadiya and Lakhimpur Frontier Tracts shall apply in the Tirap Frontier Tract, subject to any reservations or modifications with which they are applicable in the Sadiya Frontier Tract or the Lakhimpur Frontier Tract, as the case may be.

THE FIRST SCHEDULE

North and East From the mouth of the Kolia or Koria Pani stream it meets the Bhuri Dihing river up the left bank of the former to the western boundary of Bisapathar village; thence along the western boundary of this village to the path leading from Bisapathar to Bara Dumsa and Mohanggaon and thence by this path to the point where it crosses the Dirak Hka (height 493), thence a line due east to the midstream of the Noa Dihing or Diyan river and by the midstream of this latter to the Chaukan Pass over the Kumon Bum Range which here constitutes the Assam-Burma boundary; thence southwards along the Assam-Burma boundary to the point, height 10,871 .... where the Patkai Range takes off westwards.

South Thence westwards along the Patkai Range (in conformity with the agreement between the Government of Assam and the Government of Burma as to the Inter-provincial boundary) to the source of the Tirap river and Sumhak Ju.

West Thence down the midstream of that river to the mouth of a nameless stream from the west marked by a stone known as the Koiri Dhip .... thence westwards up this stream to the ridge, north-east about 2 miles of the village of Yangkang .... thence along the ridge through Wasu Peak, height 4,488, to the source of a tributary of the Dirak Nadi marked by a pillar known as the Saban (Chaban) Dhip about 1 miles east of Wasu Peak, thence down the midstream of this tributary and the Dirak Nadi as far as a point marked by an iron post .... and about 1¼ miles north-west of the village of Wangling; thence in an east-north-easterly direction along demarcated lines to a pillar on the Hesang or Hasang Hill, thence along demarcated lines eastwards to the Hesang Nadi; thence by the midstream of the Hesang Nadi to the Namdang and up the latter to the mouth of a small feeder of the Namdang river; thence up the midstream of this feeder to a point ¾ mile south-east of the Survey station of triangulation Tilak, height 1,644, thence along demarcated lines in a direction slightly north of east to the Ledo Pani, thence down the midstream of this latter to where it is crossed the foot-path from Nakbang; thence in a direction slightly south of east along demarcated line to the Matang Pani and thence down the midstream of the Matang Pani to the Likha Pani and following the latter to the point where it meets the western boundary of the Likha Pani Mining Lease grant; thence south to the boundary pillar at the south-west corner of this grant, thence along the southern boundaries of this and the Tipang Pani Mining Lease grant crossing the Tirap river to the south-east corner of the latter; thence northwards by its eastern boundary to the Tirap river, thence down the midstream of the Tirap river to the mouth of a small stream ....

Having its source on a hill, height 894; thence up this small stream to its source and over the hill to the source of the Lekha Hka and by the latter to its junction with the Kathang Hka and thence by the Kathang Hka to the Namchik river; thence down the left bank of the Namchik river to its confluence with the Namphuk or Burhi Dining river and by the right bank of the latter to the mouth of the Kolia or Koria Pani which is the starting point.

THE SECOND SCHEDULE

Commencing from the pillar at the south-west corner of the Likha Pani Mining Lease grant eastwards along this and the Tipang Pani Mining

Lease grant crossing the Tirap river to the south-east corner of the latter, thence northwards by it eastern boundary to the Tirap river; thence down the midstream of the Tirap river to the mouth of a small stream ....

Having its source on a hill, height 894; thence up this small stream to its source and over the hill to the source of the Lekha Hka and by the latter to its junction with the Kathang Hka and thence by the Kathang Hka to the Namchik river; thence down the left bank of the Namchik river to its confluence with the Namphuk or Burhi Dihing river, thence down the right bank of the Burhi Dihing river to the mouth of the Pengri Hka and up the latter to the point where it meets the eastern boundary of the upper Dihing Reserved Forest and thence southwards by the eastern boundary of this reserve to the Manmau Jan which is followed to the Burhi Dihing, thence up the midstream of the Burhi Dihing to the Tirap up the midstream of the latter to the Likha Pani, thence up the midstream of the Likha Pani to the point where it meets the western boundary of the Likha Pani Mining Lease grant and thence southwards by the western boundary of this grant to the starting point.

Note: .... wherever the boundary is said to follow a stream or path, the midstream or the centre of the path is intended unless otherwise stated.

Regulation 1 of 1944

North-East Frontier Tracts (Internal Administration) (Amendment) Regulation, 1944

Preamble *WHEREAS* it is amend the North-East Frontier Tracts (International Administration) Regulation, 1943, in the manner hereinafter appearing; now therefore in exercise of the powers conferred by sub-section (2) of section 92 of the Government of India Act, 1935, the Governor of Assam is pleased to make the following Regulation:

Short title 1. [1] This regulation may be called the North-East Frontier Tracts (Internal Administration) Regulation, 1944.

Commencement [2] It shall come into force on such date as the Governor may by notification in the official Gazette appoint.

2. For the first and second schedules of the North-East Frontier Tracts (Internal Administration) Regulation, 1943 (Regulation 1 of 1943) the following shall be substituted namely —

THE FIRST SCHEDULE

North and East From the confluence of the Kolia or Koria Pani stream and Burhi Dihing river up the left bank of the former, then following the western boundary of Bisa Pathai village, and the path *via* Bara Dumsa to Mohanggaon, to the point where this path cross the Dirak Hka (height 493 feet); thence by a straight line running eastwards to meet the Kumchai Hka, thereafter to a point (height 2,127 feet) on the Mana Bum Range, thence along this range to Champai Bum (height 10,871 feet)

.... From where the Patkai range takes off westwards.

South: Thence westwards along the Patkai Range (*vide* Inter-provincial Boundary agreement, between the Governments of Burma and Assam) to the source of the Tirap or Sumhak Ju.

West: Thence down the midstream of the Tirap or Sumhak Ju to a stone known as Koiri Dhip; thence westwards up this stream to the ridge about 2 miles north-east of Yangkang village then on to Wasu Peak (height 4,488 feet), thence by a line due east to a pillar known as Saban (Chaban) Dhip, thence along the midstream of a tributary to an iron post .... on the Dirak Nadi and thereafter in a north-easterly direction to a pillar on the Hesang Hill, thence along the demarcated line eastwards to the Hesang Nadi; and by the midstream of this river to the Namdang and up the latter to the mouth of a small feeder of the Namdang river; thence by the midstream of this feeder to a point ¾ of a mile south-east of the triangulation station Tikak (height 1,644 feet) thence along the demarcated lines to the Ledo Pani and down its midstream to where it is crossed by the foot-path from Nakbang, thence along the demarcated lines to the Matang Pani, thence down its midstream to the Likha Pani to the point where it meets the south-western corner of the Likha Pani Mining Lease grant; thence along the southern boundary of this grant and Tipang-pa Mining Lease grant and crossing the Tirap river to the south-east corner of Tipang Pani grant, thence northwards along a portion of this grant to the Tirap river and down the midstream of the Tirap river to the mouth of a small stream having its source on a hill (height 894 feet), thence up this small stream to its sources and over the hill to the source of the Lekha Hka; and by the latter to its junction with the Kathang Hka; thence by the Namchik river to its confluence with the Namphuk or Burhi Dihing river; and by the right bank of the latter to the mouth of the Kolia or Koria Pani which is the starting point.

THE SECOND SCHEDULE

Commencing from the pillar at the south-west corner of the Likha Pani Mining Lease grant eastwards along this and the Tipang Pani Mining Lease grant — crossing the Tirap river to the south-east corner of Tipang Pani grant, thence northwards along a portion of this grant to the Tirap river; thence down the midstream of the Tirap river to the mouth of a small stream having its source on a hill, (height 894 feet), thence up this small stream to its source and over the hill to the source of the Lekha Hka and by the latter to its junction with the Kathang Hka to the Namchik river; to its confluence with the Namphuk or Burhi Dihing river; thence by the right bank of the Burhi Dihing river to the mouth of the Pengri Hka and up to the latter to its source; thence along a demarcated straight line to the south-east boundary pillar of Kathang Tea Estate grant (W.L. application No. 121); thence along the southern boundary of this grant to the point where it meets the eastern boundary of the Upper Dihing Reserved Forest; thence southwards by the eastern boundary of this reserve to the Manjan which is followed to the Buri Dihing to the Tirap and up the midstream of the latter to the Likha Pani; thence up the midstream of the Lakha Pani to the point where it meets the western boundary of the Likha Pani Mining Lease grant and thence south-wards by the western boundary of this grant to the starting point.

ANNEXURE XII

Regulation 1 of 1945

The Assam Frontier (Administration of Justice) Regulation, 1945

A Regulation to consolidate and amend the law governing the administration of justice in the Frontier Tracts of Assam.

Preamble

WHEREAS it is expedient to consolidate and amend the law governing the administration of justice in the Balipara, Lakhimpur, Sadiya and Tirap Frontier Tracts of Assam.

Now, therefore, the Governor Assam, in exercise of the powers conferred by sub-section (2) of section 92 of the Government of India Act, 1935, is pleased to make the following Regulation —

Chapter I — GENERAL

Short title, extent, commencement and repeal

1. (a) This Regulation may be called the Assam Frontier (Administration of Justice) Regulation, 1945.

(b) It extends to the whole of the Balipara, Lakhimpur, Sadiya and Tirap Frontier Tracts.

(c) It shall come into force on such date at the Governor may by notification in the Assam Gazette, appoint and from such date the rules for the administration of justice in the Balipara Frontier Tract, the rules for the administration of justice in the Lakhimpur Frontier Tract, and the rules for the administration of justice in the Sadiya Frontier Tract, published with Notification Nos. 2530(f) — A.P., 2530(d) — A.P. and 2530(e) — A.P. respectively, dated the 26th March, 1937, shall be deemed to be replaced.

Definitions

2. In this Regulation, except where the contrary appears from the context:

"The Governor" means the Governor of Assam.

"Heinous offence" means and includes any of the following, namely:

Murder, culpable homicide, causing grievous hurt, rape, kidnapping or abducting in order to subject to slavery, disposing or buying of persons as slaves, habitual dealing in slaves, dacoity, robbery, rioting, house-breaking, theft of cattle, mischief by fire or any explosive substance, any offence punishable under Chapter VI or Chapter XII of the Indian Penal Code, any offence punishable under the Arms Act, and any attempt to commit or abatement of any of the aforesaid offences.

"Pleader" includes a *mukhtar* of any professional agent. "Political Officer" includes an Additional Political Officer and, so far as the Lakhimpur Frontier Tract is concerned, the Deputy Commissioner of Lakhimpur; and "Assistant Political Officer" includes, so far as that Tract is concerned, an Assistant Commissioner or an Extra Assistant Commissioner in the District of Lakhimpur appointed in this behalf by the Governor.

"The Tract" means the Balipara, Lakhimpur, Sadiya and Tirap Frontier Tracts.

Administration

3. [1] The administration of the Tracts is vested in the Governor and of each Tract in the Political Officer, the Assistant Political Officer, and the village authorities thereof, or such other officer or officers as the Governor may see fit from time to time to appoint in that behalf, subject to the provisions hereinafter contained.

[2] The Political Officer, the Assistant Political Officers of the Tracts shall be appointed by the Governor, acting in his discretion.

Jurisdiction of Assistant Political Officers

4. The Political Officer may, subject to the provisions of this Regulation, define the jurisdiction of any Assistant Political Officer and may transfer any case, civil or criminal, from one Assistant

Political Officer to another, or from an Assistant Political Officer to himself.

Village authorities 5. [1] The Political Officer shall appoint such person or persons as he considers desirable to be the members of a village authority for such village or villages as he may specify, and may modify or cancel any such order of appointment, and may dismiss any person so appointed.

[2] In any area for which no village authority has been constituted under the provisions of sub-section (1), the powers and functions of the villages authority, as provided by this Regulation, shall be exercised and performed by the Political Officer, or by any Assistant Political Officer authorized by him in this behalf.

Chapter II — POLICE

Police duties of village authorities 6. [i] The ordinary duties of police in respect of crime shall be discharged by the village authorities. They shall maintain peace and order within their jurisdiction.

[ii] The village authorities shall not be deemed to be police officers for purposes of section 25 and section 26 of the Indian Evidence Act, 1872 or the section 162 of the Code of Criminal Procedure, 1898.

Act I 1872
Act V 1898

[iii] The village authorities shall watch and report on any vagrant, or any bad or suspicious character found within their jurisdiction, and may apprehend any such person if they have reasonable grounds for suspecting that he has committed or is about to commit an offence, and shall hand over any person so apprehended to the Political Officer or an Assistant Political Officer.

Control of Police 7. Every Civil Police Station shall be under the control of the Political Officer, but its administration with regard to the pay, allowance, clothing, transfer and discipline of the staff shall be vested in the Superintendent of Police of the district which furnished the staff or such other Police Officer as the Government may appoint in this behalf, provided that transfer shall be made in consultation with the Political Officer.

Occurrence of heinous offence 8. On the commission of any heinous offence within their jurisdiction, the inhabitants of the village shall at once, if possible apprehend the offender, and in any case shall at once inform the village authority, who if the offender has not been apprehended, shall proceed without delay to the place where the offence was committed and enquire into it.

Reports by village authorities 9. It shall be the duty of the village authorities to report to the Political Officer, Assistant Political Officer as soon as possible all crimes, violent deaths, and serious accidents occurring within their jurisdiction, and all occurrences whether within or beyond their jurisdiction, which may come to their knowledge and which are likely to affect the public peace; and to arrest and deliver up offenders as soon as may be within a period of twentyfour hours of such arrest excluding the time necessary for the journey from the place of arrest to the Court having jurisdiction to try them.

Pursuit and arrest of offenders 10. A village authority may pursue beyond their jurisdiction any offender or vagrant or bad or suspicious character whom they consider it necessary to apprehend under the provisions of sub-section (3) of section 6. They shall not, however, ordinarily arrest the offender or such person without informing the village authority within whose jurisdiction he is found and inviting their assistance but may do so if there is a reasonable apprehension that he may otherwise escape.

Procedure when arrest is impossible 11. When a village authority is unable to arrest an offender, they may apply to the Political Officer, or an Assistant Political Officer or any officer empowered to make arrest, for assistance.

Aid to village authorities 12. [1] All inhabitants of the Tracts are bound to aid the village authority when required to do so for the maintenance of order or apprehending offenders, and are liable to fine for failing to give such assistance.

[2] Such fine if imposed by the village authority shall not exceed ₹ 50 and if imposed by the Political Officer or an Assistant Political Officer shall not exceed ₹ 200.

[3] An appeal shall lie from an order passed under sub-section (2) by a village authority to the Assistant Political Officer and from an order passed under sub-section (2) by an Assistant Political Officer to the Political Officer.

[4] If it appears that the community is to blame and that particular offender cannot be discovered a fine not exceeding ₹ 1,000 may be imposed upon the community by the Political Officer.

[5] Any fine imposed under sub-section (2) or sub-section (4) shall be recovered by distraint of the property of the person or persons on whom it is imposed.

Punishment of members of a village authority

13. Without prejudice to any punishment to which he may be liable under any other law, a member of a village authority shall, for any misconduct in the exercise of his functions under this Chapter, he punishable with fine which may extend to ₹ 500 or with imprisonment of either description for a term which may extend to six months, on conviction by the Political Officer or an Assistant Political Officer. An appeal shall lie from an order of Assistant Political Officer under this section to the Political Officer.

Revision

14. The Governor may at any time call for the proceedings in any matter under section 12 or section 13, and may modify or set aside an order of a village authority passed under sub-section (2) of section 12, or an order, original or appellate, passed by the Political Officer or an Assistant Political Officer under either of those sections.

Chapter III — CRIMINAL PROCEEDINGS

Administration

15. Criminal justice shall be administered by the Political Officer, the Assistant Political Officer and the village authorities.

Appointment of Additional Political Officer

16. The Governor may appoint an Additional Political Officer for the trial of particular cases when he thinks fit, and may direct that such Additional Political Officer shall, for the purpose, exercise all or any of the powers of the Political Officer.

Powers of Political Officer

17. The Political Officer shall be competent to pass any sentence warranted by law.

Powers of Assistant Political Officers

18. The Assistant Political Officer shall exercise any powers not exceeding those of a Magistrate of the first class, as defined in the Criminal Procedure Code, with which they may be invested by the Governor.

Jurisdiction of village authorities

19. The village authorities may try any case involving any of the undermentioned offences in which the person or persons accused is or are resident within their jurisdiction:

Theft, including theft in a building.

Mischief, not being mischief by fire or any explosive substances.

Simple hurt.

Criminal trespass or house trespass.

Assault or using criminal force.

Powers of village authorities

20. A village authority may impose a fine not exceeding ₹ 50 for any offence which they are competent to try, and may also award payment in restitution or compensation to the extent of the injury sustained; such fines and payments may be enforced by distraint of the property of the offender.

Compensation

21. The Political Officer or Assistant Political Officer may order compensation to be paid to any person in a criminal case out of the proceeds of fines imposed in the case.

Disposal of cases by village

22. The village authorities shall decide all cases in open Darbar in the presence of at least three

authorities & powers to compel attendance independent witnesses and of the complainant and the accused. They are empowered to order the attendance of all the foregoing, and of the witnesses to be examined in the case, and to impose a fine not exceeding ₹ 50 on any person failing to attend when so ordered.

Procedure by village authorities after sentence 23. If any person on whom a fine has been imposed a village authority fails to deposit the amount at once, or within such further time as the village authority may allow, the village authority shall send him to an Assistant Political Officer to be dealt with in such manner as he may deem fit, unless the accused person gives notice of his intention to appeal against the decision.

Appeals from village authorities 24. Any party aggrieved by a decision of a village authority may appeal within seven days to the Assistant Political Officer, who on receipt of such appeal, shall try the case *de novo*.

Appeals from Assistant Political Officers 25. An appeal shall lie from an original decision of an Assistant Political Officer to the Political Officer.

Appeal to the High Court 26. An appeal shall lie to the High Court against sentences of three years' imprisonment and upwards, and sentences of death or transportation. In other cases there shall be no right of appeal, but the High Court may entertain an appeal by special leave.

Limitation for appeals 27. [1] All appeals under sections 25 or 26 must be presented within thirty days from the date of the order appealed against, excluding the time taken in procuring a copy of the order. Provided that an appeal from a sentence of death shall be preferred within seven days from the date of the sentence, excluding the time taken in procuring a copy of the order.

[2] The Political Officer shall on passing a sentence of death, inform the person sentenced of the provisions of sub-section [1].

Powers of revision 28. The High Court or the Political Officer may call for the proceedings of any officer subordinate to it, and reduce, enhance or cancel any sentence passed, remand the case for retrial, but no offence shall be punished by a sentence exceeding that warranted by law.

Transfer of cases 29. The High Court may for any person which it considers proper transfer any original case, pending or under trial before any Court to any other Court competent to try it, which is governed by this Regulation.

Confirmation of sentence 30. [1] All sentences of death, transportation or imprisonment for seven years or more shall be subject to confirmation by the High Court, and the proceedings of all cases in which any such sentence has been passed shall be submitted to the High Court forthwith, and no such sentence shall be carried into effect unless so confirmed.

Powers in such cases [2] In any case submitted under sub-section [l], the High Court —

[a] may confirm the sentence or pass any other sentence warranted by law; or

[b] may annul the conviction and convict the accused of any other offence of which the Political Officer might have convicted him; or

[c] may order a new trial on the same or an amended charge; or

[d] may acquit the accused persons.

Provided that no order of confirmation shall be made until the period allowed for preferring an appeal has expired, or, if an appeal is presented within such period, until such appeal is disposed of.

Sentences of death 31. [1] When a sentence of death passed by the Political Officer is confirmed by the High Court, the Political Officer, shall, on receiving the order of confirmation, cause such order to be carried into effect by issuing a warrant in the form given in item No. XXXV of Schedule V of the Code of Criminal Procedure, 1898, and taking such steps as army be necessary. — Act V of 1898.

[2] The Political Officer shall fix the time and place of execution, and the time fixed shall not be less than 21 or more than 28 days from the date of issue of the warrant.

Criminal Procedure

32. The High Court, the Political Officer, and the Assistant Political Officers shall be guided in regard to procedure by the principles of the Code of Criminal Procedure, 1898, so far as they are applicable to the circumstances of the Tracts and consistent with the provisions of this Regulation. The chief exceptions are —

[a] Verbal orders or notice only shall be requisite in any case except when the regular police are employed, or when the person concerned is not a resident of or in the Tract at the time but orders of summons shall in every case be for a fixed day, and the order shall be made known to the person concerned or to some adult member of his family, and, failing this, shall be openly proclaimed at the place where he is, or was last known to be, in sufficient time to allow him, if he sees fit, to appear.

[b] The proceedings of the village authorities need not be recorded in writing, nor shall be necessary that examinations before the Political Officer, Assistant Political Officers, be signed by the parties examined, but the Political Officer, Assistant Political Officers may require the village authorities to report their proceedings in any way which appears suitable.

[c] There shall be no preliminary enquiries by regular or village police unless the Political Officer or Assistant Political Officer sees fit to direct one.

[d] Recognizance to appear shall not be taken unless it appears necessary to the Political Officer or an Assistant Political Officer.

[e] Proceedings before the Political Officer or Assistant Political Officers shall be recorded in English only.

33. ....

Suspension and remission

34. [1] The President may, either upon conditions or without conditions, suspended the execution of or remit any sentence of death, and the Governor may, in like manner suspend the execution of or remit any sentence.

[2] If any sentence has been suspend or remitted upon conditions, and in the opinion of the President or the Governor, as the case may be, those conditions have not been fulfilled, the President or the Governor may cancel the suspension or remission and there upon the person whose sentence has been suspended or remitted may, if at large, be arrested by any police without warrant and remanded to undergo the unexpired portion of his sentence or made to undergo the punishment.

Commutation

35. The President may commute any sentence of death and the governor may commute any one of the following sentences for any other mentioned after it:

Death, transportation, confiscation of property, rigorous imprisonment, whipping, simple imprisonment, fine.

Chapter IV — CIVIL PROCEEDING

Administration

36. Civil justice shall be administered by the Political Officer, the Assistant Political Officer and the village authorities.

Powers of Political Officer & Asstt. Political Officers

37. The Political Officer may try suit of any value. The Assistant Political Officers may try suits not exceedings ₹ 1,000 in value.

Arbitration

38. [1] The Political Officer and the Assistant Political Officer shall in every case in which both parties are indigenous to the Tract endeavour to persuade them to submit to arbitration by a *panchayat*.

[2] If the parties agree, each party shall nominate an equal number of the panchayat, and the Political Officer or Assistant Political Officer shall either choose, or direct the *panchayat* to choose, a further person as umpire.

[3] The names and addresses of the members of the *panchayat* and umpire, and a statement of the matter in dispute shall be recorded, and the Political Officer or Assistant Political Officer shall direct the village authority or some other person to assemble the *panchayat* and witnesses within such time as he may specify, and shall also fix a date on which the decision of the *panchayat* shall be announced before him.

[4] The umpire shall have no vote as member of the *panchayat*, but shall enter on and decide the matter in dispute if the *panchayat*, or a majority of its members, are unable to agree on their decision before the date fixed under sub-section (3).

[5] On the date fixed for the announcement of the decision, the umpire and the parties shall appear before the Court which directed the arbitration, and the Court shall record the decision together with any order which it considers reasonable for the payment, or appointment, of the costs of the *panchayat*'s proceedings.

[6] The decision so recorded shall be enforceable as if it was a decision of the Court recording it and shall be final.

Arbitration in other cases

39. [1] In the cases in which neither or only one of the parties is indigenous to the Tract, the Political Officer or Assistant Political Officer may, with the consent of both parties, order that the case be referred to arbitration by a *panchayat*, and the provisions of sub-section (2) to (5) inclusive of section 38 shall then apply except that the Political Officer or Assistant Political Officer shall give the parties an opportunity to object to the decision.

[2] Any such objection must be made within ten days of the day on which the decision of the *panchayat* or umpire is recorded and if made, shall be considered by the Political Officer, whose decision shall be final,

[3] If such objection is made the provisions of sub-section (6) of section 38 shall apply.

Powers of authorities

40. The village authorities shall try all suits without limit of value in which both the parties are indigenous to the Tract and live within their jurisdiction and which are not submitted to arbitration under the provisions of section 38. All other suits which are not submitted to arbitration under the provisions of section 39 shall be tried by the Political Officer or an Assistant Political Officer.

Powers to enforce attendance

41. The village authorities shall have power to order the attendance of the parties and of witnesses, and to fine upto a limit of ₹ 50, persons failing to attend when ordered to do so.

Unfounded & vexatious suits

42. The village authorities shall have power to award costs, as well as compensation not exceeding ₹ 50 in any case to defendants for unfounded or vexatious suits brought against them.

Assessors

43. The village authorities may appoint one or more assessors to assist them in coming to a decision, and when they do so, shall record, but shall not be bound by, the opinion of the assessor or assessors.

Hearing of cases

44. [1] All suits tried by the village authorities shall be decided in open Darbar in the presence of the parties and at least three independent witnesses.

[2] The Political Officer or an Assistant Political Officer may direct a village authority to report their proceedings in any case or class of cases in any way which may appear to him to be suitable. Save as required by such direction, no record of any proceeding shall be maintained.

[3] After hearing both parties and their witnesses, if any, the village authority shall forthwith pronounce a decision.

Procedure after pronouncement of decision

45. [1] Unless any party having a right of appeal against a decision of a village authority gives notice, when such decision is pronounced of his intention to appeal against it, the village authority shall carry out the decision forthwith, and for such purpose may proceed by distraint of any property belonging to any person liable to pay any sum under the

decision, unless such person furnish security to the satisfaction of the village authority.

[2] If notice of intention to appeal is given, the village authority shall send the parties and witnesses to the Political Officer or an Assistant Political Officer forthwith, and one of the members of the village authority or one of the independent witnesses shall accompany them.

Appeals from village authorities

46. [1] Any person aggrieved by a decision of a village authority may appeal to the Assistant Political Officer in suits not exceeding ₹ 500 in value, and to the Political Officer in suits exceeding that value.

[2] If such an appeal is filed a record shall be made of the matter in dispute, and of the decision of the village authority.

[3] The appellate Court shall, if necessary, examine the parties, and, if the decision appears to be just, shall affirm and enforce the decision as its own. If the appellate Court sees grounds to doubts the justice of the decision, it shall try the case *de novo* or refer to a *panchayat*; in any case so referred, the provisions of section 38 shall apply as if the parties had agreed to submit to arbitration.

Appeals from Assitt. Political Officer

47. An Appeal shall lie to the Political Officer from any decision, original or appellate, of an Assistant Political Officer.

48. An appeal shall lie to the High Court from an original decision of the Political Officer if the value of the suit is not less than ₹ 500 or if the suit involves a question of tribal rights or customs, or of the right to, or possession of, immovable property.

Presentation of appeals

49. An appeal which lies to the Political Officer or High Court may be presented to the Assistant Political Officer, who shall, if it is in order and presented in due time, endorse upon it the date of receipt and transmit it with the records of the case to the Political Officer.

Powers of revision

50. The High Court may, on application or otherwise, call for the proceedings of any original case or appeal decided by the Political Officer, and

not appealable under this Regulation and may pass such orders as it may deem fit.

Limitation and other conditions

51. Every petition of appeal under section 47 or section 48 and every application under section 50 shall be accompanied by a copy of the order against which the appeal or application is made, and shall be filed within thirty days of the date of such order, excluding the time taken in procuring a copy of the order.

Civil Procedure

52. The High Court, the Court of Political Officer, and Assistant Political Officer shall be guided by the spirit, but shall not be bound by the letter, of the Code of Civil Procedure, 1908, and shall follow, subject to any express provisions of these rules, the principles of the Indian Limitation Act, 1908, in disputes between persons who are not indigenous to the Tracts. — Act IX of 1908.

Execution of decrees

53. [1] If any decree is modified or amended as a result of an appeal or of an order under section 50 the decree as so modified or amended shall, for the purposes of execution, be deemed to be the decree of the original Court.

[2] Decree against persons resident beyond the jurisdiction of the Court, if satisfaction cannot be obtained within the Tract, shall be transferred for execution to a Court having jurisdiction.

Exemption from execution

54. Houses, necessary clothings, cooking utensils, or implements whereby the owner or his family subsists, shall not be attached, sold or transferred in execution of a decree, unless the house or any other thing so exempted is the actual subject matter of the suit. Land maybe sold or temporarily transferred, where custom admits of individual rights in it being recognized.

Imprisonment for debt

55. No person shall be imprisoned for debt, except when the Political Officer is satisfied that he has made a fraudulent disposition or concernment of property. In such case the debtor may be detained for a period not exceeding six months.

Representation 56. [1] No pleader shall be allowed to appear in any case before the village authorities.

[2] No pleader shall be allowed to appear in the Courts of Political Officer or Assistant Political Officers except with the Political Officer's permission. Such permission shall not be refused if the defendant at the time the cause of action arose resided beyond the jurisdiction of the Court in an area where the appearance of pleader is not restricted.

[3] The High Court may be special leave permit any pleader to appear in any case before it.

Chapter V — EVIDENCE

Oaths 57. [1] In criminal cases before the Political Officer, Assistant Political Officers, oaths shall be administered to all witnesses when the accused is charged with murder, but not in other cases unless either party so require, or the Court so determine.

[2] In civil suits before the Political Officer and Assistant Political Officers, oaths shall not be administered to parties or witnesses unless either party or require, so the Court so determine.

[3] When an oath is administered, it shall be in the manner which the Court considers most binding on the conscience of the person making it.

False evidence 58. Any person who gives false evidence in any criminal case or civil suit, whether as a party or a witness, and whether after an oath has been administered to him or otherwise, shall be deemed to have given false evidence within the meaning of the Indian Penal Code, 1860. — Act XIV of 1860.

Guidance with regard to evidence 59. The Political Officer and Assistant Political Officers shall in all criminal cases and civil suits be guided by the general principles of the Indian Evidence Act, 1872. — Act I of 1872.

The India (Provisional Constitution) Order, 1947

AND WHEREAS by paragraph [c] of sub-section [1] of section 9 of the said Act it is provided that the Governor-General shall by order make such provision as appears to him to be necessary or expedient for making omissions or additions, to, and adaptations and modifications of, the Government of India Act, 1935, in its application to the separate new Dominions:

3. [2] The following expressions shall be omitted wherever they occur, namely, "in his discretion", "acting in his discretion" and "exercising his individual judgement".

EXTRACT FROM THE CONSTITUTION OF INDIA

Powers of President to make regulations for certain Union Territories

240. The President may make regulations for the peace, progress and good Government of the Union Territory of —

[a] the Andaman & Nicobar Islands
[b] the Laccadive, Minicoy and Amindivi Islands
[c] Dadra & Nagar Haveli
[d] Goa, Daman, & Diu
[e] Pondicherry

[1] Provided that when any body is created under article 239A to function as a Legislature for the Union Territory of Goa, Daman & Diu or Pondicherry, the President shall not make any Regulation for the peace, progress and good Government of that Union Territory with effect from the date appointed for the first meeting of the Legislature.

[2] Any Regulation so made may repeal or amend any Act made by Parliament or any existing

law which is for the time being applicable to the Union Territory and, when promulgated by the President, shall have the same force and effect as an Act of Parliament which applies to that Territory.

SIXTH SCHEDULE

18. In application of the provisions of this Schedule to areas specified in Part B of the table appended to paragraph 20 [1] the Governor may —

[a] subject to the previous approval of the President, by public notification, apply all or any of the foregoing provisions of this Schedule to any tribal area specified in Part B of the table appended to paragraph 20 of this Schedule or any part of such area and thereupon such area or part shall be administered in accordance with such provisions; and

[b] with like approval, by public notification, exclude from the said table any tribal area specified in Part B of that table or any part of such area. [2] Until a notification is issued under sub-paragraph [1] of this paragraph in respect of any tribal area specified in Part B of the said table or any part of such area, the administration of such area or part thereof, as the case may be, shall be carried on by the President through the Governor of Assam as his agent and the provisions of Act 240 shall apply thereto as if such area or part thereof were a Union Territory specified in that article. [3] In the discharge of his functions under sub-paragraph [2] of this paragraph as the agent of the President the governor shall act in his discretion.

20. *Tribal areas* — [1] The areas specified in Parts A and B of the table below shall be tribal areas within the State of Assam.

[2] The United Khasi-Jaintia Hills district shall comprise the territories which before the commencement of this Constitution were known as the Khasi States and the Khasi & Jaintia Hills district,

excluding any areas for the time being comprised within the cantonment and municipality of Shillong, but including so much of the area comprised within the municipality of Shillong as formed part of the Khasi State of Mylliem.

Provided that for the purposes of clauses [e] and [f] of sub-paragraph [1] of paragraph 3, paragraph 4, paragraph 5, paragraph 6, sub-paragraph [2] clauses [a], [b] and [d] of sub-paragraph [3] and sub-paragraph [4] of paragraph 8, and clause [d] of sub-paragraph [2] of paragraph 10 of this Schedule no part of the area comprised within the municipality of Shillong shall be deemed to be within the District.

18. [2A] The Mizo district shall comprise the area which at the commencement of this Constitution was known as the Lushai Hills district].

[3] Any reference in the table below to any District [other than the United Khasi-Jaintian Hills district and the Mizo district] or administrative area shall be constructed as a reference to that district or area at the commencement of this Constitution.

Provided that the tribal areas specified in Part B of the table below shall not include any such areas in the Plain as may, with the previous approval of the President, be notified by the Governor of Assam in that behalf.

TABLE

Part — A

Part — B

1. North-east Frontier Tract including Balipara Frontier Tract, Tirap Frontier Tract, Abor Hills district and Mishmi Hills district.

2. Naga Tribal Area.

Regulation 1 of 1948

The North-East Frontier Tracts (Internal Administration) Regulation, 1948

Preamble

WHEREAS it is expedient for the good government of the North-East Frontier Tracts to divide the present Sadiya Frontier Tract into two units of administration.

Now, therefore, in exercise of the powers conferred by sub-section (2) of section 92 of the Government of India Act, 1935, as adapted by the India (Provisional Constitution) Order, 1947, the Governor of Assam is pleased to make the following Regulation:

Short title and commencement

1. [1] This Regulation may be called the North-East Frontier Tracts (Internal Administration) Regulation, 1948.

[2] It shall come into force on such date as the Governor may by notification in the official appoint.

Administrative units with boundaries

2. The Sadiya Frontier Tract as constituted at present shall be divided into two separate units of administration called the Abor Hills district and the Mishmi Hills district each comprising areas as set out in the Schedules I and II below respectively.

Application of laws

3. All laws for the time being in force in the Sadiya Frontier Tract shall apply in the Abor Hills district and the Mishmi Hills district subject to any reservations or modifications with which they are applicable in the Sadiya Frontier Tract, as the case may be.

THE SCHEDULE I

Boundary of the Abor Hills District

East: From a point, height 13,774, ... on the McMahon Line about one mile south-west of the Khangri Kharpo La pass .... the boundary run in a southerly direction along the range dividing the Siang and Dibang Valleys through points 13,337, 13,798, 13,663, 1,392, 13,921, 12,959, 13,945, 13,325, (Aborka) 13,640, 13,244, 10,820, 8,120, 6,550 to Tirap 10,310, and continuing south-eastwards through point 7,430 to point 6,844 thence down a nameless stream with its source below point 6,944 to the Egadi river; thence down the midstream of this river to the Sesseri river; thence down the midstream of this river to its junction with the Dihong at old Sessriniukh, thence the left bank of the Dihong and across the mouth of the Lohit to the left bank of the Brahmaputra which is followed as far as Rangdai Ghat ....; thence by the western boundary of the Saikhoa Reserve Forest to the Laika Jan.

South: From the above point westwards down the Laika Jan to its junction with the Brahmaputra river; thence crossing the Brahmaputra river, so as to include the Kapland and Dorkang Chapris within the area of the Abor Hills district to the point where the Burhi Suti (channel) leaves the Brahmaputra ....; thence by the right bank of Brahmaputra river keeping the Mesaki Chapri in the Abor Hills District to a point .... where the Sengajan road comes down to the Brahmaputra river; thence in a north-westerly direction by this road to the Burhi Suti .... thence by the left bank of the Burhi Suti to the mouth of the Dijmur Nadi, a branch of the Simen river and thence by the midstream of that Nadi and the parent stream to the mouth of the Dipa (Sinyang) Nadi; thence by the left bank of the Dipa (Sinyang) Nadi to where it leaves the foothills from where the line of boundary runs in a westerly direction by the path at the foot of hills so as to include all Gallong villages within the Abor Hills District to a point where the Jiya Dhol river cuts the Rajgarh Ali; thence up the right bank of the Jiya Dhol river to a point due east of a spur height 3,420, ...; thence up this spur and along it in a wersterly direction until it drops again at the junction of the Siplu and Subansiri rivers at Sipluraukh.

West: Thence by the left bank of the Subansiri river to the point where it cuts the McMahon Line on the Indo-Tibetan Frontier.

North: From the last point eastwards by the McMahon Line to the Starting point.

THE SCHEDULE II

Boundary of the Mishmi Hills District

East: From a point, height 15,283, where the McMahon Line joins the Indo-Burma Boundary .... southwards along the Indo-Burma Boundary to a point .... where the range leading westwards takes off to Dapha Bum height 15,020.

South: Westwards along this range through Dapha Bum 15,020, Jaitu 10,847 to Champai Bum height 8,244; thence in a south-westerly direction to the saddle at the east end of the Mana Bum range ....; thence a north-westerly direction along the Mana Bum range to a point, height 2,127; thence a line west-south-west crossing the Kumchai and Noa Dihing stream to the point where the path from Bara Dumsa to Mohanggaon cuts the Dirak Hka, height 493; from this point down the left bank of the Dirak Hka in a north-westerly direction to the village of Chhota Dirak (Khamti) .... thence in a westerly direction by the southern edge of the path leading from this village to the Bar Maithang to a point on the Hahkhati Jan about one mile west of the village of Chhota Dirak, near where the Hahkhati Jan turns westwards at height 450 ...., thence by the Hahkhati Jan stream known also as the Dhola and then the Dangori Nadi lower down its course, ... to a point where a small channel or khar connects it with the Ajuka Nadi; thence by this channel to the Ajuka Nadi and down the Ajuka Nadi also known as the Laika Jan lower down its course to the point where the southern end of the western boundary of the Saikhowa Reserve Forest is reached.

West: Thence northwards along western boundary of the Saikhowa Reserve Forest to Rangdai Ghat on the left bank of the Brahmaputra river; thence up along the left bank of this river across the mouth of the Lohit to the left bank of the Dihang and up the left bank of the Dihang to the mouth of the Sesseri at Sesserimukh ....; thence up the midstream of the Sesseri river to where the "Egadi" river joins the Sessiri river; thence up the midstream of the former to where it is joined on the right bank by nameless stream .... up this stream to point 6,844, and thence through, points, ... the point, height

13,744 .... on the McMahon Line about one mile south-west of the Khangri Kharpo La pass ....
....

North: Thence eastwards along the McMahon Line which forms the Indo-Tibetan Frontier to the starting point.

I have made this Regulation under sub-section (2) of section 92 of the Government of India Act, 1935.

A. HYDARI
Government of Assam

The 10th May, 1948.

I assent to this Regulation.

New Delhi,
The 3rd June, 1948.

MOUNTBATTEN OF BURMA
Governor-General

N. K. RUSTOMJI
Adviser to the Governor of Assam
For Excluded Areas & States

ANNEXURE XV

43 OF 1950
Representation of the People Act, 1950

PART II
Allocation of Seats and Delimitation of Constituencies

The House of the People

3. Allocation of seals in the House of the People — The allocation of seats to the States in the House of the People and the number of seats, if any, to be reserved for the Scheduled Castes and for the Scheduled Tribes of each State shall be as shown in the First Schedule.

4. Filling of seats in the House of the People and Parliamentary constituencies. — (1) the seat allotted in the House of the People under section 3 to the Part B tribal areas shall be the seat to be filled by a person nominated by the President.

THE FIRST SCHEDULE
(See Section 3)

Allocation of Seats in the House of the People

Name of State Union Territory or area	*Number of seats in the House as constituted on the 1st November, 1969*			*Number of seats in the House as subsequently constituted*		
	Total	*Reserved for the Scheduled Castes*	*Reserved for the Scheduled Tribes*	*Total*	*Reserved for the Scheduled Castes*	*Reserved for the Scheduled Tribes*
1	*2*	*3*	*4*	*5*	*6*	*7*
III — AREA: North-East Frontier Tract	1	—	1	—	—	—

ANNEXURE XVI

Notification No. TAD/R/35/50/109 dated the 23rd February, 1951

In exercise of the powers conferred by the provision to sub-paragraph [3] of paragraph 20 of the Sixth Schedule of the Constitution of India and with the previous approval of President, the Governor of Assam is pleased to notify the following *areas in the plains to be the areas not included in tribal areas specified in part B* of the table appended to the said paragraph 20, namely —

[1] So much of the area included in the Balipara Frontier Tract, as is comprised with the line drawn from the eastern boundary of the district of Kamrup at Pillar No. 98 on the Bar Nadi eastwards along the Inner Line of the Balipara Frontier Tract as defined in Assam Government Notification No. 6778-A.P., dated the 2nd November, 1934, till it reaches the boundary of the Lakhimpur district to the point where it meets the boundary of the Darrang district; thence westwards along the northern boundary of Kamrup district, thence northwards along this boundary to the starting point.

[2] So much of the *area included in the Abor Hills and Mishmi Hills District (Sadiya Frontier Tract)* as is comprised within the line drawn from the point 496 at Dipa in a straight line to the junction of the Romi river with a nameless stream about a mile southeast of the junction of Romi and Tode Korong rivers; thence in a straight line to point mile stone No. 4 from Kabo on the Kobo-Pasighat road; thence in a straight line to the junction of Sisseri and Gango rivers; thence along the left bank of the Gango river to its junction with the Dibang river; thence in a straight line to the confluence of Hazingnadi with Kundil river about half a mile north of the point 492 of the Kundil river; thence in a straight line to point 723 on the right bank of the Tipu-Balijan river [about 4 miles north of the confluence of Haru Nadi with Balijan]; thence down the Balijan river following its right bank of its confluence with the Lohit river thence across the Lohit river and down its left bank of Noa Dihing Mukh; thence up the right bank of the Noa Dihing river to its confluence with the Dirak river; thence up the left bank of the Dirak river to where it meets the boundary between the Sadiya Frontier Tract and the

Lakhimpur district; thence westwards along the northern boundary of the Lakhimpur district to the starting point.

[3] So much of the *area included in the Tirap Frontier Tract* as is comprised within the line drawn from the confluence of the Koria Pani and the Burhi Dihing rivers up the right bank of the Burhi Dihing river to the confluence of the Namphuk and the Namchik rivers; thence up the left bank of the Namchik river to its confluence with the Kathang river; thence up the Kathang Hka to its junction with the Lekha Hka; thence up the Lekha Hka to its source and thence to point 894; thence in a south-westerly direction down a nameless stream that originates from point 894 to its junction with the Tirap river; thence up the left bank of the Tirap to a point due east of height 2,458 on the Lungokan range; thence down the Tipang to its junction with Kumkai Wa; thence in a south-westerly direction along the ridge of Tuting Tak Kan range to the saddle between this range and Lompi Parbat range thence in north-westerly direction down the nameless stream that originates from this saddle, to its junction with Likhapani or Tel stream; thence down the Likhapani stream to its junction with the Tirap river.

Thence down the Tirap river to its junction with the Burhi Dihing river; thence down the Burhi Dihing river to its junction with the Nanmaw Jan; thence up the the Nanmaw Jan and Monggang Khasi stream as far as it forms the eastern boundary of the Upper Dihing reserve forests; thence along the eastern boundary of the Upper Dihing reserve forest [estt. Block] to the point where it meet the Pengri Hka; thence down the the Pengri Hka to the Burhi Dihing river and up the Burhi Dihing to the Starting point.

SECTION VI

The Sixth Schedule*

[Articles 244 (2) and 275 (1)]

Provisions as to the administration of Tribal areas (in the State of Assam and Meghalaya and in the Union Territory of Mizoram).

1. *Autonomous district and autonomous regions:* (1) subject to the provisions of this paragraph, the tribal areas in each item of (Parts I and II, and Part III) of the table appended to Paragraph 20 of this Schedule shall be an autonomous district.

(2). If there are different Scheduled Tribes in an autonomous district, the Governor may, by public notification, divide the area or areas inhabited by them into autonomous regions.

(3) The Governor may, by public notification —

- (a) include any area in **(any of the Parts) of the said table;
- (b) exclude any area from **(any of the Parts) of the said table;
- (c) create a new autonomous district;
- (d) increase the area of any autonomous district;
- (e) diminish the area of any autonomous district;
- (f) unite two or more autonomous districts of parts thereof so as to form one autonomous district,[1] [alter the name of any autonomous district]; and
- (g) define the boundaries of any autonomous district.

Provided that no order shall be made by the Governor under clauses (c), (d), (e) and (f) of this sub-paragraph except after consideration of the report of a Commission appointed under sub-paragraph (1) of Paragraph 14 of this Schedule.

[2][Provided further that any order made by the governor under

---

* Not applicable to the State of Jammu & Kashmir: Constitution (J&K) Order, 1954.

** Substituted by Act 81 of 1971.

this sub-paragraph may contain such incidental and consequential provisions (including any amendment of paragraph 20 and of any item in any of the Parts of the said table) as appear to the Governor to be necessary for giving effect to the provisions of the order.]

2. *Constitution of District Councils and Regional Councils:* [3][(1) There shall be a District Council for each autonomous district consisting of not more than thirty members, of whom not more than four persons shall be nominated by the Governor and the rest shall be elected on the basis of adult suffrage.]

(2) There shall be a separate Regional Council for each area constituted an autonomous region under sub-paragraph (2) of paragraph 1 of this Schedule.

(3) Each District Council and each Regional Council shall be a body corporate by the name respectively of "the District Council of (name of district)" and "the Regional Council of (name of Region)", shall have perpetual succession and a common seal and shall by the said name sue and be sued.

(4) Subject to the provisions of the Schedule, the administration of an autonomous district shall, insofar as it is not vested under this Schedule in any Regional Council within such district, be vested in the District Council for such district and the administration of an autonomous region shall be vested in the Regional Council for such region.

(5) In an autonomous district with Regional Councils, the District Council shall have only such powers with respect to the areas under the authority of the Regional Council as may be delegated to it by the Regional Council in addition to the powers conferred on it by this Schedule with respect to such areas.

(6) The Governor shall make rules for the first constitution of District Council and Regional Council in consultation with the existing Tribal Councils or other representative tribal organizations with the autonomous district or regions concerned, and such rules shall provides for —

(a) the composition of the District Councils and Regional Councils and the allocation of seats therein;

(b) the delimitation of territorial constituencies for the purpose of elections to those Councils;

(c) the qualifications for voting at such elections and the preparation of electoral rolls therefor;

(d) the qualifications for being elected at such elections as members of such Councils;

(e) the term of office of members of [3](Regional Councils);

(f) any other matter relating to or connected with elections or nominations to such Councils;

(g) the procedure and the conduct of business [4](including the power to act notwithstanding any vacancy); and

(h) the appointment of officers and staff of the District and Regional Councils.

[4][(6-A) The elected members of the District Council shall hold office for a term of five years from the date appointed for the first meeting of the Council after the general elections to the Council, unless the District Council is sooner dissolved under Paragraph 16 and a nominated member shall hold office at the pleasure of the governor:

Provided that the said period of five years may, while a Proclamation of Emergency is in operation or if circumstances exist which, in the opinion of the Governor, render the holding of elections impracticable, be extended by the Governor for a period not exceeding one year at a time and in any case where a Proclamation of Emergency is in operation not extending beyond a period of six months after the proclamation has ceased to operate:

Provided further that a member elected to fill a casual vacancy shall hold office only for the remainder of the terra of office of the member whom he replaces.]

(7) The District or the Regional Council may after its first constitution make rules [5](with the approval of the Governor) with regard to the matters specified in sub-paragraph (6) of this paragraph and may also make rules [5](with like approval) regulating —

(a) the formation of subordinate local Councils or Boards and their procedure and the conduct of their business; and

(b) generally all matters relating to the transaction of business pertaining to the administration of the district or region, as the case may be:

Provided that until rules are made by the District Council or the Regional Council under this sub-paragraph the rules made by the Governor under sub-paragraph (6) of this paragraph shall have effect in respect of elections to, the officers and staff of, and the procedure and the conduct of business in, each such Council:

(* * * * *)[6]

3. *Powers of District Council and Regional Councils to make laws:* (1) The Regional Council for an autonomous region in respect of all areas within such region and the District Council for an autonomous district in respect of all areas within the district except those which are under the authority of Regional Councils, if any, within the district shall have power to make laws with respect to —

(a) the allotment, occupation or use, or the setting apart, of land, other than any land which is reserved forest, for the purposes of agriculture or grazing or for residential or other non-agricultural proposes or for any other purposes likely to promote the interests of the inhabitants of any village or town:

Provided that nothing in such laws shall prevent the compulsory acquisition of any land, whether occupied or unoccupied for public purposes by the (Government of State concern)[7] in accordance with the law for the time being in force authorizing such acquisition;

(b) the management of any forest not being a reserved forest;

(c) the use of any canal or water-course for the purpose of agriculture;

(d) the establishment of village or town committees or councils and their powers;

(e) any other matter relating to village or town administration, including village or town police and public health and sanitation;

(f) the appointment of succession of Chiefs or Headmen;

(g) the inheritance of property;

(h) (marriage and divorce);[8] and

(i) social customs.

(2) In this paragraph, a "reserved forest" means any area which is a reserved forest under the Assam Forest Regulation, 1891, or under any other law for the time being in force in the area in question.

(3) All laws made under this paragraph shall be submitted forthwith to the Governor and, until assented to by him, shall have no effect.

4. *Administration of Justice in autonomous districts and autonomous regions:* (1) The Regional Council for an autonomous region in respect of areas within such region and the District Council for an autonomous district in respect of areas within the district other than those which are under the authority of the Regional Councils, if any within the district may constitute village councils or courts for the trial of suits and cases between the parties all of whom belong to Scheduled Tribes within such areas, other than suits and cases to which the provisions of sub-paragraph (1) of paragraph 5 of this Schedule apply, to the exclusion of any court in the State, and may appoint suitable persons to be members of such village councils or presiding officers of such courts, and may also appoint such officers as may be necessary for the administration of the laws made under paragraph 3 of this Schedule.

(2) Notwithstanding anything in this Constitution, the Regional Council for an autonomous region or any court constituted in that behalf by the Regional Council or, if in respect of any area within an autonomous district there is no Regional Council, the District Council for such district, or any court constituted in that behalf by the District Council, shall exercise the powers of court of appeal in respect of all suits and cases triable by a village council or court constituted under sub-paragraph (1) of this paragraph within such region or area as the case may be, other than those to which provisions of sub-paragraph (1) of paragraph 5 of this Schedule apply, and no other court except the High Court and the Supreme Court shall have jurisdiction over such suits or cases.

(3) The High Court (* * * *)[9] shall have and exercise such jurisdiction over the suits and cases to which the provisions of sub-paragraph (2) of this paragraph apply as the Governor may from time to time by order specify.

(4) A Regional Council or District Council, as the case may be, may with the previous approval of the governor make rules regulating —

(a) the constitution of village councils and courts and the powers to be exercised by them under this paragraph;

(b) the procedure to be followed by village councils or courts in the trial of suits and cases under sub-paragraph (1) of this paragraph;

(c) the procedure to be followed by the Regional or District Council or any court constituted by such Councils or courts in the trial of suits and cases under sub-paragraph (2) of this paragraph;

(d) the enforcement of decisions and orders of such Councils and courts;

(e) all other ancillary matters for the carrying of the provisions of sub-paragraphs (1) and (2) of this paragraph.

[10][(5) On and from such date as the President may [10a](after consulting the Government of the State concerned) by notification appoint in this behalf, this paragraph shall have effect in relation to such autonomous district or region as may be specified in the notification, as if —

(i) in sub-paragraph (1), for the words "between the parties all of whom belong to Scheduled Tribes within such areas, than suits and cases to which the provisions of sub-paragraph (1) of paragraph 5 of this Schedule apply", the words "not being suits and cases of the nature referred to in sub-paragraph (1) of paragraph 5 of this Schedule, which the Governor may specify in this behalf", had been substituted.

(ii) sub-paragraphs (2) and (3) had been omitted.

(iii) in sub-paragraph (4) —

(a) for the words "A Regional Council or District Council, as the case may be, may with the previous approval of the Governor make rules regulating", the words "the governor may make rules regulating" had been substituted; and

(b) for clause (a), the following clause had been substituted namely:

"(a) The constitution of village councils and courts, the powers to be exercised by them under this paragraph and the courts to which appeals from the decisions of village councils and courts shall lie";

(c) for clause (c), the following clause had been substituted, namely:

"(c) the transfer of appeals and other proceedings pending before the Regional or District Council or any court constituted by such Council immediately before the date appointed by the President under sub-paragraph (5)"; and

(d) in clause (e), for the words, brackets and figures "sub-paragraphs (1) and (2)", the word, brackets and figure "sub-paragraph (1)" had been substituted.]

5. *Conferment of powers under the Code of Civil Procedure, 1908, and the Code of Criminal Procedure, 1898, on the Regional and District Councils and on certain courts and officers for the trial of certain suits, cases and offences* — (1) The Governor may, for the trial of suits or cases arising out of any law in force in any autonomous district or region being a law specified in that behalf by the Governor or for the trial of offences punishable with death, transportation for life, or imprisonment for a term of not less than five years under the Indian Penal Code or under any other law for the time being applicable to such district or region, confer on the District Council or the Regional Council having authority over such district or region or on courts constituted by such District Council or on any officer appointed in that behalf by the Governor, such powers under the Code of Civil Procedure, 1908, or, as the case may be, the Code of Criminal Procedure, 1898, as he deems appropriate, and there upon the said Council, court or officer in exercise of the powers so conferred.

(2) The Governor may withdraw or modify any of the powers conferred on a District Council, Regional Council, court or officer under sub-paragraph (1) of this Paragraph.

(3) Save as expressly provided in this paragraph, the Code of Civil Procedure, 1908, and the Code of Criminal Procedure, 1898, shall not apply to the trial of any suits, cases of offences in an autonomous district or in any autonomous region to which the provisions of this paragraph apply.

[11][(4) On and from the date appointed by the President under sub-paragraph (5) of paragraph 4 in relation to any autonomous district or autonomous region, nothing contained in this paragraph shall, in its application to that district or region, be deemed to authorize the Governor to confer on the District Council or Regional Council or on courts constituted by the District Council any of the powers referred to in sub-paragraph (1) of this paragraph.]

[12][**6.** *Powers of the District Council to establish primary schools, etc.:* (1) The District Council for an autonomous district may establish, construct, or manage primary schools, dispensaries, markets, cattle pounds, ferries, roads, road transport and waterways in the district and may, with the previous approval of the Governor, make regulations for the regulation and control thereof and, in particular, may prescribe the language and the manner in which primary education shall be imparted in the primary schools in the district.

(2) The Governor may, with the consent of any District Council, entrust either conditionally or unconditionally to that Council or to its

officers, functions in relation to agriculture, animal husbandry, community projects, cooperative societies, social welfare, village planning or any other matter to which the executive power of the State [12a](* * *) extends.]

7. *District and Regional Funds:* (1) There shall be constituted for each autonomous district, a District Fund and for each autonomous region, a Regional Fund to which shall be credited all moneys received respectively by the District Council for that district and the Regional Council for that region in the course of the administration of such district or region, as the case may be, in accordance with the provisions of this Constitution.

[12a][(2) The Governor may make rules for the management of the District Fund, or, as the case may be, the Regional Fund and for the procedure to be followed in respect of payment of money into the said Fund, the withdrawal of moneys therefrom, the custody of moneys therein and any other matter connected with or ancillary to the matters aforesaid.

(3) he accounts of the District Council or, as the case may be, the Regional Council shall be kept in such form as the Comptroller and Auditor-General of India may, with the approval of the President, prescribe.

(4) The Comptroller and Auditor-General shall cause the accounts of the District and Regional Councils to be audited in such manner as he may think fit, and the reports of the Comptroller and Auditor-General relating to such accounts shall be submitted to the Governor who shall cause them to be laid before the Council.]

8. *Powers to assess and collect land revenue and to impose taxes:* (1) The Regional Council for an autonomous region in respect of all lands within such region and the District Council for an autonomous district in respect of all lands within the district except those which are in the areas under the authority of Regional Councils, if any, within the district, shall have the power to assess and collect revenue in respect of such lands in accordance with the principles for the time being followed [12b](by the Government of the State in assessing lands for the purpose of land revenue in the State of Assam generally.)

(2) The Regional Council for an autonomous region in respect of areas within such region and the District Council for an autonomous district in respect of all areas in the district except those which are under the authority of Regional Council, if any, within the district, shall have power to levy and collect taxes on lands and buildings, and tolls on persons resident within such areas.

(3) The District Council for an autonomous district shall have the power to levy and collect all or any of the following taxes within such district, that is to say —

(a) taxes on professions, trades, calling and employments;
(b) taxes on animals, vehicles and boats;
(c) taxes on the entry of goods into a market for sale therein, and tolls on passengers and goods carried in ferries; and
(d) taxes for the maintenance of schools, dispensaries or roads.

(4) A Regional Council or District Council, as the case may be, may made regulation to provide for the levy and collection of any of the taxes specified in sub-paragraphs (2) and (3) of this paragraph [13](and every such regulation shall be submitted forthwith to the Governor and, until assented to by him, shall have no effect).

9. *Licences of leases for the purpose of prospecting for, or extraction of, minerals:* (1) Such share of the royalties accruing each year from licences or leases for the purpose of prospecting for, or the extraction of, minerals granted by [13a](the Government of the State) in respect of any area within and autonomous district as may be agreed upon between [13a](the Government of the State) and the District Council of such district shall be made over to the District Council.

(2) If any dispute arises as to the share of such royalties to be made over to a District Council, it shall be referred to the Governor for determination and the amount determined by the Governor in his discretion shall be deemed to be the amount payable under sub-paragraph (1) of this paragraph to the District Council and the decision of the Governor shall be final.

10. *Powers of District Council to make regulations for the control of money-lending and trading by non-tribals:* (1) the District Council of an autonomous district may make regulations for the regulation and control of money-lending or trading within the district by persons other than Scheduled Tribes resident in the district.

(2) In particular and without prejudice to the generality of the foregoing power, such regulations may —

(a) prescribe that no one except the holder of a licence issued in that behalf shall carry on the business of money-lending;
(b) prescribe the maximum rate of interest which may be charged or be recovered by a money-lender;

(c) provide for the maintenance of accounts by money-lenders and for the inspection of such accounts by officers appointed in that behalf by the District Council; and

(d) prescribe that no person who is not a member of the Scheduled Tribes resident in the district shall carry on wholesale or retail business in any commodity except under a licence issued in that behalf by the District Council.

Provided that no regulations may be made under this paragraph unless they are passed by a majority of not less than three-fourths of the total membership of the District Council.

Provided further that it shall not be competent under any such regulations to refuse the grant of a licence to a money-lender or a trader who has been carrying on business within the district since before the time of the making of such regulations.

(3) All regulations made under this paragraph shall be submitted forthwith to the Governor and, until assented to by him, shall have no effect.

11. *Publication of laws, rules and regulations made under the Schedule:* All laws, rules and regulations made under this Schedule by a District Council or a Regional Council shall be published forthwith in the Official Gazette of the State and shall on such publication have the force of law.

12. [13b](*Application of Act of Parliament and of the Legislature of State of Assam of autonomous districts and autonomous regions in the State of Assam*): (1) Notwithstanding anything in this Constitution —

(a) no Act of the (Legislature of State of Assam)[13c] in respect of any of the matters specified in paragraph 3 of this Schedule and matters with respect to which a (District Council or a Regional Council may make laws and no Act of the Legislature of the State of Assam)[13c] prohibiting or restricting the consumption of any non-distilled alcoholic liquor shall apply to any autonomous district or autonomous region unless in either case the District Council for such district or having jurisdiction over such region by public notification so directs, and the District Council in giving such direction with respect to any Act may direct that the Act shall in its application to such district or region or any part thereof have effect subject to such exceptions or modifications as it thinks fit;

(b) the Governor may, by public notification, direct that any Act of Parliament or of the (Legislature of the State of Assam)[13c] to which the provisions of clause (a) of the sub-paragraph do not apply shall not apply to an autonomous district or an autonomous region [13d](in the State), or shall apply to such district or region or any part thereof subject to such exceptions or modifications as he may specify in the notification.

(2) Any direction given under sub-paragraph (1) of this paragraph may be given so as to have retrospective effect.

[13e][**12A.** *Application of Acts of Parliament and of the Legislature of the State of Meghalaya to autonomous district and autonomous regions in the State of Meghalaya:* Notwithstanding anything in the Constitution —

(a) if any provision of a law made by a District or Regional Council in the State of Meghalaya with respect to any matter specified in sub-paragraph (1) of paragraph 3 of this Schedule or if any provision of any regulation made by a District Council or if a Regional Council in that State under paragraph 8 or paragraph 10 of this Schedule, is repugnant to any provision of law made by the Legislature of the State of Meghalaya with respect to that matter, than, the law or regulation made by the District Council or, as the case may be, the Regional Council whether made before or after the law made by the Legislature of the State of Meghalaya, shall, to the extent of repugnancy, be void and the law made by the Legislature of the State of Meghalaya shall prevail;

(b) the President may, with respect to any Act of Parliament, by notification, direct that it shall not apply to any autonomous district or an autonomous region in the State of Meghalaya, or shall apply to such district or region or any part thereof subject to such exceptions or modifications as he may specify in the notification and any such direction may be given so as to have retrospective effect.]

[14][**12B.** *Application of Acts of Parliament and other Acts to autonomous districts and autonomous regions in the Union Territory of*

Mizoram: Notwithstanding anything in this Constitution, the President may with respect to any Act, by notification, direct that it shall not apply to an autonomous district or an autonomous region in the Union Territory of Mizoram or shall apply to such district or region or any part thereof subject to such exceptions or modifications as he may specify in the notification and any such direction may be given so as to have retrospective effect].

13. *Estimated receipts and expenditure pertaining to autonomous districts to be shown separately in the annual financial statement:* The estimated receipts and expenditure pertaining to an autonomous district which are to be credited to, or is to be made from the Consolidated Fund of the State,[15] (* * *) shall be first placed before the District Council for discussion and then after such discussion be shown separately in the annual financial statement of the State to be laid before the Legislature of the State under Article 202.

14. *Appointment of Commission to inquire into and report on the administration of autonomous districts and autonomous regions:* (1) The Governor may at any time appoint a Commission to examine and report on any matter specified by him relating to the administration of the autonomous districts and autonomous regions in the Stale, including matters specified in clauses (c), (d), (e) and (f) of sub-paragraph (3) of paragraph 1 of this Schedule, or may appoint a Commission to inquire into an report from time-to-time on the administration of autonomous districts and autonomous regions in the State generally and in particular on —

(a) the provision of educational and medical facilities and communications in such districts and regions;
(b) the need for any new or special legislation in respect of such districts and regions; and
(c) the administration of the laws, rules and regulations made by the District and Regional Councils;

and define the procedure to be followed by such Commission.

(2) The report of every such Commission with the recommendations of the Governor with respect thereto shall be laid before the Legislature of the State by the Minister concerned together with an explanatory memorandum regarding the action proposed to be taken thereon by [15a](Government of State).

(3) Allocating the business of the Government of the State among his Ministers, the governor may place one of his Ministers specially in

charge of the welfare of the autonomous districts and autonomous regions in the state.

15. *Annulment or suspension of acts and resolutions of District and Regional Councils:* (1) If at any time the Governor is satisfied that an act or resolution of a District or a Regional Council is likely to endanger the safety of India [15b](or is likely to be prejudiced to public order), he may annul or suspend such act or resolution and take such steps as he may consider necessary (including the suspension of the Council and the assumption to himself of all or any of the powers vested in or exercisable by the Council) to prevent the Commission or continuance of such act, or the giving of effect to such resolution.

(2) Any order made by the governor under sub-paragraph (1) of this paragraph together with the reasons therefor shall be laid before the Legislature of the State as soon as possible and the order shall, unless revoked by the Legislature of the State, continue in force for a period of twelve months from the date on which it was so made:

Provided that if and so often as a resolution approving the continuance in force of such order is passed by the Legislature of the State, the order shall unless cancelled by the Governor continue in force for a further period of twelve months from the date on which under this paragraph it would otherwise have ceased to operate.

16. *Dissolution of a District or a Regional Council: 16*[(1) The Governor may on the recommendation of a Commission appointed under paragraph 14 of this Schedule by public notification order the dissolution of a District or a Regional Council and —

(a) direct that a fresh general election shall be held immediately for the reconstitution of the Council; or

(b) subject to the previous approval of the Legislature of the State assume the administration of the area under the authority of such Council himself or place the administration of such area under the Commission appointed under the said paragraph or any other body considered suitable by him for a period not exceeding twelve months:

Provided that when an order under clause (a) of this paragraph has been made, the Governor may take the action referred to in clause (b) of this paragraph with regard to the administration of the area in question pending the reconstitution of the Council on fresh general election:

Provided further that no action shall be taken under clause (b) of this paragraph without giving the District or the Regional Council, as the case may be, an opportunity of placing its view before the Legislature of the State.

[17][(2) If at any time the governor is satisfied that a situation has arisen in which the administration of an autonomous district or region cannot be carried on in accordance with the provisions of this Schedule, he may, by public notification, assume to himself all or any of the functions or powers vested in or exercisable by the District Council or, as the case may be, the Regional Council and declare that such functions or powers shall be exercisable by such person or authority as he may specify in this behalf, for a period not exceeding six months:

Provided that the Governor may by a further order or orders extend the operation of the initial order by a period not exceeding six months on each occasion.

(3) Every order made under sub-paragraph (2) of this paragraph with the reasons therefor shall be laid before the Legislature of the State and shall cease to operate at the expiration of thirty days from the date on which the State Legislature first sits after the issue of the order, unless, before the expiry of that period it has been approved by the State Legislature.]

17. *Exclusion of areas from autonomous districts in forming constituencies in such districts:* For the purposes of elections to the [17a](Legislative Assembly of Assam or Meghalaya), the governor may by order declare that any area within an autonomous district [17b](in the State of Assam or Meghalaya, as the case may be) shall not form part of any constituency to fill a seat or seats in the Assembly reserved for any such district but shall form part of a constituency to fill a seat or seats in the Assembly not so reserved to be specified in the order.

18. (Omitted).[18]

19. *Transitional provisions:* (1) As soon as possible after the commencement of this constitution the Governor shall take steps for the constitution of District Council for each autonomous district in the State under this Schedule and until a District Council is so constituted for an autonomous district, the administration of such district shall be vested in the Governor and the following provisions shall apply to the administration of the areas within such district instead of the foregoing provisions of this Schedule, namely —

(a) no Act of Parliament or of the Legislature of the State shall apply to any such area unless the governor by public notification so directs; and the Governor in giving such a direction with respect to any Act may direct that the Act shall, in its application to the area or to any specified part thereof, have effect subject to such exceptions or modifications as he thinks fit; and

(b) The Governor may make regulation for the peace and good government of any such area and any regulations so made may repeal or amend any Act of Parliament or of the Legislature of the State or any existing law which is for the time being applicable to such area.

(2) Any direction given by the Governor under clause (a) of sub-paragraph (1) of this paragraph may be given so as to give retrospective effect.

(3) All regulations made under clause (b) of sub-paragraph (1) of this paragraph shall be submitted forthwith to the President and, until assented to by him, shall have no effect.

20. *Tribal areas:* (1) The areas specified in Parts I, II and III of the table below shall retrospectively be the tribal areas within the State of Assam, the State of Meghalaya and the Union Territory of Mizoram.

(2) Any reference in the table below to any district shall be construed as a reference to the territories comprised within the autonomous district of that name existing immediately before the day appointed under clause (b) of Section 2 of the North-Eastern Areas (Reorganization) Act, 1971:

Provided that for the purposes of clauses (e) and (f) of sub-paragraph (1) of paragraph 3, paragraph 4, paragraph 5, paragraph 6, sub-paragraph (2), clauses (a), (b) and (d) of sub-paragraph (3) and sub-paragraph (4) of paragraph 8 and clause (d) of sub-paragraph (2) of paragraph 10 of this Schedule, no part of the area comprised within the municipality of Shillong shall be deemed to be within the United Khasi-Jaintia Hills District.

TABLE

Part I

1. The North Cachar Hills District.
2. The Mikir Hills District.

Part II

1. The United Khasi-Jaintia Hills District.

2. The Jowai District.
3. The Garo Hills District.

Part III

The Mizo District

20A. *Interpretation:* Subject to any express provision made in this behalf, the provisions of the Schedule shall, in their application to the Union Territory of Mizoram, have effect.

(1) as if references to the Governor and Government of the State were references to the Administrator of the Union Territory appointed under article 239 and references to State (except in the expression "Government of the State") were references to the Union Territory of Mizoram,

(2) as if—

(a) in sub-paragraph (3) of paragraph 1,

(i) after clause (g), the following clause had been inserted, namely:

"(h) divide any autonomous region into two or more autonomous regions and define the boundaries thereof";

(ii) the first proviso had been omitted;

(b) in sub-paragraph (5) of paragraph 4 the provision for consultation with the Government of the State concern had been omitted;

(c) in sub-paragraph (2) of paragraph 9, the words "in his discretion" had been omitted;

(d) paragraph 13 had been omitted;

(e) sub-paragraphs (2) and (3) of paragraph 14 had been omitted;

(f) sub-paragraph (2) (including the proviso thereto) of paragraph 14 had been omitted;

(g) in paragraph 16,

(i) in sub-paragraph (1), in clause (d), the words "Subject to the previous approval of the Legislature of the State" and the second proviso to that sub-paragraph had been omitted;

(ii) "sub-paragraph (3) had been omitted".

21. *Amendment of the Schedule:* (1) Parliament may from time-to-time by law amend by way of addition, variation or repeal any of the provisions of this Schedule and, when the Schedule is so amended, any reference to this Schedule in this Constitution shall be construed as a reference to such Schedule as to amended.

(2) No such law as is mentioned in sub-paragraph (1) of this paragraph shall be deemed to be an amendment of this Constitution for the purposes of Article 368.

NOTES

1. Inserted by Act 55 of 1969.
2. Inserted by Act 81 of 1971.
3. Substituted by Act 55 of 1969.
4. Inserted by Act 55 of 1969.
5. Inserted by Act 55 of 1969.
6. Omitted by Act 55 of 1969.
7. Substituted by Act 81 of 1971.
8. Substituted by Act 55 of 1969.
9. The words "Assam" deleted by Act 81 of 1971.
10. Inserted by Act 55 of 1969.
10a. Substituted by Act 81 of 1971.
11. Inserted by Act 55 of 1969.
12. Substituted by Act 55 of 1969.
12a. Inserted by Act 81 of 1971.
12b. Substituted by Act 81 of 1971.
13. Inserted by Act 55 of 1969.
13a. Substituted by Act 81 of 1971.
13b. Substituted by Act 81 of 1971.
13c. Substituted by Act 81 of 1971.
13d. Inserted by Act 81 of 1971.
13e. Inserted by Act 81 of 1971.
14. Inserted by Act 81 of 1971.
15. Omitted by Act 81 of 1971.
15a. Substituted by Act 81 of 1971.
15b. Inserted by Act 55 of 1969.
16. Renumbered as substituted paragraph (1) by Act 55 of 1969.
17. Added by Act 55 of 1969.
17a. Substituted by Act 81 of 1971.
17b. Added by Act 81 of 1971.
18. Omitted by Act 81 of 1971.

The Manipur (Hills Areas) District Councils Act, 1971

AN ACT

to provide for the establishment of District Councils in the Hills Areas in the Union Territory of Manipur.

Be it enacted by Parliament in the Twenty-second Year of the Republic of India as follows:

CHAPTER I
Preliminary

1. *Short title and extent:* (1) This Act may be called the Manipur (Hills Areas) District Councils Act, 1971.

(2) It extends to the whole of the Union Territory of Manipur.

2. *Definitions:* In this Act, unless the context otherwise requires —

(a) "Administrator" means the administrator of the Union Territory of Manipur appointed under 239 of the Constitution;

(b) "Autonomous district" means an autonomous district referred to in sub-section (1) of section 3;

(c) "Building" includes a house, out-house, stable, latrine, urinal, shed, hut, wall (other than boundary wall) and any other structure (whether of masonry, bricks, wood, mud or other material) but does not include any portable or temporary shelter;

(d) "Constituency" means a District Council constituency provided by order made under section 5 for the purpose of elections to the District Council;

(e) "Deputy Commissioner", in relation to any District Council, means the officer appointed as such by the Administrator, by notification in the Official Gazette, to perform the functions of the Deputy Commissioner under this Act in the autonomous district for which such District Council has been constituted;

(f) "Hill Areas" means the Hill Areas determined by the President by any notification issued under sub-section (2) of section 52 of the Government of Union Territories Act, 1963 (20 of 1963) and in force immediately before the commencement of this Act;

(g) "Hill Areas Committee" means the Standing Committee referred to in section 52 of the Government of Union Territories Act, 1963 (20 of 1963);

(h) "Market" includes any place where persons assemble for the sale of, or for the purpose of exposing for sale of meat, fish, fruit, vegetables, animals intended for human food or any other articles of human food whatsoever with or without the consent of the owner of such place notwithstanding that there may be no common regulation for the concourse of buyers and sellers and whether or not any control is exercised over the business of, or the persons frequenting, the market by the owner of the place or by any other persons;

(i) "Member" means a member of District Council constituted under this Act;

(j) "Official Gazette" means the Gazette of the Union Territory of Manipur;

(k) "Person" does not include a body of persons;

(l) "Prescribed" means prescribed by rules made under this Act;

(m) "Schedule Tribes" has the same meaning assigned to it in clause (25) of article 366 of the Constitution;

(n) "Vehicle" includes a carriage, cart, hand-cart, bicycle, tricycle and every wheeled conveyance which is used or is capable of being used on a street but does not include a mechanically propelled vehicle.

CHAPTER II
Constitution of District Councils

3. *Division of Hill Areas into autonomous districts:* (1) As soon as may be after the commencement of this Act, the Administrator shall cause all the Hill Areas to be divided into not more than six autonomous districts.

(2) The Administrator may, by order notified in the Official Gazette —

(a) declare that any area in any autonomous district which is, or is intended to be, included within the limits of any municipality, cantonment or town committee shall cease to be a part of such autonomous district;
(b) increase the area of any autonomous district;
(c) diminish the area of any autonomous district;
(d) unite two or more autonomous districts or parts thereof so as to form one autonomous district;
(e) define the boundaries of any autonomous district; and
(f) alter the name of any autonomous district.

(3) No order under sub-section (2) shall be made by the Administrator except after consultation with the Hill Areas Committee.

(4) Any order made by the Administrator under sub-section (2) may contain such incidental and consequential provisions as appear to the Administrator to be necessary for giving effect to the provisions of the order.

4. *Constitution of District Councils and their composition:* (1) For each autonomous district there shall be a District Council as from such date as the Administrator may, by notification in the Official Gazette, appoint in this behalf.

(2) The total number of seats in the District Council to be filled by persons chosen by direct election on the basis of adult suffrage from territorial constituencies shall be not more than eighteen.

(3) The Administrator may nominate not more than two persons, not being persons in the service of Government, to be members of any District Council.

5. *Delimitation of constituencies:* The Administrator shall, by order, determine —

(a) the constituencies (which shall be single member constituencies) into which an autonomous district shall be divided for the purpose of election of members to the District Council of that district; and
(b) the extent of each constituency.

6. *Power to alter or amend delimitation orders:* The administrator may, from time-to-time, by order, alter or amend any order made under section 5.

7. *Qualifications for membership:* (1) A person shall not be qualified to be chosen as a member of a District Council of any autonomous district unless he is an elector for any District Council constituency in that autonomous district.

8. *Disqualifications for membership:* (1) A person shall qualified for being chosen as a member of a District Council if he is for the time being disqualified for being chosen as a member of either House of Parliament or holds any office of profit under and District Council.

(2) For the purposes of this section, a person shall not be deemed to hold an office of profit under a District Council by reason only that he is a member thereof.

9. *Electors on electoral rolls:* (1) The persons entitled to vote at elections of members of a District Council shall be the persons entitled, by virtue of the provisions of the Constitution and the Representation of the People Act, 1950 (43 of 1950), to be registered as voters at elections to the House of the People.

(2) So much of the electoral roll for any Parliamentary constituency for the time being in force as relates to the areas comprised within a constituency formed under section 5 shall to deemed to be the electoral roll for that constituency for the purposes of this Act.

10. *Right to vote:* (1) Every person whose name is, for the time being, entered in the electoral roll of a constituency shall be entitled to vote at the election of a member of the District Council from that constituency.

(2) Every person shall give one vote and no more to any one candidate at an election.

11. *Election of members:* Election of members of a District Council shall be held in accordance with the rules made under section 21 on such date or dates as the Administrator may, by notification in Official Gazette direct:

Provided that a casual vacancy shall be filled as soon as may be after the occurrence of the vacancy:

Provided further that no election shall be held to fill-up a casual vacancy occurring within four months prior to the holding of a general election under this section.

12. *Notification of results of elections:* The names of all persons elected or nominated to be members of a District Council shall be published by the Administrator in the Official Gazette.

13. *Term of office of members:* (1) Save as otherwise provided in this section, the term of office of a member shall be five years and shall commence from the date of the notification of his election or nomination under section 12 or from the date on which the vacancy in which he is elected or nominated has occurred, whichever date is later:

Provided that the Administrator may, when satisfied that it is necessary in order to avoid administrative difficulty, extend the term of office of all the members by such period not exceeding one year as he thinks fit.

(2) The term of office of a member elected to fill a casual vacancy shall commence from the date of the notification of his election and shall continue so long only as the member in whose place he is elected would have been entitled to hold office if the vacancy had not occurred.

14. *Disputes as to elections:* (1) No election of member shall be called in question except by an election petition presented to the court of the District Judge having jurisdiction in the area in which the constituency concerned is situated, within thirty days from the date of the notification of the result of the election under section 12.

(2) An election petition calling in question any such election may be presented on one or more of the grounds specified in section 16 by any candidate at such election or by any elector of the constituency.

(3) A petitioner shall join as respondents to his petition all the candidates at the election.

(4) An election petition —

(a) shall contain a concise statement of the material facts on which the petitioner relies;
(b) shall, with sufficient particulars, set forth the ground or grounds on which the election is called in question; and
(c) shall be signed by the petitioner and verified in the manner laid down in the Code of Civil Procedure, 1908 (5 of 1908), for the verification of pleadings.

15. *Relief that may be claimed by petitioner:* A petitioner may, in addition to claiming a declaration that the election of all or any of the returned candidates is void, claim a further declaration that he himself of any other candidate has been duly elected.

16. *Grounds on which an election may be called in question:* The election of a returned candidate may be called in question on any one or more of the following grounds, namely —

(a) that on the date of his election the returned candidate, was not qualified to be elected, or he was disqualified for being elected, as a member under this Act; or
(b) that the nomination paper of any candidate at the election has been improperly rejected; or
(c) that the result of the election has been materially affected by the improper acceptance of a nomination paper or by

the improper acceptance or refusal of a vote or by any other cause.

17. *Procedure to be followed by the District Judge:* The procedure provided in the Code of Civil Procedure, 1908 (5 of 1908) in regard to suits shall be followed by the court of the District Judge, as far as it can be made applicable in the trial and disposal of an election petition under this Act.

18. *Decision of the District Judge:* (1) At the conclusion of the trial of an election petition, the court of the District Judge shall make an order —

(a) dismissing the election petition; or

(b) declaring the election of all or any of the returned candidates to be void; or

(c) declaring the election of all or any of the returned candidates to be void and the petitioner or any other candidate to have been duly elected.

(2) If any person who has filed an election petition has, in addition to calling in question the election of the returned candidate, claimed a declaration that he himself or any other candidate has been duly elected and the court of the District Judge is of opinion —

(a) that in fact the petitioner or such other candidate received a majority of the valid votes; or

(b) that but for the votes obtained by the returned candidate, the petitioner or such other candidate would have obtained a majority of the valid voles;

the court of the District Judge shall, after declaring the election of the returned candidate to be void, declare the petitioner or such other candidate, as the case may be, to have been duly elected.

19. *Procedure in case of equality of votes:* If during the trial of an election petition it appears that there is equality of votes between any candidates at the election and that the addition of a vote would entitle any of those candidates to be declared elected, then, the court of the District Judge shall decided between them by lot and proceed as if the one on whom the lot falls had received an additional vote.

20. *Finality of decisions:* (1) An order of the court of the District Judge on an election petition shall be final and conclusive.

(2) An election of a member not called in question in accordance with the foregoing provisions shall be deemed to be a good and valid election.

21. *Power to make rules regulating the election of members:* The Administrator may make rules to regulate all or any of the following matters for the purpose of the holding of elections of members under the Act, namely —

(a) the manner of the splitting-up of electoral rolls for Parliamentary constituencies into parts for the purpose of constituting one or more of such parts into electoral roll for a constituency; and the officer or authority by whom such splitting-up is to be carried out;
(b) the drawing-up of the programme of election;
(c) the appointment of returning officers, presiding and polling officers for election;
(d) the nomination of candidates and the scrutiny of such nomination;
(e) the deposits to be made by candidates and the time and manner of making such deposits;
(f) the withdrawal of candidatures;
(g) the appointment of agents of candidates;
(h) the time and manner of holding elections;
(i) the general procedure at the elections including the time, place and hours of poll and the method by which votes shall be cast;
(j) the fee to be paid on an election petition;
(k) any other matter relating to elections or election disputes in respect of which the Administrator deems it necessary to make rules under this section or in respect of which this Act makes no provision or makes insufficient provision and provision is, in the opinion of the Administrator, necessary.

22. *Incorporation of District Councils:* Each District Council shall be a body corporate by the name respectively of "the District Council of (name of autonomous district)" and shall have perpetual succession and a common seal with power to acquire, hold and dispose of property and to contract and may be the said name sue and the sued.

23. *Chairman and Vice-Chairman:* (1) A District Council shall, as soon as may be, choose two members to be respectively Chairman and Vice-Chairman thereof and, so often as the office of Chairmen or Vice-Chairman becomes vacant, the Council shall choose another member to be Chairman or Vice-Chairman, as the case may be:

Provided that the Administrator may nominate the first Chairman who shall hold office for a period not exceeding one year.

(2) If a resolution for the removal of an ejected Chairman is passed by not less than two-thirds of the total membership of the Council at a meeting convened in accordance with the provision of sub-section (3) such resolution shall have the effect of removing the Chairman from his office as from the date on which the resolution is so passed and if such resolution is passed by less than two-thirds, but not less than one-half of the total membership of the Council, the Administrator may, by order in writing, remove, for reasons to be recorded, the Chairman from his office as from such date as may be specified in the order:

Provided that no such resolution shall be brought within one year from the date of election of Chairman:

Provided further that if the resolution is not passed by not less than two-thirds of the total membership of the Council, no other resolution for the removal of the Chairman shall be allowed to be considered within one year from the date on which such resolution was considered.

(3) A notice in writing of the intention to move a resolution referred to in sub-section (2) signed by not less than one-third of the total membership of the Council together with a copy of the proposed resolution shall be delivered to the Deputy Commissioner in accordance with the rules made by the Deputy Commissioner in this behalf and the Deputy Commissioner shall, after giving not less than fifteen days' notice thereon, convene for consideration of the resolution a meeting of the Council to be held in the office of the Council on a date not later than thirty days from the date on which the notice was delivered to him and he shall preside over the meeting.

(4) The Chairman of the Council shall be a whole-time functionary and shall be entitled to such salary or allowances as may be fixed by the Administrator.

24. *Oath of affirmation by members:* Every member shall, before taking his seat, make and subscribe at a meeting of the District Council, an oath or affirmation in the prescribed form.

25. *Vacation of seats:* (1) No person shall be member both of the Legislative Assembly of the Union Territory of Manipur and a District Council and if a person is chosen a member both of the Legislative Assembly and of a District Council, then at the expiration of fourteen days from the date of publication in the Official Gazette that he has been so chosen, that person's seat in the District Council shall become vacant unless he has previously resigned his seat in the Legislative Assembly.

(2) If a member —

(a) becomes subject to any of the disqualifications mentioned in section 8; or

(b) resigns his seat by writing under his hand addressed to the Chairman of the District Council,

his seat shall thereupon become vacant.

(3) If during the six successive months a member is, without the permission of the District Council, absent from all meetings thereof, the Council may declare his seat vacant.

(4) If any question arises as to whether a member has become subject to any of the disqualifications mentioned in section 8, it shall be referred to the District Judge having jurisdiction in the area in which the constituency concerned is situated and his decision shall be final.

26. *Allowances of members:* Subject to the provisions of sub-section (4) of section 23, every member shall be entitled to receive such allowances as may be determined by the Administrator.

27. *Liability of members:* Every person shall be liable for the loss, waste or misappropriation of any money or other property belonging to a District Council, if such loss, waste or misappropriation is a direct consequence of his neglect or misconduct while a member of the District Council and a suit for compensation may be instituted against him by the Council with the previous sanction of the Deputy Commissioner or by the Deputy Commissioner with the previous sanction of the Administrator.

28. *Members to be deemed to be public servants:* Every member shall be deemed to be a public servant within the meaning of section 21 of the Indian Penal Code (45 of 1860).

CHAPTER III
Functions of District Councils

29. *Functions of District Councils:* (1) Subject to such exceptions and conditions as the Administrator may make and impose, the following matters shall be under the control and administration of a District Council, namely —

(i) the maintenance and management of such property, movable and immovable, and institutions as may be transferred to that Council by the Administrator;

(ii) the construction, repair and maintenance of such of the roads, bridges, channels and buildings as may be transferred to that Council by the Administrator;

(iii) the establishment, maintenance and management of primary schools and the construction and repair of all buildings connected with these institutions and institution of scholarships;

(iv) the establishment, maintenance and management of dispensaries;

(v) the establishment and maintenance of cattle pounds including such function under the Cattle Trespass Act, 1871 (1 of 1871) as may be transferred to the Council by the Administrator;

(vi) the establishment, maintenance and management of markets and fairs and the construction, repair and maintenance of all buildings connected therewith;

(vii) the supply, storage and prevention from pollution of water for drinking, cooking and bathing purposes;

(viii) the construction, repair and maintenance of embankments and the supply, storage and control of water for agricultural purposes;

(ix) the preservation and reclamation of soil;

(x) the preservation, protection and improvement of livestock and prevention of animal diseases;

(xi) public health and sanitation;

(xii) the management of such ferries as may be entrusted to the charge of that Council by the Administrator;

(xiii) the initiation, inspection and control of relief works;

(xiv) the allotment, occupation or use or the setting apart of land, other than land acquired for any public purpose or land which is a reserved forest, for the purpose of agriculture or grazing or for residential or other non-agricultural purposes or for any other purposes likely to promote the interests of the inhabitants of any village or town situated within the autonomous district for which that council is constituted;

(xv) the management of any forest not being a reserved forest;

(xvi) the regulation of the practice of *Jhum* or other form of shifting cultivation; and

(xvii) any other matter which the Administrator may, in consultation with the Hill Areas Committee, entrust to the District Council in the field of agriculture, animal husbandry, community development, social and tribal welfare, village planning or any other matter referred to in Section 52 of the Government of Union Territories Act, 1963 (20 of 1963).

(2) It shall be competent for a District Council to recommend to the Government of the Union Territory of Manipur legislation relating to the following matters insofar as they concern members of the Scheduled Tribes, namely —

(a) appointment or succession of Chiefs;
(b) inheritance of property;
(c) marriage and divorce; and
(d) social customs.

CHAPTER IV
Procedure and Staff of District Councils

30. *Conduct of business:* A District Council shall conduct its business in such manner and in accordance with such procedure as may be prescribed.

31. *Committees:* A District Council may, from time to time, appoint out of its own body such and so many committees for the efficient discharge of its duties as may be necessary.

32. *Officers and staff:* (1) For every District Council there shall be a Chief Executive Officer, who shall be appointed by the Administrator.

(2) If a resolution for removal of the Chief Executive Officer is passed at a meeting of the District Council by a majority of not less than two-thirds of the total membership of the Council, the Administrator shall remove him forthwith.

(3) The District Council shall appoint such officers and staff as may be necessary for the proper and efficient execution of its duties and make regulations for their conditions of service.

(4) The power of appointing officers and staff (whether temporary or permanent) shall be exercised in accordance with the rules framed for the purpose by the Administrator.

(5) The conditions of service applicable to a person immediately before his appointment to a post under a District Council shall not be varied to his disadvantage except with the previous approval of the Administrator.

(6) Every officer or member of staff of a District Council shall be deemed to be a public servant within the meaning of section 21 of the Indian Penal Code (45 of 1860).

CHAPTER V
Finance of District Councils and Vesting of Property

33. *Powers of taxation:* Notwithstanding anything to the contrary contained in any other law for the time being in force, a District Council shall have the power to levy all or any of the following taxes within the autonomous district for which the Council is constituted, that is to say —

(a) taxes on professions, trades, ceilings and employments;
(b) taxes on animals, vehicles (other than mechanically propelled vehicles) and boats;
(c) taxes on entry of goods into a market for sale therein and tolls on passengers and goods carried in ferries;
(d) taxes for the maintenance of schools, dispensaries or roads; and
(e) any other tax falling under List II of the Seventh Schedule to the Constitution which the Legislature of the Union Territory of Manipur may, by law, empower the District Council to levy.

34. *Levy of fees:* A District Council may fix and levy:

(a) school fees; and
(b) fees for the use of, or benefits derived from any of the works done or services rendered under section 29.

35. *Procedure for imposing taxes:* (1) A District Council may resolve at a meeting specially convened for the purpose to propose the imposition of any of the taxes mentioned in section 33.

(2) When a resolution has been passed, the Council shall publish a notice in the Official Gazette and also in the prescribed manner, defining the class of persons or description of property proposed to be taxed, the amount or rate of tax to be imposed and the system of assessment to be adopted.

(3) Any person, directly or indirectly affected by the proposed tax and objecting to it, may, within thirty days from the publication of the notice, send his objections in writing to the Council and the Council shall, at a specially convened meeting, take all such objections into consideration.

(4) If no objection is sent within the said period of thirty days or if the objections received are deemed insufficient, the Council may submit its proposals to the Administrator with the objections, if any, and its decision thereon.

(5) The Administrator may then sanction the proposals or refuse to sanction them or return them to the council for further consideration.

(6) When the proposal in respect of a tax has been sanctioned, the Administrator shall notify its imposition in the Official Gazette and specify a date not later than three months from the date of notification on which the tax shall come into force.

36. *Abolition or reduction of taxes:* The Administrator may, by notification in the Official Gazette, and a District Council may with the previous approval of the Administrator by a resolution passed at a meeting specially convened for the purpose abolish or reduce any tax imposed under section 33.

37. *Recovery of taxes and fees:* All arrears of taxes and fees levied under this Act may be recovered under the law for the time being in force for the recovery of public dues as if such arrears were public dues.

38. *Assessment and collection of taxes and fees:* A District Council may, by notification in the Official Gazette, determine the person by whom any tax or fee shall be assessed and collected and make rules for the assessment and collection of such tax or fee and direct in what manner persons employed in the assessment or collection shall be remunerated.

39. *Appeals:* (1) In matters connected with the assessment and collection of any tax or fee levied under this Act, an appeal shall lie from the order of any person authorized to make assessment or collections to such person as the Administrator may appoint or designate for the purpose.

(2) An appeal under sub-section (1) shall be presented within thirty days from the date of the order.

(3) The order passed on the appeal shall be final.

40. *Instalments of taxes and fees:* A District Council may, by notification in the Official Gazette and with the previous approval of the Deputy Commissioner, prescribed by what instalments and what times any tax or fee shall be payable.

41. *Power to exempt from taxation:* A District Council, may with the previous approval of the Administrator, by notification in the Official Gazette, remit or reduce any tax or fee or exempt any person or class of persons or any description of property, wholly or in part, from liability as to any tax or fee and cancel any such remission, reduction or exemption.

42. *Recoveries of moneys claimable by the Council:* (1) Save as provided by section 37, all moneys claimable by a District Council may be recovered on an application to a Magistrate having jurisdiction in the area where the person from whom the money is claimable, may for the time being, be resident, by the distress and sale of any movable property or by the attachment and sale of any immovable property, within the limits of his jurisdiction belonging to such person and the cost of such proceedings shall be recoverable in the same manner as the said moneys.

(2) An application for recovery of money shall be in writing and shall be signed by an officer authorized in this behalf by order of the Chairman of the Council.

43. *Council Fund:* (1) All moneys received by or on behalf of a District Council under the provisions of this Act or any other law for the time being in force shall be credited to a fund which shall be called the "Council Fund" and it shall be held by the District Council in trust for the purposes of this Act.

(2) All expenditure of the Council shall be defrayed out of the Council Fund.

(3) The Administrator may make rules for the management of the Council Fund and for the procedure to be followed in respect of payment of money into the said Fund, the withdrawal of moneys therefrom, the custody of moneys therein and any other matter connected with or ancillary to the matters aforesaid.

(4) The accounts of a District Council shall be kept in such form as may be prescribed.

44. *Property vested in District Council:* Subject to any order of the Administrator, all property of the nature specified below and situated in the autonomous district shall vest in and belong to the District Council for which it is constituted and shall, with all other property which may become vested in the Council, be under its direction, management and control and shall be held and applied for the purposes of this Act —

(a) all public buildings, constructed or maintained out of the Council Fund;

(b) all public roads which have been constructed or are maintained out of the Council Fund and the stones and other materials thereof and also all trees, erections, materials, implements and things provided for such roads;

(c) all land or other property transferred to the District Council by the Administrator or by gift, sale or otherwise for public purposes.

45. *Budget:* (1) A District Council shall, on or before a prescribed day in each year submit to the Administrator an estimate of the income and expenditure of the Council for the next financial year in such forms as may be prescribed.

(2) The Administrator may, on or before a prescribed day, return the estimate of the Council with or without modification.

(3) When a budget is returned with modification under sub-section (2), the Council shall consider the proposed modifications, take a decision thereon and report the same to the Administrator.

(4) The budget estimate finally adopted by the Council shall be the budget of the District Council.

(5) Any subsequent alteration in the budget or reappropriation or transfer of provision within the estimate shall be made with the approval of the Administrator.

CHAPTER VI
Control

46. *Control:* (1) It shall be the duty of the Chairman of a District Council to furnish to the Deputy Commissioner a copy of the proceedings of the meetings of the Council and such other information as the Deputy Commissioner may require.

(2) The Deputy Commissioner shall have the power to give to any District Council all such directions as he may consider necessary in respect of subject, curricula, text books and standards of teaching in schools vested wholly or partly in the Council and in schools wholly or partly maintained by grants payable from the Council Fund and the Council shall comply with such direction.

(3) The Deputy Commissioner may, by order, and for reasons to be recorded, suspend the execution of any resolution or order of any District Council or prohibit the doing of any act which is about to be done, or is being done, in pursuance of or under cover of any provision of the law relating to the constitution or functions of the District Council, if, in his opinion, the resolution, order or act is in excess of the powers conferred by law or the execution of the resolution or order or the doing of the act is likely to lead to a breach of the peace, or to cause annoyance or injury to the public or to any class or body of persons:

Provided that the Council may, within fifteen days of the date of the order of the Deputy Commissioner offer such explanation as it deems fit in relation to the execution of the resolution or order which has been suspended or the doing of the act has been prohibited.

(4) When the Deputy Commissioner makes any order as aforesaid he shall forthwith send a copy of it to the Administrator with a statement of the reasons for making it and forward in due course to the Administrator the explanation, if any, offered by the Council and the Administrator may, thereupon, confirm, modify or rescind the order of the Deputy Commissioner.

47. *Supersession of the District Council:* (1) If, on receipt of a report from the Deputy Commissioner or otherwise, the Administrator is of opinion that —

(a) any District Council is not competent to perform, or persistently makes default in the performance of, the duties imposed on it by or under this Act or any other law; or

(b) any District Council exceeds or abuses its powers; or

(c) the financial position and credit position of any District Council is seriously threatened; or

(d) a situation has arisen in which the administrator of any District Council cannot be carried on in accordance with the provisions of this Act,

the Administrator may, by an order published, together with a statement of reasons therefor, in the Official Gazette, supersede such Council for such period, not exceeding one year, as may be specified in the order:

Provided that before making an order of supersession as aforesaid under clause (a) or clause (b) or clause (c), reasonable opportunity shall be given to such Council to show cause why such order of supersession should not be made:

Provided further that the period of supersession may be extended for any further period of periods not exceeding six months at a time in consultation with the Hill Areas Committee.

(2) When any District Council is superseded by an order under sub-section (1), —

(a) all the members of the Council (including the Chairman and Vice-Chairman thereof) shall, on such date as may be specified in the order, vacate their offices as such members without prejudice to their eligibility for election or nomination under clause (d);

(b) during the period of supersession of the Council, all powers and duties conferred and imposed upon the Council by or under this Act or any other law shall be exercised and performed by such officer or authority as the Administrator may appoint in this behalf;

(c) all property vested in the Council shall, until it is reconstituted, vest in the Central Government; and

(d) before the expiry of the period of supersession, election or nomination, as the case may be, of members to the Council shall be held or made for the purpose of reconstituting the Council.

48. *Effect of certain provisions during the period when the Hill Areas Committee is not functioning:* Where at any time, consequent on the dissolution of the Legislative Assembly of the Union Territory of Manipur, the Hill Areas Committee is not functioning, then, during the period when such Committee is not functioning —

(i) section 3 shall have effect as if sub-section (3) thereof had been omitted; and

(ii) clause (xvii) of section 29 and the second proviso to sub-section (1) of section 47 have effect as if the words "in consultation with the Hill Areas Committee" had been omitted therefrom.

CHAPTER VII
Offences and Penalties

49. *Penalty for obstruction:* If any person wilfully obstructs a District Council or any officer or servant of a District Council or any person authorized by the District Council in the exercise of its powers, he shall be punishable with fine which may extend to fifty rupees.

50. *Penalty for entering into any contract with the Council:* If any member, officer or other employee of a District Council enters into any contract with the Council, he shall be deemed to have committed an offence under section 168 of the Indian Penal Code (45 of 1860).

CHAPTER VIII
Rules and Bye-Laws

51. *Power of Administrator to make rules:* (1) Without prejudice to the power to make rules under any other provision of this Act, the Administrator may, after previous publication, make, by notification in the Official Gazette, rules for the purpose of carrying out the provisions of this Act.

(2) In particular and without prejudice to the generality of the foregoing power, such rules may —

(i) regulate the conduct of business of a District Council;

(ii) prescribe the forms in which the budget estimate is to be prepared and the dates for the various stages of its completion;

(iii) determine the language in which the business of a District Council will be transacted;

(iv) regulate the powers of a District Council to transfer property;

(v) regulate the powers of a District Council to contract and do other things necessary for the purposes of its constitution and the mode of executing contracts;

(vi) regulate the employment, payment, suspension and removal of officers and staff of a District Council;

(vii) protect the terms and conditions of service of Government servants transferred to a District Council;

(viii) prescribe the forms for statements, registers, estimates and accounts of a District Council and regulate the keeping, checking and publication of such accounts;

(ix) prescribe the authority by whom and the manner in which the accounts of a District Council shall be audited; and

(x) provide for any other matter for which rules have to be made under this Act.

52. *Power to make bye-laws:* (1) Subject to the provisions of this Act and of the rules made thereunder, a District Council may make bye-laws to provide for all or any of the following matters in the autonomous district for which it is constituted or in any part thereof, namely —

(a) the maintenance and management of schools and grants of stipends and scholarships;

(b) control and administration of dispensaries, their construction and repairs, the supply of medicines and the measures to be taken during the prevalence of diseases;

(c) the protection from pollution of such tanks, springs, wells or parts of rivers, streams, channels or water courses as are set apart for drinking or culinary purposes; and

(d) any other matter which is necessary for carrying out all or any of the provisions of this Act and the rules made thereunder.

(2) A bye-law made under sub-section (1) shall not have effect until it has been confirmed by the Administrator and published in such manner as he may direct.

(3) The Administrator, in confirming a bye-law, may make any change therein which appears to him to be necessary.

53. *Penalty for infringement of rules or bye-laws:* (1) In making any rule, the Administrator, and in making any bye-law, a District Council, may direct that the breach of the same shall be punishable with fine which may extend to one hundred rupees and in the case of a continuing breach with a further fine which may extend to ten rupees of every day during which the breach is continued after the offender has been convicted of such breach.

(2) In default of payment of any fine, the defaulter shall be punishable with imprisonment for a term which may extend to fifteen days.

Regulation 1 of 1954

The North-East Frontier Areas (Administration) Regulation, 1954

A Regulation to provide for the readjustment of the administrative units of the North-East Frontier Tract specified in Part B of the table annexed to the Sixth Schedule to the Constitution, and for certain matters incidental thereto.

In exercise of the powers conferred by clause (2) of article 243 of the Constitution, read with sub-paragraph (2) of paragraph 18 of the Sixth Schedule to the Constitution, the President is pleased to promulgate following Regulation made by him.

Short title and commencement

1\. (i) This Regulation may be called the North-East Frontier Areas (Administration) Regulation, 1954.

2\. It shall come into force on such date as the Governor of Assam may, by notification in the official gazette appoint.

Readjustment of administrative units

3\. On and from the commencement of this Regulation,

(a) The North-East Frontier Tract, including the Balipara Frontier Tract, the Tirap Frontier Tract, the Abor Hills district, the Mishmi Hills District shall be known as the North-East Frontier Agency.

(b) The Balipara Frontier Tract shall be divided into two separate units of administration called the Subansiri Frontier Division and the Kameng Frontier Division, each comprising the areas set out in Schedules I and II respectively.

(c) Each of the areas specified in column I of the table below shall be known by the name mentioned in the entry corresponding thereto in column 2 thereof.

Existing Name of Area	*New Name*
Tirap Frontier Tract	Tirap Frontier Division
Abor Hills District	Siang Frontier Division
Mishmi Hills District	Lohit Frontier Division

Construction of certain references in existing laws

4. Any reference in any existing law

(a) to the Balipara Frontier Tract shall be construed as a reference to the Subansiri Frontier Division and the Kameng Frontier Division; and

(b) to any of the areas specified in column 1 of the table annexed to section 2 shall be construed as a reference to the area specified in the entry corresponding thereto in column 2 of the said table.

Explanation — In this section "existing law" means any law, ordinance, order, bye-law, or regulation passed or made before the commencement of this Regulation by any Legislature, authority or person having power to make such law, ordinance, order, bye-law, rule or regulation.

5. ....

SCHEDULE I

See Section 2 [b]

Areas in the Subansiri Frontier Division

North: The McMahon Line ....

East and South: From the point where the Subansiri river cuts and McMahon Line on the India-Tibet Frontier the boundary runs down the midstream of the Subansiri river till it meets the Inner Line of the Balipara Frontier Tract at the junction of the Siplu and Subansiri rivers at Siplumukh; thence along the Inner Line of the Balipara Frontier Tract to point where it meets the Burai river south of Somma Parbat ....
....

West: From the point where the Inner Line of the Balipara Frontier Tract meets the Burai river the boundary runs in a north-westerly direction along the hill ridge that forms the watershed between the Papum and Dessing rivers to the hill top with height 6,980; thence in a north-easterly direction along the hill ridge between the Papum and Pakkui rivers to the hill top with height 7,590; thence in a north-westerly direction along the hill ridge between the Pakkui and Par rivers to the hill top with height 7,510; thence in a northerly and then a north-westerly, and westerly direction over the hill tops with height 11,710; 12,390, 11,579, 12,127, 10,004, 11,320 and among the main hill ridge that forms the watershed between the river Kameng and its tributaries on the west and the River Panir and Khru in the east ....

SCHEDULE II

See Section 2 [b]

Areas in the Kameng Frontier Division

North: The McMahon Line ....

East: The western boundary of the Subansiri Frontier Division as set out in the First Schedule, from the McMahon Line on the north to the Inner Line of the Balipara Frontier Tract to the south.

South: From the south-western corner of the Subansiri Frontier Division on the Burai river westwards along the Inner Line of the Balipara Frontier Tract as defined in the Assam Government Notification No. 6778-AP, dated the 2nd November, 1934 to the point at which the boundary between the India and Bhutan leaves Inner Line and turns northwards.

West: Along the boundary between India and Bhutan from the point where it leaves the Inner Line of the Balipara Frontier Tract to the McMahon Line.

RAJENDRA PRASAD
President

No. GA. 140/50/122, — In pursuance of sub-section (2) of section 1 of the North-East Frontier Areas (Administration) Regulation, 1954 (Regulation 1 of 1954), the Governor of Assam is pleased to appoint the 26th January, 1954, as the date on which the said Regulation shall come into force.

N.K. RUSTOMJI
Adviser to the Governor of Assam

Regulation 7 of 1965

The North-East Frontier Agency (Administration) Regulation, 1965

Promulgated by the President in the Sixteenth Year of the Republic of India.

A Regulation to make further provision for the administration of the North-East Frontier Agency and for certain matters connected therewith.

In exercise of the powers conferred by article of 240 the Constitution, read with sub-paragraph (2) of paragraph 18 of the Sixth Schedule to the Constitution, the President is pleased to promulgate the following Regulation made by him:

Short title & commencement

1. [1] This Regulation may be called the North-East Frontier Agency (Administration) Regulation, 1965.

[2] It shall come into force on such date as the Central Government may, by notification in the official Gazette, appoint.

Definition

2. In this Regulation —

1 of 1954

[a] "Division" means any of the Frontier Division referred to in section 2 of the North-East Frontier Areas (Administration) Regulation, 1954.

[b] "Existing law" means any law, ordinance, regulation, order, bye-law, rule, scheme, notification or other instrument having the force of law in India or any part thereof.

1 of 1954

[c] "North-East Frontier Agency" shall have the meaning assigned to it in the North-East Frontier Areas (Administration) Regulation, 1954.

Change of names of administrative

3. On and from the commencement of this Regulation, each of the Divisions of the North-East

units of the North-East Fr. Agency Frontier Agency specified in column 1 of the table below shall be known by the name mentioned in the entry corresponding thereto in column 2 thereof.

TABLE

Existing Name of Division	*New Name*
1	*2*
Kameng Frontier Division	Kameng District
Subansiri Frontier Division	Subansiri District
Siang Frontier Division	Siang District
Tirap Frontier Division	Tirap District

Construction of certain references in existing laws 4. Any reference in any existing law to any of the Division specified in column 1 of the table annexed to section 3 shall be construed as a reference to the District specified in the entry corresponding thereto in column 2 of the said table.

Amendment of existing laws 5. Whenever an expression mentioned in column 1 of the table below occurs in any existing law as applicable to the North-East Frontier Agency, there shall be substituted therefor the expression set opposite to it in column 2 of the said table, and there shall also be made in any sentence in which the expression occurs such consequential amendment as the rules of grammar may require.

TABLE

1	*2*
Political Officer	Deputy Commissioner
Additional Political Officer	Additional Deputy Commissioner
Assistant Political Officer	Assistant Commissioner

Sd/- S. RADHAKRISHNAN
President

Sd/- R.C.S. SARKAR
Secy. to the Government of India

Regulation 3 of 1967

The North-East Frontier Agency, Panchayati Raj Regulation, 1967

Promulgated by the President in the Eighteenth Year of the Republic India.

A Regulation to provide for the Constitution of Anchal Samitis, Zilla Parishads and Agency Council in the North-East Frontier Agency and for matters connected therewith.

In exercise of the powers conferred by article 240 of the Constitution, read with sub-paragraph (2) of Paragraph 18 of the Sixth Schedule to the Constitution, the President is pleased to promulgate the following Regulation made by him.

CHAPTER 1
Preliminary

Short title

1. (1) This Regulation may be called the North-East Frontier Agency Panchayati Raj Regulation, 1967.

Extent and commencement

(2) It extends to the whole of the North-East Frontier Agency.

(3) It shall come into force on such date as the Governor may, by notification, appoint, and different dates may be appointed for different provisions of this Regulation and for different areas.

Definitions

2. In this Regulation, unless the context otherwise requires —

(i) "Agency Council" means the Agency Council constituted under section 57;

(ii) "Anchal Samiti" means an Anchal Samiti constituted under section 4;

(iii) "Block" means such area as may be declared by the Governor under section 3 to be a Block;

(iv) "Deputy Commissioner" means the Deputy Commissioner of a District;

(v) "District" means a District of the North-East Frontier Agency;

(vi) "Governor" means the Governor of Assam;

Assam Regulation 1 of 1945 (vii) "Gram Panchayat" means a village authority constituted under the Assam Frontier (Administration of Justice) Regulation, 1945, by whatever name called;

1 of 1945 (viii) "North-East Frontier Agency" shall have the meaning assigned to it in the North-East Frontier Areas (Administration) Regulation, 1954;

(ix) "Notification" means a notification published in the official Gazette;

(x) "Prescribed" means prescribed by rules made under this Regulation;

(xi) "Sub-divisional Officer" means the Additional Deputy Commissioner or the Assistant Commissioner in charge of a Sub-division;

(xii) "Village" means an area recognized to be a village at the commencement of this Regulation and includes any area which the Governor may, by notification, declare to be a village;

(xiii) "Zilla Parishad" means a Zilla Parishad constituted under section 51.

CHAPTER II
Anchal Samitis

Declaration of Blocks 3. The Governor may, by notification, declare such contiguous areas in a District as he deems a Block for the purposes of this Regulation and may specify the *Gram Panchayats* in the Block.

Provided that no area included in a municipality, town committee or cantonment constituted under any law for the time being in force shall be included in a Block.

Constitution of Anchal Samitis and their incorporation

4. (1) The governor may, by notification, constitute an Anchal Samiti for a Block with effect from such date as may be specified therein.

(2) Every Anchal Samiti shall, by the name of the Block for which it is constituted, be a body corporate having perpetual succession and a common seal with power to acquire, hold and dispose of property and to enter into contract and shall by its corporate name sue and be sued.

Alteration in area of Block

5. (1) The Governor may, after consultation with an Anchal Samiti or Samitis concerned, at any time by notification —

(a) include any village or part of a village within the limits of a Block;

(b) exclude any village or part of a village from the limits of a Block; or

(c) amalgamate two or more Blocks into a single Block.

(2) Where, by a notification under sub-section (1), any village or part of a village is included within the limits of a Block, the jurisdiction of the Anchal Samiti established for that Block shall extend to such village or part which shall, unless the Governor otherwise directs, become subject to all notifications, rules, bye-laws and orders made under this Regulation or any other law in force in that Block.

(3) Where, by a notification under sub-section (1), any village or part of a village is excluded from the limits of a Block, the jurisdiction of the Anchal Samiti established for that block over such village or part shall thereupon cease and all notification, rules, bye-laws and orders made under this Regulation or any other law in force in that Block shall cease to apply to that village or part, as the case may be.

(4) Where, by a notification under sub-section (1), two or more Blocks are amalgamated into a single Block, the Governor may make such incidental

and consequential orders as may be necessary for effecting such amalgamation.

Composition of Anchal Samiti

6. (1) Every Anchal Samiti shall consist of—

(i) One representative elected in the prescribed manner, by the members of each Gram Panchayat falling within its jurisdiction:

Provided that where the number of villages in any Block exceeds twenty-five, the Deputy Commissioner may, by notification, divide such Block, in the prescribed manner, into not more than twenty-five constituencies, each consisting of one or more villages, and the members of Gram Panchayats included in each constituency shall elect, in the prescribed manner, one representative to the Anchal Samiti;

Provided further that, if at any time there is no Gram Panchayat in any village or, as the case may be, in any of the villages included in a constituency, or the members of the Gram Panchayat or Panchayats in a village or constituency, as the case may be, fail to elect their representative, the Deputy Commissioner may nominate a person ordinarily resident in that village or constituency, as the case may be, to be a member of the Anchal Samiti representing that village or constituency;

(ii) One representative elected, in the prescribed manner, by the chairman of the cooperative societies situated within the block from amongst themselves, *ex-officio:*

Provided that where there is only one cooperative society in a Block, the chairman of that society shall be a member of the Anchal Samiti;

(iii) Not more than five persons nominated by the Deputy Commissioner from the members of the tribes which have not secured representation in the Anchal Samiti under clause (i) or clause (ii);

(iv) The Sub-divisional Officer of the sub-division in which the Block is situated, *ex-officio:*

Provided that if the area of a Block extends to two or more sub-divisions, the Sub-divisional Officer of any one of the Sub-divisions specified by the Deputy Commissioner in this behalf shall be a member of the Anchal Samiti constituted for that Block.

(2) The Deputy Commissioner may appoint such officers as *ex-officio* members of an Anchal Samiti as may be deemed necessary:

Provided that the officers so appointed shall have the right to attend the meetings of the Anchal Samiti and take part in the proceedings thereof but shall not be entitled to vote.

Disqualifications for membership

7. A person shall be disqualified for being chosen as, and for being a member of an Anchal Samiti, if he —

(a) is not a citizen of India; or

(b) is not twenty-five years of age; or

(c) has been dismissed from the service of Government or and Anchal Samiti or any other local authority for misconduct unless a period of five years has elapsed from such dismissal; or

(d) holds any office of profit under the Government or an Anchal Samiti or any other local authority; or

(e) has directly or indirectly any share or monetary interest in any work done by, or to, the Anchal Samiti or in any contract or employment with, under, or by, or on behalf of, the Anchal Samiti; or

(f) is an undischarged insolvent; or

(g) is of unsound mind and stands so declared by a competent court; or

(h) has been convicted by a criminal court of any offence involving moral turpitude and sentenced to imprisonment for not less than six months and five years have not elapsed since his release:

Provided that the disqualifications specified in clauses (d) and (e) shall not apply to an *ex-officio* member.

President and Vice-President

8. (1) The Sub-divisional Officer who is a member of an Anchal Samiti shall be its President.

(2) In the first meeting of an Anchal Samiti, the members shall elect from among themselves, a Vice-President in the manner prescribed.

Term of office of, and vacancies among, members of Anchal Samiti

9. (1) Subject to the provisions of this section, the members of an Anchal Samiti shall hold office for a term of three years:

Provided that the Governor may, by order in writing and for reasons to be recorded therein, extend the said term by a period or periods not exceeding one year in the aggregate, and every such order shall be notified in the official gazette.

(2) The term of office of the members of an Anchal Samiti shall be deemed to commence on the date of the first meeting of the Anchal Samiti which shall be held on a date fixed by the Deputy Commissioner.

(3) The term of office of outgoing members shall be deemed to extend to and expire with the date preceding the date of the first meeting of the newly constituted Anchal Samiti.

(4) The term of office of an *ex-officio* member shall continue so long as he holds the office by virtue of which he is such a member.

(5) The Vice-President of an Anchal Samiti shall hold such office as long as he is a member of the Anchal Samiti.

(6) A member (other than an *ex-officio* member) shall be deemed to have vacated his seat if he is absent without excuse, sufficient in the opinion of the Anchal Samiti, from three consecutive ordinary meetings of the Anchal Samiti.

(7) An outgoing member shall be eligible for re-nomination or re-election.

Resignation of office and filling up of casual vacancies

10. (1) The Vice-President of an Anchal Samiti or any other member thereof, not being an *ex-officio* member, may resign his office by giving notice in writing to that effect to its President and such resignation shall take effect from the date of its receipt by the President.

(2) A casual vacancy in the office of the Vice-President or any member shall be filled by election or nomination in accordance with the provisions of this Regulation or the rules made thereunder:

Provided that a member elected or nominated under this sub-section shall hold office for the remainder of the term of the member in whose place he is elected or nominated.

Oath of office

11. (1) Every member of an Anchal Samiti shall before taking his seat make and subscribe before such officer as the Governor may specify in this behalf, an oath or affirmation in the form set out in the first Schedule.

(2) A member who has not complied with the requirements of sub-section (1), shall not vote or take part in the proceedings of any meeting of the Anchal Samiti nor shall he be included as a member of any committee constituted by the Anchal Samiti.

Officers and employees of Anchal Samiti

12. (1) The Governor shall appoint an Executive Officer for every Anchal Samiti.

(2) The Executive Officer shall act as the Secretary of the Anchal Samiti and shall, subject to the control of the President, carry out the resolutions and directions of the Anchal Samiti and discharge such other functions as may be prescribed.

(3) Subject to such rules as may be made in this behalf, the Anchal Samiti may appoint such other officers and employees and in such number as may from time to time be necessary.

Motion of no confidence

13. (1) A motion of no confidence may be moved by any member of an Anchal Samiti against its Vice-President after giving at least seven days' notice in writing to the President of the Anchal Samiti, of his intention to move such a motion.

(2) If the motion is carried by a majority of not less than two-thirds of the total number of members of the Anchal Samiti the Vice-President shall cease to hold office.

(3) Notwithstanding anything contained in this Regulation, the Vice-President of an Anchal Samiti

shall not preside at a meeting in which a motion of no confidence against him is under discussion, but he shall have the right to speak or otherwise take part in the proceedings of such meeting.

Power of Governor to remove Vice-President or member of Anchal Samiti

14. The Governor may, by order, remove from office the Vice-President or any other member of an Anchal Samiti, after giving him an opportunity of making a representation, if he —

(a) incurs any of the disqualifications specified in section 7, or

(b) refuses to act or becomes incapable of acting, or

(c) is, in the opinion of the Governor, guilty of misconduct in the discharge of his duties, or

(d) is, in the opinion of the Governor, undesirable in the public interest to be continued in office, or

(e) has caused financial loss, waste or misappropriation of any money, or property belonging to the Anchal Samiti, by neglect or misconduct in the performance of his duties; and the Vice-President or member so removed shall not be eligible for re-election or renomination to the vacancy so created.

Meetings of Anchal Samiti

15. (1) The time and place of meetings of an Anchal Samiti and the procedure at such meetings (including the quorum thereat) shall be such as may be prescribed.

(2) A member of an Anchal Samiti may, at any meeting, move any resolution and put questions to the President or the Vice-President on matters connected with the administration of the Anchal Samiti in the manner prescribed.

(3) No resolution of an Anchal Samiti shall be modified, amended, varied or cancelled by the Anchal Samiti within a period of three months from the date of passing thereof except by a resolution supported by two-thirds of the total number of members of the Anchal Samiti.

16. (1) Subject to such rules as may be made in this behalf, an Anchal Samiti may appoint from

among its members as many committees as it thinks fit to assist it in the discharge of any specified functions and may delegate to such committees such of its powers as may be deemed necessary.

(2) The President and Vice-President of an Anchal Samiti shall be the chairman and Vice-Chairman respectively of every committee appointed under sub-section (1) and the Executive Officer of the Anchal Samiti shall be an *ex-officio* member of every such committee.

(3) An Anchal Samiti may temporarily associate with any committee persons not being members of the Anchal Samiti, who have special experience and knowledge of any subject dealt with by a committee and any such person shall have the right to take part in the discussions of the committee, but shall not have the right to vote, and shall not be a member for any other purpose.

Proceedings not to be invalid

17. No act or proceeding of an Anchal Samiti or of any committee thereof shall be deemed to be invalid by reason only of the existence of any vacancy in, or defect in the constitution of, the Anchal Samiti or committee or of any informality in its proceedings.

General meeting

18. The President of an Anchal Samiti may convene a general meeting of all the members of the Gram Panchayats falling within its jurisdiction to review the action taken by the Anchal Samiti during the preceding year and to present the working plan of the Anchal Samiti for the succeeding year.

Travelling and daily allowances of members of Anchal Samiti

19. Every member of an Anchal Samiti who is not in the service of the Government shall be entitled to receive from the Anchal Samiti travelling and daily allowances for attending its meetings or the meeting of any of its committees at such rates as may be prescribed.

Powers and Functions

Functions of Anchal Samiti

20. (1) It shall be the duty of every Anchal Samiti so far as its fund and the resources at its disposal

may allow, to make reasonable provision within its jurisdiction in regard to the matters specified in the second Schedule:

Provided that it may assign to any Gram Panchayat falling within its jurisdiction all or any of its functions relating to matters specified in Part I of the said Schedule.

(2) An Anchal Samiti may also make provision for carrying out within the area under its jurisdiction, any other work or measure which is likely to promote the health, safety, education, comfort, convenience or social or economic well-being of the residents of the area.

Control of Anchal Samiti on certain properties

21. (1) The Anchal Samiti, in respect of all roads, streets, bridges, culverts and other properties placed by the Governor under sub-section (1) of section 47 under its direction, management and control, may do all things necessary for the maintenance and repair thereof and in particular, may —

(a) widen, open, enlarge or otherwise improve any such road, street, bridge or culvert and plant and preserve trees on the sides of such roads;

(b) deepen or otherwise improve any water course and other property mentioned in clause (c) of sub-section (1) of section 47; and

(c) cut any hedge or branch of any tree projecting on any such public road or street.

(2) The Anchal Samiti shall also have control of all roads, streets, waterways, bridges and culverts which are situated within its jurisdiction, not being private property or not being the property for the time being under the control of the Government, and may do all things necessary for the improvement, maintenance and repair thereof, and in particular, may —

(a) lay out and make new roads; and

(b) construct new bridges and culverts.

Transfer of any work or management of any insti-

22. (1) Subject to such rules as may be made in this behalf, and to such conditions as may be agreed upon, and Anchal Samiti may take over the

tution to, or from Anchal Samiti

execution, maintenance or repair of any work or the management of any institution within its jurisdiction on behalf of the Government or any local authority.

(2) Subject to such rules as may be made in this behalf, and to such conditions as may be agreed upon, an Anchal Samiti may, with the consent of a local authority or any person, make over to such authority or person, the execution, maintenance or repair of any work or the management of any institution within its jurisdiction.

Public charitable dispensaries and hospitals

23. (1) The Governor may, with the consent of an Anchal Samiti, by notification, direct that any public charitable dispensary or hospital falling within its jurisdiction shall be placed under the control and administration of the Anchal Samiti.

(2) On the publication of the notification referred to in sub-section (1), the Anchal Samiti shall, subject to such rules as may be made in this behalf, be charged with the control and administration of the dispensary or hospital and the construction, repair and maintenance of all buildings connected therewith.

Establishment and maintenance of dispensaries hospitals

24. Subject to such rules as may be made in this behalf, and Anchal Samiti may —

(a) establish and maintain, within its jurisdiction, dispensaries, hospitals, asylums and places for the reception of the sick or destitute or contribute towards the cost of establishment and maintenance of such institutions, etc.

(b) provide for the employment of medical practitioners and for payment of allowances to such practitioners for services rendered;

(c) provide medicines or medical assistance for persons resident within its jurisdiction or take such measures as may appear to it to be necessary during the prevalence of any disease;

(d) with the previous sanction of the Governor, contribute such annual or other sums as may be agreed upon, towards the establishment or maintenance of any dispensary, hospital, asylum or place for the reception of the sick or destitute which is situated outside its jurisdiction, but is, or may be, ordinarily used by persons resident within its jurisdiction.

Improvement of sanitation

25. (1) If an Anchal Samiti is of opinion that it is necessary so to do for the promotion of public health or for the prevention of danger to life or property, it may, by a notice in writing and within such period as may be specified therein, direct the owner or occupier of any building or land —

(i) to remove huts or privies wholly or partly; or

(ii) to remove, alter or construct private drains; or

(iii) to remove, alter or construct any public drain; or

(iv) to fill-up, clean or deepen any water-course, well, pool, ditch, tank, pond or any place containing, or used for the collection of, drainage or filth, to drain out stagnant water which appears to be injurious to health or offensive to the neighbourhood or to take such action as may be deemed necessary; or

(v) to clear any land of thick vegetation, undergrowth or jungle.

(2) If any work required to be done under sub-section (1) is not executed within the period specified in the notice, the Anchal Samiti may itself cause such work to be executed or done and the cost incurred thereon may be recovered from the owner or occupier in the prescribed manner.

(3) Any person who wilfully disobeys any direction issued under sub-section (1) shall be liable to a fine which may extend to ten rupees.

(4) If the Anchal Samiti considers that the owner or occupier or any other person has suffered loss as a result of any action taken under this section, not being due to his fault, it may award such compensation as it may deem adequate from its own funds.

Power to do certain act in the event of an epidemic

26. On the outbreak of an epidemic or an infectious disease, an Anchal Samiti shall have power to take all or any of the following measures for controlling and preventing the spread of the epidemic or disease in the area within its jurisdiction, namely —

(i) restriction of the movement of infected persons or goods within its jurisdiction;

(ii) provision for vaccination or inoculation, as the case may be;

(iii) seizure of any polluted food-stuffs;

(iv) disinfection of wells, tanks or other sources of water supply; and

(v) doing of such other acts as may be necessary.

Disinfection of buildings and articles

27. (1) If the Anchal Samiti is of opinion that the cleansing or disinfecting of a building or any part thereof, or any article therein, which is likely to retain infection, will tend to prevent or check the spread of any disease, it may, by notice, require the occupier, or where there is no occupier, the owner thereof, to cleanse or disinfect the same in the manner and within the time specified in the notice.

(2) If —

(a) within the time specified as aforesaid, the person on whom the notice is served fails to have the building or part thereof or the article cleansed or disinfected; or

(b) such person gives his consent, the Anchal Samiti may at his cost cause the building or part thereof or the article to be cleansed and disinfected:

Provided that the Anchal Samiti may, in its discretion, pay the whole or any part of such cost.

Removal of patients suffering from infections or contagious diseases to hospital

28. If any person suffering from any infectious or contagious disease is found, within the jurisdiction of any such Anchal Samiti as may be specified by the Governor by notification, to be —

(a) without proper lodging or accommodation; or

(b) living in a *sarai* or other public place, the Anchal Samiti or any person authorized by it in this behalf may, on the Advice of a medical officer not below in rank to that of an Assistant Surgeon, Grade I, remove the said person to any hospital or place at which persons suffering from such diseases are received for medical treatment and may take all reasonable measures to effect such removal.

Power to close markets

29. (1) An Anchal Samiti may by order, with a view to preventing the spread of any infectious or contagious disease, close any market or shop within its jurisdiction for such period as may be specified in the said order and may also forbid any person from entering such market or shop.

(2) An order under sub-section (ii) shall be published in such manner and at such places as the Anchal Samiti may direct and notice thereof shall also be served on the owner or occupier of the market or shop, as the case may be.

(3) The owner or occupier of the market or shop may, after complying with the provisions of the order, appeal against it to the Deputy Commissioner and the decision of the Deputy Commissioner thereon shall be final.

(4) When an order has been published under sub-section (2) and has not been set aside by the Deputy Commissioner under sub-section (3), the owner or occupier of a market or shop who fails to close such market or shop shall be liable to a fine which may extend to five hundred rupees and any person who enters such market or shop in contravention of the provisions of the order shall be liable to a fine which may extend to fifty rupees.

Licensing of market

30. (1) An Anchal Samiti may, by order, direct that no place other than markets established by, or under the control or administration of, the Anchal Samiti shall be used as a market except in accordance with the terms and conditions of a licence granted by it.

(2) The Anchal Samiti may grant a licence under the provisions of this section subject to such conditions as it may think fit as to supervision and

inspection, sanction and water supply, weights and measures to be used, rents and fees to be charged and such other matters as may be specified in the bye-laws to be framed for the purpose.

(3) The Anchal Samiti may at any time suspend, cancel or modify a licence granted under sub-section (2) for contravention of any of the conditions thereof.

(4) Any person aggrieved by an order of the Anchal Samiti under sub-section (3) may appeal against such order to the Deputy Commissioner who may, after giving such person an opportunity to represent his case, modify, annul or confirm the order.

(5) The Anchal Samiti or any officer authorized by it may close any place used as a market without a licence or the licence for which has been suspended or cancelled.

Water Supply

31. (1) The Anchal Samiti may take such action as may be necessary for proper and sufficient supply of water to any area within its jurisdiction and for this purpose may construct, repair and maintain water works, wells or tanks.

(2) The Anchal Samiti may, by order, set apart convenient tanks, springs, wells or part of rivers, streams, channels or water-courses, for the supply of water for drinking or for culinary purposes.

Compulsory vaccination:

32. An Anchal Samiti shall take such action as may be necessary for the enforcement of vaccination in the area within its jurisdiction.

Power to make contributions to Gram Panchayats;

33. Subject to such conditions as may be prescribed, an Anchal Samiti may make annual or other contributions to any Gram Panchayat falling within its jurisdiction to whom any of its powers or functions are assigned under section 20.

power to protect crops

34. An Anchal Samiti may by itself or in association with any Gram Panchayat or any other Anchal Samiti take such steps as may be necessary to scare away monkeys, squirrels, elephants, birds, locusts or other pests in order to save crops from being damaged.

Power of entry of Anchal Samiti officers

35. A member of an Anchal Samiti and any officer or other employee of the Anchal Samiti authorized by it in this behalf may enter into or upon any house, building or land with or without assistants or workmen to make any inspection or execute any work required under any of the provisions of this Regulation:

Provided that —

(a) no such entry shall be made between sunset and sunrise; and

(b) no entry into a dwelling house may be made, except with the consent of the occupier thereof and without giving the said occupier at least twenty-four hours' previous notice of the intention to make such entry signed by the President or the Vice-President of the Anchal Samiti; and due regard shall always be paid to the social and religious customs and usages of the occupants of the house so entered.

Other powers of Anchal Samiti

36. An Anchal Samiti may, within its jurisdiction —

(a) establish and maintain bungalows and *sarais* for the use of travellers and charge therefor such fees as it thinks fit; and

(b) offer rewards at such scales as may be approved by the Governor for the destruction of unclaimed or diseased dogs and animals.

Finance, Property and Accounts

Anchal Samiti Fund

37. (1) There shall be an Anchal Samiti Fund for each Anchal Samiti and the same shall be utilized for discharging its function under this Regulation.

(2) The following shall be credited to and form part of, the Anchal Samiti Fund, namely —

(i) the proceeds of any tax, fees, licence fees, cess and surcharge levied under this Regulation;

(ii) the collection charges referred to in section 46;

(iii) any grants and contributions made by the Governor or any local authority or other persons;

(iv) all sums received by way of loan or gift;

(v) the income from, or the sale proceeds of, any property of the Anchal Samiti;

(vi) the sale proceeds of all dust, dirt, dung or refuse collected by the employees of the Anchal Samiti;

(vii) all sums received in aid of, or for expenditure on, any institution or service, maintained, managed or financed by the Anchal Samiti;

(viii) any other sums paid to the Anchal Samiti.

(3) The amount in the Anchal Samiti Fund shall be kept in such custody as may be prescribed.

Raising of loans and formation of a Sinking Fund

38. Subject to such rules as may be made in this behalf, and subject to the provisions of any law for the time being in force relating to the raising of loans by local authorities, an Anchal Samiti may raise loans for discharging its functions under this Regulation, and for the repayment of such loans form a Sinking Fund.

Application of Anchal Samiti Fund

39. The Anchal Samiti Fund shall be applied for payments in the following order, namely —

(a) payment of interest on loans raised under section 38, and payments into the Sinking Fund, if formed;

(b) payment of the salaries, allowances and other remuneration of the officers and other employees of the Anchal Samiti;

(c) payment of expenses incurred by the Anchal Samiti in the discharge of its functions under this Regulation; and

(d) payment of such other administrative expenses of the Anchal Samiti as may be prescribed.

Power of taxation

40. (1) Subject to approval by the Governor and subject to such rules as may be prescribed, an Anchal Samiti may levy —

(a) a tax on brick or concrete buildings;

(b) a tax on supply of drinking water, sale of fire-wood and thatch, conservancy, lighting and slaughter-houses;

(c) a tax on cultivable land lying fallow for two consecutive years;

(d) a tax on fisheries allotted to the Anchal Samiti;

(e) a fee on the registration of cattle sold within its jurisdiction;

(f) a licence fee in respect of —

(i) tea stalls, hotels, sweetmeat shops, restaurants, bakeries and confectioneries;

(ii) collection of hides and bones;

(iii) cinema halls, circuses, professional variety shows and fairs;

(iv) brick and tile kilns;

(v) oil and rice mills;

(vi) *hats* and bamboo stall;

(vii) carts, carriages, cycles and boats;

(viii) saw, mills and timber depots;

(g) a cess for the supply of water for irrigation;

(h) a surcharge on duty for the transfer of immovable property.

(2) The taxes, fees and surcharge shall be imposed, assessed and realized at such limes and in such manner as may be prescribed.

Recovery of taxes and other duties

41. (1) When any tax or fee or other sum due to an Anchal Samiti has become payable, the Anchal Samiti shall, with the least practicable delay, cause to be sent to the person liable for the payment thereof, a demand notice in the prescribed form for the amount due from him and require him to pay the amount within a date to be specified in such notice.

(2) Every notice of demand under sub-section (1) shall be served in such manner as may be prescribed.

(3) If the sum for which a notice of demand has been served is not paid within the date specified therein, the Anchal Samiti may recover me same in the prescribed manner.

Appeal against levy of tax, etc.

42. Any person aggrieved by the assessment, levy or imposition of any tax, fee or surcharge may appeal to the Deputy Commissioner within thirty days of the date of the order imposing such tax, fee

or surcharge, and the decision of the Deputy Commissioner thereon shall be final:

Provided that an appeal may be admitted after the expiration of the period specified in this section, if the appellant statisfies the Deputy Commissioner that he had sufficient cause for not preferring the appeal within that period.

Objections to assessment

43. No objection shall be taken to any assessment made under this Regulation, nor shall the liability of any person so assessed be questioned otherwise than in accordance with the provisions of this Regulation or the rules made thereunder.

44. The Governor may, by notification, suspend the levy or imposition of any tax, fee or surcharge and may at any time in like manner rescind such suspension.

Suspension of levy of tax, etc.

45. (1) If, in the opinion of the Governor, the regular income of an Anchal Samiti falls below what is required for the proper discharge of its functions under this Regulation he may require the said Anchal Samiti to take steps to increase its income to such extent and within such period as may be specified by him.

(2) If the Anchal Samiti fails to take adequate steps to increase its income to the extent required within the period specified, the Governor may direct the Anchal Samiti to levy any of the taxes or fees specified in section 40, or increase the rate at which any such tax or fee is levied.

(3) If an Anchal Samiti fails to levy a tax or fee or enhance the rate of any tax or fee as required under sub-section (2), the Governor may, by notification, levy, or increase the rate of, such tax or fee.

Collection of tax or revenue due to Government

46. An Anchal Samiti may, in the prescribed manner, collect any class of tax or revenue or fee or due payable to the Government in respect of the area falling within its jurisdiction, being allowed a prescribed percentage of collection charges.

Properties placed under the direction management and control of Anchal Samiti

47. (1) The Governor may, if he deems fit, place all or any of the following properties situated within the jurisdiction of the Anchal Samiti, under the direction, management and control of the Anchal Samiti, namely —

(a) open sites, waste, vacant and grazing lands, not being private property, and river beds;

(b) public roads and streets;

(c) public channels, water-courses, wells, ponds, tanks (except irrigation tanks under the control of the Government) public springs, reservoirs, cisterns, fountains, aqueducts and any adjacent land (not being private property) appertaining thereto;

(d) public sewers, drains and drainage works, tunnels and culverts and things appertaining thereto and other conservancy works;

(e) sewage, rubbish and offensive matter deposited on streets or collected by the Anchal Samiti from streets, latrines, urinals, sewers, cesspools and other places; and

(f) public lamps, lamp-posts and apparatus connected therewith or appertaining thereto.

(2) All markets and fairs or such portions thereof as are held upon public land shall be managed and regulated by the Anchal Samiti and shall receive to the credit of the Anchal Samiti Fund all dues levied or imposed in respect thereof.

Accounts and Audits

48. (1) Every Anchal Samiti and every Gram Panchayat receiving contributions from an Anchal Samiti under section 33 shall maintain accounts of its receipts and expenditure in such form, as may be prescribed.

(2) The accounts of every Anchal Samiti and the Gram Panchayat referred to in sub-section (1) shall be audited annually in such manner as may be prescribed.

Preparation of budget estimate of Anchal Samiti

49. (1) An Anchal Samiti shall prepare annually on or before such date and in such form as may be prescribed a budget estimate of its income and

expenditure for the next financial year and may also prepare a supplementary budget estimate at any time during a financial year.

(2) The annual or supplementary budget estimate of an Anchal Samiti shall be submitted to the Deputy Commissioner and after being approved by him shall be binding on the Anchal Samiti.

(3) No expenditure shall be incurred by an Anchal Samiti unless it is included in the budget estimates which have been approved by the Deputy Commissioner under sub-section (2).

Administration Report

50. (1) Every Anchal Samiti shall submit annually to the Deputy Commissioner by such date as may be prescribed, a report on the administration of the Anchal Samiti during the previous year.

(2) The report shall be prepared by the Executive Officer and after it is approved by the Anchal Samiti shall be forwarded to the Deputy Commissioner with a copy of the resolution of the Anchal Samiti thereon.

CHAPTER III

Zilla Parishads

Constitution and composition of Zilla Parishad

51. (1) The Governor may, by notification, constitute a Zilla Parishad for each District with effect from such date as may be specified therein.

(2) Every Zilla Parishad shall consist of —

(i) the Vice-Presidents of all the Anchal Samitis in the District, *ex-officio*;

(ii) one representative of every Anchal Samiti in the District, to be elected by its members from amongst themselves in the prescribed manner;

(iii) not more than six persons to be nominated by the Governor from out of the tribes which have not secured representation on the Zilla Parishad:

Provided that no person shall be nominated or after having been nominated, remain a member of a Zilla Parishad, if he suffers from any of the disqualifications specified in clauses (a) to (h) of section 7;

(iv) The Deputy Commissioner in charge of the District, *ex-officio*.

Term of office of members of Zilla Parishad

52. (1) A person who is a member of a Zilla Parishad by virtue of clause (i) or clause (ii) of sub-section (2) of section 51, shall cease to be such member on his ceasing to be a Vice-President or a member as the case may be, of the Anchal Samiti.

(2) The term of office of a person nominated under clause (iii) of sub-section (2) of section 51 shall be three years:

Provided that a member nominated to fill a casual vacancy shall hold office for the remainder of the term of the member in whose place he is nominated.

President and Vice-President of Zilla Parishad

53. (1) The Deputy Commissioner shall be the president of the Zilla Parishad.

(2) As soon as may be after a Zilla Parishad is constituted, the Zilla Parishad shall elect in the prescribed manner from amongst members a Vice-President who shall, subject to the other provisions of this Regulation, hold office for a period of three years.

(3) If a casual vacancy occurs in the office of the Vice-President of a Zilla Parishad, the persons elected in the manner specified in sub-section (2) to fill such vacancy shall hold office for the remainder of the term of the Vice-President in whose place he is elected.

Resignation of Vice-President or member of Zilla Parishad

54. The Vice-President, or any member other than an *ex-officio* member, of a Zilla Parishad may resign his office by intimating in writing his intention to do so to the President of the Zilla Parishad and such resignation shall take effect from the date of its receipt by the President.

Function of Zilla Parishad

55. (1) The Zilla Parishad shall advise the Governor on all matters concerning the activities of the Gram Panchayats and Anchal Samitis situated within the District.

(2) In particular, it shall be the duty of the Zilla. Parishad —

(a) to make recommendations to the Governor in respect of —

(i) the budget estimates of the Anchal Samitis;

(ii) the distribution and allocation of funds and grants to the Anchal Samitis;

(iii) the coordination and consolidation of the plan proposed by the Anchal Samitis and drawing up of the District plan;

(iv) the coordination of the work of the Gram Panchayats and Anchal Samitis; and

(v) land settlement and raising of revenues for the Anchal Samitis.

(b) to advise on such other matters as may be referred to it by the Governor.

Meetings

56. (1) The Zilla Parishad shall meet as often as may be necessary and shall observe, subject to the provisions of sub-sections (2) and (3), such rules of procedure in regard to the transaction of business at its meetings as may be prescribed:

Provided that not more than six months shall elapse between one meeting of the Zilla Parishad and another.

(2) The president of the Zilla Parishad or in his absence, the Vice-President, or in the absence of the both, any member nominated by the president in that behalf shall preside at any meeting of the Zilla Parishad.

(3) All questions at a meeting of the Zilla Parishad shall be decided by a majority of the votes of the members present and voting and in the case of equality of votes, the President of the Zilla Parishad or in his absence, the person presiding shall have a second or casting vote.

CHAPTER IV

Agency Council

Constitution of Agency council

57. The Governor may constitute an advisory body to be called the Agency Council consisting of —

(i) the Governor;

(ii) the member of Parliament representing the North-East Frontier Agency;

(iii) the Vice-Presidents of all the Zilla Parishads;

(iv) three representatives from each of the Zilla Parishads to be elected by its members from amongst themselves in the prescribed manner; and

(v) the Adviser to the Governor, *ex-officio*.

Functions of Agency Council

58. The Agency Council may be consulted by the Governor in regard to —

(a) matters of administration involving general questions of policy relating to the North-East Frontier Agency in the State field;

(b) the Five Year Plan and the annual plan proposals for the development of the North-East Frontier Agency;

(c) the estimated receipts and expenditure pertaining to the North-East Frontier Agency to be credited to, and to be made from, the Consolidated Fund of India;

(d) proposals for undertaking legislation with respect to any of the matters enumerated in the State List in the Seventh Schedule to the Constitution; and

(e) any other matters which the Governor may refer to it for advice.

Meetings of Agency Council

59. (1) The Agency Council shall meet as often as may be necessary and not more than one year shall elapse between one meeting of the Agency Council and another meeting.

(2) The Governor shall preside at the meetings of the Agency Council.

(3) Meetings of the Agency Council shall be regulated by such procedure as may be prescribed.

(4) Subject to rules regulating the procedure of the Agency Council, and subject to the discretion of the Governor to refuse to give information or to allow discussion on any subject in the public interest, a member of the Agency Council shall have the right to ask questions on matters of public interest relating to the North-East Frontier Agency.

CHAPTER V

Control of Gram Panchayats and Anchal Samitis

Powers of inspection, supervision and control of Governor, etc.

60. The Governor, and such officers as are empowered by him in this behalf, shall have the powers of inspection, supervision and control over the performance of the functions of Gram Panchayats and Anchal Samitis and without prejudice to the generality of the foregoing powers, may —

(a) enter and inspect any immovable property in the occupation or control of, or any work in progress under the direction of, a Gram Panchayat or an Anchal Samiti;

(b) call for and inspect any document which is in the possession or control of a Gram Panchayat or an Anchal Samiti;

(c) require by an order in writing, a Gram Panchayat or an Anchal Samiti to furnish such reports, statements, accounts or proceedings as are necessary;

(d) give such advice in writing in respect of the functions and proceedings of a Gram Panchayat or an Anchal Samiti as they think fit; and

(e) institute an inquiry in respect of any matter relating to a Gram Panchayat or an Anchal Samiti and rectify any or its acts or omissions.

Inspection of construction work, etc. by members of Anchal Samiti

61. With the previous sanction of the President of the Anchal Samiti, a member of an Anchal Samiti may inspect —

(a) any work or institution constructed or maintained in whole or in part at the expense of the Anchal Samiti; or

(b) any register, books, accounts, or other documents belonging to, or in the possession of, the Anchal Samiti.

Inspector of Local Works

62. (1) The Governor may appoint an officer of Government to be Inspector of Local Works for one or more sub-divisions.

(2) The Inspector of Local Works shall —

(a) advise with regard to the construction or repairs of any Gram Panchayat or Anchal Samiti and may for this purpose enter and inspect any immovable property and every such Gram Panchayat or Anchal Samiti shall furnish such statements, estimates and reports as he may require; and

(b) perform such other functions and exercise such other powers as may be prescribed.

(3) A report of every inspection made under this section shall be prepared and a copy thereof shall be forwarded to the Gram Panchayat or Anchal Samiti concerned.

(4) Every Gram Panchayat or Anchal Samiti shall in all matters of technical details be guided by the report of the Inspector of Local Works.

Default in performance of duty by Anchal Samiti, members, officer, etc.

63. (1) If at any time it appears to the Deputy Commissioner or any officer authorized by him in this behalf that an Anchal Samiti or any member, officer or employee thereof has made wilful or persistent default in the performance of any duty imposed under this Regulation, the Deputy Commissioner or the officer may, by order in writing, fix a period for the performance of that duty, and if the duty is not performed within the period so fixed, the Deputy Commissioner or the officer may, by order, appoint any person to perform the said duty and direct that the expenses of the performance of the duty shall be paid by the defaulting Anchal Samiti within such period as he may think fit.

(2) The Deputy Commissioner or the officer exercising the power under sub-section (1) shall call for the explanation of the Anchal Samiti concerned for any default under sub-section (1) and shall forthwith report to the Governor who may, after giving notice to the Anchal Samiti officer or employee and after making such inquiry as he deems. fit, rescind, modify or confirm the order.

Suspension of execution of order or resolution of Anchal Samiti

64. (1) If, in the opinion of the Deputy Commissioner or any officer authorized by him in this behalf, the execution of any order or resolution of an Anchal Samiti or the doing of an act, which is

about to be done or is being done by, or on behalf of, an Anchal Samiti, is causing or is likely to cause injury or annoyance to the public or to lead to a breach of the peace or is unlawful, he may, by order in writing, suspend the execution of that order or resolution or prohibit the doing of that act.

(2) When the Deputy Commissioner or the officer makes an order under sub-section (1), he shall forthwith send to the Anchal Samiti affected thereby a copy of the order together with a statement of the reasons for making it.

(3) The Deputy Commissioner or the officer shall also forthwith submit to the Governor a report of the circumstances in which the order was made under this section and the Governor may, after giving notice to the Anchal Samiti and making such inquiry as he deems fit, rescind, modify or confirm the order.

Power of Deputy Commissioner to call for records relating to tax or fees and make suggestions

65. (1) The Deputy Commissioner may, at any time, call for the records of an Anchal Samiti relating to taxes or fees levied within its area and may make suggestions for alternation, addition or modification of any tax or fee so levied or the rate thereof.

(2) On receipt of a suggestion under sub-section (1), the Anchal Samiti shall reconsider the matter in a meeting and a copy of the resolution adopted shall be sent to the Deputy Commissioner.

Dissolution of an Anchal Samiti

66. (1) If, in the opinion of the Governor, an Anchal Samiti —

(a) exceeds or abuses its powers; or

(b) is incompetent to perform, or makes wilful and persistent default in the discharge of the functions imposed on it by, or under, this Regulation or any other law for the time being in force; or

(c) persistently disobeys the order of the Deputy Commissioner or the officer under sub-section (1) of section 63, the Governor may, by order in writing, dissolve the Anchal Samiti and direct that it shall be reconstituted in the manner provided in this Regulation.

(2) No order under sub-section (1) shall be passed by the Governor without giving to the Anchal Samiti a reasonable opportunity to render an explanation.

(3) When an Anchal Samiti is dissolved under sub-section (1) —

(a) all the members of the Anchal Samiti shall, from the date specified in the order, vacate their office as members; and

(b) all the functions of the Anchal Samiti shall, during the period of dissolution, be discharged by such person or persons as the Governor may appoint in this behalf.

Disputes between local authorities

67. If any dispute arises between two or more Anchal Samitis or between an Anchal Samiti and a Gram Panchayat or between two or more Gram Panchayats, it shall be referred to the Governor and his decision thereon shall be final.

Governor's power to call for proceedings

68. Notwithstanding any thing contained in this chapter, the Governor may call for and examine the records relating to any order passed by any officer or Anchal Samiti for the purpose of satisfying himself as to the legality or propriety of the order passed and may revise or modify the order as he may deem fit.

CHAPTER VI

Miscellaneous

Bar of action against Anchal Samiti, etc. and previous notice before institution

69. (1) No suit or prosecution shall lie against any member, officer, employee or agent of a Gram Panchayat or an Anchal Samiti, in respect of anything done or intended to be done in good faith under this Regulation or any rule or bye-law made thereunder.

(2) No suit or other legal proceeding shall be instituted against any Gram Panchayat or Anchal Samiti or any member, officer, employee or agent thereof, for anything done or purporting to be done under this Regulation or any rule or bye-law made thereunder, until the expiration of two months next

after notice in writing has been left or delivered at the office of the Gram Panchayat or Anchal Samiti, as the case may be, and also at the residence of the member, officer, employee, or agent thereof against whom such suit or proceeding is intended to be instituted, and the notice shall state the cause of action, the nature of the relief sought, the amount of compensation claimed and the name and place of abode of the person who intends to institute the suit or proceedings.

(3) Every suit or proceeding referred to in sub-section (2) shall be instituted within six months after the date on which the cause of action arose.

Liability of members for loss, waste or misapplication

70. (1) Every member of an Anchal Samiti shall be personally liable for the loss, waste or mis-application of any money or other property of the Anchal Samiti to which he has been a party or which has been caused or facilitated by his misconduct or wilful neglect of duty as a member amounting to fraud.

(2) If, after giving the member concerned a reasonable opportunity for showing cause to the contrary, the Deputy Commissioner or any officer authorized by him in this behalf, is satisfied, after such inquiry as he deems fit, that the loss, waste or misapplication of any money or other property of the Anchal Samiti is a direct consequence of the misconduct or wilful neglect on the part of such member, he shall, by order in writing, direct such member to pay to the Anchal Samiti before a fixed date the amount required to reimburse it for such loss, waste or misapplication:

Provided that no such order shall be made for bonafide or technical irregularities or mistakes of a member.

(3) If the amount is not so paid, the Deputy Commissioner or the officer authorized by him in that behalf shall recover it in the prescribed manner.

(4) An order of the Deputy Commissioner or the officer under sub-section (2) shall be subject to

an appeal to the Governor if made within thirty days of the date of the order.

Members, etc. to refrain from taking part at sales

71. A member of an Anchal Samiti or any officer thereof having any duty to perform in connection with any sale or contract under this Regulation shall not directly or indirectly bid for, or acquire any, interest in, any property sold at such sale or accept a contract work.

Penalty for obstructing Anchal Samitis or officers from doing anything under this Regulation, etc.

72. Whoever —

(i) obstructs an Anchal Samiti or any member, employee or agent thereof, or prevents or attempts to prevent any such member, employee or agent from doing anything which he is empowered or required to do under the provisions of this Regulation or any rule or bye-law made thereunder; or

(ii) without lawful authority removes or destroys, defaces or otherwise obliterates any notice, materials, lamp-post, direction-post, stand-post or any other property exhibited or erected by the Anchal Samiti or under its authority, shall be punishable with fine which may extend to fifty rupees.

Penalty for encroachment of road, etc.

73. Whoever encroaches upon any land, road, site, public drain, sewer, aqueduct, watercourse or other property placed under the control of an Anchal Samiti under section 47, by making any excavation or by erecting any wall, fence, rail, post, projection or other obstruction or by depositing any movable property, shall, for every such offence, be punishable with fine which may extend to fifty rupees, and, in the case of a continuing encroachment, with an additional fine which may extend to ten rupees for every day after the first during which he has persisted in the encroachment.

Intimation to be given of infectious diseases

74. If a medical practitioner who is aware of the existence of any infectious or contagious disease in any place other than a public hospital or dispensary fails to intimate forthwith the existence of such a disease to such officers as the Anchal Samiti may specify, or gives false information about the

existence of such a disease, he shall be punishable with fine which may extend to fifty rupees.

Power to compound cases

75. (1) The Anchal Samiti may, either before or after the institution of criminal proceedings under this Regulation, compound any offence against this Regulation or any rule or bye-law made thereunder on payment of such sum in cash to the Anchal Samiti Fund as may be agreed upon.

(2) Where an offence has been compounded, the offender, if in custody, shall be discharged and no further proceedings shall be taken against him in respect of the offence so compounded.

Penalty for contravention of Regulation, etc.

76. Whoever contravences any of the provisions of this Regulation or any rule made thereunder shall, if no other penalty is provided elsewhere in this Regulation for such contravention, be punishable with fine which may extend to two hundred rupees and, in the case of a continuing contravention, with an additional fine which may extend to ten rupees for every day after the first during which he has persisted in the contravention.

77. (1) The Governor may, by notification and subject to such restrictions and conditions as may be specified therein, authorize any officer subordinate to him to exercise in respect of Anchal Samitis, any of the powers which may be exercised by the Governor under this Regulation or rules framed thereunder, except the power to make rules under section 83.

(2) The Governor may also, by notification, authorize any officer subordinate to him to perform all or any of the functions of the Deputy Commissioner under this Regulation or rules framed thereunder.

(3) The Deputy Commissioner may delegate all or any of his powers under this Regulation or rules framed thereunder to any officer subordinate to him.

Cooperation with Government

78. The Anchal Samiti shall, so far as practicable, act in cooperation with, and shall assist, every

officers Government officer who works for the welfare of the rural population within its area.

Powers and duties of police in respect of offences and assistance to Anchal Samiti, etc. 79. Every police officer shall give immediate information to the Anchal Samiti of an offence coming to his knowledge which has been committed against this Regulation or any rule or bye-law made thereunder within its jurisdiction, and shall assist the members and employees of the Anchal Samiti in the exercise of their lawful authority.

Members, etc. of Anchal Samiti to be public servants 80. Every member, officer or other employee of an Anchal Samiti shall be deemed to be a public servant within the meaning of section 21 of the Indian Penal Code.

Inspection and copies of record 81. Every Anchal Samiti shall, on application made to it by any person interested, allow inspection of its records and grant certified copies thereof on payment of the prescribed fee.

Removal of difficulties 82. If any difficulty arises in giving effect to the provisions of this Regulation, the Governor may, by order published in the official gazette, make such provision, not inconsistent with the provisions of this Regulation, which appears to him to be necessary or expedient for the purpose of removing the difficulty.

Power to make rules 83. (1) Governor may, after previous publication, make rules to carry out the purposes of this Regulation.

(2) In particular, and without prejudice to the generality of the foregoing power, such rules may provide for —

(i) the manner of election of members and the Vice-President of an Anchal Samiti;

(ii) the manner of division of a Block into constituencies for the purpose of election of.members to an Anchal Samiti under clause (i) of sub-section (1) of section 6;

(iii) the functions to be discharged by the Executive Officer of an Anchal Samiti;

(iv) the appointment of the officers and employees of Anchal Samitis;

(v) the conduct of meeting of Anchal Samitis and the transaction of business thereat;

(vi) the appointment of committees of Anchal Samitis and their functions;

(vii) the travelling and other allowances to be paid to the members of the Anchal Samitis or any other person for attending meetings of Anchal Samitis or any of its committees;

(viii) the establishment, control, administration and maintenance of dispensaries, hospitals, asylums and places for the reception of the sick or destitute within the jurisdiction of the Anchal Samiti;

(ix) the custody and investment of the Anchal Samiti Fund;

(x) the raising of loans by the Anchal Samitis and the conditions subject to which an Anchal Samiti may make annual or other contributions to Gram Panchayats;

(xi) the imposition and assessment of taxes, fees and surcharge and the realization thereof;

(xii) the form of demand notices and the manner of their services;

(xiii) the manner of filling appeals under tills Regulation and hearing of such appeals;

(xiv) the collection by Anchal Samitis of any tax, fee or other due on behalf of Government and payment of collection charges therefor;

(xv) the form of accounts to be maintained by the Anchal Samitis and the Gram Panchayats receiving contributions from an Anchal Samiti and the manner of audit of such accounts;

(xvi) the form of annual estimates of Anchal Samitis and the date before which they are to be prepared;

(xvii) the manner in which any moneys due to the Anchal Samiti may be recovered;

(xviii) the manner of election of members and the Vice-President of a Zilla Parishad;

(xix) the conduct of meetings of Zilla Parishads and the procedure to be followed thereat;

(xx) the allowances to be paid to the members of the Zilla Parishad and Agency Council for attending meetings;

(xxi) the manner of election of members to the Agency Council;

(xxii) the conduct of meetings of the Agency Council and the procedure to be followed thereat;

(xxiii) the powers and functions of Inspectors of Local Works;

(xxiv) the fees to be levied by Anchal Samitis for supply of copies of documents and the procedure to be followed in furnishing such copies;

(xxv) any other matter which has to be or may be prescribed:

Provided that the rules under clause (xxii) shall be made after consultation with the Agency Council.

Power to make bye-laws

84. (1) Subject to the provisions of this Regulation and the rules made thereunder, an Anchal Samiti may frame bye-laws —

(a) to regulate the appointment, functions, powers, duties and conditions of services of its officers and employees;

(b) to prohibit or regulate the discharge of water from any drain or premises on a public street or into a river, pond, tank, well or any other place;

(c) to regulate sanitation, conservancy and drainage in the area within its jurisdiction;

(d) to prohibit or regulate the use of roads, public streets or other public places;

(e) to regulate the terms and conditions subject to which licence may be granted for the running of markets by private persons, the fees to be charged therefor and other incidental matters;

(f) to regulate the manner in which tanks, ponds, cesspools, pasture lands, playgrounds, manure pits, land for disposal of dead bodies and bathing places may be maintained and used; and

(g) to regulate any of its functions under this Regulation.

(2) Any bye-law made under sub-section (1) may provide that a contravention thereof shall be punishable with fine which may extend to twenty-five rupees and in the case of a continuing contravention, with an additional fine which may extend to five rupees for each day during which the contravention continues.

(3) The power to make bye-laws conferred under sub-section (1) is conferred subject to the condition of the bye-law being made after previous publication and any bye-law so made shall not take effect until it has been approved by the Governor and published in the official gazette.

THE FIRST SCHEDULE

Form of Oath of Office
(see Section 11)

I, ... a member of the .... Anchal Samiti, do swear in the name of God/ solemnly affirm that I will bear true faith and allegiance to the Constitution of India as by law established, that I will uphold the sovereignty and integrity of India, and that I will duly and faithfully to the best of my ability, knowledge and judgement perform the duties of my office without fear or favour or affection or ill will.

THE SECOND SCHEDULE

Matters within the Jurisdiction of Anchal Samitis
(see Section 20)

PART I

I. In the sphere of sanitation and health:

(1) Cleaning and lighting of streets.

(2) Sanitation and conservancy of the area within the jurisdiction of the Gram Panchayat and the prevention of public nuisance therein.

(3) Opening and regulation of burial and cremation grounds for the dead bodies of human beings and regulating places for disposal of dead animals and of other offensive matters.

(4) Supply of water for drinking and domestic use.
(5) Cleaning of public roads, drains, ponds, tanks, wells and other public places or works.
(6) Layout and maintenance of play-grounds for village children and of public gardens.
(7) Disposal of unclaimed corpses and unclaimed cattle.
(8) Construction and maintenance of public latrines.
(9) Taking of measures to prevent the outbreak, spread or recurrence of any infectious disease.
(10) Removal of rubbish heaps, jungle growth, the filling of disused wells, insanitary ponds, pools, ditches, prevention of water-logging in irrigated areas and improvements in sanitary conditions.
(11) Providing medical relief.
(12) Reclaiming unhealthy localities.
(13) Maternity and child welfare.
(14) Encouragement of vaccination in human beings and animals.

II. In the sphere of public works:

(1) Control, regulation and development of grazing grounds, village common and other community property.
(2) Controlling and maintaining buildings, institutions and property belonging to, or placed under, the control of the Anchal Samitis or which may be transferred to it for management.
(3) Planting of trees along the roads and public places and maintenance thereof.
(4) Establishment, maintenance and management of cattle pounds and to perform such functions as may be transferred to it by notification under section 31 of the Cattle Trespass Act, 1871 (1 of 1871).
(5) Destruction of stray and ownerless dogs.
(6) Removal of obstructions in public places and sites which are not private property.
(7) Construction, maintenance and repair of buildings waterways, public roads, drains, embankments, bunds and bridges.
(8) Control, maintenance and regulation of fairs, minor *hats* or minor bazars and cart stands.

(9) Construction and maintenance of *dharmashalas*.

(10) Construction and maintenance of houses for the staff of the Anchal Samiti.

(11) Provision and maintenance of camping grounds.

(12) Extension of village sites and the regulation of buildings.

(13) Management of community lands.

(14) Excavation, cleaning and maintenance of ponds for supply of water to animals.

(15) Construction and maintenance of minor irrigation works.

(16) Construction and maintenance of warehouses.

(17) Land management.

III. In the sphere of education and culture:

(1) Maintenance of public radio sets for the benefit of rural population.

(2) Establishment and maintenance of library, reading room, club or other places of recreation and games.

(3) Popularization of village sports, organization and celebration of national and public festivals.

(4) Spread of education to Middle English and Middle Vernacular standards.

(5) Establishment and maintenance of youth clubs and other places of recreation.

(6) Establishment and maintenance of theatres for promotion of art and culture.

IV. In the sphere of self-defence and village defence:

(1) Watch and ward of the village and of the crops therein that the cost of watch and ward shall be levied and recovered from persons resident in the village.

(2) Rendering assistance in extinguishing fires and the protection of life and property in the event of fire.

V. In the sphere of administration:

(1) Maintenance of records relating to agricultural produce, census of village industries, population census, cattle census, spinning wheels and weaving machine census, census of unemployed persons or persons having no economic holding or such other statistics as may be necessary.

(2) Registration of births, deaths, marriages and maintenance of registers for the purpose.
(3) Distribution of such reliefs as may be granted by Government or other agencies.
(4) Supplying local information to the Government or any other statutory authority.
(5) Numbering of premises.
(6) Drawing-up of programmes for increasing the output of agricultural and non-agricultural produce in the village.
(7) Preparation of a statement showing the requirements of the supplies and finance needed for carrying out rural development schemes.
(8) Control of cattle stands, threshing floors, grazing grounds and community waste-land.
(9) Reporting to proper authorities complaints which are not removable by Anchal Samitis.
(10) Preparation of plans for the development of the village.
(11) Establishment, maintenance and regulation of fairs, pilgrimages and festivals.

VI. In the sphere of the welfare of the people:

(1) Propagation of ideas connected with improved housing, encouraging people to undertake improved housing, installation of smokeless *chullas* and ventilators.
(2) Organization of welfare activities among women and children and among illiterate sections of the community.
(3) Welfare of the backward classes.
(4) Organizing voluntary labour for community works and works for the uplift of the village.

VII. In the sphere of agriculture and preservation of forests:

(1) Construction and maintenance of places for the storage of cow-dung, oil cakes and other manure and regulating its collection, removal and disposal.
(2) Tethering and grazing of cattle and encouraging stall feeding of cattle and growing feeder for the purpose.
(3) Improvement of agriculture.
(4) Establishment of granaries.
(5) Provision of agricultural finance with the assistance of Government, Cooperative and Agricultural Production.

(6) Bringing under cultivation waste and fallow lands placed by the Governor with the Anchal Samiti.
(7) Ensuring minimum standards of cultivation in the village with a view to increasing agricultural production.
(8) Ensuring conservation of mineral resources, preparation of compost and selling of manures.
(9) Establishment and maintenance of nurseries for improved seeds and provision of implements and stores.
(10) Production and use of improved seeds.
(11) Promotion of cooperative farming.
(12) Crop experiments and crop protection.

VIII. In the sphere of breeding and protecting cattle:

Improvement of cattle and cattle breeding and general care of livestock.

IX. In the sphere of village industries:

Promotion, improvement and encouragement of cottage and village industries.

PART II

I. In the sphere of sanitation and health:

(1) Public health and sanitation including curative and preventive measures in respect of an epidemic.
(2) Medical relief including establishment and maintenance of hospitals and dispensaries.
(3) Taking anti-malarial and anti-*kala azar* measures.

II. In the sphere of public works:

(1) Maintenance and regulation of the use of public buildings, grazing lands, forest lands, including lands assigned under section 28 of the Indian Forest Act, 1927 (16 of 1927), tanks and wells placed under the control of the Anchal Samiti.
(2) Control of major *hats*.
(3) Establishment and maintenance of works or provision of employment in times of scarcity.

III. In the sphere of self-defence and village defence:

Regulation of offensive and dangerous trades or practices.

IV. In the sphere of education and culture:

Spread of education above the Middle English and Middle Vernacular Standards.

V. In the sphere of administration:

(1) Collection of statistics and maintenance of records.
(2) General power over Gram Panchayats in respect of functions assigned to them.
(3) To act as agent of the Government for development works within the area where funds for specific purposes are provided.
(4) Acting as channel through which assistance given by the Governor for any purpose reaches the village.

VI. In the sphere of the welfare of people:

Relief distress caused by floods, drought, earthquake and scarcity conditions and other calamities.

VII. In the sphere of agriculture and preservation of forests:

(1) Development of agriculture and horticulture.
(2) Measures for encouraging soil conservation, land reclamation and plantation.
(3) Improvement of cattle and poultry including popularization of the use of veterinary service, cattle inoculation facilities, castration on scientific lines and establishment of artificial insemination centres.

VIII. Any other function that may be assigned to it by the Governor.

ZAKIR HUSSAIN
President

V.N. BHATIA
Secretary to the Government of India

Act No. 42 of 1957

The Naga Hills-Tuensang Area Act, 1957

AN ACT

to provide for the formation of the Naga Hills-Tuensang Area of Assam as an administrative unit.

Be it enacted by Parliament in the Eighth Year of the Republic of India as follows:

Short title and commencement

1. (1) This Act may be called the Naga Hills-Tuensang Area Act, 1957.

(2) It shall come into force on such date as the Central Government may, by notification in the official Gazette, appoint.

Formation of Naga Hills-Tuensang Area

2. As from the commencement of this Act, there shall be formed a new administrative unit in the State of Assam by the name of Naga Hills-Tuensang Area comprising the tribal areas which at such commencement were known as the Naga Hills District and Tuensang Frontier Division of the North-East Frontier Agency.

Amendment of the Sixth Schedule to the Constitution

3. In the Sixth Schedule to the Constitution, in paragraph 20 —

(a) after sub-paragraph (2A), the following sub-paragraph shall be inserted, namely —

(2B) The Naga Hills-Tuensang Area shall comprise the areas which at the commencement of this Constitution were known as the Naga Hills District and tribal Area;

(b) in sub-paragraph (3), after the words "administrative area, the brackets and words (other than the Naga Hills-Tuensang Area)" shall be inserted;

(c) in Part A of the table, item 4 shall be omitted; and

(d) in Part B of the table, for item 2, the following item shall be substituted namely: "2. The Naga Hills-Tuensang Area".

Amendment of the Delimitation Order

4. In Delimitation of Parliamentary and Assembly Constituencies Order, 1956 —

(a) in the First Schedule, in the entry in column 3 against Serial No. 37, the words "Naga Hills", shall be omitted; and

(b) in the Second Schedule, in the part relating to Assam, the heading, "Naga Hills District" and all entries against serial Nos. 16, 17 and 18 shall be omitted.

Amendment of the Representation of the People Act, 1950

5. In the Representation of the People Act, 1950 (43 of 1950) —

(a) in Part II of the First Schedule —

(i) for the entry —

"21. Part B Tribal areas the following entries shall be substituted, namely: 1"

"21. North-East Frontier Tract — 1"

"22. Naga Hills-Tuensang Area — 1"

(ii) for the figure "503", the figure "504" shall be substituted;

(b) in the Second Schedule, for the entry in column 3 against "2. Assam", the entry "105" shall be substituted.

Provision as to the sitting member of Parliament

6. Notwithstanding the alteration in the extent of the Autonomous Districts Parliamentary Constituency in Assam effected by section 4, the sitting member of the House of the People as presenting that constituency shall be deemed to have been elected to the House of the People by that constituency as so altered.

Territorial extent of laws not to be affected

7. The provisions of section 2 shall not be deemed to have effected any change in the areas to which any law in force immediately before the commencement of this Act extends or applies, and territorial references in any such law to the Naga Hills District, the Naga Tribal Area or the Tuensang Frontier Division shall, until otherwise provided by a competent

legislature or other competent authority, continue to have the same meaning.

Explanation: In this section, law means any law, ordinance, regulation, order, bye-law, rule, scheme, notification or other instrument having the force of law in India or any part thereof.

The State of Nagaland Act, 1962

AN ACT

to provide for the formation of the State of Nagaland and for matters connected therewith. (4th September, 1962)

Be it enacted by Parliament in the Thirteenth Year of the Republic of India as follows:

PART I

Preliminary

1. *Short title:* This Act may be called the State of Nagaland Act, 1962.

2. *Definitions:* In this Act, unless the context otherwise requires, —

(a) "appointed day" means the day which the Central Government may, by notification in the Official Gazette, appoint;

(b) "article" means an article of the Constitution;

(c) "assembly constituency" and "parliamentary constituency" have the same meanings as in the Representation of the People Act, 1950;

(d) "law" includes any enactment, ordinance, regulation, order, bye-law, rule, scheme, notification or other instrument or custom or usage having the force of law;

(e) "Naga Hills-Tuensang Area" means the Naga Hills-Tuensang Area specified in Part B of the Table appended to paragraph 20 of the Sixth Schedule to the Constitution, comprising the areas which at the commencement of the Constitution were known as the Naga Hills District and the Naga Tribal Area;

(f) "regional council" means the regional council referred to in Article 371-A.

PART II

Formation of the State of Nagaland

3. *Formation of the State of Nagaland:* (1) As from the appointed day, there shall be formed a new State to be known as State of Nagaland comprising the territories which immediately before that day were comprised in the Naga Hills-Tuensang Area and thereupon the said territories shall cease to form part of the State of Assam.

(2) Without prejudice to the power of the State Government to alter after the appointed day, the name, extent or boundaries of any district, the State of Nagaland shall consist of three districts to be called the Kohima district, Mokokchung district and Tuensang district, each comprising the areas respectively set out in the Schedule.

4. *Amendment of First Schedule to the Constitution:* As from the appointed day, in the First Schedule to the Constitution under the heading "I. THE STATES" —

(a) in the paragraph relating to the territories of the State of Assam, the following shall be added at the end, namely: "and the territories specified in sub-section (1) of section 3 of the State of Nagaland Act, 1962";

(b) after Entry 15, the following entry shall be inserted namely:

"16. Nagaland .... The territories specified in sub-section (1) of section 4 of the State of Nagaland Act, 1962".

5. *Amendment of Sixth Schedule to the Constitution:* As from the appointed day, in the Sixth Schedule to the Constitution —

(a) in paragraph 20 —

(i) sub-paragraph (2-B) shall be omitted;

(ii) in sub-paragraph (3) the brackets and words "(other than the Naga Hills-Tuensang Area)" shall be omitted;

(b) in the Table appended to paragraph 20, in Part B, the item "2. The Naga Hills-Tuensang Area" shall be omitted.

PART III

Representation in the Legislatures

THE COUNCIL OF STATES

6. *Representation in Council of States:* As from the appointed day —

(a) there shall be allotted one seat to the State of Nagaland in the Council of States;

(b) in the Fourth Schedule to the Constitution in the table —

(i) Entries 16 to 19 shall be renumbered as Entries 17 to 20,

(ii) after Entry 15, the following entry shall be inserted namely:
"16. Nagaland .... 1",

(iii) at the end, for the figures "224", the figures "225" shall be substituted.

7. *Election to fill vacancy:* As soon as may be after the appointed day, there shall be held an election to fill the seat allotted to the State of Nagaland in the Council of States.

8. *Term of office:* The term of office of the member for the first time elected to fill the seat allotted to the State of Nagaland in the Council of States shall expire on the 2nd day of April, 1968.

THE HOUSE OF THE PEOPLE

9. *Representation in House of the People:* (1) As from the appointed day —

(a) there shall be allotted one seat to the State of Nagaland in the House of the People;

(b) in the First Schedule to the Representation of the People Act 1950 —

(i) the Entry "25. Naga Hills-Tuensang Area ....1"

(ii) Entries 16 to 24 shall be renumbered as Entries 17 to 25;

(iii) after entry 15, the following entry shall be inserted namely:
"16 Nagaland .... 1".

(2) The whole of the State of Nagaland shall form one Parliamentary Constituency to be called the Parliamentary Constituency

of Nagaland for the purpose of filling the seat allotted to that State in the House of the People.

(3) For the period referred to in clause (2) of Article 371A, Section 13-D of the Representation of the People Act, 1950, shall apply in relation to the Parliamentary Constituency of Nagaland with the modification that it shall be necessary to prepare and revise separately the electoral roll for that part of the said Parliamentary Constituency which comprises the Tuensang District and the provisions of Part III of the Act shall apply in relation to the said part as they apply in relation to an assembly constituency.

10. *Provision as to sitting member:* The sitting member of the House of the People representing, immediately before the appointed day, the Naga Hills-Tuensang Area shall, as from that day, represent the State of Nagaland in that House and shall continue to do so until a person is elected in accordance with law to fill the seat allotted to the Parliamentary Constituency of Nagaland.

THE LEGISLATIVE ASSEMBLY

11. *Strength of Legislative Assembly:* (1) The total number of seats to be filled by persons chosen by direct election in the Legislative Assembly of Nagaland shall be 60:

Provided that for the period referred to in clause (2) of Article 371A, the total number of seats in the Legislative Assembly of Nagaland shall be 46, of which —

(a) six seats shall be allocated to the Tuensang District and shall be filled by persons chosen by the members of the regional council from amongst themselves in such manner as the Governor, after consulting that council may by notification in the Official Gazette specify; and

(b) the remaining forty seats shall be filled by persons chosen by direct election from assembly constituencies in the rest of the State of Nagaland.

(2) In the Representation of the People Act, 1950 —

(a) in section 7, the following provision shall be inserted at the end, namely:

"Provided that for the period referred to in clause (2) of Article 371A, the total number of seats allotted to the Legislative Assembly of Nagaland shall be 46, of which —

(a) Six seats shall be allocated to the Tuensang District and shall be filled by persons chosen by the members of the regional council referred to in that article from amongst themselves in such manner as the Governor, after consulting that council, may by notification in the official Gazette, specify; and

(b) the remaining forty seats shall be filled by persons chosen by direct election from assembly constituencies in the rest of the State of Nagaland"; and

(c) in the Second Schedule, after Entry 14, the following entry shall be inserted, namely:
"15. Nagaland .... 60 (for the period referred to in clause (2) of Article 371A, 46)".

(3) In the Representation of the People Act, 1951, in Section 5, in clause (c), the following proviso shall be inserted at the end, namely:

"Provided that for the period referred to in clause (2) of Article 371A, a person shall not be qualified to be chosen to fill any seat allocated to the Tuensang District in the Legislative Assembly of Nagaland unless he is a member of the regional council referred to in that article".

(4) The Election Commission shall delimit the assembly constituencies in accordance with the provisions of the Constitution on the basis of the latest census figures, and in doing so the Commission shall have regard to the following provisions, namely:

(a) all constituencies shall, as far as practicable, consist of geographically compact areas, and in delimiting them, regard shall be had to physical features, existing boundaries of administrative units, facilities of communication, public convenience and linguistic affinities of the people;

(b) all constituencies shall be single-member constituencies; and

(c) the population of each constituency shall not, as far as practicable, be more than six thousand.

(5) For the purpose of assisting the Election Commission in the performance of its functions under this section, the Commission shall associate with itself five persons of whom three shall be elected by the members of the Interim Body established under section 3 of the Nagaland

(Transitional Provisions) Regulation, 1961, from among themselves and two shall be nominated by the Central Government:

Provided that none of the said associate members shall have a right to vote or to sign any decision of the Election Commission.

(6) The Election Commission shall —

(a) formulate its proposals in regard to the matters mentioned in sub-section (4) and publish them in the Official Gazette of the State of Assam and in such other manner as the Commission may consider fit, together with a notice inviting objections and suggestions in relation to the proposals and specifying a date on or after which the proposals will be further considered by it;

(b) consider all objections and suggestions which have been received by it before the date so specified, and for the purpose of such consideration hold one or more public sittings at such place or places as it may think fit;

(c) after considering all objection and suggestions which have been received by it before the date specified, determine the matters mentioned in sub-section (4) by one or more final orders and cause such order or orders to be published in the Official Gazette of the State of Assam; and upon such publication the order or orders shall have the full force of law and shall not be called in question in any court; and

(d) amend the Delimitation of Parliamentary and Assembly Constituencies Order, 1961, so as to include therein the Parliamentary constituency of Nagaland and the Assembly constituencies delimited under this section.

12. *Rules of Procedure:* The rules as the procedure and conduct of business in force immediately before the appointed day with respect to the Legislative Assembly of Assam shall until rules are made under clause (1) of Article 208, have effect in relation to the Legislative Assembly of Nagaland subject to such modifications and adaptations as may be made therein by the Speaker thereof.

PART IV

High Court

13. *Common High Court for Assam and Nagaland:* (1) As from the appointed day,

(a) there shall be a common High Court for the State of Assam and the State of Nagaland to be called the High Court of Assam and Nagaland (hereinafter referred to as the common High Court); and

(b) the Judges of the High Court of Assam holding office immediately before that day shall, unless they have elected otherwise, become on that day Judges of the common High Court.

(2) Expenditure in respect of the salaries and allowances of the Judges of the Common High Court shall be allocated between the State of Assam and the State of Nagaland in such proportion as the President may by order determine.

14. *Provisions as to Advocates:* (1) As from the appointed day,

(a) in the Advocates Act, 1961, in section 3 in sub-section (1), for clause (b), the following clause shall be substituted, namely:

"(b) for the State of Assam and Nagaland and the Union Territory of Manipur, to be known as the Bar Council of Assam and Nagaland",

(c) the Bar Council of Assam shall be deemed to be the Bar Council of Assam and Nagaland.

(2) Any person who immediately before the appointed day is an advocate entitled to practise in the High Court of Assam shall be entitled to practise as an advocate in the common High Court.

(3) All persons who immediately before the appointed day are advocates on the roll of the Bar Council of Assam shall as from the day become advocates on the roll of the Bar Council of Assam and Nagaland.

(4) The right of audience in the common High Court shall be regulated in accordance with the like principles as, immediately before the appointed day, are in force with respect to the right of audience in the High Court of Assam:

Provided that as between the Advocate-General of Assam and the Advocate General of Nagaland the right of audience shall be determined with reference to their respective dates of enrolment as advocates.

15. *Practice and Procedure in common High Court:* Subject to the provisions of this part, the law in force immediately before the appointed day with respect to practice and procedure in the High Court of Assam shall, with necessary modifications, apply in relation to the common High Court.

16. *Custody of Seal of common High Court:* The law in force immediately before the appointed day with respect to the custody of the Seal of the High Court of Assam shall, with necessary modifications, apply with respect to the custody of the Seal of the common High Court.

17. *Form of Writs and other processes:* The law in force immediately before the appointed day with respect to the form of writs and other processes used, issued or awarded by the High Court of Assam shall, with necessary modifications, apply with respect to the form of writs and other processes used, issued or awarded by the common High Court.

18. *Power of Judges:* The law in force immediately before the appointed day with respect to the powers of the Chief Justice, single Judges and division courts of the High Court of Assam and with respect to all matters ancillary to the exercise of those powers shall, with necessary modifications, apply in relation to the common High Court.

19. *Principal Seat of common High Court:* The principal seat of the common High Court shall, unless otherwise determined by the Chief Justice after consultation with the Governors of Assam and Nagaland, be at the same place as the principal seat of the High Court of Assam immediately before the appointed day.

20. *Procedure as to appeals to Supreme Court:* The law in force immediately before the appointed day relating to appeals to the Supreme Court from the High Court of Assam and the Judges and division courts thereof shall, with necessary modifications, apply in relation to the common High Court.

21. *Pending suits, appeals and proceedings:* All suits, appeals and proceedings, civil, criminal or otherwise, pending in the High Court of Assam immediately before the appointed day shall, on that day, stand removed to the common High Court and the common High Court shall have jurisdiction to hear and determine the same, and the judgements, decrees, sentences and orders of the High Court of Assam delivered, passed or made before the appointed day shall have the same force and effect as if they had been delivered, passed or made by the common High Courts.

PART V

Financial Provisions

22. *Authorization of expenditure pending its sanction by Legislature:* The President may, at any time before the appointed day, authorize such expenditure from the Consolidated Fund of the State of Nagaland as he deems necessary for a period of not more than six months beginning with the appointed day, pending the sanction of such expenditure by the Legislature of the State of Nagaland:

Provided that the Governor of Nagaland may, after the appointed day, authorize such further expenditure as he deems necessary from the Consolidated Fund of the State of Nagaland for any period not extending beyond the said period of six months.

23. *Distribution of revenues:* The President shall by order determine the grants-in-aid of the revenues of the State of Nagaland and the share of that State in the Union duties, of excise, estate duty and taxes on income and for that purpose amend thereby the relevant provisions of the Union Duties of Excise (Distribution) Act, 1962, the additional Duties of Excise (Goods of Special Importance) Act, 1957, the Estate Duty (Distribution) Act, 1962, and the Constitution (Distribution of Revenues) Order 1962, in such manner as he thinks fit.

24. *Property, assets, rights, liabilities and obligations:* (1) All property and assets situated in, or used for, or in connection with the administration of the Naga Hills-Tuensang Area and vested in the Union immediately before the appointed day (other than any property or assets so vested for purposes of the Union) shall, as from that day, vest in the State of Nagaland:

Provided that the cash balances in the treasuries in the Naga Hills-Tuensang Area immediately before the appointed day shall as from that day vest in the State of Nagaland.

(2) All rights, liabilities and obligations of the Central Government, whether arising out of any contract or otherwise, which are, immediately before the appointed day, the rights, liabilities and obligations of the Central Government arising out of or in connection with the administration of the Naga Hills-Tuensang Area shall, as from that day, be the rights, liabilities and obligations of the Government of the State of Nagaland.

25. *Arrears of Taxes:* The right to recover arrears of any tax or duty (being a tax or duty enumerated in the State List in the Seventh Schedule to the Constitution) which have fallen due in the Naga Hills-Tuensang Area shall pass to the State of Nagaland.

PART VI

Legal and Miscellaneous Provisions

26. *Continuance of existing laws and their adaptation:* (1) All laws in force, immediately before the appointed day, in the Naga Hills-

Tuensang Area shall continue to be in force in the State of Nagaland until altered, repealed or amended by a competent Legislature or other competent authority.

(2) For the purpose of facilitating the application in relation to the State of Nagaland of any law made before the appointed day, appropriate Government may, within two years from that day, by order make such adaptations and modifications of the law, whether by way of repeal or amendment, as may be necessary or expedient and thereupon every such law shall have effect subject to the adaptations and modifications so made until altered, repealed or amended by a competent Legislature or other competent authority.

Explanation: In this section, the expression "appropriate Government" means, as respects any law relating to a matter enumerated in the Union List in the Seventh Schedule to the Constitution, the Central Government, and as respects any other law, the Government of Nagaland.

27. *Power to construe laws:* Notwithstanding that no provision or insufficient provision had been made under section 26 for the adaptation of a law made before the appointed day any court, tribunal or authority required or empowered to enforce such law may for the purpose of facilitating its application in relation to the State of Nagaland construe the law in such manner not affecting the substance as may be necessary or proper in regard to the matter before the court, tribunal or authority, as the case may be.

28. *Provisions as to continuance of courts and of officers, etc.:* (1) All courts and tribunal and all authorities discharging lawful functions throughout the Naga Hills-Tuensang Area or any part thereof immediately before the appointed day shall, unless their continuance is inconsistent with the provision of this Act or until other provision is made by a competent Legislature or other competent authority, continue to exercise their respective functions.

(2) Every person who, immediately before the appointed day, is holding or discharging the duties of any post or office in connection with the administration of the Naga Hills-Tuensang Area or any part thereof shall, except where by virtue or in consequence of the provisions of this Act such post or office ceases to exist on that day continue to hold the same post or office in the State of Nagaland, and shall be deemed, as from that day, to have been duly appointed to such post or office by the Government or other appropriate authority in, such State.

(3) Nothing in sub-section (2) shall be deemed to prevent a competent authority, after the appointed day, from passing in relation to any such person any order affecting his continuance in such post or office.

29. *Amendment of Act 27 of 1956:* As from the appointed day, in Section 15 of the States Re-organization Act, 1956, in clause (c), for the words, "and Assam" the words "Assam and Nagaland" shall be substituted.

30. *Effect of Provisions of Act inconsistent with other laws:* The provisions of this Act shall have effect notwithstanding anything inconsistent therewith contained in any other law.

31. *Power to remove difficulties:* (1) If any difficulty arises in giving effect to the provisions of this Act, the President may, by order, do anything not inconsistent with such provisions which appears to him to be necessary or expedient for the purpose of removing the difficulty.

(2) Every order made under this section shall be laid before each House of Parliament.

32. Every rule made under this section shall be laid as soon as may be after it is made, before each House of Parliament while it is in session for a total period of thirty days which may be comprised in one session or two or more successive sessions, and if, before the expiry of the session in which it is so laid or the successive sessions aforesaid, both Houses agree in making any modification in the rule or both Houses agree that the rule should not be made, the rule shall thereafter have effect only in such modified form or be of no effect, as the case may be, so however, that any such modification or annulment shall be without prejudice to the validity of anything previously done under that rule.

33. *Regulation 2 of 1961:* As from the appointed day, the Nagaland (Transitional Provisions) Regulation, 1961, shall stand repealed.

THE SCHEDULE

[(See Section 3 (2)]

1. Kohima	The areas which immediately before the 1st day of December, 1957, were comprised in the Naga Hills District excluding the areas in Mokokchung District as specified in item No. 2.
2. Mokokchung	The areas which immediately before the 1st day of December, 1957, were comprised in the Mokokchung sub-division of the Naga Hills District.
3. Tuensang	The areas which immediately before the 1st day of December, 1957, were comprised in the Tuensang Frontier Division of the North-East Frontier Agency.

ANNEXURE XXIV

The Constitution Twenty Second Amendment Act, 1969

AN ACT[1]

Further to amend the Constitution of India.

Be it enacted by Parliament in the Twentieth Year of the Republic of India as follows:

1. *Short title:* This Act may be called the Constitution Republic of India as follows:

2. *Insertion of new article 244A:* In Part X of the Constitution, after article 244, the following article shall be inserted, namely:

"244A. *Formation of an autonomous State comprising certain tribal areas in Assam and creation of Local Legislature of Council of Ministers or both therefor:* (1) Notwithstanding anything in this Constitution, Parliament may, be law, form within the State of Assam an autonomous State comprising (whether wholly or in part) all or any of the tribal areas specified in Part A of the table appended to paragraph 20 of the Sixth Schedule and create therefor —

(a) a body, whether elected or partly nominated and partly elected, to function as a Legislature for the autonomous State; or

(b) a Council of Ministers, or both with such constitution, powers and functions, in each case, as may be specified in the law.

(2) Any such law as is referred to in clause (1) may, in particular, —

(a) specify the matters enumerated in the State List or the Concurrent List with respect to which the Legislature of the autonomous State shall have power to make laws for the whole or any part thereof, whether to the exclusion of the Legislature of the State of Assam or otherwise;

(b) define the matters with respect to which the executive power of the autonomous State shall extend;

(c) provide that any tax levied by the State of Assam shall be assigned to the autonomous State insofar as the proceeds thereof are attributable to the autonomous State;

(d) provide that any reference to a State in any article of this Constitution shall be construed as including a reference to the autonomous State; and

(e) make such supplemental, incidental and consequential provisions as may be deemed necessary.

(3) An amendment of any such law as aforesaid insofar as such amendment relates of any of the matters specified in sub-clause (a) or sub-clause (b) of clause (2) shall have no effect unless the amendment is passed in each House Parliament by not less than two-third of the members present and voting.

(4) Any such law as is referred to in this article shall not be deemed to be an amendment of this Constitution for the purposes of article 368 notwithstanding that it contains any provision which amends or has the effect of amending this Constitution."

3. *Amendment of Article 275:* In article 275 of the Constitution, after clause (1), the following clause shall be inserted namely:

"(1A) On and from the formation of the autonomous State under article 244A, —

(i) any sums payable under clause (a) of the second proviso to clause (1) shall, if the autonomous State comprises as the tribal areas referred to therein, by paid to the autonomous State, and, if the autonomous State comprises only some of those tribal areas, be apportioned between the State of Assam and the autonomous State as the President may, by order specify;

(ii) these shall be paid out of the Consolidated Fund of India as grants-in-aid of the revenues of the autonomous State sums, capital and recurring, equivalent to the costs of such schemes of development as may be undertaken by the autonomous State with the approval of the Government of India for the purpose of raising the level of administration of that State to that of the administration of the rest of the State of Assam."

4. *Insertion of new Article 371B:* After article 371A of the Constitution, the following article shall be inserted, namely:

"371B. *Special provision with respect to the State of Assam:* Notwithstanding anything in this Constitution, the President may, by order made with respect to the State of Assam, provide for the constitution and functions of a committee of the Legislative Assembly of the State consisting of members of the Assembly elected from the tribal areas specified in Part A of the table appended to paragraph 20 of the Sixth Schedule and such number of other members of that Assembly as may be specified in the order and for the modifications to be made in the rules of procedure of that Assembly for the constitution and proper functioning of such committee."

NOTE

1. Received the assent of the President on 25.9.1969, *Gazette of India*, Pt. II. S. 1, Ext. p. 373.
   For statement of Objects and Reasons, see *Gazette of India*, dated 10.4.1969, Pt. II. S. 2, Ext., p. 406.

ANNEXURE XXV

The Constitution Twenty Seventh Amendment Act, 1971

AN ACT

Further to amend the Constitution of India.

Be it enacted by Parliament in the Twenty Second Year of the Republic of India as follows:

1. *Short title and commencement:* (1) This Act may be called the Constitution Twenty Seventh Amendment Act, 1971.

(2) This section and section 3 shall come into force at once and the remaining provisions of this Act shall come into force on such date, being a date not earlier than the day appointed under clause (b) of section 2 of the North-Eastern Areas (Re-organization) Act, 1971, as the Central Government may, by notification in the Official Gazette, appoint.

2. *Amendment of Article 239A:* After article 239A of the Constitution, in clause (i) for the words "Goa, Daman & Diu, Pondicherry and Mizoram" shall be substituted.

3. *Insertion of new Article 239B:* After 239A of the Constitution, the following article shall be inserted, namely —

"239B. *Power of administrator to promulgate Ordinances during recess of Legislature:* (1) If at any time, except when the Legislature of a Union Territory referred to in clause (1) of article 239A is in session, the administrator thereof is satisfied that circumstances exist which render it necessary for him to take immediate action, he may promulgate such Ordinances as the circumstances appear to him to require:

Provided that no such Ordinance shall be promulgated by the administrator except after obtaining instructions from the President in that behalf:

Provided further that whenever the said Legislature is dissolved, or its functioning remains suspended on account of any action taken under any such law as is referred to in clause (1) of article 239A, the administrator shall not promulgate any Ordinance during the period of such dissolution or suspension.

(2) An ordinance promulgated under this article in pursuance of instructions from the President shall be deemed to be an Act of the

Legislature of the Union Territory which has been duly enacted after complying with the provisions in that behalf contained in any such law as is referred to in clause (1) of article 239A, but every such Ordinance, —

(a) shall be laid before the Legislature of the Union Territory and shall cease to operate at the expiration of six weeks from the re-assembly of the Legislature or if, before the expiration of that period, a resolution disapproving it is passed by the Legislature, upon the passing of the resolution; and

(b) may be withdrawn at any time by the administrator after obtaining instructions from the President in that behalf.

(3) If and so far as an Ordinance under this article makes any provision which would not be valid if enacted in an Act of the Legislature of the Union Territory made after complying with the provisions in that behalf contained in any such law as is referred to in clause (1) of article 239A, it shall be void".

4. *Amendment of Article 240:* In article 240 of the Constitution, —

(a) in clause (1), —

(i) after entry (e), the following entries shall be inserted namely —

"(f) Mizoram;

(g) Arunachal Pradesh";

(ii) in the proviso, for the words "Union Territory of Goa, Daman & Diu or Pondicherry", the words "Union Territory of Goa, Daman & Diu, Pondicherry or Mizoram" shall be substituted; and

(iii) after the proviso as so amended, the following further proviso shall be inserted, namely —

Provided further that whenever the body functioning as a Legislature for the Union Territory of Goa, Daman & Diu, Pondicherry or Mizoram is dissolved, or the functioning of that body as such Legislature remains suspended on account of any action taken under any such law as is referred to in clause (1) of article 239A, the President may, during the period of such dissolution or suspension, make regulations for the peace, progress and good government of that Union Territory";

(b) in clause (2), for the words "any existing law", the words "any other law" shall be substituted.

5. *Insertion of new Article 371C:* After article 371B of the Constitution the following article shall be inserted, namely —

"371C. *Special provision with respect to the State of Manipur:* (1) Notwithstanding anything in this Constitution, the President may, by order made with respect to the State of Manipur, provide for the constitution and functions of a committee of the Legislative Assembly of the State consisting of members of that Assembly elected from the Hill Areas of that State, for the modifications to be made in the rules of business of the Government and in the rules of procedure of the Legislative Assembly of the State and for any special responsibility of the governor in order to secure the proper functioning of such committee.

(2) The Governor shall annually, or whenever so required by the President, make a report to the President regarding the administration of the Hill Areas in the State of Manipur and the executive power of the Union shall extend to the giving directions to the State as to the administration of the said areas.

Explanation: In this article, the expression "Hill Areas" means such areas as the President may, by order, declare to be "Hill Areas".

ANNEXURE XXVI

The Government of Union Territories (Amendment) Act, 1971

AN ACT

Further to amend the Government of Union Territory Act, 1963 and also further to amend the Sixth Schedule to the Constitution and the Representation of People Act, 1950.

Be it enacted by Parliament in the Twenty Second Year of the Republic of India as follows:

1. *Short title and Commencement:* (1) This Act may be called the Government of Union Territory (Amendment) Act, 1971.

(2) It shall come into force on such date, being a date not earlier than the day appointed under clause (b) of section 2 of the North-Eastern Areas (Re-organization) Act, 1971, as the Central Government may, by notification in the Official Gazette, appoint.

2. *Amendment of Section 1:* In section of the Government of Union Territory Act, 1963, (20 of 1963) hereinafter referred to as the principal Act, in sub-section (2), —

(i) before the existing proviso, the following proviso shall be inserted, namely —
"Provided that it shall come into force in the Union Territory of Mizoram on such date, being a dale not earlier than the date of commencement of the Government of Union Territory (Amendment) Act, 1971, as the Central Government may, by notification in the Official Gazette, appoint"; and

(ii) in the existing proviso, for the words "Provided that" the words "Provided further that" shall be substituted.

3. *Amendment of Section 2:* In section 2 of the principal Act, in sub-section (1), in clause (h), for the words "Goa, Daman & Diu, and Pondicherry", the words "Goa, Daman & Diu, Pondicherry and Mizoram" shall be substituted.

4. *Amendment of Section 3:* In section 3 of the principal Act —

(i) in sub-section (4) for the words "in the Legislative Assembly of every Union Territory other than the Union

Territory of Goa, Daman & Diu", the words "in the Legislative Assembly of the Union Territory of Pondicherry" shall be substituted;

(ii) in sub-section (4), for the words "of any Union Territory", the words "of the Union Territory of Pondicherry" shall be substituted; and

(iii) in sub-section (6), for the words "in the Legislative Assemblies of the Union Territories", the words "in the Legislative Assembly of the Union Territory of Pondicherry" shall be substituted.

5. *Amendment of Section 20:* Section 20 of the principal Act shall be re-numbered as sub-section (2) thereof and alter sub-section (1) as so re-numbered, the following sub-section shall be inserted, namely:

"(2) The provisions of article 304 shall, with the necessary modifications, apply in relation to any law passed by the Legislative Assembly of a Union Territory with respect of any of the matters referred to in that article as they apply in relation to any law passed by the Legislature of a State with respect to those matters".

6. *Substitution of new section for Section 21:* For section 21 of the principal Act, the following section shall be substituted namely, —

"21. *Inconsistency between laws made by Parliament and laws made by Legislative Assembly:* (1) If any provision of a law made by the Legislative Assembly of a Union Territory is repugnant to any provision of a law made by Parliament, then subject to the provisions of sub-section (2), the law made by Parliament, whether passed before or after the law made by the Legislative Assembly of the Union Territory, shall prevail and the law made by the Legislative Assembly of the Union Territory shall, to the extent of the repugnancy, be void:

(2) Where a law made by the Legislative Assembly of a Union Territory with respect to any of the matters enumerated in the Concurrent List or the State List in the Seventh Schedule to the Constitution contains any provision repugnant to the provisions of an earlier law made by Parliament with respect to that matter, or where a law made by the Legislative Assembly of a Union Territory with respect to any matter enumerated in the Concurrent List aforesaid is repugnant to the provisions of any earlier law, other than a law made by Parliament, with respect to that matter, than in either case, the law so made by the Legislative Assembly of the Union Territory shall, if it has been reserved for the consideration of the President and has received his assent, prevail in that Union Territory:

Provided that nothing in this sub-section shall prevent Parliament from enacting at any time any law with respect to the same matter including a law adding to, amending, varying or replacing the law so made by the Legislative Assembly of the Union Territory".

7. *Substitution of new section for Section 25:* For section 25 of the principal Act, the following sections shall be substituted namely:

"25 *Assent to Bills:* When a Bill has been passed by the Legislative Assembly of a Union Territory, it shall be presented to the Administrator and the Administrator shall declare either that he assents to the Bill or that he withholds assent therefrom or that he reserves the Bill for the consideration of the President:

Provided that the Administrator may, as soon as possible after the presentation of the Bill to him for assent, return the Bill if it is not a Money Bill together with a message requesting that the Assembly will reconsider the Bill or any specified provisions thereof, and, in particular, will consider the desirability of introducing any such amendments as he may recommend in his message and, when a Bill accordingly, and if the Bill is passed again with or without amendment and presented to the Administrator for assent, the Administrator shall declare either that he assents to the Bill or that he reserves the Bill for the consideration of the President:

Provided further that the Administrator shall not assent to, but shall reserve for the consideration of the President, any Bill which, —

(a) in the opinion of the Administrator would, if it became law, so derogate from the powers of the High Court as to endanger the position which that Court is, by the Constitution, designed to fill; or
(b) relates to any of the matters specified in clause (1) of article 31A; or
(c) the President may, by order, direct to be reserved for his consideration; or
(d) relates to matters referred to in sub-section (5) of section 7 or section 17 or section 34 of sub-section (6) of section 45 or in entry 1 or entry 2 of the State List in the Seventh Schedule to the Constitution:

Provided also that without prejudice to the provisions of the second proviso, the Administrator shall nor assent to, but shall reserve for the consideration of the President, any Bill which has been passed by the Legislative Assembly of the Union Territory of Mizoram and which relates to any area comprised in any autonomous district in that Union Territory under the Sixth Schedule to the Constitution.

Explanation: For the purposes of this section and section 25A a Bill shall be deemed to be a Money Bill if it contains only provisions dealing with all or any of the matters specified in sub-section (1) of section 23 or any matter incidental to any of those matters and, in either case, there is endorsed thereon the certificate of the Speaker of the Legislative Assembly signed by him that it is a Money Bill.

25A. *Bills reserved for consideration:* When a Bill is reserved by an Administrator for the consideration of the President, the President shall declare either that he assents to the Bill or that he withholds assent therefrom:

Provided that where the Bill is not a Money Bill, the President may direct the Administrator to return the Bill to the Legislative Assembly together with such a message as is mentioned in the first proviso to section 25 and, when a Bill is so returned, the Assembly shall reconsider it accordingly within a period of six months from the date of receipt of such message and, if it is again passed by the Assembly with or without amendment, it shall be presented again to the President for his consideration."

8. *Amendment of Section 33:* To sub-section (2) of section 33 of the principal Act, the following proviso shall be added, namely —

"Provided that the provisions of this sub-section shall apply in relation to the Legislative Assembly of the Union Territory of Mizoram as if for the words 'the State of Uttar Pradesh', the words 'the State of Assam' had been substituted".

9. *Amendment of Section 38:* In section 38 of the Principal Act, —

(i) in clause (a) the words, figures, and latter "or with the Election Commission under section 43A" shall be added at the end;

(ii) after clause (b), the following clause shall be inserted, namely:

(b) "Election Commission" means the Election Commission appointed by the President under article 324".

10. *Insertion of new Section 43A:* After section 43 of the principal Act, the following section shall be inserted, namely:

"43A. *Special provision for delimitation of constituencies of Mizoram Legislative Assembly:* (1) The provisions of sections 39 to 43 (both inclusive) shall not apply to the delimitation of constituencies for the purpose of elections to the Legislative Assembly of the Union Territory of Mizoram.

(2) The Election Commission shall, in the manner herein provided, distribute the seats assigned to the Legislative Assembly of the Union Territory of Mizoram under sub-section 2 of section 3 to single member assembly constituencies and delimit them on the basis of the latest census figures having regard to the provisions of the Constitution and the following provisions, —

(a) all constituencies shall, as far as practicable be geographically compact areas; and

(b) in delimiting the constituencies, regard shall be had to physical features, existing boundaries of administrative units, facilities of communication and public convenience.

(3) For the purpose of assisting in the performance of its functions under sub-section (2), the Election Commission shall associate with itself as associate members, —

(a) all the persons who, having been elected to the Legislative Assembly of the State of Assam for the Lungleh, Aijal East and Aijal West territorial constituencies are members of the Assembly immediately before the day appointed under clause (b) of section 2 of the North-Eastern Areas (Reorganization) Act, 1971; and

(b) such three elected members of the District Council of the Mizo District as the Chairman thereof may nominate:

Provided that none of the associate members shall have a right to vote or sign any decision of the Election Commission.

(4) If, owing to death or resignation, the office of an associate member falls vacant, it shall be filled, if practicable, in accordance with the provisions of sub-section (3).

(5) The Election Commission shall —

(a) publish its proposals for the delimitation of constituencies, together with the dissenting proposals, if any, of any associate member who desires publication thereof in the Official Gazette and in such other manner as the Commission may consider fit, together with a notice inviting objections and suggestions in relation to the proposals and specifying a date on or after which the proposals will be further considered by it;

(b) consider all objections and suggestions which may have been received by it before the date so specified; and

(c) after consideration of objections and suggestions which may have been received by it before the date so specified, determine by one or more orders the delimitation of constituencies and cause such order or orders to be published in the Official Gazette; and upon such publication the order or orders shall have the full force of law and shall not be called in question in any court.

(6) The Election Commission may, from time to time, by notification in the Official Gazette, —

(a) correct any printing mistake in any order made under sub-section (5) or any error arising therein from in advertent slip or omission; and

(b) where the boundaries or name of any territorial division mentioned in any such order or orders are or is altered, make such amendments as appear to it to be necessary or expedient for bringing such order up-to-date.

(7) Every order made under sub-section (5) and every notification issued under sub-section (6) shall be laid as soon as may be after it is made or issued before the Legislative Assembly or the Union Territory of Mizoram.

(8) All things done, and all steps taken, before the commencement of this Act in Union Territory or Mizoram with a view to delimiting territorial constituencies of that Union. Territory for purposes of elections to the Legislative Assembly of that Union Territory shall, insofar as they are in conformity with the foregoing provisions of this section, be deemed to have been done or taken under those provisions as if those provisions were in force at the time such things were done or such steps were taken".

11. *Amendment of Section 44:* In section 44 of the principal Act, —

(a) to sub-section (1), the following further proviso shall be added, namely:

"Provided further that in the Union Territory of Mizoram every decision taken by a Minister or by the Council of Ministers in relation to any matter concerning any area comprised in any autonomous district in that Union Territory under the Sixth Schedule to the Constitution shall be subject to the concurrence of the Administrator and nothing in the sub-section shall be construed as preventing the Administrator in case of any difference of opinion between him and his Ministers from taking such action in respect of the administration of such area as he, in his discretion, considers necessary"; and

(b) after sub-section (1) as so amended the following sub-section shall be inserted, namely:

"(2) In the exercise of his functions, the Administrator of the Union Territory of Mizoram shall have special responsibility for the security of the border and for that purpose he may issue such directions and take such measures as he may think necessary".

12. *Substitution of new sections for Section 54:* For section 54 of the principal Act, the following section shall be substituted, namely:

"54. *Transitional provisions for administration of justice in certain areas in the Union Territory of Mizoram:* On and from the commencement of this Act in the Union Territory of Mizoram and until other provisions in this behalf are made by a competent Legislature or other competent authority, the administration of justice in those areas of that Union Territory which are not comprised in any autonomous district under the Sixth Schedule to the Constitution shall be carried on, so far as may be, in accordance with the provisions of paragraphs 4 and 5 of that Schedule, as if those areas were comprised in an autonomous district under that Schedule and the provisions of the said paragraphs were in force in those areas and for this purpose, —

(i) all powers and functions of a District Council under the provisions of the said paragraph 4 shall be exercised and discharged by the Administrator or any officer appointed by him in this behalf;

(ii) the said paragraph 5 shall have effect as if references to the District Council, the Regional Council and the Courts constituted by the District Council, by whatever form of words, had been omitted therefrom; and

(iii) references to governor in the said paragraphs 4 and 5 shall be construed as references to the Administrator".

13. *Amendment of Sixth Schedule to the Constitution:* On and from the day on which the Legislative Assembly of the Union Territory of Mizoram has been duly constituted under and in accordance with the provisions of the principal Act, in the Sixth Schedule to the Constitution:

(i) for paragraph 12B, the following paragraph shall be substituted, namely —

"12B. *Application of Acts of Parliament and of the Legislature of the Union Territory of Mizoram to autonomous districts and autonomous regions in the Union Territory of Mizoram:* Notwithstanding anything to this constitution, —

(a) if any provision of a law made by a District Council or a Regional Council in the Union Territory of Mizoram with respect to any matter specified in sub-paragraph (1) of paragraph 3 of this Schedule or if any provision of any regulation made by a District Council or a Regional Council in that Union Territory under paragraph 8 or paragraph 10 of this Schedule, is repugnant to any provision to a law made by the Legislature of the Union Territory of Mizoram with respect to that matter, then, the law or regulation made by the District Council or, as the case may be, the regional Council, whether made before or after the law made by the Legislature of the Union Territory of Mizoram, shall, to the extent of repugnancy, be void and the law made by the Legislature of the Union Territory of Mizoram shall prevail;

(b) the President may with respect to any Act of Parliament, by notification, direct that it shall not apply to an autonomous district or an autonomous region in the Union Territory of Mizoram, or shall apply to such district or region or any part thereof subject to such exceptions or modifications as he may specify in the notification and any such direction may be given so as to have retrospective effect";

(ii) in paragraph 20, in Part III of the table, the words, "The Mizo District" shall be omitted;

(iii) for paragraph 20A, the following paragraphs shall be substituted, namely —

"20A. *Dissolution of the Mizo District Council:* (1) Notwithstanding anything in this Schedule, the District Council of the Mizo District existing immediately before the prescribed date (hereinafter referred to as the Mizo District Council) shall stand dissolved and cease to exist.

(2) The Administrator of the Union Territory of Mizoram may, by one or more orders, provide for all or any of the following matters, namely —

(a) the transfer, in whole or in part, of the assets, rights and liabilities of the Mizo District Council (including the rights and liabilities under any contract made by it) to the Union or the any other authority;

(b) the substitution of the Union or any other authority for the Mizo District Council or the addition of the Union or any other authority as a party to any legal proceedings to which the Mizo District Council is a party;

(c) the transfer or re-employment of any employees of the Mizo District Council to or by the Union or any other authority, the terms and conditions of service applicable to such employees after such transfer or re-employment;

(d) the continuance of any laws, made by the Mizo District Council and in force immediately before its dissolution, subject to such adaptation and modifications, where by way of repeal or amendment, as the Administrator may make in this behalf, until such laws are altered, repealed or amended by a competent Legislature or other competent authority; and

(e) such incidental, consequential and supplementary matters as the Administrator considers necessary.

"*Explanation:* In this paragraph and in paragraph 20B of this Schedule, the expression "prescribed date" means the date on which the Legislative Assembly of the Union Territory of Mizoram is duly constituted under and in accordance with the provisions of the Government of Union Territories Act, 1963 (20 of 1963).

20B. *Autonomous regions in the Union Territory of Mizoram to be autonomous districts and transitory provisions consequent thereto:* (1) Notwithstanding anything in this Schedule, —

(a) every autonomous region existing immediately before the prescribed date in the Union Territory of Mizoram shall, on and from that date, be an autonomous district, to that Union Territory (hereafter referred to as the corresponding new district) and the Administrator thereof may, by one or more orders, direct that such consequential amendments as are necessary to give effect to the provisions of this clause shall be made in paragraph 20 of this Schedule (including Part III of the table appended to that paragraph) and thereupon the said paragraph and the said Part shall be deemed to have been amended accordingly; and

(b) every Regional Council of an autonomous region in the Union Territory of Mizoram existing immediately before the prescribed date, (herein after referred to as the existing Regional Council) shall, on and from that date and until a District Council is duly constituted for the corresponding new district, be deemed to be the District Council or that district (hereafter referred to as the corresponding new District Council).

(2) Every member whether elected or nominated of an existing Regional Council shall be deemed to have been elected or, as the case may be, nominated to the corresponding new District Council and shall hold office until a District Council is duly constituted for the corresponding new district under this Schedule.

(3) Until rules are made under sub-paragraph (7) of paragraph 2 and sub-paragraph (4) of paragraph 4 of this Schedule by the corresponding new District Council, the rules made under the said provisions by the existing Regional Council and in force immediately before the prescribed date shall have effect in relation to the corresponding new District Council subject to such adaptations and modifications as may be made therein by the Administrator of the Union Territory of Mizoram.

(4) The Administrator of the Union Territory of Mizoram may, by one or more orders, provide for all or any of the following matters, namely, —

(a) the transfer in the whole or in part of the assets, rights and liabilities of the existing Regional Council (including the rights and liabilities under any contract made by it) to the corresponding new District Council;

(b) the substitution of the corresponding new District Council for the existing Regional Council as a party to the legal proceedings to which the existing Regional Council is a party;

(c) the transfer or re-employment of any employees of the existing Regional Council to or by the corresponding new District Council, the terms and conditions of service applicable to such employees after such transfer or re-employment;

(d) the continuance of any laws, made by the existing Regional Council and in force immediately before the prescribed date, subject to such adaptation and modifications, where by way of repeal or amendment, as the Administrator may make in this behalf, until such laws are altered, repealed or amended by a competent Legislature or other competent authority; and

(e) such incidental, consequential and supplementary matters as the Administrator considers necessary.

20C. *Interpretation:* Subject to any provision made in this behalf, the provisions of this Schedule shall, in their application to the Union Territory of Mizoram, have effect, —

(1) as if references to the Governor and Government of the State were references to the Administrator of the Union Territory appointed under article 239, references to State (except in the expression "Government of the State") were references to the Union Territory of Mizoram and references to the State Legislature were references to the Legislative Assembly of the Union Territory of Mizoram;

(2) as if —

(a) in sub-paragraph (5) of paragraph 4, the provision for consultation with the Government of the State concerned had been omitted;

(b) in sub-paragraph (2) of paragraph 6, for the words "to which the executive power of the State extends", the words "with respect to which the Legislative Assembly of the Union Territory of Mizoram has power to make laws" had been substituted; and

(c) in paragraph 13, the words and figures "under article 202" had been omitted".

14. *Amendment of Act 43 of 1950:* On and from the day on which the Legislative Assembly of the Union Territory of Mizoram has been duly constituted and in accordance with the provisions of the principal Act, in section 27A of the Representation of the People Act, 1950, —

(i) in sub-section (4), for the words "The electoral college for the Union Territory of Pondicherry", the words "The electoral college for each of the Union Territories of Pondicherry and Mizoram" shall be substituted; and

(ii) in sub-section (5), for the words "to each of the Union Territories of Mizoram and Arunachal Pradesh" the words "to the Union Territory of Arunachal Pradesh" shall be substituted.

15. *Elections to the Legislative Assembly of Mizoram:* As soon as may be after the commencement of this Act, elections shall be held in the Union Territory of Mizoram in accordance with the provisions of the principal Act as amended by this Act for constituting a Legislative Assembly for the Union Territory and every endeavour shall be made to hold such elections within a period of four months of such commencement.

ANNEXURE XXVII

The North-Eastern Areas (Reorganization) Act, 1971

AN ACT

to provide for the establishment of the State of Manipur and Tripura and to provide for the formation of the State of Meghalaya and of the Union Territories of Mizoram and Arunachal Pradesh by reorganization of the existing State of Assam and for matters connected therewith.

Be it enacted by Parliament in the Twenty Second Year of the Republic of India as follows:

PART I

Preliminary

1. *Short title:* This Act may be called the North-Eastern Areas (Reorganization) Act, 1971.

2. *Definitions:* In this Act, unless the context otherwise requires —

(a) "Administrator" means the administrator of a Union Territory appointed by the President under article 239 of the Constitution;

(b) "appointed day" means the day which the Central Government may, by notification in the Official Gazette, appoint;

(c) "article" means an article of the Constitution;

(d) "common High Court" means the Guwahati High Court (the High Court of Assam, Nagaland, Meghalaya, Manipur and Tripura) referred to in clause (b) of sub-section (1) of section 28;

(e) "Election Commission" means the Election Commission appointed by the President under article 324;

(f) "existing State of Assam" means the State of Assam as existing immediately before the appointed day;

(g) "law" includes any enactment, ordinance, regulation, order, bye-law, rule, scheme, notification or other instrument having, immediately before the appointed day, the force of law in the whole or any part of the existing State of Assam of the autonomous State of Meghalaya or the Union Territory of Manipur or the Union Territory of Tripura, as the case may be;

(h) "sitting member", in relation to either House of Parliament or the Legislative Assembly of the existing State of Assam, means a person who, immediately before the appointed day, is a member of that House or that Assembly;

(i) "successor State", in relation to existing State of Assam, means the State of Assam or Meghalaya, and includes also the Union in relation to the Union Territory of Mizoram; and

(j) "treasury" includes a sub-treasury.

PART II

Establishment of the States of Manipur and Tripura and formation of the State of Meghalaya and of the Union Territories of Mizoram and Arunachal Pradesh.

3. *Establishment of the State of Manipur:* On and from the appointed day, there shall be established a new State, to be known as the State of Manipur, comprising the territories which immediately before that day, were comprised in the Union Territory of Manipur.

4. *Establishment of the State of Tripura:* On and from the appointed day, there shall be established a new State, to be known as the State of Tripura, comprising the territories which immediately before that day were comprised in the Union Territory of Tripura.

5. *Formation of the State of Meghalaya:* On and from the appointed day, there shall be formed a new State, to be know as the State of Meghalaya, comprising, —

(a) the territories which immediately before that day were comprised in the autonomous State of Meghalaya formed under section 3 of the Assam Reorganization (Meghalaya) Act, 1969 (55 of 1969); and

(b) so much of the territories comprised within the cantonment and municipality of Shillong as did not form part of that autonomous State, and thereupon the said territories shall cease to form part of the existing State of Assam.

6. *Formation of the Union Territory of Mizoram:* On and from the appointed day, there shall be formed a new Union Territory, to be know as the Union Territory of Mizoram, comprising the territories which immediately before that day were comprised in the Mizo District in the existing State of Assam and thereupon the said territories shall cease to form part of the existing State of Assam.

7. *Formation of the Union Territory of Arunachal Pradesh:* On and from the appointed day, there shall be formed a new Union Territory, to be known as the Union Territory of Arunachal Pradesh comprising the territories which immediately before that day were comprised in the tribal areas specified in Part B of the table appended to paragraph 20 of the Sixth Schedule to the Constitution (but excluding the areas covered by Notification No. TAD/R/35/50/109, dated the 23rd February, 1951 issued by the Governor of Assam under the proviso to sub-paragraph (3) of the said paragraph (20) and known as the North-East Frontier Agency and thereupon the said territories shall cease to form part of the existing State of Assam.

8. *Territories of the State of Assam:* On and from the appointed day, the State of Assam shall comprise the territories of the existing State of Assam other than those specified in sections 5, 6 and 7.

9. *Amendment of First Schedule to the Constitution:* On and from the appointed day, in the First Schedule to the Constitution,

(a) under the heading 'I. THE STATE':

(i) in the paragraph relating to the territories of the State of Assam, the following shall be added at the end, namely, —
"and the territories specified in sections 5, 6 and 7 of the North-Eastern Area (Reorganization) Act 1971";

(ii) after entry 18, the following entries shall be inserted, namely —

"19. Manipur:	The territory which immediately before the commencement of the Constitution was being administered as if it were a Chief Commissioner's Province under the name of Manipur.
20. Tripura:	The territory which immediately before the commencement of the

	Constitution was being administered as if it were a Chief Commissioner's Province under the name of Tripura.
21. Meghalaya:	The territories specified in section 5 of the North-Eastern Areas (Reorganization) Act, 1971".

(b) under the heading 'II. THE UNION TERRITORIES':

(i) entries 2 and 3 shall be omitted and entries 4 to 9 shall be re-numbered as entries 2 to 7, respectively;

(ii) after entry 7 as so re-numbered, the following entries shall be inserted, namely —

"8. Mizoram:	the territories specified in section 6 of the North-Eastern Areas (Reorganization) Act, 1971.
9. Arunachal Pradesh:	the territories specified in section 7 of the North-Eastern Areas (Reorganization) Act, 1971".

PART III

Representation in the Legislatures

THE COUNCIL OF STATES

10. *Amendment of Fourth Schedule to the Constitution:* On and from the appointed day, in the Fourth Schedule to the Constitution, in the Table —

(a) for entries 19 to 22, the following shall be substituted namely —

"19. Manipur	1
20. Tripura	1
21. Meghalaya	1
22. Delhi	3
23. Pondicherry	1
24. Mizoram	1
25. Arunachal Pradesh	1"

(b) for the figures "226" the figures "232" shall be substituted.

11. *Allocation of sitting members representing the existing Union Territories of Manipur and Tripura:* On and from the appointed day, the sitting members of the Council of States representing the existing Union Territories of Manipur and Tripura shall be deemed to have been duly elected under clause (4) of article 80 to fill the seat allotted to each of the States of Manipur and Tripura, respectively, in that Council and the term of office of such sitting members shall remain unaltered.

12. *Election to fill the seats allotted to the State of Meghalaya and the Union Territories of Mizoram and Arunachal Pradesh:* As soon as may be after the appointed day, steps shall be taken to fill the seats in the Council of States allotted to the State of Meghalaya and the Union Territories of Mizoram and Arunachal Pradesh.

13. *Amendment of Section 27A of Act of 1950:* On and from the appointed day, in section 27A of the Representation of the People Act, 1950, —

(a) in sub-section (1), for the words "For the purpose of filling any seat" the words, brackets and figure "Subject to the provisions of sub-section (5) for the purpose of filling any seat" shall be substituted;

(b) in sub-section (4), for the words "The electoral college for each of the Union Territories of Manipur, Tripura and Pondicherry", the words "The electoral college for the Union Territory of Pondicherry" shall be substituted;

(c) after sub-section (4), the following sub-section shall be inserted, namely:

"(5) The seat allotted in the Council of States to each of the Union Territories of Mizoram and Arunachal Pradesh shall be filled by a person nominated by the President in this behalf".

THE HOUSE OF THE PEOPLE

14. *Allocation of seats in the existing House of the People:* (1) On and from the appointed day and until the dissolution of the existing House of the People, the allocation of seats to the State of Assam, Manipur, Tripura and Meghalaya and the Union Territories of Mizoram and Arunachal Pradesh in the House of the People and the number of seats, if any, to be reserved for the Scheduled Castes and for the Scheduled Tribes of each State and Union Territory, shall be as specified in the Table below and the First Schedule to the Representation of the

People Act, 1950 (43 of 1950); shall be deemed to have been amended accordingly.

The Table

Name of the State/ Union Territory	Total	Number of seats in the existing House of the People	
		Reserved for the Scheduled Castes	Reserved for the Scheduled Tribes
I. State			
1. Assam	14	1	2
2. Manipur	2	—	1
3. Tripura	2	—	1
4. Meghalaya	2	—	2
II. Union Territories			
1. Mizoram	1	—	1
2. Arunachal Pradesh	1	—	1

(2) On and from the appointed day and until the dissolution of the existing House of the People, Part A of Schedule II to the Delimitation of Parliamentary and Assembly Constituencies Order, 1966 shall stand amended as directed in the First Schedule.

15. *Parliamentary constituencies of the States of Manipur and Tripura and provision as to sitting members:* (1) On and from the appointed day and until the dissolution of the existing House of the People, —

(a) the two Parliamentary Constituencies of the existing union territory of Manipur shall be deemed to be the two Parliamentary Constituencies of the State of Manipur; and

(b) the two Parliamentary Constituencies of the existing Union Territory of Tripura shall be deemed to be the two Parliamentary Constituencies of the State of Tripura.

and the Delimitation of Parliamentary and Assembly Constituencies Order 1966 shall be construed accordingly.

(2) Every sitting member of the House of the People representing Parliamentary Constituency which on the appointed day, by virtue of the provisions of sub-section (1), becomes a Parliamentary Constituency of the State of Manipur or Tripura, as the case may be, shall, as from that day be deemed to have been elected under sub-clause (a) of clause (1) of article 81 to the House of the People from that constituency.

16. *Provision as to sitting members representing Cachar and Dhubri Parliamentary Constituencies in the House of the People and the election* *of representative from Diphu Parliamentary Constituency:* (1) The sitting member of the House of the People representing the Cachar Parliamentary Constituency which on the appointed day, by virtue of the provision of sub-section (2) of section 14, stands altered shall, as from that day, be deemed to have been elected under sub-clause (a) of clause (1) of article 81 to the House of the People from the constituency as so altered.

(2) The sitting member of the House of the People representing the Dhubri Parliamentary Constituency which on the appointed day, by virtue of the provisions of sub-section (2) of section 14, stands altered shall, as from that day, be deemed to have been elected sub-clause (a) of clause (1) of article 81 to the House of the People from that constituency so altered.

(3) As soon as may be after the appointed day election shall be held to the House of the People to elect a representative from the Diphu Parliamentary Constituency as if the seat of the member elected to the House of the People from the constituency has become vacant and the provisions of section 149 of the Representation of People Act, 1951 (43 of 1951), shall so far as may be, apply in relation to such election.

17. *Parliamentary Constituencies of the State of Meghalaya and provision as to sitting member representing the Autonomous Districts Parliamentary Constituency in the House of the People and the election of representative from Tura Parliamentary Constituency:* (1) There shall be two Parliamentary Constituencies in the State of Meghalaya to be called the Shillong Parliamentary Constituency and the Tura Parliamentary Constituency.

(2) The area falling within the Garo Hills District as it exists immediately before the appointed day shall form the Tura Parliamentary Constituency and the remaining area in the State of Meghalaya shall form the Shillong Parliamentary Constituency and the said two Parliamentary Constituencies shall be deemed to have been delimited accordingly.

(3) The sitting member of the House of the People representing immediately before the appointed day the Autonomous District Parliamentary Constituency shall be as from that day, be deemed to have been elected under sub-clause (a) of clause (1) of article 81 to the House of the People from the Shillong Parliamentary Constituency.

(4) As soon as may be after the appointed day election shall be held to the House of the People to elect a representative from the Tura Parliamentary Constituency as if the seat of the member elected to the House of the People from that constituency has become vacant and the

provisions of section 149 of the Representation of People Act, 1951 (43 of 1951) shall, so far as may be, apply in relation to such election.

18. *Parliamentary Constituency of the Union Territory of Mizoram:* The whole of the Union Territory of Mizoram shall form one parliamentary constituency to be called the Mizoram Parliamentary Constituency and as soon as may be after the appointed day election shall be held to the House of the People to elect a representative from that constituency, as if the seat of the member elected to the House of the People from that constituency has become vacant and the provisions of section 149 of the Representation of the People Act, 1951 (43 of 1951) shall, so far as may be, apply in relation to such election.

19. *Provision as to the member to represent Arunachal Pradesh in the House of the People:* The sitting member nominated to fill the seat allotted in the House of the People to the Tribal Areas of Assam specified in Part B of the Table appended to paragraph 20 of the Sixth Schedule to the Constitution, known as the North-East Frontier Agency, shall on and from the appointed day, be deemed to have been nominated to fill the seat allotted to the Union Territory to Arunachal Pradesh in the House of the People.

THE LEGISLATIVE ASSEMBLIES

20. *Allocation of seats in the Legislative Assemblies:* (1) On and from the appointed day, the total number of seats in the Legislative Assembly of the State of Assam, to be filled by persons chosen by direct election from territorial constituencies, shall be reduced from one hundred and twenty-six to one hundred and fourteen; and every sitting member of Legislative Assembly representing a constituency which ceases to be a constituency in the State of Assam by virtue of the provisions of sub-section (3) as from the appointed day, cease to be a member of that Legislative Assembly.

(2) The total number of seats in the Legislative Assembly of the State of Manipur, to be constituted at any time after the appointed day, to be filled by persons chosen by direct election from territorial constituencies shall be sixty, out of which one seat shall be reserved for the Scheduled Castes and nineteen seats shall be reserved for the Scheduled Tribes.

(3) The total number of seats in the Legislative Assembly of the State of Tripura, to be constituted at any time after the appointed day, to be filled by persons chosen by direct election from territorial constituencies shall be sixty, out of which six seats shall be reserved for

the Scheduled Castes and nineteen seats shall be reserved for the Scheduled Tribes.

(4) The total number of seats in the Legislative Assembly of the State of Meghalaya, to be constituted at any time after the appointed day, to be filled by persons chosen by direct election from territorial constituencies shall be sixty, out of which fifty seats shall be reserved for the Scheduled Tribes.

(5) On and from the appointed day, Part B of Scheduled II to the Delimitation of Parliamentary and Assembly Constituencies Order, 1966 shall stand amended as directed in the First Schedule.

21. *Amendment of Second Schedule to Act 43 of 1950:* (1) In the Second Schedule to the Representation of the People Act, 1950 —

(i) under the heading 'I. STATES' —

(a) in item 2 relating to Assam, for the figures "126", the figures "114" shall be substituted;

(b) after item 17 and the entries relating thereto the following shall be inserted, namely:

"18. Manipur	...	60	1	19
19. Tripura	...	60	6	19
20. Meghalaya	...	60	—	50";

(ii) Under the heading 'II. UNION TERRITORIES' items 3 and 5 and the entries relating thereto shall be omitted.

(2) The amendment made by clause (i) (a) of sub-section (1) shall have effect on and after the appointed day in relation to the Legislative Assembly of State of Assam and amendments made by clause (i) (b) and clause (ii) of sub-section (1) shall have effect in relation to the Legislative Assemblies of the State of Manipur, Tripura and Meghalaya to be constituted at any time after the appointed day.

22. *Delimitation of constituencies:* (1) The Election Commission shall, in the manner herein provided, distribute, whether before or after the appointed day, the seats assigned to the Legislative Assemblies of the State of Manipur, Tripura and Meghalaya under section 20 to single member territorial constituencies and delimit them on the basis of the latest census figures having regard to the provisions of the constitution and to the following provisions:

(a) all constituencies shall, so far as practicable be geographically compact areas and in delimiting them, regard shall be had to physical features, existing boundaries of administrative units, facilities of communication and public convenience;

(b) every Assembly constituency shall be so delimited as to fall only within one Parliamentary constituency;

(c) constituencies in which seats are reserved for the Scheduled Castes shall be distributed in different parts of the States and located, as far as practicable, in those areas where the proportion of their population to the total population is comparatively large; and

(d) constituencies in which seats are reserved for the Scheduled Tribes shall, as far as practicable, be located in those areas where the proportion of their population to the total population is the largest.

Explanation: In this section "latest census figures" mean the census figures with respect to the State concerned ascertainable from the the latest census of which the finally published figures are available.

(2) For the purpose of assisting in the performance of its functions under sub-section (1), the Election Commission shall associate with itself as associate members:

(a) in respect of the State of Manipur, all the sitting members of the House of the People representing the Union Territory of Manipur, or, as the case may be the State of Manipur under sub-section (2) of section 15, and such six persons who were members of the Legislative Assembly of the Union Territory of Manipur immediately before its dissolution by order of the President published in the Gazette of India, dated 16th October, 1969 with notification No. S.O. 4223, dated 16th October, 1969 of the Government of India in the Ministry of Home Affairs, as the President may, by order nominate;

(b) in respect of the State of Tripura, all the sitting members of the House of the People representing the Union Territory of Tripura or, as the case may be, the State of Tripura under sub-section (2) of section 15, and such six persons, being members of the Legislative Assembly of the Union Territory of Tripura as it functioned immediately before the 1st November, 1971, as the President may, by order, nominate;

(c) in respect of the State of Meghalaya, the member of the House of the People representing the Autonomous District Parliamentary constituency or, as the case may be, the Meghalaya Parliamentary constituency under section 17, and such of the six members of the Legislative Assembly of the Autonomous State of Meghalaya constituted under section 62 of the Assam Reorganization (Meghalaya) Act, 1969 (55 of 1969) or, as the case may be, of the Provisional Legislative Assembly of the State of Meghalaya referred to in section 27, as the President may, by order, nominate:

Provided that none of the associate members shall have a right to vote or to sign any decision of the Election Commission.

(3) If owing to death or resignation, the office of an associate member falls vacant, it shall be filled, if practicable, in accordance with the provisions of sub-section (2).

(4) A member of any Legislative Assembly nominated under clause (b) or clause (c) shall continue to be an associate member notwithstanding that he ceases to be a member of such Legislative Assembly, otherwise than consequent on the incurring of any disqualification.

(5) The Election Commission shall —

(a) publish its proposals for the delimitation of constituencies, together with the dissenting proposals, if any, of any associate member who desires publication thereof, in the Official Gazette and in such other manner as the Commission may consider fit, together with a notice inviting objections and suggestions in relation to the proposals and specifying a date on or after which the proposals will be further considered by it;

(b) consider all objections and suggestions which may have been received by it before the date so specified;

(c) after considering all objections and suggestions which may have been received by it before the date so specified, determine by one or more orders the delimitation of constituencies and cause such order or orders to be published in the Official Gazette; and upon such publication, the order shall have the full force of law and shall not be called in question in any court.

(6) As soon as may be after such publication, every such order shall be laid before the Legislative Assembly of the concerned State.

23. *Power of Election Commission to maintain delimitation orders up-to-date:* (1) The Election Commission may, from time-to-time, by notification in the Official Gazette —

(a) correct any printing mistake in any order made under section 22 or any error arising therein from inadvertent slip or omission; and

(b) where the boundaries or name of any territorial division mentioned in any such order or orders are or is altered, make such amendment as appear to it to be necessary or expedient for bringing such order up-to-date.

(2) Every notification under this section shall be laid, as soon as may be after it is issued, before the Legislative Assembly of the concerned State.

24. *Validation of acts done previous to the commencement of the Act:* All things done, and all steps taken, before the commencement of the Act with a view to delimiting the territorial constituencies of the State of Manipur, Tripura and Meghalaya for the purpose of elections of the Legislative Assemblies of those States shall, in so far as they are in conformity with the provisions of sectións 22 and 23, be deemed to have been done or taken under those sections as if those sections were in force at the time such things were done or such steps were taken.

25. *Amendment of Scheduled Castes Orders:* (1) On and from the appointed day, the Constitution (Scheduled Castes) Order, 1950 shall stand amended as directed in the Second Schedule.

(2) On and from the appointed day, the Constitution (Scheduled Castes) (Union Territories) Order, 1951 shall stand amended as directed in the Third Schedule.

26. *Amendment of Scheduled Tribes Orders:* (1) On and from the appointed day, the Constitution (Scheduled Tribes) Order, 1950 shall stand amended as directed in the Fourth Schedule.

(2) On and from the appointed day, the Constitution (Scheduled Tribes) (Union Territories) Order, 1951 shall stand amended as directed in the Fifth Schedule 27.

27. *Provisions as to provisional Legislative Assembly of the State of Meghalaya and as to Rules of Procedure and Conduct of Business of the Legislative Assemblies of the State of Meghalaya, Manipur and Tripura:* (1) On and from the appointed day and until the Legislative Assembly of the State of Meghalaya has been duly constituted and summoned to meet for the first session under the provisions of the Constitution, the Provisional Legislative Assembly of the Autonomous

State of Meghalaya, excluding the members nominated thereto, constituted under section 62 of the Assam Reorganization (Meghalaya) Act, 1969 (55 of 1969), and functioning immediately before the appointed day, shall be the Provisional Legislative Assembly of the State of Meghalaya and that Assembly shall exercise all the powers and perform all the duties conferred by the provisions of the Constitution on the Legislative Assembly of that State:

Provided that for the purposes of this sub-section, the member representing the autonomous District of United Khasi-Jaintia Hills in the said Provisional Legislative Assembly of the autonomous State of Meghalaya shall be deemed also to represent the territories specified in clause (b) of section 5.

(2) The term of office of the members of the Provisional Legislative Assembly of the State of Meghalaya shall, unless the said Legislative Assembly is sooner dissolved, expire immediately before the first meeting of the Legislative Assembly of the State of Meghalaya.

(3) The persons who, immediately before the appointed day, are the Speaker and the Deputy Speaker of the Provisional Legislative Assembly of the autonomous State of Meghalaya shall be the Speaker and the Deputy Speaker respectively of the Provisional Legislative Assembly of the State of Meghalaya.

(4) The Rules of Procedure and Conduct of Business of the Provisional Legislative Assembly of the autonomous State of Meghalaya, as in force immediately before the appointed day, shall, until rules are made under clause (1) of article 208, be the Rules of Procedure and Conduct of Business of the Provisional Legislative Assembly of the State of Meghalaya, and of the Legislative Assembly of the State of Meghalaya duly constituted under the provisions of the Constitution, subject to such adaptations as may be made therein by the Speaker of the Legislative Assembly, concerned.

(5) The Rules of Procedure and Conduct of Business of the Legislative Assembly of the Union Territory of Manipur, as in force immediately before its dissolution by order of the President published in the Gazette of India, dated the 16th October, 1969 with notification No. S.O. 4223, dated the 16th October, 1969 of the Government of India in the Ministry of Home Affairs, shall until rules are made under clause (1) of article 208, be the Rules of Procedure and Conduct of Business of the Legislative Assembly of the State of Manipur, subject to such modifications and adaptations as may be made therein by the Governor of that State.

(6) The Rules of Procedure and Conduct of Business of the Legislative Assembly of the Union Territory of Tripura as in force immediately before the 1st November, 1971, shall, until rules are made under clause (1) of article 208, be the Rules of Procedure and Conduct of Business of the Legislative Assembly of the State of Tripura subject to such modifications and adaptations as may be made therein by the Governor of that State.

PART IV

High Court

28. *Common High Court for Assam, Nagaland, Meghalaya, Manipur and Tripura:* (1) On and from the appointed day, —

(a) the High Court of Assam and Nagaland shall cease to function and is hereby abolished;

(b) there shall be a common High Court for the States of Assam, Nagaland, Meghalaya, Manipur and Tripura to be called the Guwahati High Court (the High Court of Assam, Nagaland, Meghalaya, Manipur and Tripura); and

(c) the Judges of the High Court of Assam and Nagaland holding office immediately before that day shall, unless they have elected otherwise, become on that day the Judges of the common High Court.

(2) Nothing in clause (a) of sub-section (1) shall prejudice or affect the continued operation of any notice served, injunction issued, direction given or proceedings taken before the appointed day by the High Court of Assam and Nagaland under the powers then conferred upon that Court.

29. *Jurisdiction of the common High Court:* On and from the appointed day, the common High Court shall have, in respect of the territories comprised in the States of Assam, Manipur, Meghalaya, Nagaland and Tripura, ail such jurisdiction, powers and authority as under the law in force immediately before the appointed day, are exercisable in respect o those territories by the High Court of Assam and Nagaland or the Court of the Judicial Commissioner for Manipur, or the Court of the Judicial Commissioner for Tripura, as the case may be.

30. *Abolition of certain Courts:* (1) On and from the appointed day, the Courts of Judicial Commissioners for Manipur and Tripura shall cease to function and are hereby abolished.

(2) Nothing in sub-section (1) shall prejudice or affect the continued operation by any notice served injunction issued, direction given or proceedings taken before the appointed day by any of the Courts abolished by that sub-section, under the powers then conferred upon that court.

31. *Principal seat and other places of sitting of the common High Court:* (1) The Principal seat of the common High Court shall be at the same place at which the principal seat of the High Court of Assam and Nagaland is located immediately before the appointed day.

(2) The President may by notified order provide for the establishment of a permanent bench or benches of the common High Court at one or more places within the territories to which the jurisdiction of the High Court extends, other than the principal seat of the High Court, and for any matter connected therewith:

Provided that before issuing any order under this sub-section, the President shall consult the Chief Justice of the common High Court and the Governor of the State in which the bench or benches is or are proposed to be established.

(3) Notwithstanding anything contained in sub-section (1) or sub-section (2), the Judges and division courts of the common High Court may also sit at such other place or places in the States of Assam, Manipur, Meghalaya, Nagaland or Tripura as the Chief Justice may, with the approval of the Governor of the State concerned, appoint.

32. *Extension of jurisdiction of the common High Court to the Union territories of Mizoram and Arunachal Pradesh:* On and from the appointed day, the jurisdiction of the common High Court shall extend to the Union territories of Mizoram and Arunachal Pradesh.

33. *Allocation of expenditure of the common High Court:* The expenditure in respect of salaries and allowances of the Judges of the common High Court shall be allocated amongst the States of Assam, Manipur, Meghalaya, Nagaland and Tripura and the Union in such proportion as the President may, by order, determine.

34. *Special provisions relating to advocates and Bar Council:* (1) Subject to any rule made or direction given by the common High Court in this behalf, any person, who immediately before the appointed day, is an advocate entitled to practise in the High Court of Assam and Nagaland or in the Court of the Judicial Commissioner for Manipur or in the Court of the Judicial Commissioner for Tripura, shall be entitled to practise as an advocate in the common High Court.

(2) The right of audience in the common High Court shall be regulated in accordance with the like principles as, immediately before

the appointed day, are in force with respect to the right of audience in the High Court of Assam and Nagaland:

Provided that as among the Advocates-General of the States of Assam, Manipur, Meghalaya, Nagaland and Tripura, the right of audience shall be determined with reference to their dates of enrolment as advocates.

(3) On and from the appointed day, in the Advocates Act 1961 (25 of 1961) (hereafter in this Part referred to as the Advocates Act), in section 3:

(a) in sub-section (1), —

(i) for clause (b), the following snail be substituted, namely:

"(b) for the States of Assam, Manipur, Meghalaya, Nagaland and Tripura and the Union territories of Mizoram and Arunachal Pradesh, to be known as the Bar Council of Assam, Nagaland, Meghalaya, Manipur and Tripura";

(ii) in clause (e) for the words "Union Territories of Tripura and the Andaman & Nicobar Islands", the words "Union Territory of the Andaman & Nicobar Islands" shall be substituted;

(b) in sub-section (2), in clause (b), for the words "Bar Council of Assam", the words "Bar Councils of Assam, Nagaland, Meghalaya, Manipur and Tripura" shall be substituted.

(4) The provisions of section 17 of the Advocates Act shall have effect in respect of the roll of the Bar Councils of Assam, Nagaland, Meghalaya, Manipur and Tripura subject to the Modifications that, —

(a) for clause (a) of sub-section (1) of the said section 17, the following clause shall be substituted, namely:

"(a) all persons who were entered as advocates, —

(i) on the roll of the Bar Councils of Assam and Nagaland immediately before the day appointed under clause (b) of section 2 of the North-Eastern Areas (Reorganization) Act, 1971;

(ii) on the roll of the Bar Council of West Bengal immediately before that day and who, within three months from that day, express in such manner as the Bar Council of India may, by rules, prescribe their intention in writing to practise, within the jurisdiction of the Bar Council of Assam, Nagaland, Meghalaya, Manipur and Tripura";

(b) in clause (a) of sub-section (3) of the said section 17, for the words and figures "with his date of enrolment under the Indian Bar Councils Act, 1926 (38 of 1926)" the words "with his seniority on the roll of the Bar Council of Assam and Nagaland or, as the case may be, the Bar Council of West Bengal" shall be substituted.

(5) Notwithstanding anything contained in the Advocates Act, as amended or modified by sub-sections (3) and (4); —

(a) in the case of the first Bar Councils of Assam, Nagaland, Meghalaya, Manipur and Tripura under that Act, the fifteen members required to be elected under clause (b) of sub-section (2) of section 3 of that Act, shall be nominated by the Chief Justice of the common High Court from amongst the advocates who are entitled as of right to practise in that High Court and are ordinarily practising within the territories comprised in the States of Assam, Manipur, Meghalaya, Nagaland and Tripura and the Union Territories of Mizoram and Arunachal Pradesh and the term of office of the members so nominated shall be one year from the date of the first meeting of the Council or until their successors are duly elected in accordance with the provisions of the said Act, whichever is earlier;

(b) the names of persons entered on the roll of the Bar Councils of Assam, Nagaland, Meghalaya, Manipur and Tripura from the roll of the Bar Council of West Bengal in accordance with the provisions of clause (a) of sub-section (1) of section 17 of the Advocates Act, as modified by sub-section (4), shall, as from the date or dates on which the names are so entered, stand removed from the roll of the Bar Council of West Bengal;

(c) any proceedings which were pending or which may be instituted against any person before or by the Bar Council of Assam and Nagaland or by the Bar Council of West Bengal immediately before his name is entered in the roll of the Bar Councils of Assam, Nagaland, Meghalaya, Manipur and Tripura in accordance with the provisions of clause (a) of sub-section (1) of section 17 of the Advocates Act, as modified by sub-section (4), may after such entry, be continued or instituted before or by the Bar Councils of Assam, Nagaland, Meghalaya, Manipur and Tripura;

(d) every person who, immediately before his name stands removed from the roll of the Bar Council of West Bengal in accordance with the provisions of clause (b), is a member of the Bar Council of West Bengal, shall cease to be a member of that council as from the date on which his name stands so removed from the roll of that Bar Council; and

(e) the rules made or deemed to have been made by the Bar Councils of Assam and Nagaland and in force immediately before the date on which the first Bar Councils of Assam, Nagaland, Meghalaya, Manipur and Tripura is duly constituted in accordance with the provisions of clause (a), shall, subject to such modifications and adaptations as may be made therein by the Chairman of the Bar Councils of Assam, Nagaland, Meghalaya, Manipur and Tripura, be deemed to be the rules made by that Bar Council and shall have effect accordingly.

(6) (a) As from the appointed day, the assets and liabilities of the Bar Councils of Assam and Nagaland shall pass to the Bar Councils of Assam, Nagaland, Meghalaya, Manipur and Tripura.

(b) The assets and liabilities of the Bar Council of West Bengal shall be apportioned between that Bar Council and the Bar Councils of Assam, Nagaland, Meghalaya, Manipur and Tripura in such manner and proportion as may be agreed upon by the Bar Councils and in default of agreement with reference to any matter, the matter shall be referred to the Chairman of the Bar Council of India and his decision thereon shall be final.

Explanation: Expressions used in this section, but not defined in this Act, shall have the meanings assigned to them respectively in the Advocates Act.

35. *Practice and procedure in the common High Court:* Subject to the provisions of this Part, the law in force immediately before the appointed day with respect to practice and procedure in the High Court of Assam and Nagaland shall, with the necessary modifications apply in relation to the common High Court.

36. *Custody of seal of the common High Court:* The law in force immediately before the appointed day with respect to the custody of the seal of the High Court of Assam and Nagaland shall, with the necessary modifications, apply with respect to the custody of the seal of the common High Court.

37. *Form of writs and other processes:* The law in force immediately before the appointed day with respect to the form of writs and other processes used, issued or awarded by the High Court of Assam and Nagaland shall, with the necessary modifications, apply with respect to the form of writs and other processes used, or awarded by the common High Court.

38. *Power of Judges:* The law in force immediately before the appointed day with respect to the powers of the Chief Justice single Judges and division courts of the High Court of Assam and Nagaland and with respect to all matters ancillary to the exercise of those powers shall, with the necessary modifications, apply in relation to the common High Court.

39. *Procedure as to appeals to Supreme Court:* The law in force immediately before the appointed day relating to appeals to the Supreme Court from the High Court of Assam and Nagaland and the Judges and division courts thereof shall, with the necessary modifications, supply in relation to the common High Court.

40. *Transfer of proceedings from the High Court of Assam and Nagaland and the Courts of the Judicial Commissioners to the common High Court:* (1) All proceedings pending in the High Court of Assam and Nagaland and in the Courts of the Judicial Commissioners for Manipur and Tripura immediately before the appointed day shall, from such day, stand transferred to the common High Court.

(2) Every proceeding transferred under sub-section (1) shall be disposed of by the common High Court as if such proceeding was entertained by that High Court.

(3) Any order made before the appointed day by the High Court of Assam and Nagaland or by the court of the Judicial Commissioner for Manipur or by the Court of the Judicial Commissioner for Tripura shall, for all purposes, have effect not only as an order of that High Court or,

as the case may be, of that Court but also as an order of the common High Court.

41. *Interpretation:* For the purposes of section 40:

(a) proceedings shall be deemed to be pending in a court until that court has disposed of all issues between the, parties, including any issues with respect to the taxation of the costs of proceedings and shall include appeals, applications for leave to appeal to the Supreme Court, applications for review, petitions for revision and petitions for writs; and

(b) references to a High Court shall be construed as including references to a Judge or division court thereof, and references to an order made by a court or a Judge shall be construed as including references to a sentence, judgement or decree passed or made by that court or Judge.

42. *Right to appear or act in proceedings transferred to the common High Court:* Any person who, immediately before the appointed day, is an advocate entitled to practise in the High Court of Assam and Nagaland or in the Court of the Judicial Commissioner for Manipur or in the Court of the Judicial Commissioner for Tripura and was authorized to appear or to act in any proceedings transferred from the said High Court or Courts of the Judicial Commissioners to the common High Court under section 40, shall have the right to appear or to act, as the case may be, in the common High Court in relation to those proceedings.

43. *Savings:* Nothing in this Part shall effect the application to the common High Court of any provision of the Constitution, and this Part shall have effect subject to any provision that may be made on after the appointed day with respect to that High Court by any Legislature or other authority having power to make such provisions.

PART V

Authorization of Expenditure and Distribution of Revenues

44. *Authorization of expenditure pending sanction by Legislatures:* (1) The President may, at any time before the appointed day authorize by order of such expenditure from the Consolidated Fund of the State of Manipur or of the State of Tripura as he deems necessary for a period of not more than six months beginning with the appointed day pending the sanction of such expenditure by the Legislative Assembly of the State of Manipur or the State of Tripura, as the case may be:

Provided that the Governor of Manipur or of Tripura may, after the appointed day, authorise by order such further expenditure as he deems necessary from the Consolidated Fund of the State of Manipur or, as the case may be, of the State of Tripura for any period not extending beyond the said period of six months.

(2) The President, or as the case may be, the Governor of the concerned State shall make separate orders under sub-section (1) in respect of periods falling in different financial years.

(3) The Governor of Assam, exercising the functions as Governor in relation to the autonomous State of Meghalaya by virtue of the Assam Reorganization (Meghalaya) Act, 1969, (55 of 1969) may at any time, before the appointed day, authorise by order such expenditure from the Consolidated Fund of the State of Meghalaya as he deems necessary for a period of not more than six months beginning with the appointed day pending the sanction of such expenditures by the Legislative Assembly of Meghalaya:

Provided that the Governor of Meghalaya may, after the appointed day, authorise such further expenditure as he deems necessary from the Consolidated Fund of the State of Meghalaya for any period not extending beyond the said period of six months.

(4) The Governors referred to in sub-section (3) shall make separate orders under that sub-section in respect of periods falling in different financial years.

(5) The President may, at any time, before of after the appointed day authorise by order such expenditure from the Consolidated Fund of India as he deems necessary for a period of not more than six months beginning with the appointed day for the administration of the affairs of the Union Territory of Mizoram pending the sanction of such expenditure by Parliament.

(6) The President shall make separate orders under sub-section (5) in respect of periods falling in different financial years.

45. *Appropriation of moneys for expenditure to the Union Territory of Arunachal Pradesh:* Any Act passed by Parliament for the appropriation of any money out of the Consolidated Fund of India to meet the expenditure in respect of any part of the financial year 1971-72 in, or for the purposes of the tribal areas of Assam specified in Part B of the Table appended to paragraph 20 of the Sixth Schedule to the Constitution shall, on and from the appointed day, have effect also in relation to the Union Territory of Arunachal Pradesh and it shall be lawful for the President to spend any amount in, or for the purposes of, that Union Territory out of the amounts authorized by such Act to be expended in, or for the purposes of, the said tribal areas.

46. *Reports relating to the accounts of the Union Territories of Manipur and Tripura:* (1) The reports of the Comptroller and Auditor-General of India referred to in section 49 of the Government of Union Territories Act, 1965 (20 of 1965) relating to the accounts of the Union Territory of Manipur or of the Union Territory of Tripura in respect of any period prior to the appointed day shall be submitted to the Governor of Manipur or of Tripura, as the case may be, who shall cause them to be laid before the Legislative Assembly of the State of Manipur or of the State of Tripura, as the case may be.

(2) The Governor of Manipur or of Tripura, as the case may be, may, by order, —

(a) declare any expenditure incurred out of the Consolidated Fund of the Union Territory of Manipur or of Tripura on any service in respect of any period prior to the appointed day during the financial year 1971-72, or in respect of any earlier financial year in excess of the amount granted for that service and for that year as disclosed in the reports referred to in sub-section (1) to have been duly authorized; and

(b) provide for any action to be taken on any matter arising out of the said reports.

47. *Reports relating to the accounts of the autonomous State of Meghalaya:* (1) The reports of the Comptroller and Auditor-General of India relating to the accounts of the autonomous State of Meghalaya in respect of any period prior to the appointed day shall be submitted to the Governor of Meghalaya who shall cause them to be laid before the Legislative Assembly of the State of Meghalaya.

(2) The Governor of Meghalaya may, by order, —

(a) declare any expenditure incurred out of the Consolidated Fund of the autonomous State of Meghalaya on any service in respect of any period prior to the appointed day during the financial year 1971-72 or in respect of any earlier financial year in excess of the amount granted for that service and for that year as disclosed in the reports referred to in sub-section (1) to have been duly authorized; and

(b) provide for any action to be taken on any matter arising out of the said reports.

48. *Allowances and privileges of the Governors of Assam, Manipur, Meghalaya and Tripura:* The allowances and privileges of the Governors of Assam, Manipur, Meghalaya and Tripura shall, until provision in that behalf is made by Parliament by law under clause (3) of article 158, be such as the President may, by order, determine.

49. *Distribution of revenues:* The President shall, by order, determine the grants-in-aid of the revenue of the States of Assam, Manipur, Meghalaya, and Tripura and the share of each such State in the Union duties of excise, estate duty and taxes on income and for that purpose amend thereby the relevant provisions of the Union Duties of Excise (Distribution) Act, 1962 (3 of 1962), the Additional Duties of Excise (Goods of Special Importance) Act, 1957 (58 of 1957), the Estate Duty (Distribution) Act, 1962 (9 of 1962) and the Constitution (Distribution of Revenues) Order, 1969 (G.O. 87) in such manner as he thinks fit.

PART VI

Assets and Liabilities

50. *Property, assets, rights, liabilities, obligations, etc. of the States of Manipur and Tripura:* (1) All such property and assets within the Union Territory of Manipur or of Tripura as are held immediately before the appointed day by the Union for purposes of governance of that Union Territory shall, on and from that day, pass to the State of Manipur or of Tripura, as the case may be, unless the purposes for which such property and assets are so held are Union purposes:

Provided that the cash balance in the treasuries in the Union Territory of Manipur or of Tripura before the appointed day shall, as from that day, vest in the State of Manipur or of Tripura, as the case may be.

(2) All rights, liabilities and obligations (other than those relatable to, or in connection with, a Union purpose), whether arising out of any contract or otherwise, which are, immediately before the appointed day, —

(a) the rights, liabilities and obligations of the Central Government arising out of, or in connection with, the governance of the Union Territory of Manipur or of Tripura; or

(b) the rights, liabilities and obligations of the Administrator of the Union Territory of Manipur or of Tripura in his capacity as such or of the Government of the Union Territory of Manipur or of Tripura, shall, on and from the appointed day, be the rights, liabilities and obligations of the Government of the State of Manipur or of Tripura, as the case may be.

(3) The right to recover arrears of —

(a) any tax or duty being a tax or duty enumerated in the State List in the Seventh Schedule to the Constitution; or

(b) any duty referred to in article 268; or

(c) any tax under the Central Sales Tax Act, 1956 (74 of 1956) which having fallen due in Union Territory of Manipur or of Tripura immediately before the appointed day shall, on and from that day, pass to the State of Manipur or of Tripura, as the case may be.

(4) The provisions of this section shall not apply to or in relation to, —

(a) any institution, undertaking or project the expenditure in relation to which is, immediately before the appointed day, met from and out of the Consolidated Fund of India; and

(b) any property which has been placed by the Union at the disposal of the administration of the Union Territory of Manipur or of Tripura subject to the condition that the ownership thereof will continue to vest in the Union.

Explanation: For the purposes of this section, —

(a) "liability" includes liability in respect of any civil deposit, local fund deposit, charitable or other endowment, provident fund account, pension or actionable wrong; and

(b) "Union purposes" means the purposes of Government relatable to any of the matters mentioned in the Union List in the Seventh Schedule to the Constitution.

51. *Assets and liabilities of the State of Meghalaya:* (1) All rights, liabilities and obligations whether arising out of any contract or otherwise, which are, immediately before the appointed day, the rights, liabilities and obligations of the autonomous State of Meghalaya, including the rights, liabilities and obligations apportioned or to be apportioned to the share of the autonomous State of Meghalaya by virtue of section 58, of the Assam Reorganization (Meghalaya) Act, 1969 (55 of 1969) shall, on and from the appointed day, be the rights, liabilities and obligations of the State of Meghalaya.

(2) All property and assets held by the autonomous State of Meghalaya immediately before the appointed day, including the property and assets apportioned or to be apportioned to the share of the autonomous State of Meghalaya by virtue of section 53 of the Assam Reorganization (Meghalaya by virtue of Section 53 of the Assam Reorganization (Meghalaya) Act, 1969 (55 of 1969), shall, on and from that day, pass to the State of Meghalaya.

(3) Subject to the provisions of sub-sections (1) and (2) of this section and section 52, all rights, liabilities and obligations whether arising out of any contract or otherwise, which are, immediately before the appointed day, the rights, liabilities and obligations of the existing State of Assam and all property and assets held by the existing State of Assam immediately before the appointed day shall be apportioned between the State of Assam and the State of Meghalaya in accordance with the provisions contained in the Sixth Schedule.

52. *Assets and liabilities (including public debt) relating to the Mizo District:* (1) All property and assets within the Mizo District which are, immediately before the appointed day, vested in the existing State of Assam shall, as from that day, rest in the Union.

(2) Unless the Central Government otherwise direct any stores articles and other goods belonging to the existing State of Assam and situated outside the Mizo District immediately before the appointed day shall, as from that day, pass to the Union if such stores, articles or other goods are held for, or are relatable to, the administration of that District.

(3) All rights, liabilities and obligations of the existing State of Assam in relation to the Mizo District shall, as from the appointed day, be the rights, liabilities and obligations of the Union.

(4) The liability of the existing State of Assam to the Union in respect of the loans taken by that State from the Central Government shall be reduced by an amount which bears such proportion to the total public debt of that State immediately before the appointed day as the total expenditure on all capital works and other capital outlays incurred or deemed to have been incurred up to that day by the existing State of Assam in the Mizo District bears to the total expenditure on all capital works and other capital outlays incurred or deemed to have been incurred by the existing State of Assam up to the appointed day:

Provided that for the purposes of this sub-section the total public debt of the existing State of Assam shall exclude the public debt apportioned or apportionable to the autonomous State of Meghalaya under section 58 of the Assam Reorganization (Meghalaya) Act, 1969 (55 of 1969) and the total expenditure on all capital works and other capital outlays incurred or deemed to have been incurred by the existing State of Assam shall exclude such outlays incurred or deemed to have been incurred for the purposes of the autonomous State under the said section.

(5) Nothing in this section shall apply to any amount which may be payable by the Union to the existing State of Assam in respect of the expenditure incurred by the State in connection with internal disturbances in the Mizo District.

PART VII

Provisions as to certain Corporations

53. *Provisions as to certain Corporations:* (1) The following bodies corporate constituted for the existing State of Assam, namely —

(a) the State Electricity Board constituted under the Electricity (Supply) Act, 1948, (54 of 1948); and

(b) the State Warehousing Corporation established under the Warehousing Corporations Act, 1962, (58 of 1962),

shall, on and from the appointed day, continue to function in those areas in respect of which they were functioning immediately before that day, subject to the provisions of this section and to such direction as may, from time to time, be issued by the Central Government.

(2) Any directions issued by the Central Government under sub-section (1) in respect of the Board or the Corporation may include a direction that the Act under which the Board or the Corporation was constituted shall, in its application to that Board or Corporation, have effect subject to such exceptions and modifications as the Central Government thinks fit.

(3) The Board or the Corporation referred to in sub-section (1) shall cease to function as from, and shall be deemed to be dissolved on, the expiry of a period of two years from the appointed day or such earlier date as the Central Government may, by order, appoint; and upon such dissolution, its assets, rights and liabilities shall be apportioned between the successor States in such manner as may be agreed upon

among them within one year of the dissolution of the Board or the Corporation, as the case may be, or if no agreement is reached, in such manner as the Central Government may, by order, determine.

(4) Nothing in the preceding provisions of this section shall be construed as preventing the Government of any of the successor States from constituting at any time on or after the appointed day, a State Electricity Board or a State Warehousing Corporation for that State under the provisions of the Act relating to such Board or Corporation; and if such a board or a Corporation is so constituted in any of the successor States before the dissolution of the Board or the Corporation referred to in sub-section (1), —

(a) provision may be made by order of the Central Government enabling the new Board or the new Corporation to take over from the existing Board or Corporation all or any of its undertakings, assets, rights and liabilities in that State; and

(b) upon the dissolution of the existing Board or Corporation,

(i) any assets, rights and liabilities which would otherwise have passed to that State by or under the provisions of sub-section (3) shall pass to the new Board or the Corporation instead of to that State;

(ii) any employees who would otherwise have been transferred to or re-employed by that State under sub-section (3), read with clause (i) of sub-section (5), shall be transferred to or re-employed by the new Board or the Corporation instead of to or by that State.

(5) An agreement entered into between the successor State under sub-section (3) and an order made by the Central Government under that sub-section or under clause (a) of sub-section (4) may provide for the transfer or re-employment of any employees of the Board or the Corporation referred to in sub-section (1), —

(i) to or by the successor States, in the case of an agreement under sub-section (3) or an order made under that sub-section;

(ii) to or by the new Board or the new Corporation constituted under sub-section (4), in the case of an order made under clause (a) of that sub-section; and, subject to the provisions of section 58, also for the terms and conditions of service applicable to such employees after such transfer or re-employment.

54. *Continuance of arrangements in regard to generation and supply of electric power and supply of water:* If it appears to the Central Government that the arrangement in regard to the generation or supply of electric power or the supply of water for any area or in regard to the execution of any project for such generation or supply has been or is likely to be modified to the disadvantage of that area by reason of the fact that it is, by virtue of the provisions of Part II, outside the State in which the power stations and other installations for the generation and supply of such power or the catchment area reservoirs and other works for the supply of water, as the case may be are located, the Central Government may give such directions as it deems fit, to the State Government or other authority concerned for the maintenance, so far as practicable, of the previous arrangement.

55. *Provisions as to Assam State Financial Corporation:* (1) The Assam State Financial Corporation established under the State Financial Corporations Act, 1951 (63 of 1951), shall on and from the appointed day, continue to function in those areas in respect of which it was functioning immediately before that day, subject to the provisions of this section and to such directions as may, from time to time, be issued by the Central Government.

(2) Any direction issued by the Central Government under sub-section (1) in respect of the Corporation may include a direction that the said Act, in its application to the Corporation, shall have effect subject to such exceptions and modifications as may be specified in the direction.

(3) Notwithstanding anything contained in sub-section (1) or sub-section (2), the Board of Directors of the Corporation may, with the previous approval of the Central Government and shall, if so required by the Central Government, convene at any time after the appointed day a meeting for the consideration of a scheme for the reconstitution or re-organization or dissolution as the case may be of the Corporation including proposals regarding the formation of new Corporations and the transfer thereto of the assets, rights and liabilities of the existing Corporation, and if such a scheme is approved at a general meeting by a resolution passed by a majority of the shareholders present and voting the scheme shall be submitted to the Central Government for its sanction.

(4) If the scheme is sanctioned by the Central Government either without modifications or with modifications which are approved at a

general meeting, the Central Government shall certify the scheme, and upon such certification the scheme shall notwithstanding anything to the contrary contained in any law for the time being in force, be binding on the Corporations affected by the scheme as well as the shareholders and creditors thereof.

(5) If the scheme is not so approved or sanctioned the Central Government may refer the scheme to such Judge of the common High Court as may be nominated in this behalf by the Chief Justice thereof, and the decision of the Judge in regard to the scheme shall be final and shall be binding on the Corporations affected by the scheme as well as the shareholders and creditors thereof.

(6) Nothing in the preceding provisions of this section shall be construed as preventing the Government of the State of Meghalaya from constituting, at any time after the appointed day and with the approval of the Central Government, a State Financial Corporation for that State under the State Financial Corporations Act, 1951 (63 of 1951).

56. *General provisions as to statutory corporations:* (1) Save as otherwise expressly provided by the foregoing provisions of this Part, where any body corporate constituted under a Central Act, State Act, or Provincial Act for the existing State of Assam or any part thereof has, by virtue of the provisions of Part II, become another State body corporate, then, the body corporate shall, on and from the appointed day continue to function and operate in those areas in respect of which it was functioning and operating immediately before that day, subject to such directions as may from time to time be issued by the Central Government, until other provision is made by laws in respect of the said body corporate.

(2) Any directions issued by the Central Government under sub-section (1) in respect of any such body corporate may include a direction that any law by which the said body corporate is governed shall, in its application to that body corporate, have effect, subject to such exceptions and modifications as may be specified in the direction.

57. *Temporary provisions as to continuance of certain existing road transport permits:* (1) Notwithstanding anything contained in section 63 of the Motor Vehicles Act, 1939, (4 of 1939), a permit granted by the State or a Regional Transport Authority in the existing State of Assam shall, if such permit was, immediately before the appointed day, valid and effective in any area therein, be deemed to continue to be valid and effective in that area after that day subject to the provisions of that Act, as for the time being in force in that area and it shall not be necessary for any such permit to be countersigned by any State or Regional Transport Authority for the purpose of validating it for use in such area:

Provided that the Central Government may, after consultation with the State Government or Governments concerned, add to amend or vary the conditions attached to the permit by the authority by which the permit was granted.

(2) No tolls, entrance fees or other charges of a like nature shall be levied after the appointed day in respect of any transport vehicle for its operations in any of the successor States under any such permit, if such vehicle was immediately before that day exempted from the payment of any such tolls, entrance fees or other charges for its operation within the existing State of Assam:

Provided that the Central Government may after consultation with the State Government or Governments concerned, authorizes the levy of any such tolls, entrance fees or other charges as the case may be.

58. *Special provision relating to retrenchment compensation in certain cases:* Where, on account of the reorganization of the existing State of Assam under this Act any body corporate constituted under a Central Act, State Act or Provincial Act, any cooperative society registered under any law relating to cooperative societies or any commercial or industrial undertaking of that State is reconstituted or reorganized in any manner whatsoever or is amalgamated with any other body corporate, cooperative society or undertaking, or is dissolved and in consequence of such reconstitution, reorganization, amalgamation or dissolution, any workman employed by such body corporate of any such cooperative society or undertaking, is transferred to, or re-employed by any other body corporate, or in any other cooperative society or undertaking then notwithstanding anything contained in Sections 25F, 25FF or 25FFF of the Industrial Disputes Act, 1947, (14 of 1947) such transfer or re-employment shall not entitle him to any compensation under that section:

Provided that —

(a) the terms and conditions of service applicable to the workman after such transfer or re-employment are not less favourable to the workman than those applicable to him immediately before the transfer or re-employment; and

(b) the employer in relation to the body corporate, the cooperative society or the undertaking where the workman transferred or re-employed is, by agreement or otherwise, legally liable to pay to the workman, in the event of his retrenchment, compensation under Sections 25F, 25FF or 25FFF of the Industrial Disputes Act, 1947 (14 of 1947), on the basis that his service has been continuous and has not been interrupted by the transfer or re-employment.

59. *Special provisions as to income-tax:* Where the assets, rights and liabilities of any body corporate carrying on business are under the provisions cf this Part, transferred to any other bodies corporate which after the transfer carry on the same business, the losses or profits or gains sustained by the body corporate first mentioned which, but for such transfer, would have been allowed to be carried forward and set-off in accordance with the provisions of Chapter VI of the Income-Tax Act, 1961, (43 of 1961), shall be apportioned amongst the transferee bodies corporate in accordance with the rules to be made by the Central Government in this behalf and, upon such apportionment, the share of loss allotted to each transferee body corporate shall be dealt with in accordance with the provisions of Chapter VI of the said Act, as if the transferee body corporate has itself sustained such loss in a business carried on by it in the years in which these losses were sustained.

60. *Continuance of facilities in certain State institutions:* (1) The Government of the State of Assam or Meghalaya or, as the case may be, the Central Government in relation to the Union Territory of Mizoram shall, in respect of the institutions specified in the Seventh Schedule located in that State or Union Territory, continue to provide facilities to any other Government aforesaid and the people of the States and Union Territory aforesaid which shall not, in any respect, be less favourable to such Government and people than what were being provided to them before the appointed day, for such period and upon such terms and conditions (including those relating to any contributions to be made for the provision of such facilities) as may be agreed upon between the said Governments before the expiry of a period of one year from the appointed day or, if no agreement is reached before such expiry, as may be fixed by order of the Central Government.

(2) The Central Government may at any time before the expiry of a period of one year from the appointed day, by notification in the official Gazette, specify in the Seventh Schedule any other institution existing on the appointed day in the said State and Union Territory and on the issue of such notification, the said Schedule shall be deemed to be amended by the inclusion of the said institution therein.

PART VIII

Provisions as to Services

61. *Provisions relating to All-India Services:* (1) In this section, the expression "joint cadre", —

(a) in relation to the Indian Administrative Service, has the meaning assigned to it in the Indian Administrative Service (Cadre) Rules, 1954;

(b) in relation to the Indian Police Service, has the meaning assigned to it in the Indian Police Service (Cadre) Rules, 1954; and

(c) in relation to the Indian Forest Service, has the meaning assigned to it in the Indian Forest Service (Cadre) Rules, 1966.

(2) On and from the appointed day, there shall be constituted for the States of Assam and Meghalaya a joint cadre of the Indian Administrative Service, a joint cadre of the Indian Police Service and a joint cadre of the Indian Forest Service.

(3) On and from the appointed day, there shall be constituted for the States of Manipur and Tripura a joint cadre of the Indian Administrative Service, a joint cadre of the Indian Police Service and a joint cadre of the Indian Forest Service.

(4) The initial strength and composition of the joint cadre referred to in sub-sections (2) and (3) shall be such as the Central Government may, by order, determine before the appointed day.

(5) The members of each of the said Services borne on the Assam cadre thereof immediately before the appointed day shall be allocated to the joint cadre of the same Service constituted under sub-section (2) and to the Union Territories cadre of that Service in such manner and with effect from such date or dates as the Central Government may, by order, specify.

(6) Such members of each of the said Services borne on the Union Territories cadre thereof immediately before the appointed day, as the Central Government may, by order, specify shall be allocated to the joint cadre of the same Service constituted under sub-section (3) with effect from such date or dates as may be specified in the order.

(7) Every person who, being a member of a State Civil Service of the existing State of Assam, is borne on a Select List for promotion to the Assam Cadre of an All-India Service immediately before the

appointed day shall, unless he is deemed to have been allocated to the Union under section 64, be deemed to have been included in the same order as in that List, in the Select List for promotion to the joint cadre of the same Service constituted under sub-section (2).

(8) Every person who, being a person deemed to have been allocated under section 62 for service in connection with the affairs of the State of Manipur or the State of Tripura, is borne on a Select List for promotion to the Union Territories cadre of an All-India Service immediately before the appointed day, shall be deemed to have been included in the same order as in the List, in the Select List for promotion to the joint cadre of the same Service constituted under sub-section (3).

(9) Every person who, being a person deemed to have been allocated to the. Union under section 64, is borne on a Select List for promotion to the Assam cadre of an All-India Service immediately before the appointed day, shall be deemed to have been included in the Select List for promotion to the Union Territories cadre of the same Service and his position in the said Select List shall be determined by the Central Government in consultation with the Union Public Service Commission.

(10) Nothing in this section shall be deemed to affect the operation after the appointed day of the All-India Services Act, 1951 (61 of 1951), or the rules or regulations made thereunder.

62. *Provisions relating to Services in Manipur and Tripura:* Every person who immediately before the appointed day is serving in connection with the affairs of the Union under the administrative control of the Administrator of the Union Territory of Manipur, or the Administrator of the Union Territory of Tripura (including a person who has been placed on deputation by the Administrator concerned with any other authority), shall, unless otherwise directed by an order of the Central Government, be deemed to have been allocated for service as from that day in connection with the affairs of the State of Manipur or, as the case may be, of the State of Tripura:

Provided that no direction shall be issued under this section after the expiry of a period of one year from the appointed day.

63. *Special provisions relating to members of Central Health Service:* Notwithstanding the provisions of section 62, every member of the Central Health Service who immediately before the appointed day is holding any post in the Union Territory of Manipur or the Union Territory of Tripura, being a post included to the authorized strength of that Service, shall unless otherwise directed by the Central Government, be deemed to be on deputation on and from the appointed day, to the Government of the State of Manipur or, as the case may be, of the State of Tripura on the same terms and conditions of service as are applicable to him under the Central Health Service Rules, 1963, but without any deputation allowance:

Provided that the period of such deputation shall in no case extend beyond a period of three years from the appointed day.

Explanation: In this section, "Central Health Service" means the Central Health Service constituted under the Central Health Service Rules, 1963.

64. *Provisions relating to Services in the existing State of Assam:* (1) Such persons serving in connection with the affairs of the existing State of Assam (including persons borne on any cadre of that State and serving under the Government of the autonomous State of Meghalaya or on deputation to any other Government or authority) as may be determined at any time before or after the appointed day, —

(a) by agreement between the Government of the existing State of Assam and the Government of the autonomous State of Meghalaya or between the Government of the State of Assam and the Government of the State of Meghalaya, as the case may be; or

(b) in default of any such agreement, by the Central Government may, notwithstanding anything in their terms of appointment or their conditions of service:

(i) in a case referred to in clause (a), by one or more orders made by the Government of the existing State of Assam or the Government of the State of Assam, as the case may be; or

(ii) in a case referred to in clause (b), by one or more orders made by the Central Government, be required to serve in connection with the affairs of the State of Meghalaya and every such person shall accordingly be deemed to have been allocated to that State with effect from such date as may be specified in the order.

(2) Such persons serving in connection with the affairs of the existing State of Assam (including persons borne on any cadre of the existing State of Assam and serving under the Government of the autonomous State of Meghalaya or on deputation to any other

Government or authority), as the Central Government may, at any time before or after the appointed day, determine in consultation with the Government of the existing State of Assam or the Government of the State of Assam, as the case may be, may, notwithstanding anything in the terms of their appointment or their conditions of service by one or more orders made by the Central Government, be required to serve in connection with the administration of the Union Territory of Mizoram, and every such person shall accordingly, be deemed to have been allocated to the Union with effect from such date as may be specified in the order:

Provided that every person borne on any cadre of the existing State of Assam and serving in the Mizo District immediately before the appointed day shall unless otherwise directed by the Administrator of the Union Territory of Mizoram, continue to serve on and from the appointed day, in connection with the administration of that Union Territory until an order is made under this sub-section in respect of such person or the expiry of a period of three years from the appointed day, whichever is earlier.

65. *Provisions relating to Services in the autonomous State of Meghalaya:* Every person who immediately before the appointed day is serving in connection with the affairs of the autonomous State of Meghalaya (including a person on deputation from the Government of that autonomous State to any other Government or authority) not being a person to whom section 64 applies, shall be deemed to have been allocated to serve as from that day in connection with the affairs of the State of Meghalaya.

66. *Other provisions relating to Services:* (1) Nothing in this section or sections 62 to 65 (both inclusive) shall be deemed to affection or after the appointed day the operation of the provisions of Chapter I of Part XIV of the Constitution in relation to determination of conditions of service of persons serving in connection with the affairs of the States of Manipur, Meghalaya or Tripura or the Union Territory of Mizoram:

Provided that the conditions of service applicable immediately before the appointed day in the case of any person deemed to have been allocated to the State of Manipur or the State of Tripura under section 62 or to the State of Meghalaya under sub-section (1) of section 64 or section 65 or to the Union under sub-section (2), of section 64 shall not be varied to his disadvantage except with the previous approval of the Central Government.

(2) All services prior to the appointed day rendered by a person —

(a) if he is deemed to have been allocated to any State under section 62 or section 64 or section 65, shall be deemed to have been rendered in connection with the affairs of the State; and

(b) if he is deemed to have been allocated to the Union in connection with the administration of the Union Territory of Mizoram, shall be deemed to have been rendered in connection with the affairs of the Union, for the purposes of the rules regulating his conditions of service.

(3) The provisions of sections 62, 64 and 65 shall not apply in relation to members of any All-India Service.

67. *Provisions as to continuance of officers in same posts:* (1) Every person who, immediately before the appointed day is holding or discharging the duties of any post or office in connection with the administration of the Union Territory of Manipur or Union Territory of Tripura, shall continue to hold the same post or office in the State of Manipur, or, as the case may be, in the State of Tripura and shall be deemed, on and from that day, to have been duly appointed to the post or office by the Government of, or other appropriate authority in the State concerned.

(2) Where a person who immediately before the appointed day is holding or discharging the duties of any post or office in connection with the affairs of the existing State of Assam and as from the appointed day, such duties become duties in connection with affairs of the State of Meghalaya or administration of the Union Territory of Mizoram, then, he shall continue to hold the same post or office in that State or Union Territory and shall be deemed on and from that day, to have been duly appointed to the post or office by the Government or Administrator of, or other appropriate authority in that State or Union Territory, as the case may be.

(3) Where a person who immediately before the appointed day is holding or discharging the duties or any post or office in connection with the affairs of the autonomous State of Meghalaya and, as from the appointed day, such duties become duties in connection with the affairs of the State of Meghalaya, then, he shall continue to hold the same post or office in the State of Meghalaya and shall be deemed on and from that day, to have been duly appointed to the post or office by the Government of, or other appropriate authority in the State of Meghalaya.

(4) Nothing in sub-section (1) or sub-section (2) or sub-section (3) shall be deemed to prevent a competent authority, on and from the

appointed day, from passing in relation to any person referred to in that sub-section, any order affecting his continuance in such post or office.

68. *Advisory Committees:* The Central Government may, by order, establish one or more Advisory Committees for the purpose of assisting it in regard to —

(a) the discharge of any of its functions under this Part; and

(b) the ensuring of fair and equitable treatment to all persons affected by the provisions of this Part and the proper consideration of any representation made by such persons.

69. *Power of Central Government to give directions:* The Central Government may give such directions to the State Governments of Assam, Manipur, Meghalaya and Tripura and to the Administrator of the Union Territory of Mizoram as may appear to it to be necessary for the purpose of giving effect to the foregoing provisions of this Part and the State Governments and the Administrator shall comply with such directions.

70. *Provisions as to State Public Service Commission:* (1) The Public Service Commission for the existing State of Assam shall, on and from the appointed day, be deemed to be the Public Service Commission for the State of Assam.

(2) Every person holding office immediately before the appointed day as Chairman or other member of the Public Service Commission for the existing State of Assam shall, as from the appointed day, be the Chairman or, as the case may be, the other member of the Public Service Commission for the State of Assam.

(3) Every person who becomes Chairman or other member of the Public Service Commission for the State of Assam on the appointed day under sub-section (2) shall —

(a) be entitled to receive from the Government of the State of Assam conditions of service not less favourable than those to which he was entitled under the provisions applicable to him immediately before the appointed day; and

(b) subject to the provision to clause (2) of article 316, hold office or continue to hold office until the expiration of his term of office as determined under the provisions applicable to him immediately before the appointed day.

PART IX

Legal and Miscellaneous Provisions

71. *Amendment of Articles 210, 239A, 241A, 275, 332, 371B and Fifth and Sixth Schedules to the Constitution:* On and from the appointed day —

(a) in article 210, in the proviso to clause (2) for the words "Legislature of the State of Himachal Pradesh", the words "Legislatures of the States of Himachal Pradesh, Manipur and Meghalaya and Tripura" shall be substituted;

(b) in article 239A, in clause (1) the words "Manipur, Tripura", shall be omitted;

(c) in article 244, —

(i) in clause (1), for the words "the State of Assam" the words "the States of Assam and Meghalaya" shall be substituted;

(ii) in clause (2), for the words "the State of Assam" the words "the State of Assam and Meghalaya and the Union Territory of Mizoram" shall be substituted;

(d) in article 244A, in clause (1), for the word and letter "Part A", the word and figure "Part 1" shall be substituted;

(e) in article 275, in clause (a) of the second proviso to clause (1), for the word and letter "Part A" the word and figure "Part 1" shall be substituted;

(f) in article 332, —

(i) in clause (5), the words "except in the case of the constituency comprising the cantonment and municipality of Shiliong" shall be omitted;

(ii) in clause (6), the words "except from the constituency comprising the cantonment and municipality of Shillong" shall be omitted;

(g) in article 371B, for the word and letter "Part A" the word and figure "Part 1" shall be substituted;

(h) in the Fifth Schedule to the Constitution, in paragraph 1, for the words "State of Assam" the words "States of Assam and Meghalaya" shall be substituted;

(i) the Sixth Schedule to the Constitution shall stand amended as directed in the Eighth Schedule.

72. *Amendment of Act 2 of 1934:* On and from the appointed day, in section 21A, of the Reserve Bank of India Act, 1934, in sub-section (1), the brackets and words "(including the autonomous State of Meghalaya)" shall be omitted.

73. *Amendment of Act 64 of 1950:* On and from the appointed day, in section 47A of the Road Transport Corporations Act, 1950, in the Explanation to sub-section (1), after clause (ii) the following clause shall be inserted, namely:

"(iii) in relation to the Assam State Road Transport Corporation, shall mean the Government of the State of Assam or of Meghalaya as formed under the North-Eastern Areas (Reorganization) Act, 1971".

74. *Amendment of Act 37 of 1956:* On and from the appointed day, in the States Reorganization Act, 1956, —

(a) for clause (c) of section 15, the following clause shall be substituted, namely:

"(c) the Eastern Zone, comprising the States of Bihar, West Bengal and Odisha";

(b) in sub-section (1) of section 16, clause (d) shall be omitted.

75. *Amendment of Act 20 of 1963:* On and from the appointed day, in the Government of Union Territories Act, 1963, —

(a) in clause (h) of sub-section (1) of section 2, the words "Manipur, Tripura", shall be omitted;

(b) in section 44, sub-section (2) shall be omitted; and

(c) section 52 shall be omitted.

76. *Amendment of Act 56 of 1955, and the Tripura (Courts) Order, 1950:* On and from the appointed day, —

(a) the Manipur (Courts) Act, 1955, shall stand amended as directed in the Ninth Schedule; and

(b) the Tripura (Courts) Order, 1950, shall stand amended as directed in the Tenth Schedule.

77. *Territorial extent of laws:* The provisions of Part II shall not be deemed to have effected any change in the territories to which any law in force immediately before the appointed day extends or applies, and the territorial references in any such law to the existing State of Assam or the autonomous State of Meghalaya or the Union Territorial references in any such law to the existing State of Assam or the autonomous State of Meghalaya or the Union Territory of Manipur or the Union Territory of Tripura or the North-East Frontier Agency shall, until otherwise provided by a competent Legislature or other competent authority, be construed as meaning the territories within that State or autonomous State or Union Territory or Agency immediately before the appointed day.

78. *Continuance of existing District Councils and Regional Council and members thereof:* For the removal of doubt, it is hereby declared that all District Councils and the Regional Council constituted under the provisions of the Sixth Schedule to the Constitution and functioning immediately before the appointed day in the respective autonomous districts and in the autonomous region shall, as from that day, be deemed to have been constituted under the said Schedule as amended by clause (i) of section 71, with the Eighth Schedule and accordingly, —

(a) every such District Council and the Regional Council shall, unless sooner dissolved, continue to function in the respective autonomous districts and in the autonomous region notwithstanding that any such district or region ceases to be comprised in the territories of the State of Assam, by virtue of the provisions of Part II; and

(b) every member of such District Council or Regional Council shall continue to be a member thereof for the unexpired term of his office as such.

79. *Power to adapt laws:* For the purpose of facilitating the application of any law in relation to any of the States or Union Territories formed or established by the provisions of Part II the appropriate Government may before the expiration of two years from the appointed day by order, make such adaptations and modifications of the law, whether by way of repeal or amendment, as may be necessary or expedient, and thereupon every such law shall have effect subject to the adaptations and modifications so made until altered, repealed or amended by a competent Legislature or other competent authority.

Explanation: In this section, the expression "the appropriate Government" means:

(a) as respects any law relating to a matter enumerated in the Union List in the Seventh Schedule to the Constitution, the Central Government; and

(b) as respects any other law, —

(i) in its application to a State, the State Government; and

(ii) in its application to a Union Territory, the Central Government.

80. *Power to construe laws:* (1) Notwithstanding that no provision or insufficient provision has been made under section 79 for the adaptation of a law made before the appointed day, any court, tribunal or authority required or empowered to enforce such law may for the purpose of facilitating its application in relation to the States of Assam, Manipur, Meghalaya or Tripura or to the Union Territory of Mizoram or Arunachal Pradesh construe the law in such manner without affecting the substance, as may be necessary or proper in regard to the matter before the court, tribunal or authority.

(2) Any reference to the High Court of Assam or the High Court of Assam and Nagaland or to the Court of the Judicial Commissioner for Manipur or the Court of the Judicial Commissioner for Tripura in any law shall, unless the context otherwise requires, be construed, on and from the appointed day, as a reference to the common High Court.

81. *Power to name authorities, etc. for exercising statutory junctions:* The Central Government, as respects the Union Territory of Mizoram or Arunachal Pradesh and the State Government as respects any new State established or formed by the provisions of Part II may, by notification in the Official Gazette, specify the authority, officer or person who, as from the appointed day, shall be competent to exercise such functions exercisable under any law in force on that day as may be mentioned in that notification and such law shall have effect accordingly.

82. *Legal proceedings:* (1) Where immediately before the appointed day the Union is a party to any legal proceedings with respect to any property, right or liability and such property, right or liability devolves on the State of Manipur or the State of Tripura under this Act, then, the State of Manipur or, as the case may be, the State of Tripura shall be deemed to be substituted for the Union as a party to these proceedings and the proceedings may continue accordingly.

(2) Where immediately before the appointed day the autonomous State of Meghalaya is a party to any legal proceedings with respect to any property, right or liability of that State, and such property, right or liability devolves on the State of Meghalaya under this Act, then, the State of Meghalaya shall be deemed to be substituted for the autonomous State of Meghalaya as a party to those proceedings and the proceedings may continue accordingly.

(3) Where immediately before the appointed day the existing State of Assam is a party to any legal proceeding with respect to any

property, rights or liabilities subject to appointment under this Act, the successor State, which succeeds to, or acquires a share in that property or those rights or liabilities by virtue of any provision of this Act, shall be deemed to be substituted for the existing State of Assam as a party to those proceeding or added as a party thereto, as the case may be, and the proceeding may continue accordingly.

83. *Rights of pleaders to practise in certain cases:* Any person who, immediately before the appointed day, is entrolled as a pleader entitled to practise in any subordinate courts in the existing State of Assam shall, for a period of one year from that day, continue to be entitled to practise in those courts, notwithstanding that the whole or any part of the territories within jurisdiction of those courts has been transferred to the State of Meghalaya or to a Union Territory.

84. *Transfer of pending proceedings:* (1) Every proceeding pending immediately before the appointed day before a court (other than a High Court), tribunal, authority or officer in any area which on that day falls within a State or Union Territory shall, if it is a proceeding relating exclusively to the territories which as from that day are the territories of another State or Union Territory, stand transferred to the corresponding court, tribunal, authority or officer in that other State or Union Territory, as the case may be.

(2) If any question arises as to whether any proceedings should stand transferred under sub-section (1), it shall be referred to the common High Court and the decision of that High Court shall be final.

(3) In this section, —

(a) "proceeding" includes any suit, case or appeal; and

(b) "corresponding court, tribunal, authority or officer" in a State or a Union Territory means —

(i) the court, tribunal, authority or officer in that State or Union Territory to which or before whom the proceeding would have lain if it had been instituted after the appointed day; or

(ii) in case of doubt, such court, tribunal, authority or officer in that State or Union Territory as may be determined after the appointed day by the Government of that State or the Central Government, as the case may be, or before the appointed day by the Government of the existing State of Assam or the Government of the autonomous State of Meghalaya or the Central Government, as the case may be, to be the corresponding court, tribunal, authority or officer.

85. *Provisions as to continuance of courts, etc.:* All courts and tribunals and all authorities discharging lawful functions throughout the existing State of Assam or the Union Territory of Manipur or the Union Territory of Tripura or any part of such State or Union Territory immediately before the appointed day shall, unless their continuance is inconsistent with the provisions of this Act or until other provision is made by a competent Legislature or other competent authority, continue to exercise the respective functions.

86. *Effect of provisions of the Act inconsistent with other laws:* The provisions of this Act shall have effect notwithstanding anything inconsistent therewith contained in any other law.

87. *Power to remove difficulties:* (1) If any difficulty arises in giving effect to the provisions of this Act, the President may, by order, do anything not inconsistent with such provisions which appears to him to be necessary or expedient for the purpose of removing the difficulty.

(2) Every order made under this section shall be laid before each House of Parliament.

88. *Power to make rules:* (1) The Central Government may, by notification in the Official Gazette, make rules to give effect to the provisions of this Act.

(2) Every rule made under this section shall be laid, as soon as may be after it is made, before each House of Parliament while it is in session for a total period of thirty days which may be comprised in one session or in two successive sessions and if, before the expiry of the session in which it is so laid or the session immediately following, both Houses agree in making any modification in the rule or both Houses agree that the rule should not be made, the rule shall thereafter have effect only in such modified or be of no effect, as the case may be, so, however, that any such modification or annulment shall be without prejudice to the validity of anything previously done under that rule.

THE FIRST SCHEDULE

[See Sections 14(2) and 20(5)]

Amendments to the Delimitation of Parliamentary and Assembly Constituencies Order, 1966

In Schedule II to the Delimitation of Parliamentary and Assembly Constituencies Order, 1966, —

(1) In Part A: PARLIAMENTARY CONSTITUENCIES, —

(a) for serial No. 1 and the entries relating thereto, the following shall be substituted, namely:

"1. Cachar — (11) Silchar, (12) Sonai, (13) Dholai, (14) Lakhimpur, (15) Udharbond, (16) Borkhola";

(b) for serial No. 3 and the entries relating thereto, the following shall be substituted, namely:

"3. Diphu (S.T.) — (18) Haflong, (19) Bokajan, (20) Howaraghat, (21) Baithalangso";

(c) for serial No. 4 and the entries relating thereto, the following shall be substituted, namely:

"4. Dhubri — (31) Mankachar, (32) South Salmara, (33) Dhubri, (34) Gauripur, (35) Golakganj, (36) Bilasipara";

(2) In Part B — ASSEMBLY CONSTITUENCIES, serial Nos.: 1, 2, 3 and 22 to 30 (both inclusive) and the entries relating thereto shall be omitted.

THE SECOND SCHEDULE

[See Section 25 (1)]

Amendments to the Constitution (Scheduled Castes) Order, 1950

In the Constitution (Scheduled Castes) Order, 1950 —

(1) in paragraph 2, for the figures "XIV" the figures "XVII" shall be substituted.

(2) in paragraph 4, —

(a) for the words and figures "and any reference in Part XIV", the words and figures "any reference in Part XIV" shall be substituted;

(b) the following shall be added at the end, namely: "and any reference in Parts XV, XVI and XVII to a State shall be construed as a reference to the State constituted as from the day appointed under clause (b) of section 2 of the North-Eastern Areas (Reorganization) Act, 1971";

(3) in the Schedule, after Part XIV, the following Parts shall be inserted, namely:

Part XV — MANIPUR

Throughout the State:

1. Dhupi or Dhobi
2. Lois
3. Muchi or Ravidas
4. Namasudra
5. Patni
6. Sutradhar
7. Yaithibi.

Part XVI — MEGHALAYA

Throughout the State:

1. Bansphor
2. Bhuinmali or Mali
3. Brittial-Bania or Bania
4. Dhupi or Dhobi
5. Dugla or Dholi
6. Hira
7. Jalkeot
8. Jhalo, Malo or Jhalo-Malo
9. Kaibartta or Jaliya
10. Lalbegi
11. Mahara
12. Mehtar or Bhangi
13. Muchi or Rishi
14. Namasudra
15. Patni
16. Sutradhar.

Part XVII — TRIPURA

Throughout the State:

1. Bagdi
2. Baiti
3. Bhuimali
4. Bhunar
5. Chamar or Muchi
6. Dandasi
7. Dhenuar
8. Dhoba
9. Duai
10. Dum
11. Ghasi
12. Gour
13. Gunar
14. Gur
15. Gorang
16. Jalia Kaibarta
17. Kahar
18. Kalindi
19. Kan
20. Kanda
21. Kanugh
22. Keot
23. Khadit
24. Kharia
25. Khemcha
26. Koch
27. Koir
28. Kol
29. Kora
30. Kotal
31. Mahisyadas
32. Mali
33. Mehtor
34. Musahar
35. Namasudra
36. Patni
37. Sabar.

THE THIRD SCHEDULE

[See Section 25(2)]

Amendments to the Constitution (Scheduled Castes) (Union Territories) Order, 1951

In the Constitution (Scheduled Castes) (Union Territories) Order, 1951, —

(1) for paragraph 4, the following paragraph shall be sub-stituted, namely:

"4. any reference in this Order to a Union Territory in Part I of the Schedule shall be construed as a reference to the territory constituted as a Union Territory as from the 1st day of November, 1956, any reference to a Union Territory in Part II of the Schedule shall be construed as a reference to the territory constituted as a Union Territory as from the 1st day of November, 1966 and any reference to a Union Territory as from the day appointed under clause (b) of section 2 of the North-Eastern Areas (Reorganization) Act, 1971."

(2) in the Schedule, —

(a) Parts III and IV shall be omitted;

(b) Part V shall be renumbered as Part II and after that Part as so renumbered, the following Parts shall be inserted, namely:

Part III — MIZORAM

Throughout the Union Territory:

1. Bansphor
2. Bhuinmali or Mali
3. Brittial-Bania or Bania
4. Dhupi or Dhobi
5. Dugla or Dholi
6. Hira
7. Jalkeot
8. Jhalo, Malo or Jhalo-Malo
9. Kaibartta or Jaliya
10. Lalbegi
11. Mahara
12. Mehtar or Bhangi
13. Muchi or Rishi
14. Namasudra
15. Patni
16. Sutradhar.

Part IV — ARUNACHAL PRADESH

Throughout the Union Territory:

1. Bansphor
2. Bhuinmali or Mali
3. Brittial-Bania or Bania
4. Dhupi or Dhobi

5. Dugla or Dholi
6. Hira
7. Jalkeot
8. Jhalo, Malo or Jhalo-Maio
9. Kaibartta or Jaliya
10. Lalbegi
11. Mahara
12. Mehtar or Bhangi
13. Muchi or Rishi
14. Namasudra
15. Patni
16. Sutradhar.

THE FOURTH SCHEDULE

[See Section 26(1)]

Amendments to the Constitution (Scheduled Tribes) Order, 1950

In the Constitution (Scheduled Tribes) Order, 1950, —

(1) In paragraph 2, for the figures "XIII", the figures "XVI" shall be substituted;

(2) In paragraph 3, —

(a) for the words and figures "and any reference in Part XIII", the words and figures "any reference in Part XIII" shall be substituted;

(b) the following shall be added at the end, namely:
"and any reference in Parts XIV to XVI to a State shall be construed as a reference to the State constituted as from the day appointed under clause (b) of section 2 of the North-Eastern Areas (Reorganization) Act, 1971";

(3) In the Schedule:

(a) in Part II — Assam, paragraph 2 shall be omitted and in paragraph 3, for the words "excluding the Tribal areas"; the words "excluding the autonomous districts" shall be substituted;

(b) after Part XIII, the following Parts shall be inserted, namely:

Part XIV — MANIPUR

Throughout the State:

1. Aimol
2. Anal
3. Angami
4. Chiru
5. Chothe
6. Gangte
7. Hmar
8. Kabui
9. Kacha Naga
10. Khoirao
11. Koireng
12. Kom

13. Lamgang
14. Any Mizo (Lushai) tribes
15. Maram
16. Maring
17. Mao
18. Monsang
19. Moyon
20. Paite
21. Purum
22. Ralte
23. Sema
24. Simte
25. Suhte
26. Tangkhul
27. Thadou
28. Vaiphui
29. Zou.

Part XV — MEGHALAYA

Throughout the State:

1. Chakma
2. Dimasa (Kachari)
3. Garo
4. Hajong
5. Hmar
6. Khasi and Jaintia (including Khasi, Synteng or Pnar, War, Bhoi or Lyngngam)
7. Any Kuki Tribes including
   - (i) Biate or Biete
   - (ii) Changsan
   - (iii) Chongloi
   - (iv) Doungel
   - (v) Gamalhou
   - (vi) Gangte
   - (vii) Guite
   - (viii) Hanneng
   - (ix) Haokip or Haupit
   - (x) Haolai
   - (xi) Hengna
   - (xii) Hongsungh
   - (xiii) Hrangkhwal or Rangkhoi
   - (xiv) Jongbe
   - (xv) Khawchung
   - (xvi) Khawathlang or Khothalong
   - (xvii) Khelma
   - (xviii) Kholhou
   - (xix) Kipgen
   - (xx) Kuki
   - (xxi) Lengthang
   - (xxii) Lhangum
   - (xxiii) Lhoujem
   - (xxiv) Lhouvun
   - (xxv) Lupheng
   - (xxvi) Mangjel
   - (xxvii) Misao
   - (xxviii) Riang
   - (xxix) Sairhem
   - (xxx) Selnam
   - (xxxi) Singson
   - (xxxii) Sitlhou
   - (xxxiii) Sukte
   - (xxxiv) Thado
   - (xxxv) Thangngeu
   - (xxxvi) Uibuh
   - (xxxvii) Vaiphei
8. Lakher
9. Man (Tai-Speaking)
10. Any Mizo (Lushai) tribes
11. Mikir
12. Any Naga tribes
13. Pawi
14. Synteng.

Part XVI — TRIPURA

Throughout the State:

1. Lushai
2. Mag
3. Kuki, including the following sub-tribes:
   - (i) Balte
   - (ii) Belahut
   - (iii) Chhalya
   - (iv) Fun
   - (v) Hajango
   - (vi) Jangtoi
   - (vii) Khareng
   - (viii) Khephong
   - (ix) Kuntei
   - (x) Laifang
   - (xi) Lantei
   - (xii) Mizel
   - (xiii) Namte
   - (xiv) Paitu Paite
   - (xv) Rangchan
   - (xvi) Rangkhole
   - (xvii) Thangluya
4. Chakraa
5. Garoo
6. Chaimal
7. Halam
8. Khasia
9. Bhutia
10. Munda including Kaur
11. Orang
12. Lepcha
13. Santal
14. Bhil
15. Tripura or Tripuri, Tippera
16. Jamatia
17. Noatia
18. Riang
19. Uchai.

THE FIFTH SCHEDULE

[See Section 26 (2)]

Amendments to the Constitution (Scheduled Tribes) (Union Territories) Order, 1951

In the Constitution (Scheduled Tribes) (Union Territories) Order, 1951, —

(1) In paragraph 2, for the words and figures "Parts I to IV", the words and figures "Parts I to III" shall be substituted;

(2) For paragraph 3, the following paragraph shall be substituted namely:

"(3) Any reference in this Order to a Union Territory in Part I of the Schedule shall be construed as a reference to that territory constituted as a Union Territory as from the 1st day of November, 1956 and any reference to a Union Territory in Parts II and III of the Schedule shall be construed as a reference to the territory constituted as a Union Territory as from the day appointed under clause (b) of section 2 of the North-Eastern Areas (Reorganization) Act, 1971".

(4) In the Schedule, —

(a) Parts II and III shall be omitted; and

(b) Part IV shall be renumbered as Part I and after that part as so re-numbered, the following Parts shall be inserted, namely:

"Part II — MIZORAM

Throughout the Union Territory:

1. Chakma
2. Dimasa (Kachari)
3. Garo
4. Hajong
5. Hmar
6. Khasi and Jaintia (including Khasi, Synteng or Pnar, War, Bhoi or Lyngngam)
7. Any Kuki tribes including:
   - (i) Baite or Biete
   - (ii) Changsan
   - (iii) Chongloi
   - (iv) Doungel
   - (v) Gamalhou
   - (vi) Gangte
   - (vii) Guite
   - (viii) Hanneng
   - (ix) Haokip or Haupit
   - (x) Haolai
   - (xi) Hengna
   - (xii) Hongsungh
   - (xiii) Hrangkhwal or Rangkhol
   - (xiv) Jongbe
   - (xv) Khawchung
   - (xvi) Khawathlang or Khothalong
   - (xvii) Khelma
   - (xviii) Kholhou
   - (xix) Kipgen
   - (xx) Kuki
   - (xxi) Lengthang
   - (xxii) Lhangum
   - (xxiii) Lhoujem
   - (xxiv) Lhouvun
   - (xxv) Lupheng
   - (xxvi) Mangjel
   - (xxvii) Missao
   - (xxviii) Riang
   - (xxix) Sairhem
   - (xxx) Salnam
   - (xxxi) Singson
   - (xxxii) Sitihou
   - (xxxiii) Sukte
   - (xxxiv) Thado
   - (xxxv) Hangngeu
   - (xxxvi) Uibuh
   - (xxxvii) Vaiphei
8. Lakher
9. Man (Tai-Speaking)
10. Any Mizo (Lushai) tribes,
11. Mikir
12. Any Naga tribes
13. Pawi
14. Synteng."

"Part III — ARUNACHAL PRADESH

Throughout the Union Territory:

All tribes of the Union Territory including:

1. Abor
2. Aka
3. Apatani
4. Dafla
5. Galong
6. Khampti
7. Khowa
8. Mishmi
9. Momba
10. Any Naga tribes
11. Sherdukpen
12. Singpho."

THE SIXTH SCHEDULE

[See Section 51(3)]

Apportionment of Assets and Liabilities

1. *Definitions:* In this Schedule:

(a) "population ratio", in relation to the States of Assam and Meghalaya, means the ratio of 93:58 to 6:42; and

(b) "transferred territories" means the territories which, as from the appointed day, become the territories of the State of Meghalaya under section 5.

2. *Provisions of the Schedule to be applied to the apportionment of certain assets and liabilities:* Where any asset or liability is required to be apportioned to the autonomous State of Meghalaya by virtue of section 58, of the Assam Reorganization (Meghalaya) Act, 1969 (55 of 1969), but has not been so apportioned before the appointed day, the provisions of this Schedule shall be applied after apportionment under the said section has been effected.

3. *Apportionment of land, stores, etc.:* (1) Subject to the other provisions contained in this Schedule, all land and all stores, articles and other goods belonging to the existing State of Assam shall, on and from the appointed day, —

(a) in a case where such land, stores, articles and other goods are situated within the transferred territories, pass to the State of Meghalaya; and

(b) in any other case, pass to the State of Assam:

Provided that where the Central Government is of the opinion that any goods or class of goods should be distributed among the States of Assam and Meghalaya otherwise than according to the situation of the goods, the Central Government may issue such directions, as it thinks fit, for a just and equitable distribution of the goods and the goods shall pass to the States of Assam and Meghalaya accordingly.

(2) (a) Such of those lands and buildings as are held by the existing State of Assam within the limits of the cantonment and municipality of Shillong immediately before the appointed day as may be agreed upon between the States of Assam and Meghalaya shall be available for the use of the State of Assam on the appointed day and thereafter for such period as may be agreed upon between the said States.

(b) Where no agreement is reached between the States of Assam and Meghalaya on any of the matters referred to in clause (a), the Central Government shall decide such matte. and the decision of the Central Government thereon shall be binding on the said States.

(c) Different periods may be agreed upon under clause (a) or decided under clause (b) for different lands and buildings.

(d) Where any land or building is made available to the State of Assam under this sub-paragraph on or after the appointed day, then, notwithstanding anything contained in this Schedule, the debt or other liabilities in respect of such land or building shall pass to the State of Meghalaya only from the date from which possession of the land or building is given to the State of Meghalaya and the amount of such debt or other liability shall be determined by agreement between the States of Assam and Meghalaya or, in default of any such agreement by the Central Government.

(e) For so long as any land or building referred to in clause (a) is held by the State of Assam for its use, it shall be the responsibility of that State to properly maintain such land or building from its own funds.

(3) Stores relating to the Secretariat and the offices of Heads of departments having jurisdiction over the areas comprised partly in the transferred territories and partly in the State of Assam and unissued stores shall be divided between the State of Assam and Meghalaya in

accordance with such directions as the Central Government may think fit to issue for a just and equitable distribution thereof.

Explanation: In this paragraph, the expression "land" includes immovable property of every description and any rights in or over such property, and the expression "goods" does not include coins, bank notes, and currency notes.

4. *Arrears of taxes:* The State of Meghalaya shall have the right to recover the arrears of tax or any duty, including the arrears of land revenue, on property situated in the transferred territories, and shall also have the right to recover the arrears of any other tax or duty if the place of assessment of that tax or duty is located in the transferred territories.

5. *Right to recover loans and advances:* (1) Save as provided in sub-paragraph (2) of paragraph 6, the right to recover any loans or advances made before the appointed day by the existing State of Assam to any local body, society, agriculturist or other person in the transferred territories shall belong to the State of Meghalaya.

(2) The right to recover loans and advances of pay and travelling allowances to a Government servant made before the appointed day by the existing State of Assam shall pass to the State of Meghalaya if, after the appointed day, that Government servant is required to serve in connection with the affairs of Meghalaya.

6. *Investments:* (1) The investments of the existing State of Assam immediately before the appointed day in any company or private commercial or industrial undertaking, insofar as such investments have not been made or deemed not to have been made from the Cash Balance Investment Account, shall pass to the State of Meghalaya, if the principal seat of business of the company or undertaking is located in the transferred territories and where on that day the principal seat of business of the company or undertaking is located in the transferred territories and where on that day the principal seat of business of the company or undertaking is located outside the territories of the existing State of Assam, such investments shall be divided between the States of Assam and Meghalaya in the population ratio:

Provided that such investments in any Government company shall be divided between the States of Assam and Meghalaya in such proportion as may be agreed upon between those States or —

(a) in default of such agreement; or

(b) at the expiry of a period of one year from the appointed day, whichever is earlier, in such proportion as the Central Government may, by order, determine:

Provided further that nothing in this paragraph shall apply to any investment made by the existing State of Assam on or after the 2nd day of April, 1970 in any company or private commercial or industrial undertaking located outside the territories of the existing State of Assam.

(2) Where any body corporate constituted under a Central Act, State Act or Provincial Act or the existing State of Assam or any part thereof has, by virtue of the provisions of Part II, become an inter-State body corporate, the investments in, or loans or advances to, any such body corporate by the existing State of Assam made before the appointed day shall, save as otherwise expressly provided by or under this Act, be divided between the States of Assam and Meghalaya in the same proportion in which the assets of the body corporate are divided under the provisions of Part VII.

7. *Assets and liabilities of State Undertakings:* (1) The assets and liabilities relating to any commercial or industrial undertaking of the existing State of Assam shall pass to the State of Meghalaya if the undertaking is located in the transferred territories.

(2) Where a depreciation reserve fund is maintained by the existing State of Assam for any commercial or industrial undertaking the securities held in respect of investments made from that fund shall pass to the State of Meghalaya if the undertaking is located in the transferred territories.

(3) Where any such undertaking is located partly in the State of Assam and partly in the State of Meghalaya, the assets and liabilities and the securities referred to in sub-paragraphs (1) and (2) respectively shall be divided in such manner as may be agreed upon between the Governments of the two States within one year from the appointed day, or in default of such agreement, as the Central Government may, by order, direct.

8. *Public debt:* (1) The public debt of the existing State of Assam attributable to loans raised by the issue of Government securities and outstanding with the public immediately before the appointed day shall continue to be the public debt of the State of Assam, and the State of Meghalaya shall be liable to pay to the State of Assam a share of the sums due from time to time for the servicing and repayment of the debt and for the purpose of determining the said share, the debt shall be deemed to be divided between the States of Assam and Meghalaya as if it were a debt referred to in sub-paragraph (5).

Explanation: In this sub-paragraph, the "public debt of the existing State of Assam", excludes the portion of such public debt the liability for servicing and repayment of which has been apportioned to the autonomous State of Meghalaya by virtue of section 58 of the Assam Reorganization (Meghalaya) Act, 1969, (55 of 1969).

(2) Where a sinking fund or depreciation fund is maintained by the existing State of Assam for repayment of any loan raised by it, the securities held in respect of investment made from that fund shall be divided between the States of Assam and Meghalaya in the same proportion in which the total public debt is divided between the two States under this paragraph.

(3) The public debt of the existing State of Assam attributable to loans taken from the Central Government, the National Cooperative Development Cooperation or the Central Warehousing Cooperation or the Khadi and Village Industries Commission or from any other source for the express purpose of re-lending the same to a specific institution and outstanding immediately before the appointed day shall —

(a) if re-lent to the Assam State Electricity Board, or any other institution which becomes an inter-State body corporate on the appointed day, be divided between the States of Assam and Meghalaya in the same proportion in which the assets of such body corporate are divided under the provisions of Part VII.

(b) if re-lent to any local body, body corporate or other institution in any local area, be the debt of the State in which the local area is included on the appointed day.

(4) Out of so much of the public debt of the existing State of Assam, other than the public debt referred to in sub-paragraphs (1) and (3), as is equal to loans and advances made by that State and outstanding on the appointed day, the share of the liability of the State of Meghalaya shall be for an amount equal to the loans and advances (not being re-lent amounts referred to in sub-paragraph (3) and outstanding immediately before the appointed day) recoverable by the State of Meghalaya under paragraph 5.

(5) The remaining public debt of the existing State of Assam attributable to loans taken from the Central Government, the Reserve Bank of India or any other body or bank outstanding immediately before the appointed day, shall be divided between the State of Assam and Meghalaya in proportion to the total expenditure on all capital works and other capital outlays incurred or deemed to have been incurred by the existing State of Assam up to the appointed day in the territories remaining in the State of Assam and the total expenditure on all capital

works and other capital outlays incurred or deemed to have been incurred by the existing State of Assam up to the appointed day in the transferred territories, other than such outlays incurred or deemed to have been incurred before the 2nd day of April, 1970 in the autonomous State of Meghalaya for the purposes of the autonomous State as defined in paragraph 1 of the Third Schedule to the Assam Reorganization (Meghalaya) Act, 1969 (55 of 1969).

(6) For the purpose of this paragraph "Government security" means a security created and issued by the existing State of Assam for the purpose of raising a public loan and having any of the forms specified in, or prescribed under, clause (2) of Section 2 of the Public Debt Act, 1944 (18 of 1944).

(7) For the purpose of this paragraph, "the public debt of the existing State of Assam attributable to the loans taken from the Central Government" means the public debt of the State as reduced in accordance with the provisions of sub-section (4) of section 52.

9. *Refund of taxes collected in excess:* After the appointed day it shall be the liability of the State of Meghalaya to refund any tax or duty on property, including land revenue, collected in excess or any property situate in the transferred territories or any other tax or duty collected in excess, if the place of assessment of that tax or duty is situate in the transferred territories.

10. *Deposits, etc.:* (1) The liability of the existing State of Assam in respect of any civil deposit or local fund deposit, made before the appointed day in any place situate in the transferred territories shall become the liability of the State of Meghalaya.

(2) The liability of the existing State of Assam in respect of any charitable or other endowment shall, as from the appointed day, be the liability of the State of Meghalaya, if the institution entitled to the benefit of the endowment is located in the transferred territories, or if the objects of the endowment, under the terms thereof, are confined to the transferred territories.

11. *Arrears of pay and allowances:* The liability of the existing State of Assam in respect of any arrears of pay or allowances due to any Government servant for the period prior to the appointed day shall, if the Government servant is required to serve in connection with the affairs of the State of Meghalaya, be the liability of the State of Meghalaya.

12. *Provident Fund, etc.:* The liability of the existing State of Assam in respect of the Provident Fund and Special Deposit Fund accounts of a Government servant required to serve in connection with the affairs of the State of Meghalaya shall, on and from the appointed day, be the liability of the State of Meghalaya.

13. *Pensions:* The liability of the State of Assam or the State of Meghalaya in respect of pensions shall be apportioned between the two States in such manner as may be agreed upon between them or in default of such agreement, in such manner as the Central Government may, by order, specify.

14. *Contracts:* (1) Where, before the appointed day, the existing State of Assam has made any contract in exercise of its executive power for any purposes of that State, that contract shall be deemed to have been made in the exercise of the executive power, —

(a) if such purposes are, as from the appointed day, exclusively purposes of either the State of Assam or the State of Meghalaya, of the State of Assam or, as the case may be, of the State of Meghalaya; and

(b) in any other case, of the State of Assam, and all rights and liabilities which have accrued or may accuse under any such contract shall, to the extent to which they would have been rights or liabilities of the existing State of Assam, be rights or liabilities of the State of Assam, or, as the case may be, of the State of Meghalaya:

Provided that in any such case as is referred to in clause (b), the initial allocation of rights and liabilities made under this sub-paragraph shall be subject to such financial adjustment as may be agreed upon between the States of Assam and Meghalaya, or, in default of such agreement, as the Central Government may, by order, direct.

(2) For the purposes of this paragraph, there shall be deemed to be included in the liabilities which have accrued or may accure under any contract, —

(a) any liability to satisfy an order or award made by any court or tribunal in proceedings relating to the contract; and

(b) any liability in respect of expenses incurred in, or in connection with, any such proceedings.

(3) This paragraph shall have effect subject to the other provisions of this Schedule relating to the apportionment of liabilities in respect of loans, guarantees and other financial obligations; and bank balances and securities shall, notwithstanding that they partake of the nature of contractual rights, be dealt with under those provisions.

15. *Liability in respect of actionable wrong:* Where, immediately before the appointed day, the existing State of Assam is subject to any liability in respect of any actionable wrong, other than breach of contract, that liability shall, —

(a) if the cause of action arose wholly within the territories, which as from that day, are the territories of the State of Assam or the State of Meghalaya, be the liability of the State of Assam or, as the case may be, of the State of Meghalaya; and

(b) in any other case, be initially the liability of the State of Assam, but subject to such financial adjustment as may be agreed upon between the States of Assam and Meghalaya or, in default of any such agreement, as the Central Government may, by order, direct.

16. *Liability as guarantor:* Where, immediately before the appointed day, the existing State of Assam is liable as guarantor in respect of any liability of a registered cooperative society or other person, that liability shall, —

(a) if the area of operation of such society or person is limited to the territories which, as from that day, are the territories of the State of Assam or of the State of Meghalaya, be the liability of the State of Assam or, as the case may be, of the State of Meghalaya; and

(b) in any other case, be initially the liability of the State of Assam, subject to such financial adjustment as may be agreed upon between the State of Assam and Meghalaya or, in default of such agreement, as the Central Government may, by order, direct.

17. *Items in suspense:* If any item in suspense is ultimately found to affect an asset or liability of the nature referred to in any of the foregoing provisions of this Schedule, it shall be dealt with in accordance with that provision.

18. *Residuary provisions:* The benefit or burden of any asset or liability of the existing State of Assam not dealt with in the foregoing paragraphs of this Schedule shall pass to the State of Assam in the first instance, subject to such financial adjustment as may be agreed upon between the States of Assam and Meghalaya within one year from the appointed day or, in default of such agreement, as the Central Government may, by order, direct.

19. *Apportionment of assets and liabilities by agreement:* Where the States of Assam and Meghalaya agree that the benefit or burden of any particular asset or liability should be apportioned between them in a manner other than that as provided for in the foregoing paragraphs of this Schedule, then, notwithstanding anything contained therein, the benefit or burden of that asset or liability shall be apportioned in the manner so agreed upon.

20. *Power of Central Government to order allocation or adjustment in certain cases:* Where, by virtue of any of the provisions of this Schedule, the State of Assam or the State of Meghalaya is entitled to any property, or obtains any benefits or becomes subject to any liability, and the Central Government is of opinion on a reference made to it within a period of three years from the appointed day by the State of Assam or the State of Meghalaya, as the case may be, that it is just and equitable, that property or those benefits should be transferred to one of the two States or shared between them, or that a contribution towards that liability should be made by either of the States, the said property or benefits shall be allocated in such manner, or the State of Meghalaya or the State of Assam shall make to the other State primarily subject to the liability such contribution in respect thereof, as the Central Government may, after consultation with the Government of Assam and the Government of Meghalaya, by order, determine.

THE SEVENTH SCHEDULE

[See Section 60(1)]

List of Institutions where existing facilities shall be continued:

1. Assam Forest Training School, Jhalukbari.
2. Survey School for Mandals, Guwahati.
3. Assam Survey Training School, Guwahati.
4. Assam Cooperative Training Centre, Joysagar.
5. Gram Sevikas Training Centre, Jorhat.
6. Police Training College, Dergaon.
7. Forensic Science Laboratory, Guwahati.
8. Finger Print Bureau, Shillong.
9. Public Health Laboratory, Shillong.
10. Administrative Training School, Guwahati.
11. Reid Chest T.B. Hospital, Shillong.
12. Gauhati Medical College, Guwahati.
13. Assam Medical College, Dibrugarh.

14. Medical College, Silchar.
15. Pasteur Institute, Shillong.
16. State Malaria Institute, Shillong.
17. Ayurvedic College, Guwahati.
18. Mental Hospital, Tezpur.
19. Primary Health Centre, Chabua.
20. Assam Engineering College, Jhalukbari.
21. Jorhat Engineering College, Jorhat.
22. Assam Government Press, Shillong.
23. Assam Agriculture College. } Under the Agricultural
24. Assam Veterinary College. } University, Jorhat.

THE EIGHTH SCHEDULE

[See Section 71 (i)]

Amendments to the Sixth Schedule to the Constitution

1. In the Sixth Schedule to the Constitution (hereafter in this Schedule referred to as the Sixth Schedule), in the heading, for the word "Assam", the words "the States of Assam and Meghalaya and in the Union Territory of Mizoram" shall be substituted.

2. In paragraph 1 of the Sixth Schedule, —

(i) in sub-paragraph (1), for the word and letter "Part A", the words and figures "Parts I and II and in Part III" shall be substituted;

(ii) in sub-paragraph (3), —

(a) in clauses (a) and (b), for the word and letter "Part A" the words "any of the Parts" shall be substituted;

(b) after the existing proviso, the following proviso shall be inserted, namely:

"Provided further that any order made by the Governor under this sub-paragraph may contain such incidental and consequential provisions (including any amendment of paragraph 20 and of any item in any of the Parts of the said table) as appear to the Governor to be necessary for giving effect to the provisions of the order".

3. In paragraph 3 of the Sixth Schedule, in the proviso the clause (a) of sub-paragraph (1) for the words "by the Government of Assam or the Government of Meghalaya", the words "by the Government of the State concerned" shall be substituted.

4. In paragraph 4 of the Sixth Schedule, —

(i) in sub-paragraph (3), the words "of Assam" shall be omitted.

(ii) in sub-paragraph (5), for the words "after consulting the Government of Assam or, as the case may be, the Government of Meghalaya", the words "after consulting the Government of the State concerned" shall be substituted.

5. In paragraph 6 of the Sixth Schedule, in sub-paragraph (2), the words "of Assam or Meghalaya, as the case may be", shall be omitted.

6. In paragraph 8 of the Sixth Schedule, in sub-paragraph (1), for the words "by the Government of Assam in assessing lands for the purpose of land revenue in the State of Assam generally", the words "by the Government of the State in assessing lands for the purpose of land revenue in the State generally" shall be substituted.

7. In paragraph 9 of the Sixth Schedule, in sub-paragraph (1), for the words "the Government of Assam", in both the places where they occur, the words "the Government of the State" shall be substituted.

8. In paragraph 12 of the Sixth Schedule, —

(i) for the heading, the following heading shall be substituted, namely:
"Application of Acts of Parliament and of the Legislature of the State of Assam to autonomous districts and autonomous regions in the State of Assam";

(ii) in sub-paragraph (1):

(a) in clause (a), for the words "Legislature of the State" in both the places where they occur, the words "Legislature of the State of Assam" shall be substituted and after the words "any autonomous district or autonomous region" the words "in that State" shall be inserted;

(b) in clause (b), for the words "Legislature of the State", the words "Legislature of the State of Assam", shall be substituted and after the words "an autonomous district or an autonomous region", the words "in that State" shall be inserted.

9. For paragraph 12A of the Sixth Schedule, the following paragraphs shall be substituted, namely:

"12A. *Application of Acts of Parliament and of the Legislature of the State of Meghalaya to autonomous districts and autonomous regions in the State of Meghalaya:* Notwithstanding anything in this Constitution:

(a) if any provision of a law made by a District or Regional Council in the State of Meghalaya with respect to any matter specified in sub-paragraph (1) of paragraph 3 of this Schedule or if any provision of any regulation made by a District Council or a Regional Council in that State under paragraph 8 or paragraph 10 of this Schedule, is repugnant to any provision of a law made by the Legislature of the State of Meghalaya with respect to that matter, then, the law or regulation made by the District Council or as the case may be, the Regional Council whether made before or after the law made by the Legislature of the State of Meghalaya, shall, to the extent of repugnancy, be void and the law made by the Legislature of the State of Meghalaya shall prevail; and

(b) the President may, with respect to any act of Parliament, by notification, direct that it shall not apply to an autonomous district or an autonomous region in the State of Meghalaya, or shall apply to such district or region or any part thereof subject to such exceptions or modifications as he may specify in the notification and any such direction may be given so as to have retrospective effect.

12B. *Application of Acts of Parliament and other Acts to autonomous districts and autonomous regions in the Union Territory of Mizoram:* Notwithstanding anything in this Constitution, the President may with respect to any Act of Parliament and the Administrator may with respect to any other Act, by notification, direct that it shall not apply to an autonomous district or an autonomous region in the Union Territory of Mizoram or shall apply to such district or region or any part thereof subject to such exceptions or modifications as he may specify in the notification and any such direction may be given so as to have retrospective effect".

10. In paragraph 13 of the Sixth Schedule, the words "of Assam" shall be omitted.

11. In paragraph 14 of the Sixth Schedule, in sub-paragraph (2), for the words "the Government of Assam", the words "the Government of the State" shall be substituted.

12. In paragraph 17 of the Sixth Schedule, for the words "the Legislative Assembly of Assam", the words "the Legislative Assembly of Assam or Meghalaya" shall be substituted and after the words "autonomous district", the words "in the State of Assam or Meghalaya, as the case may be", shall be inserted.

13. Paragraph 18 of the Sixth Schedule, shall be omitted.

14. For paragraphs 20 and 20A of the Sixth Schedule, the following paragraphs shall be substituted, namely, —

"20. *Tribal areas:* (1) The areas specified in Parts I, II and III of the table below shall respectively be the tribal areas with in the State of Assam, the State of Meghalaya and the Union Territory of Mizoram.

(2) Any reference in the table below to any district shall be construed as a reference to the territories comprised within the autonomous district of that name existing immediately before the appointed day under clause (b) of section 2 of the North-Eastern Areas (Reorganization) Act, 1971:

Provided that for the purposes of clauses (e) and (f) of sub-paragraph (1) of paragraph 3, paragraph 4, paragraph 5, paragraph 6, sub-paragraph (2), clauses (a), (b) and (d) of sub-paragraph (3) and sub-paragraph (4) of paragraph 8 and clause (d) of sub-paragraph (2) of paragraph 10 of this Schedule, no part of the area comprised within the raunicipality of Shillong shall be deemed to be within the United Khasi-Jaintia Hills District".

TABLE

Part I

1. The North Cachar Hills District.
2. The Mikir Hills District.

Part II

1. The United Khasi-Jaintia Hills District.
2. The Jowai District.
3. The Garo Hills District.

Part III

The Mizo District.

20A. *Interpretation:* Subject to any express provision made in this behalf, the provisions of this Schedule shall, in their application to the Union Territory of Mizoram, have effect —

(1) as if references to the Governor and Government of the State were references to the Administrator of the Union Territory appointed under article 239 and references to State (except in the expression "Government of the State") were references to the Union Territory of Mizoram;

(2) as if —

(a) in sub-paragraph (3) of paragraph 1, —

(i) after clause (g), the following clause had been inserted, namely:

"(h) divide any autonomous region into two or more autonomous regions and define the boundaries thereof";

(ii) the first proviso had been omitted;

(b) in sub-paragraph (5) of paragraph 4 the provision for consultation with the Government of the State concerned had been omitted;

(c) in sub-paragraph (2) of paragraph 9, the words "in his discretion" had been omitted;

(d) paragraph 13 had been omitted;

(e) sub-paragraphs (2) and (3) of paragraph 14 had been omitted;

(f) sub-paragraph (2) (including the proviso thereto) of paragraph 15 had been omitted;

(g) in paragraph 16, —

(i) in sub-paragraph (1), in clause (b), the words "subject to the previous approval of the Legislature of the State" and the second proviso to that sub-paragraph had been omitted;

(ii) sub-paragraph (3) had been omitted".

THE NINTH SCHEDULE

[See Section 76(a)]

Amendments to the Manipur (Courts) Act, 1955

In the Manipur (Courts) Act, 1955 (56 of 1955):

(i) through the Act save as otherwise expressly provided, —

(a) for the words "Chief Commissioner", the words "State Government" shall be substituted, and for the words "Judicial Commissioner", the words "High Court" shall be substituted, and such consequential amendments, as the rules of grammar may require, shall be made;

(b) for the words "Union Territory of Manipur", the words "State of Manipur" shall be substituted;

(ii) in the long title, the words "a Judicial Commissioner's Court and other" shall be omitted.

(iii) in section 2, —

(a) clause (i) shall be omitted;

(b) after clause (iii), the following clause shall be inserted, namely:

(iiia) "High Court", means the Guwahati High Court (the High Court of Assam, Nagaland, Meghalaya, Manipur and Tripura);

(iv) Chapter II shall be omitted;

(v) in section 16, the words "the Court of the Judicial Commissioner and" shall be omitted;

(vi) in section 17, —

(a) the brackets and figure "(1)" shall be omitted;

(b) sub-section (2) shall be omitted;

(vii) in section 18, for sub-section (1), the following sub-section shall be substituted, namely:

"(1) When the business pending before the court of a district judge requires the aid of an additional district judge for its speedy disposal, one or more additional district judges may be appointed";

(viii) section 19 shall be omitted;

(ix) for section 23, the following section shall be substituted, namely:

"23. *Local limits of the jurisdiction of courts of sub-ordinate judges and munsiffs:* (1) The local limits of the jurisdiction of the court of a subordinate judge or a munsiff shall be such as the State Government may, after consultation with the High Court, by notification in the Official Gazette define.

(2) When a subordinate judge is posted to a district, the local limits of the district shall, in the absence of any direction to the contrary, be the local limits of his jurisdiction";

(x) in section 25, sub-section (4) shall be omitted;

(xi) sections 33, 34, 35 and 40 shall be omitted;

(xii) in sub-section (1) of section 43, the words "the Court of the Judicial Commissioner and" shall be omitted;

(xiii) section 46 shall be omitted.

THE TENTH SCHEDULE

[See Section 76(b)]

Amendments to the Tripura (Courts) Order, 1950

In the Tripura (Courts) Order, 1950 —

(i) throughout the Order, save as otherwise expressly provided, for the words "Chief Commissioner", the words "State Government" shall be substituted, and for the words "Judicial Commissioner" or "Court of the Judicial Commissioner", the words "High Court", shall be substituted, and such consequential amendments, as the rules of grammar may require, shall be made;

(ii) in paragraph 2, —

(a) clause (i) shall be omitted;

(b) for clause (iii), the following clauses shall be substituted, namely:

(iii) "High Court" means the Guwahati High Court (the High Court of Assam, Nagaland, Meghalaya, Manipur and Tripura);

(iiia) "Tripura" means the State of Tripura;

(iii) Chapter II shall be omitted;

(iv) in paragraph 15, the words "the Court of the Judicial Commissioner and" shall be omitted;

(v) in paragraph 16, —

(a) the brackets and figure (1) shall be omitted;

(b) sub-paragraph (2) shall be omitted.

(vi) in paragraph 17 for sub-paragraph (1), the following sub-paragraph shall be substituted, namely:

"(1) When the business pending before the Court of District Judge requires the aid of an Additional Judge or Judges for its speedy disposal, one or more Additional District Judges may be appointed";

(vii) paragraph 18 shall be omitted;

(viii) for paragraph 22, the following paragraph shall be substituted, namely —

22. *Local limits of jurisdiction of Courts of Subordinate Judges and Munsiffs:* (1) The local limits of the jurisdiction of the Court of a Subordinate Judge or Munsiff shall be such as the State Government may, after consultation with the High Court, by notification in the Official Gazette, define.

(2) When a Subordinate Judge is posted to a district, the local limits of the district shall, in the absence of any directions to the contrary, be the local limits of his jurisdiction";

(ix) paragraph 31 shall be omitted;

(x) for paragraph 32, the following paragraph shall be substituted, namely:

"32 *Finality of appellate decrees of District Court:* Subject to the provisions of section 100 of the Code of Civil Procedure, 1908 (5 of 1908), an appellate decree of a District Court shall be final";

(xi) paragraphs 33, 34, 35 and 41 shall be omitted;

(xii) in sub-paragraph (1) of paragraph 42, the words "the Court of Judicial Commissioner and" shall be omitted.

(3) The Council shall, —

(a) review, from time-to-time, the implementation of the projects and schemes included in the regional plan and recommend measures for effecting coordination among the Governments of the States concerned in the matter of implementation of such projects and schemes;

(b) where a project or scheme is intended to benefit two or more States, recommend the manner in which, —

(i) such project or scheme may be executed or implemented and managed or maintained; or

(ii) the benefits therefrom may be shared; or

(iii) the expenditure thereon may be incurred;

(c) on a review of progress of the expenditure, recommend to the Central Government the quantum of financial assistance to be given, from time-to-time, to the State or States entrusted with the execution or implementation of any project or scheme included in the regional plan; and

(d) recommend to the Government of the State concerned or to the Central Government the undertaking of necessary surveys and investigation of projects in any State represented in the Council to facilitate consideration of the feasibility of including new projects in the regional plan.

(4) The Council shall review from time-to-time the measures taken by the States represented in the Council for the maintenance of security and public order therein and recommend to the Governments of the States concerned further measures necessary in this regard.

5. *Meetings of the Council:* (1) The Council shall meet at such times as the Chairman of the Council may appoint in this behalf and shall, subject to the other provisions of this section, observe such rules of procedure in regard to transaction of business at its meetings as it may lay down from time-to-time.

(2) The Chairman or in his absence the Vice-Chairman, if any, or in the absence of both the Chairman and the Vice-Chairman, any other member chosen by the members present from amongst themselves, shall preside at a meeting of the Council.

(3) The proceedings of every meeting of the Council shall be forwarded to the Central Government and also to the Government of each State represented on the Council.

6. *Nomination of certain Officers to attend the meeting of the Council:* In order to assist the Council in the discharge of its functions, each of the Ministries of the Central Government dealing with matters relating to Defence, Finance, Home Affairs and Planning shall nominate an officer to attend the meetings of the Council.

7. *Officers and Staff of the Council:* (1) The Council shall have a Secretarial Staff consisting of a Secretary, a Planning Adviser, a Financial Adviser and a Security Adviser and such other officers and employees as the Central Government may, by order, determine.

(2) The Secretarial Staff of the Council shall function under the direction, supervision and control of the Chairman of the Council.

(3) The office of the Council shall be located at such place as may be determined by the Council.

(4) The Administrative expenses of the said office, including the salaries and allowances payable to, or in respect of, members of the Secretarial Staff of the Council, shall be brone by the Central Government out of the moneys provided by Parliament for the purpose.

8. *Repeal:* The North-Eastern Council Act, 1970 (26 of 1970) is hereby repealed.

ANNEXURE XXIX

Constitutional Provisions about NER

A. PART IX

The Panchayats

1. *Article 243M:* Part not to Apply to Certain Areas.

2. *Article 243ZC:* Part not to Apply to Certain Areas.

B. PART X

The Scheduled and Tribal Areas

1. *Article 244:* Administration of Scheduled Areas and Tribal Areas.

2. *Article 244A:* Formation of an autonomous State comprising certain tribal areas in Assam and creation of local Legislature or Council of Ministers or both therefore.

C. PART XXI

Temporary, Transitional and Special Provisions

1. *Article 371A:* Special provision with respect to the State of Nagaland.

2. *Article 371B:* Special provision with respect to the State of Assam.

3. *Article 371C:* Special provision with respect to the State of Manipur.

4. *Article 371F:* Special provisions with respect to the State of Sikkim.

5. *Article 371G:* Special provision with respect to the State of Mizoram.

6. *Article 371H:* Special provision with respect to the State of Arunachal Pradesh.

D. SIXTH SCHEDULE

[Articles 244(2) and 275(1)]

Provisions as to the Administration of Tribal Areas in the States of Assam, Meghalaya, Tripura and Mizoram

SIXTH SCHEDULE
[Articles 244(2) and 275(1)]

Provisions as to the Administration of Tribal Areas in the States of Assam, Meghalaya, Tripura and Mizoram

1. *Autonomous districts and autonomous regions:* (1) Subject to the provisions of this paragraph, the tribal areas in each item of Parts I, II and IIA and in Part III of the table appended to paragraph 20 of this Schedule shall be an autonomous district.

(2) If there are different Scheduled Tribes in an autonomous district, the Governor may, by public notification, divide the area or areas inhabited by them into autonomous regions.

(3) The Governor may, by public notification, —

(a) include any area in any of the Parts of the said table;

(b) exclude any area from any of the Parts of the said table;

(c) create a new autonomous district;

(d) increase the area of any autonomous district;

(e) diminish the area of any autonomous district;

(f) unite two or more autonomous districts or parts thereof so as to form one autonomous district;

(ff) alter the name of any autonomous distric; and

(g) define the boundaries of any autonomous district:

Provided that no order shall be made by the Governor under clauses (c), (d), (e) and (f) of this sub-paragraph except after consideration of the report of a Commission appointed under sub-paragraph (1) of paragraph 14 of this Schedule:

Provided further that any order made by the Governor under this sub-paragraph may contain such incidental and consequential provisions (including any amendment of paragraph 20 and of any item in any of the Parts of the said Table) as appear to the Governor to be necessary for giving effect to the provisions of the order.

1. Paragraph 1 has been amended in its application to the State of Assam by the Sixth Schedule to the Constitution (Amendment)

Act, 2003 (44 of 2003), Section 2, so as to insert the following proviso after sub-paragraph (2), namely:

"Provided that nothing in this sub-paragraph shall apply to the Bodoland Territorial Areas District".

2. *Constitution of District Councils and Regional Councils:* (1) There shall be a District Council for each autonomous district consisting of not more than thirty members, of whom not more than four persons shall be nominated by the Governor and the rest shall be elected on the basis of adult suffrage.

(2) There shall be a separate Regional Council for each area constituted an autonomous region under sub-paragraph (2) of paragraph 1 of this Schedule.

(3) Each District Council and each Regional Council shall be a body corporate by the name respectively of "the District Council of (name of district)" and "the Regional Council of (name of region)", shall have perpetual succession and a common seal and shall by the said name sue and be sued.

(4) Subject to the provisions of this Schedule, the administration of an autonomous district shall, in so far as it is not vested under this Schedule in any Regional Council within such district, be vested in the District Council for such district and the administration of an autonomous region shall be vested in the Regional Council for such region.

(5) In an autonomous district with Regional Councils, the District Council shall have only such powers with respect to the areas under the authority of the Regional Council as may be delegated to it by the Regional Council in addition to the powers conferred on it by this Schedule with respect to such areas.

(6) The Governor shall make rules for the first Constitution of District Councils and Regional Councils in consultation with the existing tribal Councils or other representative tribal organizations within the autonomous districts or regions concerned, and such rules shall provide for —

(a) the composition of the District Councils and Regional Councils and the allocation of seats therein;

(b) the delimitation of territorial constituencies for the purpose of elections to those Councils;

(c) the qualifications for voting at such elections and the preparation of electoral rolls therefor;

(d) the qualifications for being elected at such elections as members of such Councils;
(e) the term of office of members of Regional Councils;
(f) any other matter relating to or connected with elections or nominations to such Councils;
(g) the procedure and the conduct of business (including the power to act notwithstanding any vacancy) in the District and Regional Councils; and
(h) the appointment of officers and staff of the District and Regional Councils.

(6A) The elected members of the District Council shall hold office for a term of five years from the date appointed for the first meeting of the Council after the general elections to the Council, unless the District Council is sooner dissolved under paragraph 16 and a nominated member shall hold office at the pleasure of the Governor:

Provided that the said period of five years may, while a Proclamation of Emergency is in operation or if circumstances exist which, in the opinion of the Governor, render the holding of elections impracticable, be extended by the Governor for a period not exceeding one year at a time and in any case where a Proclamation of Emergency is in operation not extending beyond a period of six months after the Proclamation has ceased to operate:

Provided further that a member elected to fill a casual vacancy shall hold office only for the remainder of the term of office of the member whom he replaces.

(7) The District or the Regional Council may after its first Constitution make rules with the approval of the Governor with regard to the matters specified in sub-paragraph (6) of this paragraph and may also make rules with like approval regulating —

(a) the formation of subordinate local Councils or Boards and their procedure and the conduct of their business; and
(b) generally all matters relating to the transaction of business pertaining to the administration of the district or region, as the case may be:

Provided that until rules are made by the District or the Regional Council under this sub-paragraph the rules made by the Governor under sub-paragraph (6) of this paragraph shall have effect in respect of elections to, the officers and staff of, and the procedure and the conduct of business in, each such Council.

1. Paragraph 2 has been amended in its application to the State of Assam by the Sixth Schedule to the Constitution (Amendment) Act, 2003 (44 of 2003), Section 2, so as to insert the following proviso after sub-paragraph (1), namely —

   "Provided that the Bodoland Territorial Council shall consist of not more than forty-six members of whom forty shall be elected on the basis of adult suffrage, of whom thirty shall be reserved for the Scheduled Tribes, five for non-tribal communities, five open for all communities and the remaining six shall be nominated by the Governor having same rights and privileges as other members, including voting rights, from amongst the un-represented communities of the Bodoland Territorial Areas District, of which at least two shall be women".

2. Paragraph 2 has been amended in its application to the State of Assam by the Sixth Schedule to the Constitution (Amendment) Act, 1995 (42 of 1995), Section 2, so as to insert the following proviso after sub-paragraph (3), namely —

   "Provided that the District Council constituted for the North Cachar Hills District shall be called as the North Cachar Hills Autonomous Council and the District Council constituted for the Karbi Anglong District shall be called as the Karbi Anglong Autonomous Council."

3. Paragraph 2 has been amended in its application to the State of Assam by the Sixth Schedule to the Constitution (Amendment) Act, 2003 (44 of 2003), Section 2, so as to insert the following proviso after sub-paragraph (3), namely:

   "Provided further that the District Council constituted for the Bodoland Territorial Areas District shall be called the Bodoland Territorial Council".

3. *Powers of the District Councils and Regional Councils to make laws:* (1) The Regional Council for an autonomous region in respect of all areas within such region and the District Council for an autonomous district in respect of all areas within the district except those which are under the authority of Regional Councils, if any, within the district shall have power to make laws with respect to:

(a) the allotment, occupation or use, or the setting apart, of land, other than any land which is a reserved forest for the purposes of agriculture or grazing or for residential or other non-agricultural purposes or for any other purpose likely to promote the interests of the inhabitants of any village or town:

Provided that nothing in such laws shall prevent the compulsory acquisition of any land, whether occupied or unoccupied, for public purposes by the Government of the State concerned in accordance with the law for the time being in force authorizing such acquisition;

(b) the management of any forest not being a reserved forest;

(c) the use of any canal or water-course for the purpose of agriculture;

(d) the regulation of the practice of *jhum* or other forms of shifting cultivation;

(e) the establishment of village or town committees or councils and their powers;

(f) any other matter relating to village or town administration, including village or town police and public health and sanitation;

(g) the appointment or succession of Chiefs or Headmen;

(h) the inheritance of property;

(i) marriage and divorce; and

(j) social customs.

(2) In this paragraph, a "reserved forest" means any area which is a reserved forest under the Assam Forest Regulation, 1891, or under any other law for the time being in force in the area in question.

(3) All laws made under this paragraph shall be submitted forthwith to the Governor and, until assented to by him, shall have no effect.

1. Paragraph 3 has been amended in its application to the State of Assam by the Sixth Schedule to the Constitution (Amendment) Act, 2003 (44 of 2003), Section 2, so as to substitute sub-paragraph (3) as under, —

"(3) Save as otherwise provided in sub-paragraph (2) of paragraph 3A or sub-paragraph (2) of paragraph 3B, all laws made under this paragraph or sub-paragraph (1) of paragraph 3A or sub-paragraph (1) of paragraph 3B shall be submitted forthwith to the Governor and, until assented to by him, shall have no effect".

2. After paragraph 3, the following paragraph has been inserted in its application to the State of Assam by the Sixth Schedule to the Constitution (Amendment) Act, 1995 (42 of 1995), Section 2 and after paragraph 3A, the following paragraph has been inserted in its application to the State of Assam by the Sixth Schedule to the Constitution (Amendment) Act, 2003 (44 of 2003), Section 2, namely —

"**3A.** *Additional powers of the North Cachar Hills Autonomous Council and the Karbi Anglong Autonomous Council to make laws:* (1) Without prejudice to the provisions of paragraph 3, the North Cachar Hills Autonomous Council and the Karbi Anglong Autonomous Council within their respective districts, shall have power to make laws with respect to —

(a) industries, subject to the provisions of entries 7 and 52 of List I of the Seventh Schedule;

(b) communications, that is to say, roads, bridges, ferries and other means of communication not specified in List I of the Seventh Schedule; municipal tramways, ropeways, inland waterways and traffic thereon subject to the provisions of List I and List III of the Seventh Schedule with regard to such waterways; vehicles other than mechanically propelled vehicles;

(c) preservation, protection and improvement of stock and prevention of animal diseases; veterinary training and practice; cattle pounds;

(d) primary and secondary education;

(e) agriculture, including agricultural education and research, protection against pests and prevention of plant diseases;

(f) fisheries;

(g) water, that is to say, water supplies, irrigation and canals, drainage and embankments, water storage and water power subject to the provisions of entry 56 of List I of the Seventh Schedule;

(h) social security and social insurance; employment and unemployment;

(i) flood control schemes for protection of villages, paddy fields, markets, towns, etc. (not of technical nature);

(j) theatre and dramatic performances, cinemas subject to the provisions of entry 60 of List I of the Seventh Schedule; sports, entertainments and amusements;

(k) public health and sanitation, hospitals and dispensaries;

(l) minor irrigation;

(m) trade and commerce in, and the production supply and distribution of, food stuffs, cattle fodder, raw cotton and raw jute;

(n) libraries, museums and other similar institutions controlled or financed by the State; ancient and historical monuments and records other than those declared by or under any law made by Parliament to be of national importance; and

(o) alienation of land.

(2) All laws made by the North Cachar Hills Autonomous Council and the Karbi Anglong Autonomous Council under paragraph 3 or under this paragraph shall, in so far as they relate to matters specified in List III of the Seventh Schedule, be submitted forthwith to the Governor who shall reserve the same for the consideration of the President.

(3) When a law is reserved for the consideration of the President, the President shall declare either that he assents to the said law or that he withholds assent therefrom:

Provided that the President may direct the Governor to return the law to the North Cachar Hills Autonomous Council or the Karbi Anglong Autonomous Council, as the case may be, together with a message requesting that the said Council will reconsider the law or any specified provisions thereof and, in particular, will consider the desirability of introducing any such amendments as he may recommend in his message and, when the law is so returned, the said Council shall consider the law accordingly within a period of six months from the date of receipt of such message and, if the law is again passed by the said Council with or without amendment it shall be presented again to the President for his consideration".

3. After paragraph 3A, the following paragraph has been inserted in its application to the State of Assam by the Sixth Schedule to the Constitution (Amendment) Act, 2003 (44 of 2003), Section 2, namely —

3B. *Additional powers of the Bodoland Territorial Council to make laws:* (1) Without prejudice to the provisions of paragraph 3, the Bodoland Territorial Council within its areas shall have power to make laws with respect to:

(i) agriculture, including agricultural education and research, protection against pests and prevention of plant diseases;

(ii) animal husbandry and veterinary, that is to say, preservation, protection and improvement of stock and prevention of animal diseases, veterinary training and practice, cattle pounds;

(iii) cooperation;

(iv) cultural affairs;

(v) education, that is to say, primary education, higher secondary including vocational training, adult education, college education (general);

(vi) fisheries;

(vii) flood control for protection of village, paddy fields, markets and towns (not of technical nature);

(viii) food and civil supply;

(ix) forests (other than reserved forests);

(x) handloom and textile;

(xi) health and family welfare;

(xii) intoxicating liquors, opium and derivatives, subject to the provisions of entry 84 of List I of the Seventh Schedule;

(xiii) irrigation;

(xiv) labour and employment;

(xv) land and revenue;

(xvi) library services (financed and controlled by the State Government);

(xvii) lotteries (subject to the provisions of entry 40 of List I of the Seventh Schedule), theatres, dramatic performances and cinemas (subject to the provisions of entry 60 of List I of the Seventh Schedule);

(xviii) markets and fairs;

(xix) municipal corporation, improvement trust, district boards and other local authorities;

(xx) museum and archaeology institutions controlled or financed by the State, ancient and historical monuments and records other than those declared by or under any law made by Parliament to be of national importance;

(xxi) panchayat and rural development;

(xxii) planning and development;

(xxiii) printing and stationery;

(xxiv) pubic health engineering;

(xxv) public works department;

(xxvi) publicity and public relations;

(xxvii) registration of births and deaths;

(xxviii) relief and rehabilitation;

(xxix) sericulture;

(xxx) small, cottage and rural industry subject to the provisions of entries 7 and 52 of List I of the Seventh Schedule;

(xxxi) social welfare;

(xxxii) soil conservation;

(xxxiii) sports and youth welfare;

(xxxiv) statistics;

(xxxv) tourism;

(xxxvi) transport (roads, bridges, ferries and other means of communications not specified in List I of the Seventh Schedule, municipal tramways, ropeways, inland waterways and traffic thereon subject to the provision of List I and List III of the Seventh Schedule with regard to such waterways, vehicles other than mechanically propelled vehicles);

(xxxvii) tribal research institute controlled and financed by the State Government;

(xxxviii) urban development — town and country planning;

(xxxix) weights and measures subject to the provisions of entry 50 of List I of the Seventh Schedule; and

(xl) welfare of plain tribes and backward classes:

Provided that nothing in such laws shall —

(a) extinguish or modify the existing rights and privileges of any citizen in respect of his land at the date of commencement of this Act; and

(b) disallow and citizen from acquiring land either by way of inheritance, allotment, settlement or by any other way of transfer if such citizen is otherwise eligible for such acquisition of land within the Bodoland Territorial Areas District.

(2) All laws made under paragraph 3 or under this paragraph shall in so far as they relate to matters specified in List III of the Seventh Schedule, be submitted forthwith to the Governor who shall reserve the same for the consideration of the President.

(3) When a law is reserved for the consideration of the President, the President shall declare either that he assents to the said law or that he withholds assent therefrom:

Provided that the President may direct the Governor to return the law to the Bodoland Territorial Council, together with the message requesting that the said Council will reconsider the law or any specified provisions thereof and, in particular, will consider the desirability of introducing any such amendments as he may recommend in his message and, when the law is so returned, the said Council shall consider the law accordingly within a period of six month from the date of receipt of such message and, if the law is again passed by the said Council with or without amendments it shall be presented again to the President for his consideration".

4. *Administration of justice in autonomous districts and autonomous regions:* (1) The Regional Council for an autonomous region in respect of areas within such region and the District Council for an autonomous district in respect of areas within the district other than those which are under the authority of the Regional Councils, if any, within the district may constitute village councils or courts for the trial of suits and cases between the parties all of whom belong to Scheduled Tribes within such areas, other than suits and cases to which the provisions of sub-paragraph (1) of paragraph 5 of this Schedule apply, to the exclusion of any court in the State, and may appoint suitable persons to be members of such village councils or presiding officers of such courts, and may also appoint such officers as may be necessary for the administration of the laws made under paragraph 3 of this Schedule.

(2) Notwithstanding anything in this Constitution, the Regional Council for an autonomous region or any court constituted in that behalf by the Regional Council or, if in respect of any area within an autonomous district there is no Regional Council, the District Council for such district, or any court constituted in that behalf by the District Council, shall exercise the powers of a court of appeal in respect of all suits and cases triable by a village council or court constituted under sub-paragraph (1) of this paragraph within such region or area, as the case may be, other than those to which the provisions of sub-paragraph (1) of paragraph 5 of this Schedule apply, and no other court except the High Court and the Supreme Court shall have jurisdiction over such suits or cases.

(3) The High Court shall have and exercise such jurisdiction over the suits and cases to which the provisions of sub-paragraph (2) of this paragraph apply as the Governor may from time to time by order specify.

(4) A Regional Council or District Council, as the case may be, may with the previous approval of the Governor make rules regulating:

(a) the constitution of village councils and courts and the powers to be exercised by them under this paragraph;

(b) the procedure to be followed by village councils or courts in the trial of suits and cases under sub-paragraph (1) of this paragraph;

(c) the procedure to be followed by the Regional or District Council or any court constituted by such Council in appeals and other proceedings under sub-paragraph (2) of this paragraph;

(d) the enforcement of decisions and orders of such councils and courts; and

(e) all other ancillary matters for the carrying out of the provisions of sub-paragraphs (1) and (2) of this paragraph.

(5) On and from such date as the President may, after consulting the Government of the State concerned, by notification appoint in this behalf, this paragraph shall have effect in relation to such autonomous district or region as may be specified in the notification, as if —

(i) in sub-paragraph (1), for the words "between the parties all of whom belong to Scheduled Tribes within such areas, other than suits and cases to which the provisions of sub-paragraph (1) of paragraph 5 of this Schedule apply,", the words "not being suits and cases of the nature referred to in sub-paragraph (1) of paragraph (5) of this Schedule, which the Governor may specify in this behalf," had been substituted;

(ii) sub-paragraphs (2) and (3) had been omitted;

(iii) in sub-paragraph (4) —

(a) for the words "A Regional Council or District Council, as the case may be, may with the previous approval of the Governor make rules regulating", the words "the Governor may make rules regulating" had been substituted;

(b) for clause (a), the following clause had been substituted, namely —

"(a) the constitution of village councils and courts, the powers to be exercised by them under this paragraph and the courts to which appeals from the decisions of village councils and courts shall lie";

(c) for clause (c), the following clause had been substituted, namely —

"(c) the transfer of appeals and other proceedings pending before the Regional or District Council or any court constituted by such Council immediately before the date appointed by the President under sub-paragraph (5)"; and

(d) in clause (e), for the words, brackets and figures "sub-paragraphs (1) and (2)", the word, brackets and figure "sub-paragraph (1)" had been substituted.

1. Paragraph 4 has been amended in its application to the State of Assam by the Sixth Schedule to the Constitution (Amendment) Act, 2003 (44 of 2003), Section 2, so as to insert the following sub-paragraph after sub-paragraph (5), namely —

"(6) Nothing in this paragraph shall apply to the Bodoland Territorial Council constituted under the proviso to sub-paragraph (3) of paragraph 2 of this Schedule".

5. *Conferment of powers under the Code of Civil Procedure, 1908, and the Code of Criminal Procedure, 1898, on the Regional and District Councils and on certain courts and officers for the trial of certain suits, cases and offences:* (1) The Governor may, for the trial of suits or cases arising out of any law in force in any autonomous district or region being a law specified in that behalf by the Governor, or for the trial of offences punishable with death, transportation for life, or imprisonment for a term of not less than five years under the Indian Penal Code or under any other law for the time being applicable to such district or region, confer on the District Council or the Regional Council having authority over such district or region or on courts constituted by such District Council or on any officer appointed in that behalf by the Governor, such powers under the Code of Civil Procedure, 1908, or, as the case may be, the Code of Criminal Procedure, 1898, as he deems appropriate, and thereupon the said Council, court or officer shall try the suits, cases or offences in exercise of the powers so conferred.

(2) The Governor may withdraw or modify any of the powers conferred on a District Council, Regional Council, court or officer under sub-paragraph (1) of this paragraph.

(3) Save as expressly provided in this paragraph, the Code of Civil Procedure, 1908, and the Code of Criminal Procedure, 1898, shall not apply to the trial of any suits, cases or offences in an autonomous district or in any autonomous region to which the provisions of this paragraph apply.

(4) On and from the date appointed by the President under sub-paragraph (5) of paragraph 4 in relation to any autonomous district or autonomous region, nothing contained in this paragraph shall, in its application to that district or region, be deemed to authorize the Governor to confer on the District Council or Regional Council or on courts constituted by the District Council any of the powers referred to in sub-paragraph (1) of this paragraph.

1. See now the Code of Criminal Procedure, 1973 (Act 2 of 1974).

6. *Powers of the District Council to establish primary schools, etc.:* (1) The District Council for an autonomous district may establish, construct, or manage primary schools, dispensaries, markets, cattle pounds, ferries, fisheries, roads, road transport and waterways in the district and may, with the previous approval of the Governor, make regulations for the regulation and control thereof and, in particular, may prescribe the language and the manner in which primary education shall be imparted in the primary schools in the district.

(2) The Governor may, with the consent of any District Council, entrust either conditionally or unconditionally to that Council or to its officers functions in relation to agriculture, animal husbandry, community projects, cooperative societies, social welfare, village planning or any other matter to which the executive power of the State extends.

7. *District and Regional Funds:* (1) There shall be constituted for each autonomous district, a District Fund and for each autonomous region, a Regional Fund to which shall be credited all moneys received respectively by the District Council for that district and the Regional Council for that region in the course of the administration of such district or region, as the case may be, in accordance with the provisions of this Constitution.

(2) The Governor may make rules for the management of the District Fund, or, as the case may be, the Regional Fund and for the procedure to be followed in respect of payment of money into the said Fund, the withdrawal of moneys therefrom, the custody of moneys therein and any other matter connected with or ancillary to the matters aforesaid.

(3) The accounts of the District Council or, as the case may be, the Regional Council shall be kept in such form as the Comptroller and Auditor-General of India may, with the approval of the President, prescribe.

(4) The Comptroller and Auditor-General shall cause the accounts of the District and Regional Councils to be audited in such manner as he may think fit, and the reports of the Comptroller and Auditor-General relating to such accounts shall be submitted to the Governor who shall cause them to be laid before the Council.

8. *Powers to assess and collect land revenue and to impose taxes:* (1) The Regional Council for an autonomous region in respect of all lands within such region and the District Council for an autonomous district in respect of all lands within the district except those which are in the areas under the authority of Regional Councils, if any, within the district, shall have the power to assess and collect revenue in respect of such lands in accordance with the principles for the time being followed by the Government of the State in assessing lands for the purpose of land revenue in the State generally.

(2) The Regional Council for an autonomous region in respect of areas within such region and the District Council for an autonomous district in respect of all areas in the district except those which are under the authority of Regional Councils, if any, within the district, shall have power to levy and collect taxes on lands and buildings, and tolls on persons resident within such areas.

(3) The District Council for an autonomous district shall have the power to levy and collect all or any of the following taxes within such district, that is to say —

(a) taxes on professions, trades, callings and employments;
(b) taxes on animals, vehicles and boats;
(c) taxes on the entry of goods into a market for sale therein, and tolls on passengers and goods carried in ferries; and
(d) taxes for the maintenance of schools, dispensaries or roads.

(4) A Regional Council or District Council, as the case may be, may make regulations to provide for the levy and collection of any of the taxes specified in sub-paragraphs (2) and (3) of this paragraph and every such regulation shall be submitted forthwith to the Governor and, until assented to by him, shall have no effect.

9. *Licences or leases for the purpose of prospecting for, or extraction of, minerals:* (1) Such share of the royalties accruing each year from licences or leases for the purpose of prospecting for, or the extraction of, minerals granted by the Government of the State in respect of any area within an autonomous district as may be agreed upon between the

Government of the State and the District Council of such district shall be made over to that District Council.

(2) If any dispute arises as to the share of such royalties to be made over to a District Council, it shall be referred to the Governor for determination and the amount determined by the Governor in his discretion shall be deemed to be the amount payable under sub-paragraph (1) of this paragraph to the District Council and the decision of the Governor shall be final.

1. Paragraph 9 has been amended in its application to the States of Tripura and Mizoram by the Sixth Schedule to the Constitution (Amendment) Act, 1988 (67 of 1988), Section 2, so as to insert the following sub-paragraph after sub-paragraph (2), namely —

"(3) The Governor may, by order, direct that the share of royalties to be made over to a District Council under this paragraph shall be made over to that Council within a period of one year from the date of any agreement under sub-paragraph (1) or, as the case may be, of any determination under sub-paragraph (2)".

10. *Power of District Council to make regulations for the control of money-lending and trading by non-tribals:* (1) The District Council of an autonomous district may make regulations for the regulation and control of money-lending or trading within the district by persons other than Scheduled Tribes resident in the district.

(2) In particular and without prejudice to the generality of the foregoing power, such regulations may —

(a) prescribe that no one except the holder of a licence issued in that behalf shall carry on the business of money-lending;

(b) prescribe the maximum rate of interest which may be charged or be recovered by a money-lender;

(c) provide for the maintenance of accounts by money-lenders and for the inspection of such accounts by officers appointed in that behalf by the District Council;

(d) prescribe that no person who is not a member of the Scheduled Tribes resident in the district shall carry on wholesale or retail business in any commodity except under a licence issued in that behalf by the District Council:

Provided that no regulations may be made under this paragraph unless they are passed by a majority of not less than three-fourths of the total membership of the District Council: Provided further that it shall not be competent under any such regulations to refuse the grant of a licence to a money-lender or a trader who has been carrying on business within the district since before the time of the making of such regulations.

(3) All regulations made under this paragraph shall be submitted forthwith to the Governor and, until assented to by him, shall have no effect.

1. Paragraph 10 has been amended in its application to the States of Tripura and Mizoram by the Sixth Schedule to the Constitution (Amendment) Act, 1988 (67 of 1988), Section 2, as under — (a) in the heading, the words "by non-tribals" shall be omitted; (b) in sub-paragraph (1), the words "other than Scheduled Tribes" shall be omitted; (c) in sub-paragraph (2), for clause (d), the following clause shall be substituted, namely —

   "(d) prescribe that no person resident in the district shall carry on any trade, whether wholesale or retail, except under a licence issued in that behalf by the District Council".

2. Paragraph 10 has been amended in its application to the State of Assam by the Sixth Schedule to the Constitution (Amendment) Act, 2003 (44 of 2003), Section 2, so as to insert the following sub-paragraph after sub-paragraph (3), namely —

   "(4) Nothing in this paragraph shall apply to the Bodoland Territorial Council constituted under the proviso to sub-paragraph (3) of paragraph 2 of this Schedule".

11. *Publication of laws, rules and regulations made under the Schedule:* All laws, rules and regulations made under this Schedule by a District Council or a Regional Council shall be published forthwith in the Official Gazette of the State and shall on such publication have the force of law.

12. *Application of Acts of Parliament and of the Legislature of the State of Assam to autonomous districts and autonomous regions in the State of Assam:* (1) Notwithstanding anything in this Constitution, —

(a) no Act of the Legislature of the State of Assam in respect of any of the matters specified in paragraph 3 of this Schedule as matters with respect to which a District

Council or a Regional Council may make laws, and no Act of the Legislature of the State of Assam prohibiting or restricting the consumption of any non-distilled alcoholic liquor shall apply to any autonomous district or autonomous region in that State unless in either case the District Council for such district or having jurisdiction over such region by public notification so directs, and the District Council in giving such direction with respect to any Act may direct that the Act shall in its application to such district or region or any part thereof have effect subject to such exceptions or modifications as it thinks fit; and

(b) the Governor may, by public notification, direct that any Act of Parliament or of the Legislature of the State of Assam to which the provisions of clause (a) of this sub-paragraph do not apply shall not apply to an autonomous district or an autonomous region in that State, or shall apply to such district or region or any part thereof subject to such exceptions or modifications as he may specify in the notification.

(2) Any direction given under sub-paragraph (1) of this paragraph may be given so as to have retrospective effect.

1. Paragraph 12 has been amended to its application to the State of Assam by the Sixth Schedule to the Constitution (Amendment) Act, 1995 (42 of 1995), Section 2, as under, —

   "in paragraph 12, in sub-paragraph (1), for the words and figure "matters specified in paragraph 3 of this Schedule", the words, figures and letter "matters specified in paragraph 3 or paragraph 3A of this Schedule" shall be substituted".

2. Paragraph 12 has been amended in its application to the State of Assam by the Sixth Schedule to the Constitution (Amendment) Act, 2003 (44 of 2003), Section 2, as under, —

   "in paragraph 12, in sub-paragraph (1), in clause (a), for the words, figures and letter "matters specified in paragraph 3 or paragraph 3A of this Schedule", the words, figures and letter "matters specified in paragraph 3 or paragraph 3A or paragraph 3B of this Schedule" shall be substituted".

12A. *Application of Acts of Parliament and of the Legislature of the State of Meghalaya to autonomous districts and autonomous regions* *in the State of Meghalaya:* Notwithstanding anything in this Constitution, —

(a) if any provision of a law made by a District or Regional Council in the State of Meghalaya with respect to any matter specified in sub-paragraph (1) of paragraph 3 of this Schedule or if any provision of any regulation made by a District Council or a Regional Council in that State under paragraph 8 or paragraph 10 of this Schedule, is repugnant to any provision of a law made by the Legislature of the State of Meghalaya with respect to that matter, then, the law or regulation made by the District Council or, as the case may be, the Regional Council whether made before or after the law made by the Legislature of the State of Meghalaya, shall, to the extent of repugnancy, be void and the law made by the Legislature of the State of Meghalaya shall prevail; and

(b) the President may, with respect to any Act of Parliament, by notification, direct that it shall not apply to an autonomous district or an autonomous region in the State of Meghalaya, or shall apply to such district or region or any part thereof subject to such exceptions or modifications as he may specify in the notification and any such direction may be given so as to have retrospective effect.

12AA. *Application of Acts of Parliament and of the Legislature of the State of Tripura to the autonomous districts and autonomous regions in the State of Tripura:* Notwithstanding anything in this Constitution, —

(a) no Act of the Legislature of the State of Tripura in respect of any of the matters specified in paragraph 3 of this Schedule as matters with respect to which a District Council or a Regional Council may make laws, and no Act of the Legislature of the State of Tripura prohibiting or restricting the consumption of any non-distilled alcoholic liquor shall apply to any autonomous district or autonomous region in that State unless, in either case the, District Council for such district or having jurisdiction over such region by public notification so directs, and the District Council in giving such direction with respect to any Act may direct that the Act shall, in its application to that district or such region or any part thereof have effect subject to such exceptions or modifications as it thinks fit;

(b) the Governor may, by public notification, direct that any Act of the Legislature of the State of Tripura to which the provisions of clause (a) of this sub-paragraph do not apply, shall not apply to the autonomous district or any autonomous region in that State, or shall apply to that district or such region, or any part thereof, subject to such exceptions or modifications, as he may specify in the notification; and

(c) the President may, with respect to any Act of Parliament, by notification, direct that it shall not apply to the autonomous district or an autonomous region in the State of Tripura, or shall apply to such district or region or any part thereof, subject to such exceptions or modifications as he may specify in the notification and any such direction may be given so as to have retrospective effect.

12B. *Application of Acts of Parliament and of the Legislature of the State of Mizoram to autonomous districts and autonomous regions in the State of Mizoram:* Notwithstanding anything in this Constitution, —

(a) no Act of the Legislature of the State of Mizoram in respect of any of the matters specified in paragraph 3 of this Schedule as matters with respect to which a District Council or a Regional Council may make laws, and no Act of the Legislature of the State of Mizoram prohibiting or restricting the consumption of any non-distilled alcoholic liquor shall apply to any autonomous district or autonomous region in that State unless, in either case, the District Council for such district or having jurisdiction over such region, by public notification, so directs, and the District Council, in giving such direction with respect to any Act, may direct that the Act shall, in its application to such district or region or any part thereof, have effect subject to such exceptions or modifications as it thinks fit;

(b) the Governor may, by public notification, direct that any Act of the Legislature of the State of Mizoram to which the provisions of clause (a) of this sub-paragraph do not apply, shall not apply to an autonomous district or an autonomous region in that State, or shall apply to such district or region, or any part thereof, subject to such exceptions or modifications, as he may specify in the notification; and

(c) the President may, with respect to any Act of Parliament, by notification, direct that it shall not apply to an autonomous district or an autonomous region in the State of Mizoram, or shall apply to such district or region or any part thereof, subject to such exceptions or modifications as he may specify in the notification and any such direction may be given so as to have retrospective effect.

13. *Estimated receipts and expenditure pertaining to autonomous districts to be shown separately in the annual financial statement:* The estimated receipts and expenditure pertaining to an autonomous district which are to be credited to, or is to be made from, the Consolidated Fund of the State shall be first placed before the District Council for discussion and then after such discussion be shown separately in the annual financial statement of the State to be laid before the Legislature of the State under article 202.

14. *Appointment of Commission to inquire into and report on the administration of autonomous districts and autonomous regions:* (1) The Governor may at any time appoint a Commission to examine and report on any matter specified by him relating to the administration of the autonomous districts and autonomous regions in the State, including matters specified in clauses (c), (d), (e) and (f) of sub-paragraph (3) of paragraph 1 of this Schedule, or may appoint a Commission to inquire into and report from time-to-time on the administration of autonomous districts and autonomous regions in the State generally and in particular on —

(a) the provision of educational and medical facilities and communications in such districts and regions;

(b) the need for any new or special legislation in respect of such districts and regions; and

(c) the administration of the laws, rules and regulations made by the District and Regional Councils;

and define the procedure to be followed by such Commission.

(2) The report of every such Commission with the recommendations of the Governor with respect thereto shall be laid before the Legislature of the State by the Minister concerned together with an explanatory memorandum regarding the action proposed to be taken thereon by the Government of the State.

(3) In allocating the business of the Government of the State among his Ministers the Governor may place one of his Ministers

specially in charge of the welfare of the autonomous districts and autonomous regions in the State.

1. Paragraph 14 has been amended in its application to the State of Assam by the Sixth Schedule to the Constitution (Amendment) Act, 1995 (42 of 1995), Section 2, as under, —

   "in paragraph 14, in sub-paragraph (2), the words "with the recommendations of the Governor with respect thereto" shall be omitted".

15. *Annulment or suspension of acts and resolutions of District and Regional Councils:* (1) If at any time the Governor is satisfied that an act or resolution of a District or a Regional Council is likely to endanger the safety of India or is likely to be prejudicial to public order, he may annul or suspend such act or resolution and take such steps as he may consider necessary (including the suspension of the Council and the assumption to himself of all or any of the powers vested in or exercisable by the Council) to prevent the commission or continuance of such act, or the giving of effect to such resolution.

(2) Any order made by the Governor under sub-paragraph (1) of this paragraph together with the reasons therefor shall be laid before the Legislature of the State as soon as possible and the order shall, unless revoked by the Legislature of the State, continue in force for a period of twelve months from the date on which it was so made: Provided that if and so often as a resolution approving the continuance in force of such order is passed by the Legislature of the State, the order shall unless cancelled by the Governor continue in force for a further period of twelve months from the date on which under this paragraph it would otherwise have ceased to operate.

1. Paragraph 15 has been amended in its application to the States of Tripura and Mizoram by the Sixth Schedule to the Constitution (Amendment) Act, 1988 (67 of 1988), Section 2, as under, —

   "(a) in the opening paragraph, for the words "by the Legislature of the State", the words "by him" shall be substituted; (b) the proviso shall be omitted".

16. *Dissolution of a District or a Regional Council:* (1) The Governor may on the recommendation of a Commission appointed under paragraph 14 of this Schedule by public notification order the dissolution of a District or a Regional Council, and —

(a) direct that a fresh general election shall be held immediately for the reconstitution of the Council; or

(b) subject to the previous approval of the Legislature of the State assume the administration of the area under the authority of such Council himself or place the administration of such area under the Commission appointed under the said paragraph or any other body considered suitable by him for a period not exceeding twelve months: Provided that when an order under clause (a) of this paragraph has been made, the Governor may take the action referred to in clause (b) of this paragraph with regard to the administration of the area in question pending the reconstitution of the Council on fresh general election:

Provided further that no action shall be taken under clause (b) of this paragraph without giving the District or the Regional Council, as the case may be, an opportunity of placing its views before the Legislature of the State.

(2) If at any time the Governor is satisfied that a situation has arisen in which the administration of an autonomous district or region cannot be carried on in accordance with the provisions of this Schedule, he may, by public notification, assume to himself all or any of the functions or powers vested in or exercisable by the District Council or, as the case may be, the Regional Council and declare that such functions or powers shall be exercisable by such person or authority as he may specify in this behalf, for a period not exceeding six months:

Provided that the Governor may by a further order or orders extend the operation of the initial order by a period not exceeding six months on each occasion.

(3) Every order made under sub-paragraph (2) of this paragraph with the reasons therefor shall be laid before the Legislature of the State and shall cease to operate at the expiration of thirty days from the date on which the State Legislature first sits after the issue of the order, unless, before the expiry of that period it has been approved by that State Legislature.

1. Paragraph 16 has been amended in its application to the States of Tripura and Mizoram by the Sixth Schedule to the Constitution (Amendment) Act, 1988 (67 of 1988) Section 2, as under, —

"(a) in sub-paragraph (1), the words "subject to the previous approval of the Legislature of the State" occurring

in clause (b), and the second proviso shall be omitted;
(b) for sub-paragraph (3), the following sub-paragraph shall be substituted, namely —

"(3) Every order made under sub-paragraph (1) or sub-paragraph (2) of this paragraph, along with the reasons therefor shall be laid before the Legislature of the State".

17. *Exclusion of areas from autonomous districts in forming constituencies in such districts:* For the purposes of elections to the Legislative Assembly of Assam or Meghalaya or Tripura or Mizoram, the Governor may by order declare that any area within an autonomous district in the State of Assam or Meghalaya or Tripura or Mizoram, as the case may be, shall not form part of any constituency to fill a seat or seats in the Assembly reserved for any such district but shall form part of a constituency to fill a seat or seats in the Assembly not so reserved to be specified in the order.

1. Paragraph 17 has been amended in its application to the State of Assam by the Sixth Schedule to the Constitution (Amendment) Act, 2003 (44 of 2003), Section 2, so as to insert the following proviso, namely:

   "Provided that nothing in this paragraph shall apply to the Bodoland Territorial Areas District".

19. *Transitional provisions:* (1) As soon as possible after the commencement of this Constitution the Governor shall take steps for the constitution of a District Council for each autonomous district in the State under this Schedule and, until a District Council is so constituted for an autonomous district, the administration of such district shall be vested in the Governor and the following provisions shall apply to the administration of the areas within such district instead of the foregoing provisions of this Schedule, namely: —

(a) no Act of Parliament or of the Legislature of the State shall apply to any such area unless the Governor by public notification so directs; and the Governor in giving such a direction with respect to any Act may direct that the Act shall, in its application to the area or to any specified part thereof, have effect subject to such exceptions or modifications as he thinks fit;

(b) the Governor may make regulations for the peace and good government of any such area and any regulations so made may repeal or amend any Act of Parliament or of the Legislature of the State or any existing law which is for the time being applicable to such area.

(2) Any direction given by the Governor under clause (a) of sub-paragraph (1) of this paragraph may be given so as to have retrospective effect.

(3) All regulations made under clause (b) of sub-paragraph (1) of this paragraph shall be submitted forthwith to the President and, until assented to by him, shall have no effect.

1. Paragraph 19 has been amended in its application to the State of Assam by the Sixth Schedule to the Constitution (Amendment) Act, 2003 (44 of 2003), Section 2, so as to insert the following sub-paragraph after sub-paragraph (3), namely —

"(4) As soon as possible after the commencement of this Act, and Interim Executive Council for Bodoland Territorial Areas District in Assam shall be formed by the Governor from amongst leaders of the Bodo movement, including the signatories to the Memorandum of Settlement, and shall provide adequate representation to the non-tribal communities in that area:

Provided that Interim Council shall be for a period of six months during which endeavour to hold the election to the Council shall be made.

Explanation: For the purposes of this sub-paragraph, the expression "Memorandum of Settlement" means the Memorandum signed on the 10th day of February, 2003 between Government of India, Government of Assam and Bodo Liberation Tigers".

20. *Tribal areas:* (1) The areas specified in Parts I, II, IIA and III of the table below shall respectively be the tribal areas within the State of Assam, the State of Meghalaya, the State of Tripura and the State of Mizoram.

(2) Any reference in Parts I, II or Part III of the table below to any district shall be construed as a reference to the territories comprised within the autonomous district of that name existing immediately before the day appointed under clause (b) of section 2 of the North-Eastern Areas (Reorganization) Act, 1971:

Provided that for the purposes of clauses (e) and (f) of sub-paragraph (1) of paragraphs 3, 4, 5 and 6, sub-paragraph (2), clauses (a), (b) and (d) of sub-paragraphs (3) and (4) of paragraph 8 and clause (d) of sub-paragraph (2) of paragraph 10 of this Schedule, no part of the area comprised within the municipality of Shillong shall be deemed to be within the Khasi Hills District.

(3) The reference in Part IIA in the table below to the "Tripura Tribal Areas District" shall be construed as a reference to the territory comprising the tribal areas specified in the First Schedule to the Tripura Tribal Areas Autonomous District Council Act, 1979.

TABLE

PART I

1. The North Cachar Hills District.
2. The Karbi Anglong District.
3. The Bodoland Territorial Area District.

PART II

1. Khasi Hills District.
2. Jaintia Hills District.
3. The Garo Hills District.

PART IIA

Tripura Tribal Areas District.

Part III

1. The Chakma District.
2. The Mara District.
3. The Lai District.

20A. *Dissolution of the Mizo District Council:* (1) Notwithstanding anything in this Schedule, the District Council of the Mizo District existing immediately before the prescribed date (hereinafter referred to as the Mizo District Council) shall stand dissolved and cease to exist.

(2) The Administrator of the Union territory of Mizoram may, by one or more orders, provide for all or any of the following matters, namely: —

(a) the transfer, in whole or in part, of the assets, rights and liabilities of the Mizo District Council (including the rights and liabilities under any contract made by it) to the Union or to any other authority;

(b) the substitution of the Union or any other authority for the Mizo District Council, or the addition of the Union or any other authority, as a party to any legal proceedings to which the Mizo District Council is a party;

(c) the transfer or re-employment of any employees of the Mizo District Council to or by the Union or any other authority, the terms and conditions of service applicable to such employees after such transfer or re-employment;

(d) the continuance of any laws, made by the Mizo District Council and in force immediately before its dissolution, subject to such adaptations and modifications, whether by way of repeal or amendment, as the Administrator may make in this behalf, until such laws are altered, repealed or amended by a competent Legislature or other competent authority; and

(e) such incidental, consequential and supplementary matters as the Administrator considers necessary.

Explanation: In this paragraph and in paragraph 20B of this Schedule, the expression "prescribed date" means the date on which the Legislative Assembly of the Union territory of Mizoram is duly constituted under and in accordance with the provisions of the Government of Union Territories Act, 1963.

20B. *Autonomous regions in the Union territory of Mizoram to be autonomous districts and transitory provisions consequent thereto:* (1) Notwithstanding anything in this Schedule, —

(a) every autonomous region existing immediately before the prescribed date in the Union territory of Mizoram shall, on and from that date, be an autonomous district in that Union territory (hereafter referred to as the corresponding new district) and the Administrator thereof may, by one or more orders, direct that such consequential amendments as are necessary to give effect to the provisions of this clause shall be made in paragraph 20 of this Schedule (including Part III of the table appended to that paragraph) and thereupon the said paragraph and the said Part III shall be deemed to have been amended accordingly;

(b) every Regional Council of an autonomous region in the Union territory of Mizoram existing immediately before the prescribed date (hereafter referred to as the existing Regional Council) shall, on and from that date and until a District Council is duly constituted for the corresponding new district, be deemed to be the District Council of that district (hereafter referred to as the corresponding new District Council).

(2) Every member whether elected or nominated of an existing Regional Council shall be deemed to have been elected or, as the case may be, nominated to the corresponding new District Council and shall hold office until a District Council is duly constituted for the corresponding new district under this Schedule.

(3) Until rules are made under sub-paragraph (7) of paragraph 2 and sub-paragraph (4) of paragraph 4 of this Schedule by the corresponding new District Council, the rules made under the said provisions by the existing Regional Council and in force immediately before the prescribed date shall have effect in relation to the corresponding new District Council subject to such adaptations and modifications as may be made therein by the Administrator of the Union territory of Mizoram.

(4) The Administrator of the Union territory of Mizoram may, by one or more orders, provide for all or any of the following matters, namely:

(a) the transfer in whole or in part of the assets, rights and liabilities of the existing Regional Council (including the rights and liabilities under any contract made by it) to the corresponding new District Council;

(b) the substitution of the corresponding new District Council for the existing Regional Council as a party to the legal proceedings to which the existing Regional Council is a party;

(c) the transfer or re-employment of any employees of the existing Regional Council to or by the corresponding new District Council, the terms and conditions of service applicable to such employees after such transfer or re-employment;

(d) the continuance of any laws made by the existing Regional Council and in force immediately before the prescribed date, subject to such adaptations and modifications, whether by way of repeal or amendment, as the Administrator may make in this behalf until such laws are altered, repealed or amended by a competent Legislature or other competent authority; and

(e) such incidental, consequential and supplementary matters as the Administrator considers necessary.

1. After paragraph 20B, the following paragraph has been inserted in its application to the State of Assam by the Sixth Schedule to the Constitution (Amendment) Act, 1995 (42 of 1995), Section 2, namely —

"20BA. Exercise of discretionary powers by the Governor in the discharge of his functions. — The Governor in the discharge of his functions under sub-paragraphs (2) and (3) of paragraph 1, sub-paragraphs (1), (6), sub-paragraph (6A) excluding the first proviso and sub-paragraph (7) of paragraph 2, sub-paragraph (3) of paragraph 3, sub-paragraph (4) of paragraph 4, paragraph 5, sub-paragraph (1) of paragraph 6, sub-paragraph (2) of paragraph 7, sub-paragraph (4) of paragraph 8, sub-paragraph (3) of paragraph 9, sub-paragraph (3) of paragraph 10, sub-paragraph (1) of paragraph 14, sub-paragraph (1) of paragraph 15 and sub-paragraphs (1) and (2) of paragraph 16 of this Schedule, shall, after consulting the Council of Ministers and the North Cachar Hills Autonomous Council or the Karbi Anglong Autonomous Council, as the case may be, take such action as he considers necessary in his discretion".

2. After paragraph 20B, the following paragraph has been inserted in its application to the States of Tripura and Mizoram, by the Sixth Schedule to the Constitution (Amendment) Act, 1988 (67 of 1988), Section 2, namely —

"20BB. Exercise of discretionary powers by the Governor in the discharge of his functions. The Governor, in the discharge of his functions under sub-paragraphs (2) and (3) of paragraph 1, sub-paragraphs (1) and (7) of paragraph 2, sub-paragraph (3) of paragraph 3, sub-paragraph (4) of paragraph 4, paragraph 5, sub-paragraph (1) of paragraph 6, sub-paragraph (2) of paragraph 7, sub-paragraph (3) of paragraph 9, sub-paragraph (1) of paragraph 14, sub-paragraph (1) of paragraph 15 and sub-paragraphs (1) and (2) of paragraph 16 of this Schedule, shall, after consulting the Council of Ministers, and if he thinks it necessary, the District Council or the Regional Council concerned, take such action as he considers necessary in his discretion".

20C. *Interpretation:* Subject to any provision made in this behalf, the provisions of this Schedule shall, in their application to the Union territory of Mizoram, have effect — (1) as if references to the Governor and Government of the State were references to the Administrator of the Union territory appointed under article 239, references to State (except in the expression "Government of the State") were references to the Union territory of Mizoram and references to the State Legislature were references to the Legislative Assembly of the Union territory of Mizoram.

(2) as if —

(a) in sub-paragraph (5) of paragraph 4, the provision for consultation with the Government of the State concerned had been omitted;

(b) in sub-paragraph (2) of paragraph 6, for the words "to which the executive power of the State extends", the words "with respect to which the Legislative Assembly of the Union territory of Mizoram has power to make laws" had been substituted; and

(c) in paragraph 13, the words and figures "under article 202" had been omitted.

21. *Amendment of the Schedule:* (1) Parliament may from time to time by law amend by way of addition, variation or repeal any of the provisions of this Schedule and, when the Schedule is so amended, any reference to this Schedule in this Constitution shall be construed as a reference to such Schedule as so amended.

(2) No such law as is mentioned in sub-paragraph (1) of this paragraph shall be deemed to be an amendment of this Constitution for the purposes of article 368.

ANNEXURE XXX

Memorandum of Settlement on Bodoland Territorial Council (BTC)

New Delhi, 10th February, 2003

1. The Government of India and the Government of Assam have been making concerted efforts to fulfil the aspirations of the Bodo people relating to their cultural identity, language, education and economic development. Towards this end, a series of talks were held between Government of India, Government of Assam and Bodo Liberation Tigers (BLT) since March 2000. As a result, it is agreed to create a self-governing body for the Bodo Areas in the State of Assam as follows:

2. *Objectives:* The objectives of the agreement are: to create an Autonomous self-governing body to be known as Bodoland Territorial Council (BTC) within the State of Assam and to provide Constitutional protection under Sixth Schedule to the said Autonomous Body; to fulfil economic, educational and linguistic aspirations and the preservation of land-rights, socio-cultural and ethnic identity of the Bodos; and speed-up the infrastructure development in BTC area.

3. *Area:*

3.1. The area of proposed BTC shall comprise all the 3,082 villages and areas to be so notified by the State Government. The above mentioned villages and areas shall be divided into 4 contiguous districts after reorganization of the existing districts of Assam within a period of 6 months of the signing of the agreement on the lines of the proposal given by BLT subject to clearance of the Delimitation Commission.

3.2 A committee comprising one representative each from Governments of India and Assam and BLT will decide by consensus on the inclusion of additional villages and areas in the BTC from out of 95 villages and areas on the basis of the criteria of tribal population being not less than 50 per cent, contiguity or any other agreed relevant criteria within a period of three months of signing of this MoS.

4. *Status of Bodoland Territorial Council:* The provision of the Sixth Schedule and other relevant Articles of the Constitution of India will apply to BTC, *mutatis mutandis* in terms of this agreement. The safeguards/modifications for the non-tribals in BTC area, *inter-alia*, will include the following:

4.1. Provision of para 1(2) of Sixth Schedule regarding Autonomous Regions will not be applicable to BTC.

4.2. A provision will be made in para 2(1) of the Sixth Schedule for increasing the number of members for BTC up to 46 out of which 30 will be reserved for Scheduled Tribes, 5 for non-tribal communities, 5 open for all communities and 6 to be nominated by Governor of Assam from the unrepresented communities for BTC area of which atleast two should be women. Nominated members will have the same rights and privileges as other members, including voting rights. Election from the 40 constituencies of BTC shall be on the basis of adult franchise. The term of the elected members of BTC shall be for 5 years.

4.3. Safeguards for the settlement rights, transfer and inheritance of property etc. of non-tribals will be suitably incorporated in para 3 of the Sixth Schedule. Any such law as may be made by the BTC in this regard will not, in particular: (a) Extinguish the rights and privileges enjoyed by an citizen of India in respect of their land at the commencement of BTC, and (b) Bar any citizen from acquiring land either by way of inheritance, allotment, settlement or by way of transfer if such citizens were eligible for such *bonafide* acquisition of land within the BTC area.

4.4. Provision will be added in para 6 of Sixth Schedule that in BTC area, language and medium of instruction in educational institutions will not be changed without approval of the State Government.

4.5. Provision of para 8 of Sixth Schedule regarding power to assess and collect land revenue and impose taxes shall be applicable to BTC.

4.6. Para 10 of the Sixth Schedule will not be applicable to BTC area.

4.7. Provision of Article 332(6) of the Constitution will be so modified that the existing status of representation of BTC area in the State Assembly is kept intact. After the creation of BTC, the Parliamentary and Assembly Constituencies shall be delimited by the Delimitation Commission in accordance with the provisions of the Constitution.

4.8. In the event, Panchayati Raj system ceases to be in force in the council area, the powers of the Panchayati Raj Institutions in such matters shall be vested with the Council. The Amendments to the Sixth Schedule shall include provisions in such a manner that non-tribals are not disadvantaged in relation to the rights enjoyed by them at the commencement of BTC and their rights and privileges including land rights are fully protected.

5. *Power and Functions:*

5.1. The Council shall have legislative powers in respect to subjects transferred to it as enumerated below. All laws made under this paragraph shall be submitted forthwith to the Governor and until assented to by him, shall have no effect. The BTC shall have executive, administrative and financial powers in respect of subjects transferred to it. Subjects to be entrusted to BTC by Assam Government 1. Small, Cottage and Rural Industry, 2. Animal Husbandry and Veterinary, 3. Forest, 4. Agriculture, 5. PWD, 6. Sericulture, 7. Education [Primary Education, Higher Secondary including Vocational Training, Adult Education, College Education (General)], 8. Cultural Affairs, 9. Soil Conservation, 10. Cooperation, 11. Fisheries, 12. Panchayat and Rural Development, 13. Handloom and Textile, 14. Health and Family Welfare, 15. Public Health Engineering, 16. Irrigation, 17. Social Welfare, 18. Flood Control, 19. Sports and Youth Welfare, 20. Weights and Measures, 21. Library Services, 22. Museum and Archaeology, 23. Urban Development — Town and Country Planning, 24. Tribal Research Institute, 25. Land and Revenue, 26. Publicity/Public Relations, 27. Printing and Stationery, 28. Tourism, 29. Transport, 30. Planning and Development, 31. Municipal Corporation, Improvement Trust, District Boards and other local authorities, 32. Welfare of Plan Tribes and Backward

Classes, 33. Markets and Fairs, 34. Lotteries, Theatres, Dramatic Performance and Cinema, 35. Statistics, 36. Food and Civil Supply, 37. Intoxicating liquors, opium and derivatives, etc., 38. Labour and Employment, 39. Relief and Rehabilitation, and 40. Registration of Births and Deaths.

5.2. There shall be an Executive Council comprising of not more than 12 Executive Members, one of whom shall be the Chief and another one the Deputy Chief of the said Executive Council. There shall be adequate representation for the non-tribal members in the Executive Council. The Chief and the Deputy Chief of the Council shall have the status equivalent to the Cabinet Minister and the other Executive Members equivalent to the Minister of the State of Assam for protocol purposes in BTC area.

5.3. The BTC shall have the full control over the officers and staff connected with the delegated subjects working in the BTC area and shall be competent to transfer officers and staff within the BTC area. ACRs of these officers shall also be written by the appropriated BTC authority.

5.4. BTC shall also be competent to make appointments for all posts under its control in accordance with the rules of appointment followed by the Government of Assam. However, the posts, where recruitment is made on the recommendation of APSC, shall not be covered under this provision. The Council may constitute a Selection Board for appointments to be made by it and may also make rules, with the approval of the Governor of Assam to regulate appointments and to ensure adequate representation for all communities living in the Council area.

5.5. No posts shall be created by BTC without concurrence of the Government of Assam and it shall also abide by the decision of the Government of Assam in respect of abolition of temporarily keeping vacant any post.

5.6. Development functions and bodies within the competence of BTC shall be transferred to BTC. In respect of DRDA, concurrence of Government of India will be obtained.

5.7. The offices of the Dy. Commissioner and Superintendent of Police will be outside the superintendence and control of BTC.

5.8. The State Government would provide an amount, to be decided every year on population ratio basis, as grants-in-aid in two equal instalments to the BTC for executing development works. The proportionate share for the BTC shall be calculated on the basis of the plan funds available after setting aside the funds required for earmarked sectors and the salary. This amount may be reduced proportionately if the state plan allocation is reduced or there is plan cut due to resource problem. In addition, the Council will be paid a suitable amount of plan funds and non-plan funds to cover the office expenses and the salaries of the staff working under their control. The BTC shall disburse the salaries of the staff under their control and would ensure strict economy in the matter.

5.9. BTC authority shall prepare a plan with the amounts likely to be available for development works, both under State share and Central share, covering any or all the activities of the departments under their control. The Council shall have full discretion in selecting the activities and choosing the amount for the investment under the same in any year covering all groups of people in a fair and equitable manner. This plan will be a sub set of the State plan and would be treated as its integral part. Once the plan of the State, including BTC plan, gets the approval of the Planning Commission the BTC authority will start execution of their plan in the BTC area. Modifications, if any, made by the Planning Commission in the BTC proposal, shall be binding on the BTC authority. The State Government shall not divert the funds allocated to the BTC to other heads and also ensure its timely release. BTC may have Planning Department to prepare the plans for BTC area to be submitted to Planning Commission through the Government of Assam.

5.10. The executive functions of the BTC shall be exercised through its Principal Secretary who shall be an officer of the rank not below of Commissioner/Secretary to Government of Assam. The sanctioning powers of the Government of Assam shall be vested with the Principal Secretary of BTC and sanctioning powers of head(s) of the Department(s) including for technical sanction shall be conferred on the senior most officer of that Department preferably not below the rank of Additional Director, who may be designated as Director of BTC for that department. The Principal Secretary and other officers shall exercise their powers under the overall guidance and supervision of BTC.

6. *Law and Order:* To strengthen the Police Administration, Government of Assam shall appoint an IGP for 4 districts of BTC and the jurisdiction of the DIG Kokrajhar shall also be modified to cover these 4 districts.

7. *Revision of list of ST:* Consequent to the inclusion of BTC area into the Sixth Schedule, the list of ST for the State of Assam shall be so modified so as to ensure that the tribal status of Bodos and other tribals living outside the BTC are does not get affected adversely.

8. *Grant of ST status of Bodo Kacharis of Karbi Anglong and NC Hills districts:* The Government of India agrees to consider sympathetically, the inclusion of the Bodo Kacharis living in Karbi Anglong and NC Hills Autonomous Council area in the ST (Hill) List of State of Assam.

9. *Development of Bodo Language:*

9.1. The Government of India agrees to consider favourably the inclusion of Bodo Language in Devnagri Script in the Eighth Schedule of the Constitution.

9.2. Bodo language shall be the official language of BTC subject to the condition that Assamese and English shall also continue to be used for official purpose.

10. *Additional Development Package for BTC:*

10.1. The State Government, within the limitation of financial and other constraints, may offer or allow the Council to offer, possible and sustainable additional incentives for attracting private investment in the Council area and would also support projects for external funding.

10.2. In order to accelerate the development of the region and to meet the aspirations of the people, the Government of India will provide financial assistance of ₹ 100 crore per annum for 5 years for projects to develop the socio-economic infrastructure in BTC areas over and above the normal plan assistance to the State of Assam. The size of the Corpus will be reviewed after a period of 5 years. Suitable mechanism will be built in the system to ensure that the funds are transferred to BTC in time and at regular intervals. An illustrative list of projects which may be considered to be taken-up in BTC given below: *List of projects:* 1. To establish a centre for development and research of Bodo language; 2. Upgradation of existing educational infrastructure by way of renovation/addition of buildings, providing modern facilities for teaching such as computers, science laboratories etc. from primary level to college level in BTC area; 3. A cultural complex to be established at Kokrajhar to promote and develop Bodo tradition and cultural heritage; 4. To establish a super-speciality hospital with all modern facilities at Kokrajhar Government Hospitals shall be established in all district, sub-divisional and block headquarter; 5. To establish sports complexes in all the district headquarters; 6. Food processing plants and clod storage facilities at Kokrajhar, Kajolgaon, Udalguri and Tamulpur; 7. Construction of a bridge over River Aai to connect Koilamoila, Amguri etc. with the rest of the district; 8. To build a Bodoland Bhawan in Delhi; 9. To set-up integrated agro-processing park and textile-*cum*-apparel park; 10. Revitalization of Kokilabari Agricultural Farm; 11. To develop adequate infrastructure to promote Manas sanctuary as an international tourist spot; 12. To complete Champa, Suklai and Dhansiri irrigation projects; 13. To construct a highway on the Indo-Bhutan border from Jamduar to Bhairabkunda to connect remote places located adjacent to the border; 14. To set-up model dairy, fishery, horticulture and poultry farms/training centres at different places in all the 4 districts to encourage youth for self-employment; and 15. To enhance the existing facilities in veterinary hospitals in BTC area.

10.3. Government of India will provide necessary one time financial assistance required for development of administrative infrastructure in the newly created district headquarters, sub-divisional headquarters and book headquarters, besides the BTC Secretariat Complex at Kokrajhar.

11. *Centrally funded University:*

11.1. A centrally funded Central Institute of Technology (CIT) will be set-up to impact education in various technological/ vocational disciplines such as Information Technology, Bio-Technology, Food Processing, Rural Industries, Business Management, etc.

11.2. The CIT will be subsequently upgraded to a Centrally funded State University with technical and non-technical disciplines to be run by the BTC.

12. *Relief and Rehabilitation:*

12.1. The BLT would join the national mainstream and shun the path of violence in the interest of peace and development. After the formation of the interim council of BTC, BLT will dissolve itself as an organization and surrender with arms within a week of swearing-in of the interim council. The State Government would provide full support to relief and rehabilitation of the members of BLT who would surrender with arms in this process in accordance with the existing policy of the State. Financial support in such cases, however shall be limited to be provisions of the scheme prepared and funded by the Government of India. Withdrawal of cases against such persons and those related to overground Bodo movement since 1987 shall be considered according to the existing policy of the State of Assam.

12.2. The Government of India will initiate steps for review of action against the Bodo employees of Government of India and subordinate officers as well as in respect of Central Government Undertakings. Similar action would be taken by the Government of Assam.

12.3. Bodo youth will be considered for recruitment in Police, Army and Paramilitary forces to increase their representation in these forces.

13. *Special Rehabilitation Programme for the people affected by ethnic disturbances:* The Special Rehabilitation Programme (SRP) for the people affected by ethnic disturbances in Assam, who are at present living at relief camps in Kokrajhar, Bongaigaon, etc. shall be completed by the Government of Assam with active support of BTC. Necessary funds for their rehabilitation shall be provided by the Government of India and lands which are free from all encumbrances required for such rehabilitation shall be made available by the BTC.

14. *Interim Council:* Immediately after signing of the agreement, Interim Executive Council for BTC shall be formed by Governor of Assam from amongst the leaders of the present Bodo movement, including the signatories to this settlement, and shall include adequate representation to the non-tribal communities in BTC area. The Interim Council shall not continue for a period beyond 6 months during which period election to the Council shall be held. Government of Assam shall dissolve the Bodoland Autonomous Council (BAC) and repeal the BAC Act.

15. Government of Assam will consider inclusion of all tribals including Bodos in RHAC/MAC/LAC in consultation with leaders of these Councils.

16. The Implementation of the provision of the Memorandum of Settlement shall be periodically reviewed by a Committee comprising representatives of Government of India, Government of Assam and BTC. Signed on 10th February, 2003 at New Delhi in the presence of Shri L.K. Advani, Hon'ble Deputy Prime Minister of India and Shri Tarun Gogoi, Chief Minister of Assam; Hagrama Basumatary, Chairman Bodo Liberation Tigers; P.K. Dutta, Chief Secretary Government of Assam; R.C.A. Jain, Secretary (BM) Ministry of Home Affairs, Government of India.

Annexure:

Memorandum of Settlement, pages 1-9; 2. List of Villages I, pages 10-51; 3. List of Additional villages II, pages 52-55 demanded by the BLT; 4. List of Subjects to be entrusted III, pages 56-57; 5. Illustrative list of Projects IV (website).

ANNEXURE XXXI

The Mising Autonomous Council Act, 1995 As Amended by Assam Act No. VIII of 2001 and Assam Act No. XXI of 2005

AN ACT

To provide for the establishment of an [1][.....] authority in the name and style of "THE MISING AUTONOMOUS COUNCIL" and for certain matters incidental thereto and connected therewith.

Preamble: [2][*WHEREAS* it is expedient to provide for the establishment of a Mising Autonomous Council within the State of Assam with maximum autonomy within the framework of the Constitution, comprising of the Satellite Areas and Core Areas for social, economic, educational, ethnic and cultural advancement of the Mising Community residing therein.]

It is hereby enacted in the Forty Sixth Year of the Republic of India, as follows:

CHAPTER I

Preliminary

Short title extent and commencement:

1. (1) This Act may be called the Mising Autonomous Council Act, 1995.
   (2) It extends to the whole of the State of Assam.
   (3) It shall come into force on such date as the State Government may, by a notification in the official gazette, appoint and different dates may be appointed for different provisions of the Act or different areas.

Definition:

2. In this Act, unless the context otherwise requires, —

(a) 'bye-law' means the bye-law framed by the General Council.

(b) 'Constitution' means the Constitution of India.

(c) 'Constituency' means the constituency referred to in section 48.

(d) 'Council Area' means the Mising Autonomous Council Area.

(e) 'Executive Council' means the executive body of the General Council of the Mising Autonomous Council Constituted under sections 3 (3) and 24.

(f) 'Elector' in relation to a constituency means a person whose name is entered in the electoral roll of that constituency.

(g) 'General Council Fund' and 'Village Council Fund' means the funds constituted under section 61.

(h) 'Government' means the State Government of Assam.

(i) 'Governor' means the Governor of Assam.

(j) 'General Council' means the General Council of the Mising Autonomous Council referred to in section 3.

(k) 'Gaon Panchayat', 'Anchalik Panchayat' and 'Zilla Parishad' have the same meaning as defined in the Assam Panchayat Act, 1994. **Assam Act XVIII of 1994**

(l) 'Member' means a member of the Village Council or the General Council or the Executive Council, as the case may be.

(m) 'Municipality' has the same meaning as in the Assam Municipal Act, 1956.

(n) 'Notification' means the notification issued under this Act. **Assam Act XV of 1957**

(o) 'Official Gazette' means the Official Gazette of Assam.

(p) 'Prescribed' means prescribed by rules made under this Act.

(q) [3]['Satellite Areas' mean the area or areas consisting of non-contiguous cluster of villages predominantly inhabited by Scheduled Tribes population having 50 per cent and above as a whole in the cluster and not necessarily in the individual villages.]

(r) 'Village Council' means the Village Councils referred to in section 4; and

(s) 'Village Council Area' means the area declared to be the area of a Village Council by the Government by notification in the Official Gazette.

[4](t) "Commission" means the Assam State Election Commission constituted *vide* Government Notification No. PDA 116/94/ 6 dated 31-5-1994.

(u) [3]["Core Areas" means the compact and contiguous areas predominantly inhabited by Scheduled Tribes population having 50 per cent and above as a whole in the area and not necessarily in the individual villages.]

(v) "Tribal Belts/Blocks/Tribal Sub-Plan Areas" means areas notified as such under the Assam Land and Revenue Regulation, 1886 and also identified by the Department of Welfare of Plains Tribes & Backward Classes, Government of Assam.]

Assam Regulation 1 of 1886

Mising Autonomous Council:

3. (1) There shall be an autonomous council to be called the Mising Autonomous Council within the State of Assam comprising of the areas of the Village Councils as may be [5][notified] by the Government [6][...] in the Official Gazette.

(2) The Mising Autonomous Council shall have maximum autonomy within the framework of the Constitution.

(3) The Mising Autonomous Council shall have a General Council and an Executive Council as provided hereinafter.

Village Council:

4. [7][(1) There shall be a Village Council for each block of villages as may be notified by the Government under sub-section (1) of section 3 consisting of approximately 6,000 to 8,000 tribal population.]

(2) For the purposes of sub-section (1) above, there shall be as many village councils as may be specified by the Government by notification in the Official Gazette.

CHAPTER II

The General Council

Incorporation of the General Council:

5. The General Council shall be a body corporate having perpetual succession and a common seal with powers to acquire, hold and

dispose of property and to contract and shall sue or be sued by its corporate name.

Constitution of the General Council:

6. (1) [8][The General Council Shall consist of 40 (forty) members of which 36 (thirty six) shall be directly elected and 4 (four) shall be nominated by the Government with the concurrence of the Mising Autonomous Council from amongst the group of communities residing in the Council area and not otherwise represented in the General Council. Out of 40 (forty) seats [9][25 (twenty five)] seats shall be reserved for [9][Scheduled Tribes] and 6 (six) seats shall be reserved for women of any community".

(2) The Members of Parliament and the Members of the Legislative Assembly, Assam belonging to Scheduled Tribes Reserved Constituencies of the Council Area shall be *ex-officio* members of the General Council.

(3) Every member of the General Council shall be entitled to such allowances as may be fixed by the General Council and approved by the Government.

(4) [10][the elected members of the General Council shall, at the first meeting to be convened by an officer authorized by the Government after the election for the purpose of Constitution of the Executive Council, elect from amongst themselves by a secret ballot one of the members to be Chairman of the meeting to conduct the proceeding where he shall also cast his vote and elect from amongst themselves in the manner prescribed:

(i) One member to be the Chairman.

(ii) One member to be the Deputy Chairman.

(iii) One Chief Executive Councillor of the Executive Council.

(iv) As many Executive Councillor as may be decided by the General Council, but not exceeding one third of the total number of members of the General Council.]

Term of Office:

7. (1) The term of office of the General Council shall be five years from the date of the first meeting as appointed by the

Government after the election of the members, unless dissolved earlier under section 68.

(2) Notwithstanding anything contained in sub-section (1) above, the Chief Executive Councillor of the Executive Councillors shall cease to hold office as such forthwith if he, for any reason, ceases to be a member.

(3) Notwithstanding anything contained in sub-section (1) the Governor may, if he is satisfied that circumstances so exist which render the holding of the election, as provided, impracticable, extend the term for a period not exceeding one year.

Resignation of Members of the General Council:

8. (1) Any member of the General Council may, at any time, by giving notice in writing addressed to the Chief Executive Councillor, resign his office.

Provided that in case of the Chief Executive Councillor, the notice shall be addressed to any of the Executive Councillors.

(2) Such resignation shall take effect from such date as specified in the notice or if no such date is specified, from the date of its receipt by the office bearer addressed.

Removal of Members of the General Council:

9. (1) The Chief Executive Councillor or the Executive Councillors or any one of them or all of them may be removed from office by a resolution carried by a majority of the total number of the elected members at a special meeting of the General Council called for the purpose upon a requisition made in writing by not less than one third of the members of the General Council.

(2) The Government, after giving an opportunity to an elected member of the General Council to show cause against the action proposed to be taken against him and after giving a reasonable opportunity of being heard, may by order, remove him from the office, if he —

(a) After his election, is convicted by a criminal court of an offence involving moral turpitude punishable with imprisonment for any period exceeding six months; or

(b) Incurs any of the disqualifications mentioned in section

54 after his election as member of the General Council; or

(c) Is absent from three consecutive meetings of the General Council.

(3) Any member of the General Council who is removed from the office under sub-section (2) above, may within thirty days from the date of the order, appeal to such Judicial Authority as the Government may prescribe and the authority so prescribed after admitting an appeal may, after complying with the normal and fundamental principles of Judicial proceedings, pass such order or orders either confirming or modifying or setting aside the order appealed against and pending the final disposal of the appeal may pass such other interlocutory order or orders including stay of operation of the order appealed against.

(4) The order, passed, by the Judicial Authority referred to in sub-section (3) above, on such appeal shall be final.

Salaries, allowances and other emoluments:

10. (1) The Chief Executive Councillor and the Executive Councillors shall be whole time functionaries and shall be paid out of the General Council Fund such salaries and allowances as may be prescribed.

(2) The other term and conditions of service of the Chief Executive Councillor and the Executive Councillors shall be such as may be prescribed.

Filling-up of vacancies:

11. (1) Where the office of any member falls vacant by reason of his death, resignation, removal or otherwise, the vacancy shall be filled-up by election in accordance with the provisions of this Act and the rules framed there under, may be.

Provided that any vacancy in the office of the Chief Executive Councillor or the Executive Councillors shall be filled-up by the General Council by electing a member thereof in the manner prescribed for the election of the Chief Executive Councillor or the Executive Councillors, as the case may be.

(2) Any member elected in accordance with the provisions of sub-section (1) above, shall hold such office only for the

remainder of the term of the General Council or the period extended under sub-section (3) of section 7.

Powers, Functions and Duties of the Chief Executive Councillor:

12. (1) The Chief Executive Councillor shall —

(a) Be responsible for the maintenance of the records of the General Council.

(b) Have general responsibility for the financial and executive administration of the General Council.

(c) Exercise administrative supervision and control over the officers and employees of the General Council and the officers and employees whose services s may be placed at the disposal of the General Council by the Government.

(d) For transaction of business under this Act, or for the purpose of making any order under this Act, exercise such powers, perform such functions and discharge such duties as may be exercised, performed or discharged by the General Council under this Act or the rules made there under.

Provided that the Chief Executive Councillor shall not exercise such powers, perform such functions or discharge such duties as may be required by the rules made under this Act to be exercised, performed or discharged by the General Council at a meeting.

(e) Exercise such other powers, perform such other duties as the General Council may, by general or special resolution, direct or as the Government may, by rules made in this behalf, prescribe.

Meeting of the General Council:

13. (1) The General Council shall meet at least once in every three months for transaction of its business.

(2) The meeting of the General Council shall be held at the headquarter of the Mising Autonomous Council at such time as may be notified by the Chief Executive Councillor.

Provided that the first meeting of the General Council after the election shall be held on such date as may be appointed by the Government.

Oath of affirmation by members:

14. Every member of the General Council shall before taking his seat, make and subscribe before such person as may be appointed by the Governor in this behalf an oath or affirmation in the manner and forms as may be prescribed.

Quorum:

15. The quorum necessary for transaction of business at a meeting of the General Council shall be 10 members and the decision of the General Council shall be by a single majority of votes of the members present.

Head Quarter of the General Council:

16. The Government may, by notification in the official Gazette, declare any place within the Council Area to be the head quarter of the General Council.

Secretariat of the Mising Autonomous Council:

17. (1) There shall be a secretariat for the Mising Autonomous Council at the head-quarter of the General Council headed by a Principal Secretary to be appointed by the Government in consultation with the Chief Executive Councillor.

(2) The Principal Secretary shall be the Principal Executive Officer of the General Council and all other officers of the General Council shall be subordinate to him.

(3) The Principal Secretary shall be present and take part in the discussion of all the meeting of the General Council or the Executive Council or any committee of the General Council and may, with the consent of the Chief Executive Councillor or any other person presiding over such meeting for the time being, as the case may be, at any time make a statement or give explanation of the facts and circumstances, but shall not be entitled to vote in any such meeting.

(4) The Principal Secretary and the other officers of the Secretariat shall be paid out of the General Council Fund.

(5) The term of appointment of the Principal Secretary shall be for a period of three years but may be extended by the Government in consultation with the Chief Executive Councillor.

(6) The Government may appoint such other Secretaries for the General Council on such terms and conditions as the Government may, in consultation with the Chief Executive Councillor, determine.

(7) The Government may, in consultation with the Chief Executive Councillor, depute such other officers or experts, as may be required to assist the General Council on such terms and conditions as may be determined by the Government.

(8) The Government may from time to time post officers of the rank of class II and above within the Council Area in accordance with the exigencies, but while making such postings due regard may be given to the views of the General Council.

(9) All officers and other staff posted in the Council Area shall be accountable to the General Council for their performance and assessment of their works recorded by the Executive Council shall be incorporated in their Annual Confidential Reports by the Government.

(10) Notwithstanding anything contained in sub-section (5) above, the Government may, at any time in consultation with the Chief Executive Councillor, withdraw the principal secretary or any other officer posted or appointed by it in the secretariat.

CHAPTER III

Powers and Functions of the General Council

Subjects to be under Control and Administration of the General Council:

18. Notwithstanding anything contained in any other law or rules for the time being in force, the General Council shall have executive powers in relation to the Council Area over the following subjects:

(1) Cottage Industry.
(2) Animal Husbandry and Veterinary.
(3) Forest other than reserved forest.
(4) Agriculture.
(5) Rural Roads and Bridges.
(6) Sericulture.
(7) Education:

(i) Adult Education.

(ii) Primary Education.

(iii) Up to Higher Secondary including Vocational Training.

(8) Cultural Affairs.

(9) Soil Conservation.

(10) Cooperation.

(11) Fisheries.

(12) Panchayat and Rural Development.

(13) Handloom and Textile.

(14) Public Health Engineering — Drinking Water.

(15) Minor Irrigation.

(16) Social Welfare.

(17) Flood Control Schemes for Protection of Villages (not of highly technical nature).

(18) Sports and Youth Welfare.

(19) Weights and Measures.

(20) Library Services.

(21) Museum and Archaeology.

(22) Urban Development, Town and Country Planning.

(23) Tribal Research.

(24) Land and Land Revenue [11][provided that no allotment or settlement of land shall be made in the Council area without the recommendation of the Executive Council].

(25) Publicity and Public Relation.

(26) Tourism.

(27) Transport.

(28) Any other matter connected with development.

(29) Municipal Board, Improvement Trust, District of Boards and other local-self Government of Village Administration.

(30) Tribal Welfare.

(31) Market and Fair.

(32) Lotteries, Theatres, Dramatic performances and Cinema.

(33) Vital Statistics including registration of birth and deaths.

(34) Food and Civil Supplies.

Other matter to be under the Control of Administration of the General Council:

19. Subject to the general policy of the Government, the General Council shall —

(1) Formulate integrated development plans for the Council Area.

(2) Implement schemes and programmes for the development of the Council Area.

(3) Have powers to appoint Class III and Class IV staff within the Council Area.

(4) Have powers to regulate trade and commerce within the council area in accordance with the existing laws including issue of permit or licenses to individuals within the Council Area.

(5) Guide customs and traditions and social justice of the Mising community according to the traditional laws.

(6) Organize special recruitment drive into Army, Navy, and other Para-military Forces, Police Forces and other Central Government establishment for appointments of the persons belong to the Mising Community.

(7) Allot permits for trade and commerce to the people residing in the Council Area preference being given to the Mising Community.

Powers to impose, levy and collect taxes:

20. (1) Subject to the provisions of any other law for the time being in force, the General Council shall have the powers to collect within the council area such taxes as are payable under the law for time being in force in the manner as may be prescribed.

Provided that the tax or taxes as aforesaid shall be collected from such date as may be appointed by the Government by notification in this behalf in the Official Gazette.

(2) Subject to sub-section (1) and such maximum rates as the Government may prescribe, the General Council shall —

(a) Levy tolls on persons, vehicles or animals of any class, for the use of any bridge or road other than *kaccha* road, or ferry constructed or established and managed by it.

(b) Levy the following fees and rates, namely —

(i) Fees on the registration of boats or vehicles.

(ii) Fees for providing sanitary arrangements at such places of worship, pilgrimage, fairs, melas, other public places within the Council Area as may be specified by the Government by notification in the Official Gazette.

(iii) Fees for Licenses.

(iv) Water rates, where arrangements for irrigation or drinking water is made by it within the Council Area.

(v) Lighting rate where arrangements for lighting of public street or places are made by it within the Council Area.

(3) Notwithstanding anything contained in the foregoing sub-sections, the General Council shall not undertake registration of any vehicle or levy any fee in respect thereof and shall not provide sanitary arrangements at places of worship, pilgrimage, fairs, *melas* or other public places within the Council Area or levy and fees in respect thereof if such vehicle has already been registered by any other authority under the law for the time being in force, or if such provisions for sanitary arrangements has already been made by the Government or any other local authority.

(4) The collection of tolls, fees or rates and the terms and conditions for the imposition thereof shall be such as may be prescribed by the bye-laws. Such bye-laws may international provide for exemption from all or any class of cases.

(5) The General Council may levy fees or taxes on any or all the subjects assigned to the village council.

Power to Entrust Functions:

21. Notwithstanding anything contained in this Act, the Government may, in consultation with the General council, entrust either conditionally or without any condition, to the General Council or their officers any function in relation to any matter not enumerated in section 18 to which the executive power of the Government extends.

Power to Acquire, Hold and Dispose of Property:

22. Notwithstanding anything contained in section 5, the General Council, subject to the previous approval of the Government and subject to such terms and conditions as may be imposed by the Government, shall have the power to acquire, hold or dispose of any immovable property or movable property the value of which

exceeds rupees one lakh and to enter into any contract or agreement with any party or authority.

Power to Make Bye-laws:

23. (1) The General Council may, subject to the provisions of this Act and the rules made there under and subject to the approval of the Government, make bye-laws to be applicable within the council area with respect to all or any of the matters enumerated in sections 18, 19, 43 and 44 for the regulation, control and administration thereof.

(2) All bye-laws made under sub-section (1) above, shall have effect upon their publication in the official Gazette.

CHAPTER IV

The Executive Council

The Executive Council:

24. (1) The Executive Council shall consist of the Chief Executive Councillor and [12][.....] Executive Councillors elected in accordance with the provisions of sub-section (4) of section 6.

(2) The Chief Executive Councillor shall be the Chairman of the Executive Council and shall preside over the meetings thereof.

(3) Any casual vacancy among the members of the Executive Council occurring by reasons of death, resignation removal or otherwise shall be filled through election by the members of the General Council in the same manner as provided in sub-section (4) of section 6.

Provided that no act or proceeding of the Executive Council shall be called in question or shall become invalid merely by reason of any vacancy among its members.

(4) The manner of transaction of business of the Executive Council shall be such as may be determined by the General Council by bye-laws made by it with the approval of the Government.

(5) The Executive Council shall be collectively responsible to the General Council.

Term of Office of the Executive Council:

25. A member of the Executive Council shall hold office until he —

(a) Ceases to be a member of the General Council; or

(b) Resigns his office in writing under his hand addressed to the Chief Executive Councillor in which case the resignation shall take effect from the date of acceptance thereof.

Provided that tin case of the Chief Executive Councillor, the resignation shall be addressed to any one of the Executive Councillors.

Powers and Functions of the Executive Council:

26. (1) The executive powers of the General Council shall vest in the Executive Council.

(2) All orders or instructions made or executed by the Executive Council shall be deemed to have been made or executed by or under the authority of the General Council.

(3) Every order made or instruction issued or resolution passed by the General Council shall be authenticated by the signature of the Chief Executive Councillor, or in his absence, by any one of the Executive Councillors.

General Powers of the Chief Executive Councillor:

27. (1) The Chief Executive Councillor shall be the Chief of the Mising Autonomous Council and shall exercise such powers and discharge such functions as are conferred on him by or under this act or the rules made there under.

(2) The Chief Executive Councillor shall, for the smooth and convenient transaction of business of the Executive Council, allocate among the Executive Councillors such business in such manner as he may deem fit.

Special Power of the Chief Executive Councillor:

28. (1) The Executive Council may, in cases where the Chief Councillor is required to take in accordance with the provisions of this Act or Rules made there under, or any other law for the time being in force, any action subject to the approval of the Executive Council by a general or special resolution, authorize the Chief Executive Councillor to take such action subject to such condition, if any, as may be specified therein, in anticipation of such approval.

(2) Whenever the Chief Executive Councillor takes any action

under sub-section (1) above, he shall inform the Executive Council forthwith and shall obtain the approval thereof.

Meeting of the Executive Council:

29. (1) The Executive Council shall meet at least once in every three months for transaction of its business at such place and time as the Chief Executive Councillor may direct.

(2) The meeting shall be convened by the Chief Executive Councillor by giving seven clear days notice in writing to each member of the Executive Council.

Quorum:

30. [13][The quorum for transaction of business at a meeting of the Executive Council shall be one-third of the total strength of the Executive Councillors. The meeting shall be conducted by the Chief Executive Councillors by giving 7 (seven) days clear notice in writing to each member of the Executive Council.]

CHAPTER V

The Village Council

Incorporation of the Village Council:

31. The Village Council shall be a body corporate having perpetual succession and a common seal with powers to acquire, hold and dispose of property and shall sue or be sued by its corporate name.

Constitution of the Village Council:

32. (1) The Village Council shall consist of 10 (ten) members of which 5 (five) seats shall be reserved for the Mising Community out of which at least one shall be a woman.

(2) Every member of the Village Council shall be entitled to such sitting allowances as may be fixed by the Village Council subject to the approval of the General Council and the Government.

(3) The elected members of the Village Council shall, at he first meeting after the election, elect from among themselves, in the manner prescribed,

(i) One member to be the President who shall also be the Chief of the Village Council; and

(ii) One member to be the Vice President who shall be the Deputy Chief of the Village Council.

Term of Office:

33. (1) The term of Office of the Village Council shall be five years from the date of the first meeting as appointed by the Government after the election of the members, unless dissolved earlier under section 68.

Provided that the Governor may, if he is satisfied that circumstances exist which render the holding of election, as provided, impracticable, extend the term for a period not exceeding one year.

(2) Notwithstanding anything contained in sub-section (1) above, the President or the Vice President of a Village Council shall cease to hold office as such forthwith if he, for any reason, ceases to be a member.

(3) Notwithstanding anything contained in sub-section (1) or sub-section (2) above, the term of the Village Council shall be co-terminus with the general council.

Resignation of Members of the Village Council:

34. (1) Any members of the Village Council may, at any time, by giving notice in writing addressed to the President, resign his office.

(2) Such resignation shall take effect from such date as specified in the notice or if no such date is specified from the date of its receipt by the office bearer addressed.

Removal of Members of the Village Council:

35. (1) The President or the Vice President or both of a Village Council may be removed from office by a resolution carried by a majority of the total number of the elected members at a special meeting of the Village Council called for the purpose upon requisition made in writing by not less than one third of the members of the village council.

(2) The Government, after giving an opportunity to an elected member of the Village Council to show cause against the

action proposed to be taken against him and after giving a reasonable opportunity of being heard, may by order remove him from the office if he —

(a) After his election, is convicted by a criminal court of an offence involving moral turpitude punishable with imprisonment for any period exceeding six months; or

(b) Incurs any of the disqualifications mentioned in section 54 after his election as member of the Village Council; or

(c) Is absent from three consecutive meetings of the village council.

(3) Any members of the Village Council who is removed from the office under sub-section (2) above may, within thirty days from the date of the order, appeal to such judicial authority as the Government may prescribe and the authority so prescribed after admitting an appeal may, after complying with the normal and fundamental principles of judicial proceedings, pass such order or orders either confirming or modifying or setting aside the order appealed against and pending the final disposal of the appeal, may pass such other interlocutory order or orders including stay of operation of the order appealed against.

(4) The order passed by the Judicial Authority referred to in sub-section (3) above, on such appeal shall be final.

Filling-up of Vacancy in Office of the President or Vice-President:

36. Any vacancy in the office of the President or Vice-President by reason of death, resignation, removal or otherwise, shall be filled-up within one month from the date of occurrence thereof, from amongst the elected members of the Village Council in the same manner as has been provided in section 32 for the election of the President or the Vice-President as the case may be.

Salaries, Allowances and Other Emoluments:

37. (1) The President and the Vice-President shall be whole time functionaries and shall be paid out of the Village Council fund such salaries and allowances as may be prescribed.

(2) The other terms and conditions of service of the President and the Vice-President shall be such as may be prescribed.

Powers, Functions and Duties of the President and Vice-Presidents:

38. (1) The President of the Village Council shall be responsible for the maintenance of records of the Village Council, for the administrative control and supervision of all officers and employees in the Village Council.

(2) The President shall exercise such powers, discharge such duties and perform such functions as may be entrusted by the Village Council.

(3) The Vice-President of the Village Council shall exercise such of the powers, perform such of the functions and discharge such of the duties of the President as the President may, from time-to-time subject to the rules if any made in this behalf by the Government, delegate to him in writing.

(4) Notwithstanding anything contained in the foregoing sub-sections, neither the President nor the Vice-President shall exercise such powers, perform such functions or discharge such duties as may be required by the rules made under this act to be exercised, performed or discharged by the Village Council at a meeting.

Meeting of the Village Council:

39. (1) The Village Council shall meet at least once in every three months for transaction of its business.

(2) The meeting of the Village Council shall be held at the office of the Village Council or at such other convenient place at such time as may be notified by the President.

Provided that the first meeting of the Village Council after the election shall be held on such date and time as may be appointed by the Government.

Oath of Affirmation:

40. Every member of the Village Council shall, before taking his seat, make and subscribe, before such person as may be appointed by the Governor in this behalf, an oath or affirmation in the manner and form as may be prescribed.

41. The quorum necessary for transaction of business at a meeting of the Village Council shall be 4 (four) members and the decision of the Village Council shall be by a single majority of votes of the members present.

Office of the Village Council:

42. (1) There shall be an office of the Village Council at such place as may be determined by the Village Council with the approval of the Government.

(2) The Government shall, in consultation with the President of the Village Council, appoint a secretary to the Village Council.

(3) The Secretary to the Village Council shall be the Chief Executive of the Village Council and shall act under the direction and control of the President. All other officers and staff shall be subordinate to him.

(4) The secretary shall be present and take part in the discussion of all the meeting of the Village Council or any committee of the Village Council and may, with the consent of the President or any other person presiding ever such meeting for the time being, as the case may be, at any time make a statement or give explanation of the facts and circumstances, but shall not be entitled to vote in any such meeting.

(5) The Government may, in consultation with the President, depute such other officers or experts, as may be required, to assist the Village Council on such terms and conditions as may be determined by the Government.

(6) The Government may, from time-to-time post such other officers or staff as may be required so as to meet the exigencies, but while making such posting due regard may be given to the views of the Village Council.

(7) All officers and staff posted in the Village Council office, shall be accountable to the Village Council for their performances and assessment of their works recorded by the Village Council shall be incorporated in their Annual Confidential reports by the Government.

(8) Notwithstanding anything contained in any of the foregoing sub-section, the Government may, at any time, in consultation with the President, withdraw the secretary or any other officer of staff posted or appointed by it in the office of the Village Council.

CHAPTER VI

Powers and Functions of the Village Council

Subjects to be under the Control and Administration of the Village Council:

43. Notwithstanding anything contained in any other law or rules for the time being in force, Village Council shall have the Executive Power in relation to the Village Council area over the following subjects:
    (1) Agriculture including agricultural extension.
    (2) Animal Husbandry, Dairy Development and Poultry.
    (3) Fisheries.
    (4) Social and Farm Forestry/Minor Forest produce, fuel and fodder.
    (5) *Khadi*, village and cottage Industries.
    (6) Rural Housing.
    (7) Drinking water.
    (8) Road, building, culverts, bridges, tunnels, waterways and other means of communication.
    (9) Rural Electrification.
    (10) Non-conventional Energy Sources.
    (11) Poverty Alleviation programme.
    (12) Education including Primary Schools.
    (13) Adult and Non-formal Education.
    (14) Libraries.
    (15) Cultural Activities.
    (16) Markets and Fairs.
    (17) Rural Sanitation.
    (18) Public Health and Family Welfare.
    (19) Women and Child Development.
    (20) Social Welfare including welfare of handicapped and mentally retarded.
    (21) Welfare of weaker section and in particular the SC/ST.
    (22) Public Distribution System.
    (23) Maintenance of Community assets.
    (24) Construction and maintenance of cattle sheds, similar institutions.
    (25) Construction and maintenance of cattle sheds, pounds and cart stands.

(26) Maintenance of public parks and play grounds.
(27) Construction and maintenance of slaughter houses.
(28) Maintenance and regulation of manure.
(29) Such other functions as may be entrusted by the Government from time-to-time.

Other Matters to be under the Control of Administration of the Village Council:

44. (i) Subject to the General policy of the Government and subject to the general control and supervision of the General Council, the Village Council shall —
Formulate integrated development plans for the Village Council Area;
(ii) Implement schemes and programmes for the development of the Village Council Area;
(iii) Have powers to appoint Class III and Class IV staff of the village council;
(iv) Have powers to regulate trade and commerce within the Village Council area in accordance with the existing laws including issue of permits or licenses to individuals within the Village Council area;
(v) Guide customs and traditions and social justice of Mising Community according to their traditional laws; and
(vi) Allot permits for trade and commerce to the people residing in the Village Council area preference being given to the Mising Community.

Power to Impose, Levy and Collect Taxes:

45. (1) Subject to the provisions of any other laws for the time being in force and subject to the previous approval of the General Council, the Village Council shall have the power to collect within the Village Council area such taxes as are payable under the law for the time being in force in the manner as may be prescribed.
Provided that the tax or taxes as aforesaid shall be collected from such date as may be appointed by the Government by notification in this behalf in the Official Gazette.
(2) Subject to sub-section (1) and such maximum rates as the Government may prescribe, the Village Council shall —

(a) Levy tolls on persons, vehicles or animals of any class for the use of any bridge, or road other than *kaccha* road, or ferry constructed or established by it.

(b) Levy the following fees and rates namely:

(i) Fees on the registration of boats or vehicles.

(ii) Fees for providing sanitary arrangements as such places or worships, pilgrimage, fairs, *melas* or other public places within the Village Council area as may be specified by the Government by notification in the Official Gazette.

(iii) Fees for licenses.

(iv) Water rates where arrangements for irrigation or drinking water is made by it within the Village Council area.

(v) Lighting rate where arrangements for lighting on public streets or places are made by it within the Village Council area.

(3) Notwithstanding anything contained in the foregoing sub-sections, the Village Council shall not undertake registration of any vehicle or levy any fee in respect thereof and shall not provide sanitary arrangements at places of worship, pilgrimage, fairs, *melas* or other public places within the Village Council area or levy any fees in respect thereof, if such vehicle has already been registered by any other authority under the law for the time being in force or if such provision for sanitary arrangements has already been made by the Government or any other local authority.

(4) The collection of tolls, fees or rates and the terms and conditions for the imposition thereof shall be such as may be prescribed by the bye-laws, such bye-laws may international provide for exemption from all or any class of cases.

Power to Entrust Functions:

46. Notwithstanding anything contained in this act, the Government may, in consultation with the village council, entrust either conditionally or without any condition to the Village Council or its officers any functions in relation to any matter not enumerated in section 43 to which the executive power of the Government extends.

Power to Acquire, Hold and Dispose of Property:

47. Notwithstanding anything contained in section 3, the Village Council subject to the previous approval of the Government and subject to such terms and conditions as may be imposed by the Government, shall have the power to acquire, hold and dispose of any immovable property or movable property the value of which exceeds rupees fifty thousand and to enter into any agreement or contract with any party or authority.

CHAPTER VII

Election

Delimitation:

48. (1) There shall be 10 (ten) constituencies in a Village Council area for electing members to the Village Council. Each such constituency shall be a single member constituency and shall be territorial.

(2) [14][There shall be 36 (thirty six) constituencies in the Council Area for electing members to the General Council. Each constituency shall be a single member constituency.]

The Government shall, by order published in the Official Gazette, determine the territorial limits of the constituencies into which the Village Council area or the Council Area shall be delimited for the purpose of election of members to the Village Council and the General Council.

Power to Amend or Alter Delimitation:

49. Notwithstanding anything contained in section 48 above, the Government may, by order published in the Official Gazette, alter or amend the order made under section 48.

Provided that no such order shall be made after the comment of the election process.

Electoral Rolls:

50. (1) Subject to the provisions of this Act and the rules made there under, so much of the electoral roll for the assembly constituency in force on the last date of nomination, as is relatable to a Village Council constituency, as defined in

clause (b) of section 2, shall be the electoral roll for that Village Council constituency.

(2) The electoral rolls of the Village Council constituencies as are relatable to a constituency of the General Council, as defined in clause (b) of section 2, shall be the electoral roll for the constituency of the General Council.

(3) Persons whose names are included in the electoral roll as aforesaid in sub-section (1) or (2) above, shall be the electorate for the election of members of the Village Council or the General Council, as the else may be.

(4) The [15][Commission] shall, at the time and in the manner prescribed, cause to be published the electoral roll in respect of a constituency.

Right to Vote:

51. (1) Save as otherwise provided in this act every person whose name is entered in the electoral roll for the time being in force, of any constituency shall be entitled to vote in that constituency.

(2) No person shall vote at an election in any constituency, if he is subject to any of the disqualification referred to in section 10 of the Representation of Peoples Act, 1951. **Central Act 43 of 1951**

(3) No person shall vote in more than one constituency.

(4) No person shall vote in the same constituency more than once.

(5) No person shall vote at any election if he is confirmed in a prison, whether under a sentence of imprisonment or otherwise or in the lawful custody of police.

Provided that nothing in this sub-section shall apply to a person subjected to preventive detention under any law for the time going in force.

Election of Members:

52. [16][Election of members for the purpose of constituting the General Council and the Village Council shall be held on such date or dates as may be notified by the Commission in consultation with the Government.]

Qualification for Membership of Village Council or General Council:

53. [17][A person shall be qualified to be elected either to the Village Council or to the General Council if he is an elector as defined in clause (e) of section 2.]

Disqualification for Membership of Village Council or General Council:

54. (1) A person shall not be qualified for being elected either to the Village Council or the General Council, if —

(a) He is not a citizen of India.

(b) He is less than 18 years of age on such date as may be fixed by the Government. Or

(c) He has been elected to any Municipality Panchayat within the State of Assam. Or

(d) He is in service of the Central or State Government, Municipality or other authority. Or

(e) He has either directly or indirectly by himself, or by the person or employer or employee, any share or interest in any contract with, by or on behalf of the Village Council, General Council or a Municipality or Panchayat within the Council Area. **Central Act of 1956**

Provided that no person shall be deemed to be so disqualified by reason only of his having a share or interest in a public company, as defined in the Companies Act, 1956, which contracts with or is employee by a Municipal Authority or Panchayat within the Council Area. Or

(f) He has been dismissed from the services of the Central or State Government or a local authority or a Cooperative Society or a Government Company as defined the Companies Act, 1956 or a Corporation owned or controlled by the Central or the State Government for misconduct involving moral turpitude and five years have not elapsed from the date of such dismissal. Or **Central Act of 1956**

(g) He has been adjudged by a competent court to be of unsound mind. Or

(h) He has been convicted by a court of an offence involving moral turpitude punishable with imprisonment for a period of more than six months or an offence under Chapter IXA of the Indian Penal Code or Chapter III, Part III or Part VII of the Representation of Peoples Act, 1951 and five years have not elapsed from the date of expiration of the sentence.

Provided that a person shall not be disqualified under this section, by reason only of his being a member, President or Vice-President of the Village Council or a member, Chief Executive Councillor or Executive Councillor of the General Council.

Filling-up of Vacancies:

55. Where the office of any member becomes vacant by reason of his death, resignation, removal or otherwise, the vacancy shall be filled by election in accordance with the provisions of this act and the rules made there under.

Validation:

56. Where the members elected at an election are restrained from functioning on account of the election as a whole being set aside by order of a court, anything done or any action taken by such members before they are so restrained or before the election is so set aside, as the case may be, shall be deemed to have been validly done or take.

Publication of Results of Elections:

57. The names of all persons elected to Village Councils and the General Council shall be published by the [18][Commission] in the Official Gazette and upon such publication, the Village Councils and the General Council shall be deemed to have been duly constituted.

Vacation of Post:

58. If an elected member is chosen to be a Member of Parliament or the State Legislature, and of General Council in case of a member of the Village Council, then at the expiration of fourteen days from the date of publication in the Gazette of India or the Official

Gazette, as the case may be, of the declaration that he has been so chosen the seat of such member in the General Council or the Village Council, as the case may be shall become vacant unless he has previously resigned his seat in the Parliament or the State Legislature or the General Council, as the case may be.

Disputes Regarding Elections:

59. (1) No election shall be called in question except by an election petition presented in such manner as may be prescribed and before such authority as may be appointed by the Government, from time-to-time by notification in the Official Gazette.

Provided that no person below the rank of assistant District Judge, in case of member of Village Council and District Judge, within the meaning of article 236 of the Constitution, in case of member of the General Council, shall be appointed for the purpose.

(2) No election shall be called into question except on any one or more of the following grounds; namely —

(a) That on the date of his election the returned candidate was not qualified or disqualified, to be chosen to fill the seat in the Village Council or the General Council, as the case may be.

(b) That corrupt practice has been committed by a returned candidate or his election agent or by any other person with the consent of the returned candidate or his election agent. Corrupt practice shall mean any of the corrupt practices specified in section 123 of the Representation of Peoples Act, 1951. **Central Act 43 of 1956**

Explanation:

(c) That any nomination has been improperly rejected.

(d) That the result of the election in so far as it concerns the returned candidate has been materially affected:

(i) By the improper acceptance of any nomination; or

(ii) By any corrupt practice committed in the interest of the returned candidate by an agent other than his election agent; or

(iii) By improper reception, refusal or rejection of any vote; or

(iv) By reception of any vote which is void; or

(v) By any non-compliance with the provisions of this act, or of any rules or order made there under.

(3) At the conclusion of trial of any election petition, the authority appointed sub-section (1) shall make an order —

(a) Dismissing the election petition; or

(b) Declaring the election of all or any of the returned candidates to be void; or

(c) Declaring the election of all or any of the returned candidates to be void and the petitioner or any other candidate to have been duly elected.

(4) If a petitioner, in addition to calling in question the election of a returned candidate, make a declaration that he himself or any other candidate has been duly elected and the authority under sub-section (1) is of the opinion that —

(a) In fact the petitioner or such other candidate has received the majority votes; or

(b) But for the votes obtained by the returned candidate by corrupt practice the petitioner or such other candidate would have obtained the majority of the valid votes the authority as aforesaid shall, after declaring the election of the returned candidate to be void, declare the petitioner or such other candidate, as the case may be, to have been duly elected.

Powers to make Rules Regulating the Election of the Members:

60. The Government may, by notification in the Official Gazette make rules to regulate all or any of the following matters for the purpose of holding election to the Village Councils and to the General Council under this act:

(a) [19][the designation of the officer or authority to whom the power to determine the territorial limits of the constituencies under section 48 may be delegated, and the manner in which the electoral roll shall be maintained by the Commission.]

(b) The appointment of returning officers, presiding officers and Polling Officers for Election.

(c) The drawing-up of programme for election.

(d) The nomination of candidates and security of nominations.

(e) The deposits to be made by the candidates and the time and manner of making such deposits.

(f) Withdrawal of Candidature.

(g) Appointment of agents of candidates.

(h) The filling-up of casual vacancies.

(i) The general procedure at the election including the time, place and hours of poll and the methods by which votes shall be cast.

(j) The fee to be paid on election petition.

(k) Any other matter relating to election or election disputes in respect of which the Government deems it necessary to make rules under this section or in respect of which there is no provision in this act or the provision is insufficient and in the opinion of the Government, adequate provision is necessary.

CHAPTER VIII

Funds, Audit and Budget

General Council Fund and Village Council Fund:

61. (1) There shall be two funds to be called respectively the General Council Fund, meant for the General Council and the Village Council Fund meant for the Village Councils.

(2) Each fund as aforesaid shall be under separate sub-heads within the statė budget to be held for the purpose of this act and all moneys realized or realizable under this act and all moneys otherwise received by the General Council or the Village Council, as the case may be shall be credited to its respective fund.

(3) The Government shall provide funds to the General Council Fund and the Village Council Fund from the Tribal Sub-plan and other resources in accordance with the appropriate formulas to be worked out keeping in mind the resources of the Government, priorities or development works in other areas including other tribal areas along with other relevant deciding factors.

(4) The following shall be deposited to the Village Council fund:

(a) Contributions and grants received from the Government.
(b) Contributions and grants from the General Council.
(c) All receipts on account of donation, rates, fees, taxes, etc.
(d) All other sums received by or on behalf of the village council.
(e) Land revenue and local rates, if any, on land including Tea Garden, which falls in the Village Council area.

(5) The allocation made under these sub-heads shall be in keeping with the guidelines laid down by the Government of India from time-to-time in the spirit of the Constitution of India.

(6) The Government shall not divert the fund allocated under these sub-heads except in exigencies, when there is inhabitable budget deficit.

(7) All funds, as may be allocated by the Central Government or the State Government for the General Council or the Village Council, as the case may be shall be assigned to it and shall be credited to the General Council Fund or the Village Council Fund, as the case may be.

(8) The General Council or the Village Council, as the case may be, subject to the provisions of loans by any law relating to the raising of local authorities, raise with the approval of the Government loans for the purposes of this Act and create a sinking fund for the repayment of such loan.

(9) The money credited to the General Council Fund or the Village Council fund shall be applied for the payment of all sums, charges and costs necessary for carrying out the purposes of this act.

(10) No payment shall be made out of the General council fund or the Village Council fund unless such expenditure is covered by a current budget grant.

Provided that the General Council or the Village Council as the case may be may make payments in terms of refund of deposits by contractors or for urgent works under undertaken in an emergency or when required by the Government in the interest of the public or under the decree or order of a civil or criminal court against the General Council or the Village Council, as the case may be, and for such others cases as may be prescribed.

Provided further that such expenditure shall be reported to the General Council or the Village Council as the case may be, for taking such action under the provisions of this act as may appear to it to be feasible for covering the amount of such payments.

(11) Surplus moneys standing at the credit of the General Council or the Village Council, as the case may be, at the end of the financial year, shall be invested in accordance with such bye-laws as may be made by the General Council in this behalf.

Provided that no funds standing at the credit of the General Council or the Village Council, as the case may be, shall be lapsed, but shall be carried over to the budget of the next financial year.

(12) The General Council shall make bye-laws for the management of the General Council Fund and the Village Council Fund and for the procedure to be followed in respect of payment of money into the said funds, withdrawal of moneys therefore, the custody of the moneys therein and any other matter incidental thereto or connected therewith.

(13) The accounts of the General Council and the Village Council shall be kept in such form and manner as may be prescribed in consultation with the accountant general, Assam.

Audit:

62. Subject to the provisions of the Comptroller and Auditor-General's (Duties, Power and Conditions of Service) Act, 1971 and the rules and the orders made there under, the audit of the accounts of the General Council and Village Council shall be entrusted by the Government to the Comptroller and Auditor-General of India who may submit to governor such report therein as it may deem fit. The Government shall transmit the report to the General Council and the Village Councils for discussion and consideration. The General Council and the Village Councils shall return the report to the Government with comments, if any. The Government shall lay such report along with the comments of the General Council and the Village Councils before the State Legislature. **Act 56 of 1971**

Budget:

63. (1) The General Council shall at such time and in such manner as may be prescribed prepare in each financial year a budget of its estimated receipts and disbursements for the following

financial year and submit it to the Government by 1st November of the current financial year. The Village Councils also shall prepare its budget in the like manner and shall submit the same to the General Council for consideration and onward transmission to the Government on or before the 1st October of the current financial year.

(2) The Government may within such time as may be prescribed, either approve the budget or return it to General Council or the Village Council concerned, as the case may be, for reconsideration on the observations of the Government, if any. The General Council or the Village Council concerned as the case may be, shall thereupon resubmit the budget along with its cements on the observation and if the approval of the Government upon such submission or resubmission as the case may be, is not received by the General Council or the Village Councils as the case may be, the budget shall be deemed to have been approved by the Government.

(3) No expenditure shall be incurred unless the budget of the General Council as well as the budget of the Village Councils are either approved or deemed to have been approved by the Government.

(4) [20][The General Council may prepare in each financial year a supplementary estimate providing for any modification of its budget for the year and may submit to the Government for approval.]

CHAPTER IX
Miscellaneous

Effect of Bye-law, etc.:

64. All the bye-laws, regulations made, orders passed and notification issued under this Act by the General Council or the Executive Council or the Village Councils as the case may be shall be subject to maintenance of security and safety of the State of Assam and Government shall have the powers to take such steps as may be deemed necessary for the purpose.

Power to Issue Instructions:

65. The Government shall have the general power to issue instructions from time-to-time for the purpose of implementation of this act.

Protection of the Right of the Non-tribal and other Ethnic Groups:

66. All rights and interest of the non-tribal citizens and other ethnic groups other than the Mising community within the Council Area as exist at the commencement of this act, in matters pertaining to their language, literature, culture, religion, customs and traditions, trade and commerce, industry, land, etc. shall be protected.

Properties situated in the Council Area:

67. (1) Subject to such restriction as the Government may impose all properties specified below and situated in the Council Area shall vest in and belong to General Council namely:

(a) All public buildings constructed or maintained out of the General Council Fund.

(b) All pubic roads which have been constructed and maintained out of the General Council Fund and stones and other materials thereof and also trees, erections, materials implements and things provided for such roads.

(c) All land and other properties movables or immovable transferred to the General Council by the Government.

(d) Such properties owned and controlled by the Municipality or the Panchayat as may be assigned, to the General Council by the Government.

(2) Notwithstanding anything contained in sub-section (1) above all the properties specified in sub-section (1) and construction and maintenance of which has been done out of the Village Council fund shall vest in and belong to the Village Council within the area in which the property is situated.

(3) The properties vested under sub-section (1) or (2) above and all other properties, which may become vested in the General Council, as the case may be, shall be under the management, direction and control of the General Council or the Village Council concerned as the case may be.

Dissolution of the General Council, Executive Council and the Village Council:

68. (1) The Governor may, if he is satisfied, on receipt of a report or otherwise and in consultation with the Judicial Department of the Government that a situation has arisen in which the

administration of the Council Area cannot be carried out in accordance with the provisions of the law for the time being in force or the general or the special instructions issued by the Government from time-to-time, by notification in the Official Gazette, dissolve the General Council, the Executive Council and the Village Council before the expiry of the term and assume to himself all or any of the powers and functions of the General Council, the Executive Council and the Village Council, the Executive Council and the Village Councils and declare that such powers and functions shall be exercised by such persons or authority as the may specify in this behalf for a period not exceeding six months at a time.

(2) Every order made under sub-section (1) above shall be laid before the State Legislature for approval and unless approved by the State Legislature shall cease to operate on the expiry of thirty days from the date on which the Assam Legislative Assembly first sits after the issue of the orders.

Effect of Dissolution:

69. When an order of dissolution is made under section 68, with effect from the date of the orders:

(a) All the members of the General Council, the Executive Council and the Village Councils shall vacate their offices; and

(b) All powers, duties, functions of the General Council, the Executive Council and the Village Council shall be exercised, discharge and performed by such authorities or as may be appointed by the Governor in this behalf.

Special Provision for Council Areas:

70. (1) The Government shall consult and give due regard to the views of the General Council before any law is made and implemented in the Council Area on the following subjects, namely —

(i) The religions and social practice of the Mising Community.

(ii) The customary laws and procedures of the Mising Community.

(iii) Ownership and transfer of land within the Council Area.

Reservation for Services:

71. Subject to the provisions of the law for the time being in force the General Council shall have the power to reserve jobs for the scheduled tribes within its jurisdiction.

Members, Officers and Employees to be Public Servants:

72. The Chief Executive Councillor, the Executive Councillors, the President and the Vice-President of the Village Councils shall be deemed to be public servants within the meaning of section 21 of the Indian Panel Code.

Validation:

73. No Act or proceedings of the General Council or the Executive Council or the Village Council, as the case may be, shall be deemed to be invalid merely by reason of existence of any vacancy therein or any defect or irregularity in the constitution thereof.

Indemnity:

74. No suit or other legal proceedings shall lie against the General Council or the Executive Council or the Village Council or any member, or officer or employee thereof for anything done in good faith or intended to be done in pursuance of this Act, or any rules or bye-law made there under.

Interpretation:

75. If any question arises as to the interpretation of this act of the rules made there under the same shall be referred to the Government whose decision therein shall be final.

Removal of Difficulties:

76. If any difficulty arises in giving effect to any provision of this Act, the Government may, by order, do anything not inconsistent with the provisions of this Act as may appear necessary or expedient for the purpose of removing the difficulty.

Special Status:

77. The General Council shall, within the laws for the time being in force, take steps to protect the demographic complexion of the areas falling within its jurisdiction.

Application of Acts of the Legislature of the State:

78. If any provision of the bye-law made by the General Council is repugnant to any provision of the law made by the Legislature of the State of Assam, with respect to that matter then the bye-law so made, whether before or after the laws made by the Legislature of the State of Assam shall to the extent of repugnancy be void and the law made by the Legislature shall prevail.

Power to Make Rules:

79. (1) The Government may make rules providing for any matter which with any provision of this act is required to be prescribed or to be provided for by rules.

(2) Every rules made under this section shall be laid, as soon as may be after it is made before the State Legislature, while it is in session for a total period of fourteen days which may be comprised in one session or in two or more successive sessions and if before the expiry of the sessions immediately following the session or the successive sessions aforesaid, the State Legislature agrees in making any modification in the rule or the State Legislature agrees that the rule should not be made, the rule shall thereafter have effect only in such modified form or be of no effect, as the case may be.

Provided however that any such modification or annulment shall be without prejudice to the validity of anything previously done under the rule.

Transitional Provision:

80. The Government shall, as soon as possible, take steps for the Constitution of an Interim Mising Executive Council by nomination until the General Council is constituted under this Act. The Interim Executive Council shall, in addition, look after the duties of the Village Councils till the same are constituted under this Act.

Saving:

81. Nothing in this act shall affect the application of any law, whether made before or after this act, to the Council Area unless such law specifically provides for exclusion of the Council Area of such application.

Explanation:

For the purpose of this section 'Law' shall, include any enactment, ordinance, regulation, order, bye-law, rule, scheme, notification or other instrument having the force of law.

M.K. DEKA

Joint Secretary and I/C Secretary to the Government of Assam Legislative Department

NOTES

1. Word "Administrative" omitted by Assam Act no. VIII of 2001.
2. Clause substituted by Assam Act no. XXI of 2005.
3. Clause substituted by Assam Act no. XXI of 2005.
4. Clause (t), (u) and (v) inserted by Assam Act no. VIII of 2001.
5. Word substituted by Assam Act no. VIII of 2001.
6. Word omitted by Assam Act no. VIII of 2001.
7. Substituted by Assam Act no. VIII of 2001.
8. Clause substituted by Assam Act no. VIII of 2001.
9. Words substituted by Assam Act no. XXI of 2005.
10. Clause substituted by Assam Act no. VIII of 2001.
11. Words inserted by Assam Act no. XXI of 2005.
12. Words omitted by Assam Act no. VIII of 2001.
13. Clause substituted by Assam Act no. VIII of 2001.
14. Clause substituted by Assam Act no. VIII of 2001.
15. Word substituted by Assam Act no. VIII of 2001.
16. Clause substituted by Assam Act no. VIII of 2001.
17. Clause substituted by Assam Act no. VIII of 2001.
18. Word substituted by Assam Act no. VIII of 2001.
19. Clause substituted by Assam Act no. VIII of 2001.
20. Clause inserted by Assam Act no. XXI of 2005.

ANNEXURE XXXII

The Manipur (Hill Areas) District Councils Act, 1971

Act No. 76 of 1971 [26th December, 1971]

AN ACT

to provide for the establishment of District Councils in the Hill Areas in the Union territory of Manipur.

Be it enacted by Parliament in the Twenty Second Year of the Republic of India as follows: —

CHAPTER I
Preliminary

1. Short Title and Extent

(1) This Act may be called the Manipur (Hill Areas) District Councils Act, 1971.

(2) It extends to the whole of the Union territory of Manipur.

2. Definitions

In this Act, unless the context otherwise requires, —

(a) "Administrator" means the administrator of the Union territory of Manipur appointed under article 239 of the Constitution;

(b) "autonomous district" means an autonomous district referred to in sub-section (1) of section 3;

(c) "building" includes a house, out-house, stable, latrine, urinal, shed, hut, wall (other than boundary wall) and any other structure (whether of masonry, bricks, wood, mud or other material), but does not include any portable or temporary shelter;

(d) "constituency" means a District Council constituency provided by order made under section 5 for the purpose of elections to the District Council;

(e) "Deputy Commissioner", in relation to any District Council, means the officer appointed as such by the Administrator, by notification in the Official Gazette, to perform the functions of the Deputy Commissioner under this Act in the autonomous district for which such District Council has been constituted;

(f) "Hill Areas" means the Hill Areas determined by the President by any notification issued under sub-section (2) of section 52 of the Government of Union Territories Act, 1963 (20 of 1963) and in force immediately before the commencement of this Act;

(g) "Hill Areas Committee" means the Standing Committee referred to in section 52 of the Government of Union Territories Act, 1963 (20 of 1963);

(h) "Market" includes any place where persons assemble for the sale of, or for the purpose of exposing for sale of meat, fish, fruit, vegetables, animals intended for human food or any other articles of human food whatsoever with or without the consent of the owner of such place notwithstanding that there may be no common regulation for the concourse of buyers and sellers and whether or not any control is exercised over the business of, or the persons frequenting, the market by the owner of the place or by any other persons;

(i) "member" means a member of a District Council constituted under this Act;

(j) "Official Gazette" means the Gazette of the Union territory of Manipur;

(k) "person" does not include a body of persons;

(l) "prescribed" means prescribed by rules made under this Act;

(m) "Scheduled Tribes" has the same meaning assigned to it in clause (25) of article 366 of the Constitution; and

(n) "vehicle" includes a carriage, cart, hand-cart, bicycle, tricycle and every wheeled conveyance which is used or is capable of being used on a street but does not include a mechanically propelled vehicle.

CHAPTER II

Constitution of District Councils

3. Division of Hill Areas into Autonomous Districts

(1) As soon as may be after the commencement of this Act, the

Administrator shall cause all the Hill Areas to be divided into not more than six autonomous districts.

(2) The Administrator may, by order notified in the Official Gazette, —

(a) declare that any area in any autonomous district which is, or is intended to be, included within the limits of any municipality, cantonment or town committee shall cease to be a part of such autonomous district;
(b) increase the area of any autonomous district;
(c) diminish the area of any autonomous district;
(d) unite two or more autonomous districts or parts thereof so as to form one autonomous district;
(e) define the boundaries of any autonomous district;
(f) alter the name of any autonomous district.

(3) No order under sub-section (2) shall be made by the Administrator except after consultation with the Hill Areas Committee.

(4) Any order made by the Administrator under sub-section (2) may contain such incidental and consequential provisions as appear to the Administrator to be necessary for giving effect to the provisions of the order.

4. Constitution of District Councils and their Composition

(1) For each autonomous district there shall be a District Council as from such date as the Administrator may, by notification in the Official Gazette, appoint in this behalf.

(2) The total number of seats in the District Council to be filled by persons chosen by direct election on the basis of adult suffrage from territorial constituencies shall be not more than eighteen.

(3) The Administrator may nominate not more than two persons, not being persons in the service of Government, to be members of any District Council.

5. Delimitation of Constituencies

The Administrator shall, by order, determine —

(a) the constituencies (which shall be single member constituencies) into which an autonomous district shall be divided for the purpose of election of members to the District Council of that district; and

(b) the extent of each constituency.

6. Power to Alter or Amend Delimitation Orders

The Administrator may, from time to time, by order, alter or amend any order made under section 5.

7. Qualifications for Membership

A person shall not be qualified to be chosen as a member of a District Council of any autonomous district unless he is an elector for any District Council constituency in that autonomous district.

8. Disqualifications for Membership

(1) A person shall be disqualified for being chosen as a member of a District Council if he is for the time being disqualified for being chosen as a member of either House of Parliament or holds any office of profit under any District Council.

(2) For the purposes of this section, a person shall not be deemed to hold an office of profit under a District Council by reason only that he is a member thereof.

9. Electors on Electoral Rolls

(1) The persons entitled to vote at elections of members of a District Council shall be the persons entitled, by virtue of the provisions of the Constitution and the Representation of the People Act, 1950, (43 of 1950) to be registered as voters at elections to the House of the People.

(2) So much of the electoral roll for any Parliamentary Constituency for the time being in force as relates to the areas comprised within a constituency formed under section 5 shall be deemed to be the electoral roll for that constituency for the purposes of this Act.

10. Right to Vote

(1) Every person whose name is, for the time being, entered in the electoral roll of a constituency shall be entitled to vote at the election of a member of the District Council from that constituency.

(2) Every person shall give one vote and no more to any one candidate at an election.

11. Election of Members

Election of members of a District Council shall be held in accordance with the rules made under section 21 on such date or dates as the Administrator may, by notification in the Official Gazette, direct:

Provided that a casual vacancy shall be filled as soon as may be after the occurrence of the vacancy:

Provided further that no election shall be held to fill-up a casual vacancy occurring within four months prior to the holding of a general election under this section.

12. Notification of Results of Elections

The names of all persons elected or nominated to be members of a District Council shall be published by the Administrator in the Official Gazette.

13. Term of Office of Members

(1) Save as otherwise provided in this section, the term of office of a member shall be five years and shall commence from the date of the notification of his election or nomination under section 12 or from the date on which the vacancy in which he is elected or nominated has occurred, whichever date is later:

Provided that the Adminstrator may, when satisfied that it is necessary in order to avoid administrative difficulty, extend the term of office of all the members by such period not exceeding one year as he thinks fit.

(2) The term of office of a member elected to fill a casual vacancy shall commence from the date of the notification of his election and shall continue so long only as the member in whose place he is elected would have been entitled to hold office if the vacancy had not occurred.

14. Disputes as to Elections

(1) No election of a member shall be called in question except by an election petition presented to the court of the District Judge having jurisdiction in the area in which the constituency concerned is situated, within thirty days from the date of the notification of the result of the election under section 12.

(2) An election petition calling in question any such election may be presented on one or more of the grounds specified in section 16 by any candidate at such election or by any elector of the constituency.

(3) A petitioner shall join as respondents to his petition all the candidates at the election.

(4) An election petition —

(a) shall contain a concise statement of the material facts on which the petitioner relies;

(b) shall, with sufficient particulars, set forth the ground or grounds on which the election is called in question; and

(c) shall be signed by the petitioner and verified in the manner laid down in the Code of Civil Procedure, 1908 (5 of 1908) for the verification of pleadings.

15. Relief that may be Claimed by Petitioner

A petitioner may, in addition to claiming a declaration that the election of all or any of the returned candidates is void, claim a further declaration that he himself or any other candidate has been duly elected.

16. Grounds on which an Election may be Called in Question

The election of a returned candidate may be called in question on any one or more of the following grounds, namely: —

(a) that on the date of his election the returned candidate was not qualified to be elected, or he was disqualified for being elected, as a member under this Act; or

(b) that the nomination paper of any candidate at the election has been improperly rejected; or

(c) that the result of the election has been materially affected by the improper acceptance of a nomination paper or by the improper acceptance or refusal of a vote or by any other cause.

17. Procedure to be followed by the District Judge

The procedure provided in the Code of Civil Procedure, 1908 (5 of 1908) in regard to suits shall be followed by the court of the District Judge, as far as it can be made applicable, in the trial and disposal of an election petition under this Act.

18. Decision of the District Judge

(1) At the conclusion of the trial of an election petition, the court of the District Judge shall make an order —

(a) dismissing the election petition; or
(b) declaring the election of all or any of the returned candidates to be void; or
(c) declaring the election of all or any of the returned candidates to be void and the petitioner or any other candidate to have been duly elected.

(2) If any person who has filed an election petition has, in addition to calling in question the election of the returned candidate, claimed a declaration that he himself or any other candidate has been duly elected and the court of the District Judge is of opinion —

(a) that in fact the petitioner or such other candidate received a majority of the valid votes; or
(b) that but for the votes obtained by the returned candidate, the petitioner or such other candidate would have obtained a majority of the valid votes, the court of the District Judge shall, after declaring the election of the returned candidate to be void, declare the petitioner or such other candidate, as the case may be, to have been duly elected.

19. Procedure in Case of Equality of Votes

(1) If during the trial of an election petition it appears that there is equality of votes between any candidates at the election and that the addition of a vote would entitle any of those candidates to be declared elected, then, the court of the District Judge shall decide between them by lot and proceed as if the one on whom the lot falls had received an additional vote.

20. Finality of Decisions

(1) An order of the court of the District Judge on an election petition shall be final and conclusive.
(2) An election of a member not called in question in accordance with the foregoing provisions shall be deemed to be a good and valid election.

21. Power to Make Rules Regulating the Election of Members

The Administrator may make rules to regulate all or any of the following matters for the purpose of the holding of elections of members under this Act, namely: —

(a) the manner of the splitting-up of electoral rolls for Parliamentary Constituencies into parts for the purpose of constituting one or more of such parts into electoral roll for a constituency; and the officer or authority by whom such splitting-up is to be carried out;
(b) the drawing-up of the programme of election;
(c) the appointment of returning officers, presiding and polling officers for election;
(d) the nomination of candidates and the scrutiny of such nomination;
(e) the deposits to be made by candidates and the time and manner of making such deposits;
(f) the withdrawal of candidatures;
(g) the appointment of agents of candidates;
(h) the time and manner of holding elections;
(i) the general procedure at the elections including the time, place and hours of poll and the method by which votes shall be cast;
(j) the fee to be paid on an election petition; and
(k) any other matter relating to elections or election disputes in respect of which the Administrator deems it necessary to make rules under this section or in respect of which this Act makes no provision or makes insufficient provision and provision is, in the opinion of the Administrator, necessary.

22. Incorporation of District Councils

Each District Council shall be a body corporate by the name respectively of "the District Council of (name of autonomous district)" and shall have perpetual succession and a common seal with power to acquire, hold and dispose of property and to contract and may by the said name sue and be sued.

23. Chairman and Vice-Chairman

(1) A District Council shall, as soon as may be, choose two members to be respectively Chairman and Vice-Chairman

thereof and so often as the office of Chairman or Vice-Chairman becomes vacant, the Council shall choose another member to be Chairman or Vice-Chairman, as the case may be:

Provided that the Administrator may nominate the first Chairman who shall hold office for a period not exceeding one year.

(2) If a resolution for the removal of an elected Chairman is passed by not less than two-thirds of the total membership of the Council at a meeting convened in accordance with the provisions of sub-section (3), such resolution shall have the effect of removing the Chairman from his office as from the date on which the resolution is so passed and if such resolution is passed by less than two-thirds, but not less than one-half of the total membership of the Council, the Administrator may, by order in writing, remove, for reasons to be recorded, the Chairman from his office as from such date as may be specified in the order:

Provided that no such resolution shall be brought within one year from the date of election of the Chairman:

Provided further that if the resolution is not passed by not less than two-thirds of the total membership of the Council, no other resolution for the removal of the Chairman shall be allowed to be considered within one year from the date on which such resolution was considered.

(3) A notice in writing of the intention to move a resolution referred to in sub-section (2) signed by not less than one-third of the total membership of the Council together with a copy of the proposed resolution shall be delivered to the Deputy Commissioner in accordance with the rules made by the Deputy Commissioner in this behalf and the Deputy Commissioner shall, after giving not less than fifteen days' notice thereon, convene for consideration of the resolution a meeting of the Council to be held in the office of the Council on a date not later than thirty days from the date on which the notice was delivered to him and he shall preside over the meeting.

(4) The Chairman of the Council shall be a whole-time functionary and shall be entitled to such salary or allowances as may be fixed by the Administrator.

24. Oath or Affirmation by Members

Every member shall, before taking his seat, make and subscribe at a meeting of the District Council, an oath or affirmation in the prescribed form.

25. Vacation of Seats

(1) No person shall be a member both of the Legislative Assembly of the Union territory of Manipur and of a District Council and if a person is chosen a member both of the Legislative Assembly and of a District Council, then, at the expiration of fourteen days from the date of publication in the Official Gazette that he has been so chosen, that person's seat in the District Council shall become vacant unless he has previously resigned his seat in the Legislative Assembly.

(2) If a member —

(a) becomes subject to any of the disqualifications mentioned in section 8; or

(b) resigns his seat by writing under his hand addressed to the Chairman of the District Council, his seat shall thereupon become vacant.

(3) If during the six successive months a member is, without the permission of the District Council, absent from all meetings thereof, the Council may declare his seat vacant.

(4) If any question arises as to whether a member has become subject to any of the disqualifications mentioned in section 8, it shall be referred to the District Judge having jurisdiction in the area in which the constituency concerned is situated and his decision shall be final.

26. Allowances of Members

Subject to the provisions of sub-section (4) of section 23, every member shall be entitled to receive such allowances as may be determined by the Administrator.

27. Liability of Members

Every person shall be liable for the loss, waste or misappropriation of any MONEY or other property belonging to a District Council, if such loss, waste or misappro-priation is a direct consequence of his neglect or misconduct while a member of the District Council and a suit for compensation may be instituted against him by the Council with the previous sanction of the Deputy Commissioner or by the Deputy Commissioner with the previous sanction of the Administrator.

28. Members to be Deemed to be Public Servants

Every member shall be deemed to be a public servant within the meaning of section 21 of the Indian Penal Code (45 of 1860).

CHAPTER III

Functions of District Councils

29. Functions of District Councils

(1) Subject to such exceptions and conditions as the Administrator may make and impose, the following matters shall be under the control and administration of a District Council, namely: —

(i) the maintenance and management of such property, movable and immovable, and institutions as may be transferred to that Council by the Administrator;

(ii) the construction, repair and maintenance of such of the roads, bridges, channels and buildings as may be transferred to that Council by the Administrator;

(iii) the establishment, maintenance and management of primary schools and the construction and repair of all buildings connected with these institutions and institution of scholarships;

(iv) the establishment, maintenance and management of dispensaries;

(v) the establishment and maintenance of cattle pounds including such functions under the Cattle-trespass Act, 1871 (1 of 1871) as may be transferred to that Council by the Administrator;

(vi) the establishment, maintenance and management of MARKETS and fairs and the construction, repair and maintenance of all buildings connected therewith;

(vii) the supply, storage and prevention from pollution of water for drinking, cooking and bathing purposes;

(viii) the construction, repair and maintenance of embankments and the supply, storage and control of water for agricultural purposes;

(ix) the preservation and reclamation of soil;

(x) the preservation, protection and improvement of live-STOCK and prevention of animal diseases;

(xi) public health and sanitation;

(xii) the management of such ferries as may be entrusted to the charge of that Council by the Administrator;

(xiii) the initiation, inspection and control of relief works;

(xiv) the allotment, occupation or use, or the setting apart of land, other than land acquired for any public purpose or land which is a reserved forest, for the purpose of agriculture or grazing or for residential or other non-agricultural purposes or for any other purposes likely to promote the interests of the inhabitants of any village or town situated within the autonomous district for which that council is constituted;

(xv) the management of any forest not being a reserved forest;

(xvi) the regulation of the practice of *Jhum* or other form of shifting cultivation; and

(xvii) any other matter which the Administrator may, in consultation with the Hill Areas Committee, entrust to the District Council in the field of agriculture, animal husbandry, community development, social and tribal welfare, village planning or any other matter referred to in section 52 of the Government of Union Territories Act, 1963 (20 of 1963).

(2) It shall be competent for a District Council to recommend to the Government of the Union Territory of Manipur Legislation relating to the following matters in so far as they concern members of the Scheduled Tribes, namely: —

(a) appointment or succession of Chiefs;

(b) inheritance of property;

(c) marriage and divorce; and

(d) social customs.

CHAPTER IV

Procedure and Staff of District Councils

30. Conduct of Business

A District Council shall conduct its business in such manner and in accordance with such procedure as may be prescribed.

31. Committees

A District Council may, from time-to-time, appoint out of its own body such and so many committees for the efficient discharge of its duties as may be necessary.

32. Officers and Staff

(1) For every District Council there shall be a Chief Executive Officer, who shall be appointed by the Administrator.
(2) If a resolution for removal of the Chief Executive Officer is passed at a meeting of the District Council by a majority of not less than two-thirds of the total membership of the Council, the Administrator shall remove him forthwith.
(3) The District Council shall appoint such officers and staff as may be necessary for the proper and efficient execution of its duties and make regulations for their conditions of service.
(4) The power of appointing officers and staff (whether temporary or permanent) shall be exercised in accordance with the rules framed for the purpose by the Administrator.
(5) The conditions of service applicable to a person immediately before his appointment to a post under a District Council shall not be varied to his disadvantage except with the previous approval of the Administrator.
(6) Every officer or member of staff of a District Council shall be deemed to be a public servant within the meaning of Section 21 of the Indian Penal Code (45 of 1860).

CHAPTER V

Finance of District Councils and Vesting of Property

33. Powers of Taxation

Notwithstanding anything to the contrary contained in any other law for the time being in force, a District Council shall have the power to levy all or any of the following taxes within the autonomous district for which the Council is constituted, that is to say —

(a) taxes on professions, Trades, callings and employments;
(b) taxes on animals, vehicles (other than mechanically propelled vehicles) and boats;
(c) taxes on entry of goods into a Market for sale there in and tolls on passengers and goods carried in ferries;
(d) taxes for the maintenance of schools, dispensaries or roads; and
(e) any other tax falling under List II of the Seventh Schedule to the Constitution which the Legislature of the Union territory of Manipur may, by law, empower the District Council to levy.

34. Levy of Fees

A District Council may fix and levy —

(a) school fees; and
(b) fees for the use of, or benefits derived from, any of the works done or services rendered under section 29.

35. Procedure for Imposing Taxes

(1) A District Council may resolve at a meeting specially convened for the purpose to propose the imposition of any of the taxes mentioned in section 33.
(2) When a resolution has been passed, the Council shall publish a notice in the Official Gazette and also in the prescribed manner, defining the class of persons or description of property proposed to be taxed, the amount or rate of tax to be imposed and the system of assessment to be adopted.
(3) Any person, directly or indirectly affected by the proposed tax and objecting to it, may, within thirty days from the publication of the notice, send his objections in writing to the Council and the Council shall, at a specially convened meeting, take all such objections into consideration.
(4) If no objection is sent within the said period of thirty days or if the objections received are deemed insufficient, the Council may submit its proposals to the Administrator with the objections, if any, and its decision thereon.

(5) The Administrator may then sanction the proposals or refuse to sanction them or return them to the Council for further consideration.

(6) When the proposal in respect of a tax has been sanctioned, the Administrator shall notify its imposition in the Official Gazette and specify a date not later than three months from the date of notification on which the tax shall come into force.

36. Abolition or Reduction of Taxes

The Administrator may, by notification in the Official Gazette, and a District Council may with the previous approval of the Administrator by a resolution passed at a meeting specially convened for the purpose, abolish or reduce any tax imposed under section 33.

37. Recovery of Taxes and Fees

All arrears of taxes and fees levied under this Act may be recovered under the law for the time being in force for the recovery public dues as if such arrears were public dues.

38. Assessment and Collection of Taxes and Fees

A District council may, by notification in the Official Gazette, determine the person by whom any tax or fee shall be assessed and collected and make rules for the assessment and collection of such tax or fee and direct in what manner persons employed in the assessment or collection shall be remunerated.

39. Appeals

(1) In matters connected with the assessment and collection of any tax or fee levied under this Act, an appeal shall lie from the order of any person authorised to make assessment or collections to such person as the Administrator may appoint or designate for the purpose.

(2) An appeal under sub-section (1) shall be presented within thirty days from the date of the order.

(3) The order passed on the appeal shall be final.

40. Instalments of Taxes and Fees

A District Council may, by notification in the Official Gazette and with the previous approval of the Deputy Commissioner, prescribe by what instalments and at what times any tax or fee shall be payable.

41. Power to Exempt from Taxation

A District Council may, with the previous approval of the Administrator, by notification in the Official Gazette, remit or reduce any tax or fee or exempt any persons or class of persons or any description of property, wholly or in part, from liability to any tax or fee and cancel any such remission, reduction or exemption.

42. Recoveries of Moneys Claimable by the Council

(1) Save as provided by section 37, all moneys claimable by a District Council may be recovered on an application to a Magistrate having jurisdiction in the area where the person from whom the MONEY is claimable may, for the time being, be resident, by the distress and sale of any movable property or by the attachment and sale of any immovable property, within the limits of his jurisdiction belonging to such person and the cost of such proceedings shall be recoverable in the same manner as the said moneys.

(2) An application for recovery of money shall be in writing and shall be signed by an officer authorised in this behalf by order of the Chairman of the Council.

43. Council Fund

(1) All moneys received by or on behalf of a District Council under the provisions of this Act or any other law for the time being in force shall be credited to a FUND which shall be called the "Council Fund" and it shall be held by the District Council in trust for the purposes of this Act.

(2) All expenditure of the Council shall be defrayed out of the Council Fund.

(3) The Administrator may make rules for the management of the Council Fund and for the procedure to be followed in respect of payment of money into the said Fund, the withdrawal of moneys therefrom, the custody of moneys therein and any other matter connected with or ancillary to the matters aforesaid.

(4) The accounts of a District Council shall be kept in such form as may be prescribed.

(5) The accounts of a District Council shall be audited in such manner as may be prescribed.

44. Property Vested in District Council

Subject to any order of the Administrator, all property of the nature specified below and situated in the autonomous district shall vest in and belong to the District Council for which it is constituted and shall, with all other property which may become vested in the Council, be under its direction, management and control and shall be held and applied for the purposes of this Act —

(a) all public buildings, constructed or maintained out of the Council Fund;

(b) all public roads which have been constructed or are maintained out of the Council Fund and the stones and other materials thereof and also all trees, erections, materials, implements and things provided for such roads;

(c) all land or other property transferred to the District Council by the Administrator or by gift, sale or otherwise for public purposes.

45. Budget

(1) A District Council shall, on or before a prescribed day in each year submit to the Administrator an estimate of the income and expenditure of the Council for the next Financial year in such form as may be prescribed.

(2) The Administrator may, on or before a prescribed day, return the estimate of the Council with or without modifications.

(3) When a budget is returned with modifications under sub-section (2), the Council shall consider the proposed modifications, take a decision thereon and report the same to the Administrator.

(4) The budget estimate finally adopted by the Council shall be the budget of the District Council.

(5) Any subsequent alteration in the budget or reappropriation or transfer of provision within the estimate shall be made with the approval of the Administrator.

CHAPTER VI

Control

46. Control

(1) It shall be the duty of the Chairman of a District Council to furnish to the Deputy Commissioner a copy of the proceedings of the meetings of the Council and such other information as the Deputy Commissioner may require.

(2) The Deputy Commissioner shall have the power to give to any District Council all such directions as he may consider necessary in respect of subjects, curricula, text books and standards of teaching in schools vested wholly or partly in the Council and in schools wholly or partly maintained by grants payable from the Council Fund and the Council shall comply with such directions.

(3) The Deputy Commissioner may, by order, and for reasons to be recorded, suspend the execution of any resolution or order of any District Council or prohibit the doing of any act which is about to be done, or is being done, in pursuance of or under cover of any provision of the law relating to the constitution or functions of the District Council, if, in his opinion, the resolution, order or act is in excess of the powers conferred by law or the execution of the resolution or order or the doing of the act is likely to lead to a breach of the peace, or to cause annoyance or injury to the public or to any class or body of persons:

Provided that the Council may, within fifteen days of the date of the order of the Deputy Commissioner offer such explanation as it deems fit in relation to the execution of the resolution or order which has been suspended or the doing of the act has been prohibited.

(4) When the Deputy Commissioner makes any order as aforesaid, he shall forthwith send a copy of it to the Administrator with a statement of the reasons for making it and forward in due course to the Administrator the explanation, if any, offered by the Council and the Administrator may, thereupon, confirm, modify or rescind the order of the Deputy Commissioner.

47. Supersession of District Council

(1) If, on receipt of a report from the Deputy Commissioner or otherwise, the Administrator is of opinion that —

(a) any District Council is not competent to perform, or persistently makes default in the performance of, the duties imposed on it by or under this Act or any other law; or

(b) any District Council exceeds or abuses its powers; or

(c) the financial position and credit position of any District Council is seriously threatened; or

(d) a situation has arisen in which the administration of any District Council cannot be carried on in accordance with the provisions of this Act, the Administrator may, by an order published, together with a statement of reasons therefor, in the Official Gazette, supersede such Council for such period, not exceeding one year, as may be specified in the order:

Provided that before making an order of supersession as aforesaid under clause (a) or clause (b) or clause (c), reasonable opportunity shall be given to such Council to show cause why such order of supersession should not be made:

Provided further that the period of supersession may be extended for any further period or periods not exceeding six months at a time in consultation with the Hill Areas Committee.

(2) When any District Council is superseded by an order under sub-section (1), —

(a) all the members of the Council (including the Chairman and Vice-Chairman thereof) shall, on such date as may be specified in the order, vacate their offices as such members without prejudice to their eligibility for election or nomination under clause (d);

(b) during the period of supersession of the Council, all powers and duties conferred and imposed upon the Council by or under this Act or any other law shall be exercised and performed by such officer or authority as the Administrator may appoint in this behalf;

(c) all property vested in the Council shall, until it is reconstituted, vest in the Central Government; and

(d) before the expiry of the period of supersession, election or nomination, as the case may be, of members to the

Council shall be held or made for the purpose of reconstituting the Council.

48. Effect of certain provisions during the period when the Hill Areas Committee is not functioning. Where at any time, consequent on the dissolution of the Legislative Assembly of the Union territory of Manipur, the Hill Areas Committee is not functioning, then, during the period when such Committee is not functioning, —

(i) section 3 shall have effect as if sub-section (3) thereof had been omitted;

(ii) clause (xvii) of section 29 and the second proviso to sub-section (1) of section 47 have effect as if the words "in consultation with the Hill Areas Committee" had been omitted therefrom.

CHAPTER VII

Offences and Penalties

49. Penalty for Obstruction

If any person wilfully obstructs a District Council or any officer or servant of a District Council or any person authorised by the District Council in the exercise of its powers, he shall be punishable with fine which may extend to fifty rupees.

50. Penalty for Entering into any Contract with the Council

If any member, officer or other employee of a District Council enters into any contract with the Council, he shall be deemed to have committed an offence under section 168 of the Indian Penal Code.

CHAPTER VIII

Rules and Bye-laws

51. Power of Administrator to Make Rules

(1) Without prejudice to the power to make rules under any other provision of this Act, the Administrator may, after previous publication, make, by notification in the Official Gazette, rules for the purpose of carrying out the provisions of this Act.

(2) In particular and without prejudice to the generality of the foregoing power, such rules may —

(i) regulate the conduct of business of a District Council;
(ii) prescribe the forms in which the budget estimate is to be prepared and the dates for the various stages of its completion;
(iii) determine the language in which the business of a District Council will be transacted;
(iv) regulate the powers of a District Council to transfer property;
(v) regulate the powers of a District Council to contract and do other things necessary for the purposes of its constitution and the mode of executing contracts;
(vi) regulate the employment, payment, suspension and removal of officers and staff of a District Council;
(vii) protect the terms and conditions of service of Government servants transferred to a District Council;
(viii) prescribe the forms for statements, registers, estimates and accounts of a District Council and regulate the keeping, checking and publication of such accounts;
(ix) prescribe the authority by whom and the manner in which the accounts of a District Council shall be audited; and
(x) provide for any other matter for which rules have to be made under this Act.

52. Power to Make Bye-laws

(1) Subject to the provisions of this Act and of the rules made thereunder, a District Council may make bye-laws to provide for all or any of the following matters in the autonomous district for which it is constituted or in any part thereof, namely: —

(a) the maintenance and management of schools and grants of stipends and scholarships;
(b) control and administration of dispensaries, their construction and repairs, the supply of medicines and the measures to be taken during the prevalence of diseases;
(c) the protection from pollution of such tanks, springs, wells or parts of rivers, streams, channels or water courses as are set apart for drinking or culinary purposes; and

(d) any other matter which is necessary for carrying out all of any of the provisions of this Act and the rules made thereunder.

(2) A bye-law made under sub-section (1) shall not have effect until it has been confirmed by the Administrator and published in such manner as he may direct.

(3) The Administrator, in confirming a bye-law, may make any change therein which appears to him to be necessary.

53. Penalty for Infringement of Rules or Bye-laws

(1) In making any rule, the Administrator, and in making any bye-law, a District Council, may direct that the breach of the same shall be punishable with fine which may extend to one hundred rupees and in the case of a continuing breach with a further fine which may extend to ten rupees of every day during which the breach is continued after the offender has been convicted of such breach.

(2) In default of payment of any fine, the defaulter shall be punishable with imprisonment for a term which may extend to fifteen days.

Assam Act No. XXV of 2005 (Received the assent of the Governor 8th May, 2005)

The Deori Autonomous Council Act, 2005

AN ACT

to provide for the establishment of an administrative authority in the name and style of Deori Autonomous Council and for certain matters incidental thereto and connected therewith.

Preamble *WHEREAS* it is expedient to provide for the establishment of a Deori Autonomous council within the State of Assam with maximum autonomy within the framework of the Constitution, comprising of the satellite areas of Village Councils formed out of blocks of contiguous revenue villages, each having 50 per cent and above Deori and other Scheduled Tribes population without having any compact area for social, economic, educational, ethnic and cultural advancement of the Deori and other Scheduled Tribes communities residing therein.

It is hereby enacted in the Fifty-sixth Year of the Republic of India, as follows:

CHAPTER I

Preliminary

Short title, extent and commence 1. (1) This Act may be called the Deori Autonomous Council Act, 2005.

(2) It extends to the whole of the state of Assam.

(3) It shall come into force on such date as the State Government may, by notification in the

Official Gazette, appoint and different dates may be appointed for different provisions of the Act or different areas.

Definitions

2. In this Act, unless the context otherwise requires —

(a) 'Bye-law' means the bye-law framed by the General Council,

(b) 'Constitution' means, the Constitution of India,

(c) 'Constituency' means a constituency referred to in section 48.

(d) 'Council Area' means the Deori Autonomous Council Area.

(e) 'Core Areas' means the compact and contiguous areas predominantly inhabited by Deori community and having more than 50 per cent Scheduled Tribes populations as a whole in the area and not necessarily in the individual villages.

(e) 'Executive Council' means the executive body of the General Council of the Deori Autonomous Council constituted under sections 3(3) and 24.

(f) 'Elector' in relation to a constituency means a person whose name is entered in the electoral roll of that constituency.

(g) 'General Council Fund' and 'Village Council Fund' means the funds constituted under section 61.

(h) 'Government' means the State Government of Assam.

(i) 'Governor' means the Governor of Assam. **Assam Act XVIII of 1994**

(j) 'General Council' means the General Council of the Deori Autonomous Council referred to in section 3.

(k) 'Gaon Panchayat', 'Anchalik Panchayat' and 'Zilla Parishad' have the same meaning defined in the Assam Panchayat Act, 1994.

(l) 'Member' means a member of the Village Council or the General Council or the Executive Council, as the case may be.

Assam Act XV of 1957

(m) 'Municipality' has the same meaning as in the Assam Municipal Act, 1956.

(n) 'Notification' means the notification issued under this Act.

(o) 'Official Gazette' means the Official Gazette of Assam.

(p) 'Prescribed' means prescribed by rules made under this Act.

(q) 'Satellite area' means the area or areas consisting of non-contiguous cluster of villages predominantly inhabited by Deori community and having more than 50 per cent Schedule Tribes population as a whole in the cluster and not necessarily in the individual villages.

(r) 'Village Council' means the Village Councils referred to in section 4; and

(s) 'Village Council Area' means the area declared to be the area of a Village Council by the Government by notification in the Official Gazette.

Deori Autonomous Council

3. (1) There shall be an autonomous council to be called the Deori Autonomous Council within the State of Assam comprising of the areas of the Village Councils as may be specified by the Government by notification in the Official Gazette.

(2) The Deori Autonomous Council shall have maximum autonomy within the frame work of the Constitution.

(3) The Deori Autonomous Council shall have a General Council and an Executive Council as provided hereinafter.

Village Council

4. (1) There shall be a Village Council for each block of villages, each Village having 50 per cent or more Scheduled Tribe population.

(2) Each Village Council area shall consist of approximately 3,000 to 5,000 population.

(3) Each Village Council area shall consist of 10 (ten) elected members out of which 5 (five) will be form Scheduled Tribe community. Out of 5 (five) reserved seats 1 (one) shall be reserved for a women member.

Bibliography

Referred Books

Aitchison, C.U. (1982). *Treaties, Engagements and Sanads*, Kolkata, 1931, Delhi.

Alemchiba, M. (1970). *A Brief Historical Account of Nagaland*, Kohima, Directorate of Art and Culture, Nagaland.

Bardoloi Commission Report.

Bareh, H. (1970). *Gazetteer of India*, Kohima district, Kohima.

Basu, D.D. (1977). *Constitutional Law of India*, New Delhi.

Bhattacharya, J.B. (ed.) (1982). *Social Tension in North-East India*, Kolkata: Research India Publication.

Barpujari, H.K. (1981). *Problems of the Hill Tribes in North-Eastern Frontier*, Vol. III, 1873-1962, Guwahati.

Baveja, J.D. (1970). *The Land Where Bamboo Flowers*, Guwahati Publication Board.

Bose, M.L. (1979). *Historical and Constitutional Documents of North-Eastern India*, New Delhi.

Chakraborty, B.C. (1981). *British Relations with the Hill Tribes of Assam since 1858*, Kolkata.

Chaube, S.K. (1973). *Hill Politics in North-East India*, Delhi.

Dubey, S.M. (ed.) (1978). *North-East India: A Sociological Study*, New Delhi.

Das, R.K. (1985). *Manipur Tribal Scene — Studies in Society and Change*, New Delhi.

Elvin, V. (1964). *A Philosophy of NEFA*, Shillong.

Elvin, V. (1961). *Nagaland*, Shillong.

Gassah, L.S. (ed.) (1992). *Regional Political Parties in North-East India*, New Delhi: Omsons Publications.

Kumar, B.B. (ed.) (1993). *Modernization in Naga Society*, New Delhi: Omsons Publications.

Luthra, P.N. (1974). *Nagaland from District to a State*, Shillong.

MacKenjie, A. (1979). *North-East Frontier of India, 1884*, Delhi.

Nibedon, Nirmal (1981). *North-East India — The Ethnic Explosion*, New Delhi.

Nag, Amit (1984). *The Mizo Dilemma*, Silchar: Tribal Publications.

Rao, V.V., *A Century of Government and Politics in North-East India*, New Delhi, Vol. I (Assam), 1983, Vol. II (Meghalaya), 1984, Vol. IV (Manipur), 1991.

Sarin, V.K. (1980). *North-East India in Flames*, New Delhi.

Sema, Hokishe, *Emergence of Nagaland*, New Delhi.

Singh, K.S. (1972). *Tribal Situation in India*, Shimla: IIAS.

Singh, K.S., *Tribal Movements in India*, New Delhi, 1982.

Singh, C. (1989). *Emergence of Arunachal Pradesh as a State*, New Delhi.

Stracey, P.D. (1968). *Nagaland Nightmare*, New Delhi.

Thanga, L.B., *The Mizo — A Study in Racial Personality*, Guwahati.

Youno, Asoso (1974). *The Rising Nagas*, New Delhi.

Papers

Kumar, B.B., *Social Tension in North-East India*.

Sinha, Nirmal C. (1977). *The Shimla Convention 1914*, A Chinese Puzzle, Gangtok, Bulletin of Tibetology, No. 1 (N.S.).

INDEX